"Whenever Nancy bakes or cooks she wins over even the most discerning palate! When it comes to the home or professional baker this book is a MUST!"

—WOLFGANG PUCK

"Nancy is such a talented author and an accomplished baker, and in her new book she perfected and personalized many familiar recipes of pies, cookies, and cakes. It is always refreshing and motivating to see a new book that pays homage to the classics. And everyone should know that Nancy will always add a personal and delicious twist."

—DANIEL BOULUD, chef and restaurateur

"Nancy is a curious chef and baker. She wants to try things to understand if they are as good as they are supposed to be or not, or even better than expected. I am not as curious as she. Nancy is taking classic desserts, baked treats, and asking, 'I know this is the classic recipe but can we do it better? Make it more delicious?' If I were ever to make a peanut butter cookie, do you know where I am going to look for the recipe? Right here in this cookbook. Because I know that Nancy wouldn't let me down. Not when it is so important to her to get it right. That is why we all need this book."

—MASSIMO BOTTURA,
restaurateur and chef patron, Osteria Francescana

The Cookie
That Changed
My Life

The Cookie That Changed My Life

And More
Than 100 Other
Classic Cakes,
Cookies, Muffins,
and Pies That
Will Change
Yours

Nancy Silverton

with Carolynn Carreño

Photographs by Anne Fishbein

Alfred A. Knopf
New York
2023

THIS IS A BORZOI BOOK
PUBLISHED BY ALFRED A. KNOPF

www.aaknopf.com

Library of Congress Cataloging-in-Publication Data
Names: Silverton, Nancy, author. | Carreño, Carolynn, other. |
Fishbein, Anne, photographer.
Title: The cookie that changed my life: and more than 100 other
classic cakes, cookies, muffins, and pies that will change yours /
Nancy Silverton with Carolynn Carreño; photographs by Anne Fishbein.
Description: New York: Alfred A. Knopf, 2023. | Includes index.
Identifiers: LCCN 2022034670 | ISBN 9780593321669 (hardcover) |
ISBN 9780593321676 (ebook)
Subjects: LCSH: Baking. | Desserts. | LCGFT: Cookbooks.
Classification: LCC TX763 .S525 2023 | DDC 641.81/5—dc23/eng/20220810
LC record available at https://lccn.loc.gov/2022034670

Cover photograph by Anne Fishbein
Cover design by Linda Huang

Manufactured in China
Published November 14, 2023
Second Printing, July 2023

Here's to that unforgettably delicious yellow birthday cake with chocolate frosting that we savored as kids, and here's to those aromas wafting from your kitchen today that bring those sweet memories back.

Here's to the lingering scent of cinnamon rolls drifting from your oven, sending you in a time machine back to the enchanting scents of your mother's, aunt's, and grandma's kitchens.

And here's to that peanut butter cookie that lighted me in a dark hour.

Contents

The Cookie
That Changed
My Life

Introduction

~~~~~~~~~~~

It all started with a peanut butter cookie. Add to that a year-long pandemic lockdown, and what you get is this book, a collection of over 100 recipes for the classic baked goods you know and love, tweaked to absolute perfection. It happened like this:

It was week one of the pandemic and I was at home, with nothing to do but watch movies, field phone calls, and ponder the fate of my employees and my restaurants. I have a big woven basket in the corner of my kitchen where one knows to go to look for treats. It's full of things that were given to me in goody bags, brought home from restaurants (including my own), or that I picked up during my travels.

One morning, my eyes wandered to the basket, and there it was: Inside a brown bag, grease-stained with butter, was a giant, soft peanut butter cookie. My partner, Michael Krikorian, never leaves a bakery without a cookie, specifically, a chocolate chip, oatmeal raisin, or peanut butter cookie. He wants to see how they do with those classics, and if they do well, he'll try their other offerings. That's how the cookie ended up there. The cookie came from Friends & Family, a Los Angeles bakery owned and operated by Roxana Jullapat, a talented baker who worked with me at Campanile and then worked in many exceptional Los Angeles restaurants before opening her own. I reached in and took out the cookie, and I immediately noted that Roxana's cookie had a beautifully crackled top and perfectly rounded edges, both signs of success in this type of cookie. I took a bite, and I thought: Wow! This is *good*. It was everything one could ask for in a peanut butter cookie: It was moist and chewy—and it really tasted like peanut butter. If I were leading a Global Peanut Butter Cookie Perfection Task Force, I would have said to the troops, "Let's go home. Our work here is done."

Lucky for me, prior to this, I had been asked to write a blurb for Roxana's book, *Mother Grains,* so I had a copy of the galleys (the prepublication edition of a book) on my phone. I found the recipe, ordered the ingredients online, and the day they were delivered, I made the cookies. The cookies I baked were just as good as the one from Friends & Family. Naturally, I wasn't content to leave well enough alone, and like I said, I had a lot of time on my hands. So throughout the day I played with the recipe and eventually landed on a cookie that consisted of Roxana's cookie as a base dressed up with a spoonful of peanut butter in the center, into which I nestled a pile of roasted and salted Spanish peanuts: It was as peanutty as a peanut butter cookie could possibly be and now had these added textural components. Now, I thought, we'd reached absolute perfection. I snapped a photo and sent it to my agent and my editor.

Whenever I finish a book, before I have recovered from the "childbirth" of delivering the manuscript, they ask me what my next book is going to be, and I always say: Never again! But it never turns out to be true. "This is my next book," I texted them, along with a photo of the peanut butter cookie masterpiece. "Making the absolute best version of the familiar baked goods that we all know and love." They were all for it.

Over the next year, while the rest of the country was obsessed with learning to make sourdough bread, I, too, found that I had the inclination to bake. But rather than tackling bread, which, of course, I'd already done, I took on classic American baked goods. One by one, I looked at familiar favorites, made them time after time, adjusted this and that, until I felt I had made each item as good as I believed it could be. Together with Shiri Nagar, whom I'd enlisted to help with the recipe testing and development for this book, we took on one classic after another: apple crisp (deceptively simple); yellow cake with fudge frosting (about which everyone, including my grandson Ike, has an opinion); corn bread (I just wanted it to taste like corn; too much to ask?);

and lemon bars (purists beware!). The majority of the recipes here are the results of that tinkering. Some are inspired by other bakers, but I put my touch on them, as I did with Roxana's peanut butter cookies. Some have appeared in previous books of mine, but I tweaked and updated them for this book; for instance, I took the base for my "Oreos" and piled a walnut-studded fudge topping on top to create the Ultimate Chocolate Cookie. And a few others, still, are recipes that I sought out from my baking colleagues when I realized that they had made something that simply could not be improved upon. The Ginger Stout Cake (page 243) from Claudia Fleming is the perfect example.

Although I think you'll recognize the vast majority of the recipes here, there are a handful that are probably not among your childhood memories. Portuguese Custard Tarts (page 385) is one of those. Another is the Black Sesame White Chocolate Cookies (page 100) from Hart Bageri in Copenhagen. In the case of the custard tarts, they are a classic if you grew up in Portugal. The black sesame cookies are a complete and absolute product of the times: One hundred years from now, tahini and black sesame seeds will both be traced back to this decade by food anthropologists as a trend of this decade. Even though these recipes are not American classics now, I believe they belong here in my book of "bests." And if I have anything to do with it, ten years from now they will have made their way into the American Bakery lexicon, just like Basque Cheesecake (yes, it's here on page 252) did in this past decade.

If you're asking yourself right now, "Who needs another recipe for banana bread?" Let me just say that I hear you. There are so many cookbooks out there, not to mention a seemingly infinite number of recipes on the Internet. But I'm confident that when you see and taste the banana bread in this book, even though you didn't think you needed another banana bread recipe, you'll realize that you did.

Having been baking professionally now for fifty years (fifty years! I can hardly believe it myself), I have seen and done my share of innovating, inventing, and envelope pushing. In fact, I would say that innovating has defined American baking during this time. In the last ten years, as both baking and cooking have reached competitive levels, with ingredients from around the globe available at the touch of a button and the influences of Instagram sending ideas soaring, innovation in baking has exploded. We've innovated in every way conceivable—and even some ways that are still hard to conceive. Maybe it is my age setting in, but more and more I find myself asking: Do we really need matcha in our pound cake? Lavender in shortbread? Pie on a stick? Cake in a jar? Or bacon in any dessert? The answer, for me, is a definite "No."

Creative, yes. But for me, these creations aren't craveable, and that was the ultimate criterion for a recipe to make it into this book. It needs to be something you *crave*. Or can't get enough of. The way for me to judge what is craveable is to start with what *I* crave. If you want to thrill me, give me a perfect brownie, dense, fudgy, and packed with quality chocolate; a tender, lightly browned shortbread cookie made with French butter; or a strawberry-rhubarb pie that tastes like the essence of springtime. Nothing excites me more than when I bite into one of these familiar treats only to discover that it has been done to perfection. This book is a collection of those superb recipes.

Although some of these recipes have many steps (a small price to pay for perfection), none of the steps is complicated. These are by and large easy recipes. They're meant to be just the kind of project the home baker wants to and can take on. The home baker, that is, that isn't looking to take on a croissant-making challenge, but for something to put in their kids' lunch boxes or bring to a friend's house for dinner. You won't find any sophisticated baking or pastry-making technique here. The techniques you will encounter in these recipes are those we grew up with when making cookies, cakes, and pies: creaming butter, whipping egg whites, rolling out dough, and dropping, cutting, or slicing cookie dough. And since these are not plated desserts (except for the one: the Chocolate Decadence Cake with Cocoa-Covered Almonds and Hot Fudge Sauce, page 291), the majority of the recipes consist of just one component; two if you count pie and tart crusts, frostings, or glazes.

I don't cook or bake from cookbooks often, but I do like to flip through them for ideas. When I do, I don't like to flip back and forth between pages to look at cross-referenced recipes. I don't ask you to do that either. Each recipe stands on its own, containing all the detail that even the most novice baker needs to get the desired results. (The only exception being pies and tarts that utilize basic doughs.) I do not send you to another page for subrecipes, "master classes," or "definitions." I put all that information in the recipes.

Having taught countless young bakers over the course of my career to achieve a very specific result, I understand that the difference between something turning out "fine" and something being flawless lies in the details. The tricks, tips, and specifics you need are all here, in every recipe, where you need them, so the cakes, cookies, pies, and biscuits that you pull out of your oven are as beautiful and delicious as they were when I pulled them out of mine. More experienced bakers may find more information than they need. If you know how to roll pie dough, check a custard tart for doneness, remove a cake from a cake pan, or add egg whites to cake batter, be my guest and skim over the details when you get to that part of a recipe.

With all the classics under one roof, as it were, this is a book that I want on my shelf, and I hope one that you will want on yours. It is the book I hope you will reach for on an ordinary day when you want to bake a birthday cake for your kids, cookies for a backyard barbecue, or a special little something, let's say, to celebrate the end of a long and grueling pandemic. Working on this book allowed me to revisit favorites from my past, such as Bran Muffins (page 40) and Tarte Tatin (page 353), and to make a few things that I knew were dear to your heart, such as Lemon Bars (page 349) and German Chocolate Cake (page 286), but that I had never made before. I had a lot of fun with the old and the new, and I hope you do, too.

A Note About Your Oven

Every oven bakes differently: Some are hotter in the front, others hotter in the back. In some ovens, the heat comes from above, and in others, it comes from the bottom of the oven. The more you bake, the more you will get to know your oven and recognize its idiosyncrasies. It's a good idea to have your oven recalibrated from time to time; often your local gas company will come out and do this free of charge. You can also place an oven thermometer in your oven to cross-check the temperature. These recipes were tested in a standard home oven and except for Madeleines (page 225), all the recipes assume you're using a conventional oven. If you have a convection oven, reduce the oven temperature by 25°F and use a low fan if you have that option. The baking time in a convection oven may also be as much as 25 percent shorter. In any case, always pay as much if not more attention to the indicators for doneness than to the time. The more you bake, the more you will rely on sight, smell, and touch to tell you when your baked goods are ready to come out of the oven.

Storage

I chose not to tell you how to store things and for how long. I store everything at room temperature. If you have a cake dome, great. If you have sealed storage containers, those are good, too. The only items I refrigerate are Brownies (page 117), because I like them cold, not because they need to be stored that way, and those that are heavy on the cream, like cream pies and Bread Pudding (page 238).

Likewise, I don't specify that you can freeze dough for every recipe. Yes, you can freeze dough. In the case of pie or tart dough that needs to be rolled out, place it in the refrigerator overnight to thaw it. For cookies, form the dough before you freeze it and bake straight from the freezer.

Tools and Equipment

A thoughtfully equipped kitchen can really make the difference between a baking endeavor going smoothly and even the simplest recipe turning into an unpleasant project. So here it is, a list of baking tools, some basic and others more specialized, that will allow you to bake through these recipes with comfort and ease. Some items are available at restaurant supply stores. Others you will find at specialty cooking and baking supply stores and from online sources.

Baking Pans and Molds

In these recipes, I took advantage of the vast selection and variety of baking pans and molds that are available today. Using baking pans in different shapes and sizes, with various decorative details, allowed me to get creative in a way that appeals to my sensibility as a baker. In each recipe, I specify the pan or mold that I used in the photo. I also include the cup capacity of the pan or mold so you can use an alternative with the same results.

Baking Sheets

The only baking sheets to consider are heavy-duty sheet pans, with a rolled steel edge. The baking sheet I call for throughout these recipes and refer to as a "large baking sheet" is a half-sheet pan (13 × 18 inches). I suggest you have at least four on hand. They are relatively inexpensive, easy to store, and they make the production process of baking, especially small, repetitive items such as cookies, so much easier. I also suggest you have one or two quarter-sheet pans (9½ × 13 inches) on hand for toasting nuts, seeds, coconut, and other items in small quantities.

Bench Knife

A simple, inexpensive tool for scraping dough off your work surface and for cutting dough without damaging your knives.

Bowls

We've all been there: juggling ingredients from one bowl to another when you have too few. Or trying to mix ingredients in a bowl that is too small—or too big. It's such a simple thing to remedy. Bowls are inexpensive. I suggest you buy a selection of nesting stainless steel bowls from a kitchen supply store or online source. Additionally, stock a set (or two) of deep nesting bowls for baking. Having all of the following would be the ideal, but even half of these will change your baking life.

Three 4- to 5-inch

Two 8-inch

Two or three 12-inch

One 14-inch

One 16-inch

One 18-inch

One or two sets of deep mixing bowls

Candy Thermometer

For making doubt-free work of cooking sugar and making lemon curd.

Cardboard Cake Rounds

This stalwart of the professional kitchen makes the project of iced cakes and layer cakes much easier for the home baker as well. They are the best option for inverting cakes and pies. And they are essential if you are baking tarts with a flan ring.

Corn Creamer

Corn creamers are an inexpensive tool; they don't just take the kernels off the cob, they also break the kernels, creaming the corn. There really is no substitute. This tool is essential in making Corn Muffins (page 35) and Corn Bread (page 458).

Cutters

I suggest you make the small investment in two sets of graduated round cutters, one fluted and one straight sided.

Digital Kitchen Scale

When I started baking and writing cookbooks, kitchen scales designed for the home baker (or cook) did not exist, so I wrote all my recipes using volume measurements. Today, kitchen scales are easy to find. I've included both weights and measures for all these recipes for those who may be intimidated by the idea of weighing ingredients rather than measuring, but I recommend you give weighing a try. You'll soon discover how easy it is, and you'll never look back. Weighing is also more accurate.

Flan Rings and Fluted Tart Rings

Also called a tart ring, a flan ring is like a tart pan with no bottom. You set the ring on a parchment-lined baking sheet and the baking sheet serves as the bottom of the pan. When I started baking professionally, half a century ago, removable-bottom tart pans were not available. Fluted-edged tart pans are widely available now, but straight-sided, removable-bottom tart pans are still scarce. While fluted-edged tarts can be pretty, I prefer the clean look of a tart with straight sides. If you can't find a flan ring, use a removable-bottom tart pan in its place, and if a fluted-edged pan is the only one you have access to, that will work. I use 10-inch and 12-inch rings for tarts, and small, 3- to 4-inch rings for cookies.

Food Processor

You will need a full-size (approximately 9-cup capacity) food processor for recipes that require grinding, such as nuts for nut-based doughs— like Linzer Cookies (page 139) and Hazelnut Plum Tart (page 411)—and graham crackers for graham cracker crusts. When grinding a small amount of ingredients, a mini–food processor is essential. They're also inexpensive. I love mine and use it often.

Knives

You'll use knives in these recipes to chop nuts, cut bread and cookie dough, release baked goods from the pans they were baked in, and slice finished baked goods. I suggest you have a quality chef's knife, large serrated knife, and paring knife.

Measuring Cups and Spoons

Traditionally, measuring cups with lines denoting various measures are used for measuring liquids. Nesting measuring cups, with each cup a specific measure, are used for measuring dry ingredients. In the case of dry ingredients, scrape the cup to get a level measure rather than shaking it, which compacts the ingredients and will give you a false measure. Also, I don't suggest you go in for novelty measuring cups and spoons because they are less accurate. You'll want to have one set of nesting measuring cups, one set of nesting measuring spoons, and one 4-cup liquid measuring cup.

Microplanes

Handheld Microplane graters have replaced the box grater for nearly all my grating needs. I use a fine Microplane for grating citrus zest, hard cheeses, nutmeg, and fresh ginger. I use a medium Microplane for grating hard-cooked eggs and semihard cheeses.

Offset Spatulas

These recipes call for you to use an offset spatula, a narrow spatula that is offset from the handle, making it easier to fit into baking pans where it might not otherwise. I also call for you to use them to smooth out batter before putting cakes in the oven, to spread filling, and to frost cakes. I recommend you have one large and one small.

Pastry Brush

You will use a pastry brush to wash dough with egg or cream before baking, to clean the sides of a saucepan when cooking sugar, and for dabbing glazes onto cakes.

Pie Weights

These are small metal or ceramic weights made for weighing down pie and tart crusts when par-baking the crust. If you don't have pie weights, dried beans can be used instead; the beans can be reused as pie weights, but don't try cooking them once they've been used as weights.

Piping Bag

I call for large disposable piping bags in this book; you cut the tip for these to whatever size you want. If you are not using a decorative tip, you do not need a tip at all. These are also convenient in that you don't have to wash them out. Using a piping bag makes clean and easy work of filling small baking molds, such as madeleine molds. Although I don't call for it, you can also use a pastry bag to fill tins for muffins and cupcakes.

Rolling Pin

There are two basic types of rolling pins: those with handles and those without. I prefer a handleless rolling pin. Because the palms of your hands are directly on the pin, you can feel how much pressure you are putting on the dough, which gives you more control. There are two types of handless pins: one that is straight all the way across, called a dowel pin, and one with tapered ends, also called a French rolling pin, which is my favorite. A rolling pin is necessary throughout these recipes for rolling tart dough, pie dough, and cookie dough. In my recipe for Shortbread Cookies (page 179), I suggest an embossed rolling pin for rolling a decorative stamp onto the dough.

Rolling Pastry Cutter

This small tool is handy for cutting dough with the guide of a ruler. I use a straight-edged pastry cutter to cut dough for such things as the Lattice-Topped Apple Pie (page 319); I use a fluted-edged pastry cutter to create pretty zigzag edges on Iced Raisin Bars (page 173) and other items.

Saucepans and Sauté Pan

You will need small, medium, and large saucepans as well as a large sauté pan for various stove-top tasks including cooking butter, warming milk or cream, improvising a double boiler with a bowl on top, cooking sugar, and making rice pudding, among other uses. Invest in heavy-duty pans (preferably stainless steel) with a light-colored bottom. All-Clad's stainless steel pots and pans are the classic, and a lifelong investment. The brand Made In has more recently entered the arena with a collection of stainless steel pots and pans that are equally great. Heavy-gauge pans such as these conduct heat evenly and help prevent you from burning ingredients. Using a pan with a light-colored interior is helpful so that you can see the color of what you're cooking, which is especially important when making brown butter (see Brown Butter Cream Cheese Frosting, page 281) or golden butter (see New York Crumb Cake, page 65), and when cooking sugar to make caramel.

Silicone Baking Mat

Silicone baking mats, such as the Silpat brand, can be used in place of parchment paper to line a baking sheet. In a few recipes in which the baked goods really want to stick to the baking pan, such as Alaska Cookies with Chocolate Chunks (page 113) and Coconut Macaroons (page 191), I call for you to use a baking mat instead of parchment paper to ensure that you can lift the baked goods off.

Silicone Spatulas

Look for those that are large, heavy-duty, heatproof, and flexible. Have several on hand; you'll use them constantly for scraping down bowls, mixing batters, and stirring.

Spice Grinder

An electric spice grinder is essential for grinding spices. Freshly ground spices, in particular cinnamon and cardamom, really make a difference in the flavor of any baked good that utilizes those spices. (Any coffee grinder that you can wipe out to clean can be used as a spice grinder.)

Stand Mixer

Most of the recipes in this book call for you to use a stand mixer. If you already own a stand mixer, use what you have. If you are buying a stand mixer for the purpose of this book, I recommend you buy one that has a bowl with a 5- or 6-quart capacity and that has a lift mechanism that allows you to get your hand or a rubber spatula down in the bowl without getting the batter all over. (You can't mix some of the smaller quantities of ingredients if you use a mixer with a bowl any larger than 6 quarts.) It's also handy to have an extra bowl for your stand mixer for those recipes that require you to whip egg whites and then fold them into batter.

Ruler

A handy and perhaps unexpected tool for your pastry kitchen. You will use a ruler to measure the thickness and dimension when rolling out dough and as a guide to cut straight lines in dough with a knife or rolling pastry cutter.

Star Tip

This is a classic, easy-to-use frosting tip and the only tip used in these recipes, for piping frosting onto cupcakes and whipped cream onto a cream pie.

Powdered Sugar Shaker

This is handy to have around if you bake a lot, but you can use a sieve or tamis for the same purpose.

Kitchen Shears

Kitchen shears are an unsung hero in the kitchen. They trim dough and cut parchment paper, and are useful for other tasks.

Sieve

For straining custards, pastry cream, sauces, and other items; and dusting pastries with powdered sugar or cocoa. A conical strainer called a chinois is my preferred fine sieve for liquids.

Tamis

A drum-shaped mesh strainer, a tamis is my preferred tool for sifting flour, cocoa powder, powdered sugar, and other dry ingredients, and for dusting baked goods with powdered sugar or cocoa powder. The flat surface makes it easy to use. They come in various sizes.

Tart Pans

I use two styles of tart pan. For baking the Poppy Seed Cake (page 201), Chocolate Almond Dot Cake (page 303), and Financiers (page 228), I use classic French tart pans, with fluted edges and removable bottoms. For tarts, I use straight-sided flan rings instead, but if you can't find a flan ring, a tart pan can be used in its place.

Vegetable Peeler

You'll need this for peeling citrus zest and, of course, for peeling fruits and vegetables. I've tried a lot of vegetable peelers and as far as I'm concerned, a Honsen peeler, which is not expensive, is the only one to buy. It works so well, it makes peeling a pleasure rather than a chore.

Wire Whisks

I like a long (12- to 14-inch) heavy-duty whisk. It's nice to have a variety. You'll find yourself reaching for a different shape and size depending on what you're whisking or stirring, or how big the vessel is that you are whisking or stirring in. You'll use it in these recipes for stirring dry ingredients, whisking wet ingredients, and making many batters.

Supplies

Aluminum Foil

Heavy-duty aluminum foil is the only kind of aluminum foil I keep in the kitchen. In this book, I use it for wrapping springform pans that are going into a water bath, to ensure they don't take on any water. You can find it in standard supermarkets.

Parchment Paper

I use parchment paper in almost every recipe in this book. I use it for lining baking sheets whenever I'm baking directly on them. This isn't crucial, but it helps prevent baked goods from sticking to the baking sheet; it also eliminates the step of scrubbing baking sheets. I also roll out some of the stickier doughs—such as that for Iced Raisin Bars (page 173) and Sweet Tart Dough (page 329)—between sheets of parchment paper. It may seem awkward if you've never done it before, but it makes rolling much easier. I recommend you buy parchment paper sheets, which are cut specifically to fit a half-sheet pan, as opposed to parchment paper that comes in a roll, which can be frustrating to use because it wants to roll back up. Parchment sheets can be found at cooking supply stores and online sources. If you're in a pinch and need to buy the parchment at a grocery store, you will see it sold alongside aluminum foil and wax paper.

Plastic Wrap

I call for plastic wrap often in this book, for wrapping doughs and covering doughs and containers before placing them in the refrigerator.

Buy professional-grade plastic wrap in a large roll at a cooking or restaurant supply store. It is the only plastic wrap I have found that sticks and creates a seal around whatever you're wrapping.

Ingredients

The following are some staple ingredients that I use throughout these recipes and about which I have some thoughts to share. When an ingredient is used only once or twice in the book, I discuss it in the headnote to the recipe rather than here.

Almond Meal and Almond Flour

Made of almonds ground to a fine meal, almond meal lends a moist, chewy quality to baked goods. I prefer unblanched almond meal, which is made with almonds with their skins. Bob's Red Mill Unblanched Almond Meal is widely available in grocery stores and online. I call for almond meal in these recipes, rather than asking you to grind whole almonds into meal, because almond meal is so accessible these days. Grinding your own nuts requires you to break out your food processor, but if you prefer to start with whole almonds (I do!), I give you that alternative in each recipe. Almond flour is a similar product; it is slightly more refined. It's used in this book only once, in Marge Manzke's chewy Oatmeal Raisin Cookies (page 103).

Almond Paste

Almond paste is made from ground almonds and sugar. I use it to impart almond flavor and moisture to baked goods, such as Chewy Almond Cookies (page 189), Marzipan Cake (page 211), and Chocolate Almond Dot Cake (page 303). Almond paste is like marzipan, though marzipan is sweeter and has a smoother texture. I prefer unblanched almond paste, which is made from almonds with their skins; you can find it at baking and cooking supply stores or from online sources. Almond paste made from skinless almonds is widely available in the baking section of grocery stores; either will work in these recipes.

Buckwheat Flakes

Buckwheat is a gluten-free grain with an intense, earthy flavor. You can find buckwheat flakes at health food stores or from online sources. They add a nice flavor and textural component to the Seedy Crackers (page 472). That recipe was shared with me by a friend; until then, I had never heard of buckwheat flakes. I also use them in the Granola Bar Bites (page 71) to give those another textural, grainy component. You can buy buckwheat flakes at natural foods stores and from online sources.

Butter

Unsalted butter is the only type of butter used in this book, or that I ever bake with. In those recipes in which the butter is the star, such as Shortbread Cookies (page 179), Pound Cake (page 221), and Rough Puff Pastry Dough (page 357), I call for European-style, cultured butter, which has a higher fat content than common varieties of butter (82% to 85% as opposed to 80% for common brands). My favorite brand of cultured butter is Rodolphe Le Meunier, but any cultured butter will be a delicious addition to your baked goods.

Chocolate

High-quality chocolate, such as Valrhona, Callebaut, or Ghirardelli, is widely available these days and really make a difference. I like the convenience of Valrhona chocolate *feves*, or disks, which I use for everything (except for unsweetened chocolate, because Valrhona doesn't make them). Using feves eliminates the step of chopping chocolate in instances when it's melted. When used as chunks in Chocolate Chunk Cookies (page 95) or Brownies (page 117), I cut some in half and leave others whole. With a few exceptions when I call for milk chocolate, white chocolate, or unsweetened chocolate, I use bittersweet chocolate, which contains 70% cacao: The higher the percentage of cacao, the more intense the chocolate. (Unsweetened chocolate, for instance, is 100% cacao.) When shopping for milk chocolate, look for one with a relatively high percentage of cacao so it's not too sweet; I like Valrhona Jivara, which has 39% cacao. When shopping for white chocolate, remember that quality is equally important, so it's not too sweet; again, I use Valrhona.

Cocoa Powder

There are three types of cocoa powder on the market: natural cocoa powder, which is the most common, and what I call for throughout these recipes; Dutch process, also called "alkalized," cocoa powder, which is not used in this book; and black, or nonalkalized, cocoa powder, which has a slightly bitter taste and, as the name suggests, is almost black in color. The only recipe in which I call for black cocoa powder is the base portion of the Ultimate Chocolate Cookies (page 135); it's the only cocoa powder that really imparts that true black color and whose slightly bitter flavor is reminiscent of the flavor of Oreos. When buying natural cocoa powder for these recipes, seek out a quality brand; I use Valrhona.

Coconut Oil

I had never cooked with coconut oil before working on this book. I found that the texture really varies from brand to brand, even when I was sticking strictly with virgin, or unprocessed, coconut oil. Some brands are so hard you can barely get a spoon into them; these need to be liquefied (melted) before you can use it in the recipe. Other brands are solid, like Crisco, but they're soft and light and they will melt when you add them to a recipe. Use your best judgment, and if in doubt, melt the oil. (If you have a microwave, use that, otherwise melt it in a small saucepan over low heat.)

Cooking Spray

I call exclusively for cooking spray to grease pans, tins, and molds. When I started baking, the only cooking spray available had an artificial butter flavor. Today, you can find neutral-flavored spray, as well as organic varieties made with healthy oils. It's much easier to spray than to grease a pan with butter and it's also more effective as it gets into the nooks, crannies, and corners of whatever you're spraying. If you prefer to grease with butter, that's fine, too.

Eggs

I use extra-large eggs throughout the recipes. I always prefer organic, cage-free, or farm-fresh eggs.

Flour

As a professional baker, I use many types of white flour, including cake flour, bread flour, pastry flour, and unbleached all-purpose flour. The difference between these flours has to do with their protein content. The higher the protein content, the more gluten the flour produces, and the less tender the resulting baked goods. In these recipes, I used unbleached all-purpose flour whenever possible. However, in instances when I have called for a different type of white flour, rest assured, I first tried the recipe with all-purpose flour and then determined that a different protein level—either lower protein, such as pastry or cake flour, or higher protein, such as bread flour—was a necessary ingredient for success.

Bread flour This flour has a higher protein content than all-purpose flour. The protein produces gluten, so it is used to make bread. It is only called for in a few recipes that I got from another source, such as Chewy Ginger Cookies (page 110) and Cinnamon Rolls (page 86). The original recipes called for bread flour, and I wanted to stay true to the originals. You can use all-purpose flour in its place.

Cake flour A low-protein flour ground to a fine consistency, cake flour makes for a light, soft cake. I use it to make Corn Muffins (page 35) and Angel Food Cake (page 205). The softer flour helps produce a cake with a lighter crumb.

Pastry flour A low-protein flour, but not as low in protein as cake flour. I call for this flour in the Cream Biscuits (page 452), Madeleines (page 225), and Almond Biscotti (page 159). I felt that in these recipes, the softer flour would really make a difference.

Rice flour is milled from medium- or long-grain white rice. I use it in small quantities in the pastry cream for Coconut Cream Slab Pie (page 360) and in Onion and Sage Focaccia (page 455). Sweet rice flour is made from sticky rice and is much starchier; it is not an acceptable substitute. Use stone-ground rice flour if you can find it.

Rye flour (dark) Milled from whole rye berries (also called rye kernels), including the germ and bran, dark rye flour has a distinct, nutty taste and dark, grayish hue. I use it in the dough for Chocolate Chunk Cookies (page 95) to add a hint of flavor. (I also use it to give character to my homemade pizza dough, but that's another story, in another book . . .) If you can't find dark rye flour, medium or light rye flour will also work.

Self-Rising Flour A premixture of all-purpose flour, baking powder, and salt, self-rising flour is often seen in baking recipes from the American South. You can find it many grocery stores and online, or make your own using a ratio of 1 cup flour, 1½ teaspoons baking powder, and ¼ teaspoon Diamond Crystal kosher salt.

Spelt flour Spelt is an heirloom grain in the same family as wheat. Using spelt flour adds a layer of whole-grain flavor to baked goods without giving them a heavy or grainy "health food" texture. It is used in the Oat Currant Scones (page 53); it's also part of a mix of flours in the dough for the Onion and Sage Focaccia (page 455); and, of course, it plays a starring role in Spelt Digestivi (page 476).

Unbleached all-purpose flour A versatile white flour, this is the flour I use most often in this book; it is made from wheat berries from which the germ and bran have been removed, making a refined product. Bleached all-purpose flour, by contrast, is treated with chemicals; it is whiter in color and finer in texture. It looks like something you'd use to make Twinkies; I never use it. In many recipes that call for other white flours, such as bread flour and pastry flour, I give unbleached flour as an alternative. Measure the alternatives by volume, not weight.

Whole wheat flour, like white flour, is made of wheat berries. The difference in the case of wheat flour is that the berries are ground with the bran and germ intact, so it has a higher fiber content than white flour, such as all-purpose flour called for in these recipes. I call for it whenever I want to add a bit of wheat flavor, texture, or even color, as in Granola Bar Bites (page 71), to keep them feeling healthy; and in Rough Puff Pastry Dough (page 357) and the streusel atop the Rustic Pear Tarts (page 432) to give them color; whole-wheat flour also plays a starring role in the Spiced Graham Crackers (page 165).

Italian Leavening

I call for Italian leavening in a handful of Italian or Italian-inspired recipes. I don't know what it is, but there is something about Italian leavening that makes pastries taste . . . Italian. The most common brand is Paneangeli. You can find it in Italian specialty markets and from online sources. If you can't find Italian leavening, substitute half baking soda and half baking powder.

Nuts

I use a lot of nuts in baking (I like the flavor and texture they add to baked goods); you will see peanuts, almonds, walnuts, pecans, pistachios, and hazelnuts throughout these recipes. I prefer to buy whole or halved nuts rather than chopped nuts or nut pieces. Buy nuts from a source that carries fresh products and has a lot of turnover, as nuts contain a lot of oil and go rancid quickly. Store the nuts in the refrigerator or freezer in an airtight container until you're ready to use them.

Oil

Neutral-flavored oil My preferred varieties of neutral-flavored oils are grapeseed and safflower oil.

Olive oil When baking with olive oil, such as for the Carrot Cake (page 281) and Olive Oil Cakes (page 232), I use a quality extra-virgin olive oil.

Polenta

Polenta is the Italian version of cornmeal or ground dried corn kernels; it is generally coarser than cornmeal, although both are available in a variety of grinds. I use fine yellow polenta in some recipes and coarse yellow polenta in others. In both cases, I use Anson Mills Stone Ground Polenta. In some recipes, polenta is a star, such as Meyer Lemon Polenta Cake (page 399), Corn Muffins (page 35), and Corn Bread (page 458). In other recipes, such as Pineapple Upside-Down Cake (page 217), I sneak it in to add a bit of texture to the cake.

Potato Starch

In an effort not to use refined corn products in these recipes, I eliminated cornstarch and used potato starch in its place. You can find potato starch in grocery stores. If you can't find potato starch, use an equal amount of cornstarch.

Raisins

Look for fresh, plump raisins from a good source. Farmers' markets and Middle Eastern markets are both good options. I recently discovered green raisins, which have so much flavor. If you find them, they'd be delicious in any recipe where raisins are called for. Not everyone has easy access to farmers' markets or might want to make the trip just for raisins. I get it. Do the best you can.

Rolled Oats

I call for rolled oats in several recipes, including Oatmeal Raisin Cookies (page 103), Granola Bar Bites (page 71), Oat Currant Scones (page 53), and, of course, Granola (page 67). I use Bob's Red Mill Organic Old-Fashioned Rolled Oats. Use any brand of old-fashioned oats you like, but don't use thick-cut oats (a Bob's Red Mill product, which are great, but which will not work the same in these recipes), steel-cut oats, quick-cooking oats, or instant oats.

Salt

I think it's safe to say that every recipe that follows in these pages calls for kosher salt. Salt adds a necessary contrast to sugar in baked goods, bringing out the sweetness and the other flavors in the recipe; without it, the flavor of even the best baked goods falls a bit flat. The interaction between salt and sweet is brought to another level when the baked goods are topped with flaky sea salt. For adding to batters and doughs, I use Diamond Crystal kosher salt. I call for this salt by brand to ensure that the amount you use is accurate; if you use another brand or another texture of salt, it will measure differently, and your baked goods will be too salty or not salty enough. For topping baked goods, I use Maldon sea salt, an English brand; I like the texture of its large, tender flakes on top of baked goods. Maldon is widely available, even at many grocery stores. Jacobsen Salt Co.'s "pure flake sea salt," from Oregon, is another good option for flaky sea salt.

Sesame Seeds

Whether I'm using white or black sesame seeds, I use only toasted sesame seeds. They're much more flavorful than untoasted, and in terms of the white seeds, I also prefer the light golden color over the stark pearly white of those that are untoasted. Toasted sesame seeds, both white and black, are sold in shaker canisters in the Japanese section of supermarkets or at Asian grocery stores or from online sources. If you can't find toasted sesame seeds, use unhulled sesame seeds.

Spices

Grinding your own spices makes a big difference in terms of flavor and aroma. Except for nutmeg, which is grated using a Microplane (see page 12), whole spices are easy to grind in a spice grinder or most coffee grinders, electric or manual. You can freshly grind any of the spices in this book, including cinnamon, nutmeg, cloves, allspice, black pepper, and cardamom.

Black pepper I use black pepper sparingly, but when I do use it, I want it to have an intense taste and aroma. Tellicherry black peppercorns are my preferred variety. I call for coarsely ground black pepper in these recipes, which you can achieve using a pepper mill, mortar and pestle, or by pulsing the peppercorns in a spice grinder.

Cardamom This Indian spice has a strong, unique aroma that you will recognize as the dominant flavor in chai. Cardamom comes in both green and black. Either works equally well in these recipes. It is one spice that is considerably better, and always worth the effort, freshly ground.

Cinnamon Freshly ground cinnamon, made by grinding cinnamon sticks, is far superior to preground cinnamon. Look for cinnamon sticks that are loosely coiled; they seem to be softer, oilier, and more flavorful.

Nutmeg This spice comes in the form of a whole nut about twice the size of a shelled almond. Use a fine Microplane to grate it onto a small sheet of parchment paper, then pick up the parchment and use it like a funnel to funnel the nutmeg into a measuring spoon.

Sugar

Dark brown sugar A mixture of granulated sugar and molasses, which is a by-product of the sugar-refining process, this sugar gives molasses flavor to baked goods and is also responsible for the chewy quality in many American-style baked goods, such as Chocolate Chunk Cookies (page 95). I call for dark brown sugar in these recipes, which has a higher molasses content than light brown sugar. I figure if I want to add molasses flavor to something, then I want a *lot* of molasses flavor. Lightly pack brown sugar when measuring. Light brown sugar contains less molasses. If you use it in place of dark brown sugar, your baked goods will turn out, but they won't have the same color or depth of flavor.

Demerara and Turbinado Sugar These coarse, crunchy sugars have a slight molasses flavor. I call for demerara to coat the Snickerdoodles (page 107), which imparts a nice crunch to the cookies' exterior. I call for demerara or turbinado sugar to be sprinkled on the Strawberry-Rhubarb Pie crust (page 401) to add a crunchy, sparkling finish. The two sugars can be used interchangeably. But these sugars aren't just for sprinkling. The Chewy Ginger Cookies (page 110) use turbinado sugar in the dough, and the Financiers call for demerara in the dough.

Granulated sugar This is the most refined of all sugars and of course it is a staple in a dessert baking book. In addition to making things sweet, it also adds moisture to baked goods. These recipes were tested using conventional brands such as C&H and Domino.

Molasses A thick, viscous by-product of the sugar-refining process, molasses is a component in brown sugar and muscovado sugar. It has a strong, earthy, minerally taste. It imparts a unique flavor to baked goods and gives them a chewy texture, making molasses (in the form of brown sugar) essential in American drop cookies such as Chocolate Chunk Cookies (page 95) and Oatmeal Raisin Cookies (page 103). It is one of the defining flavors in Chewy Ginger Cookies (page 110). Look for unsulphured molasses, which hasn't been treated with chemicals. Blackstrap molasses is a less refined product and has a slightly bitter taste; I don't recommend it.

Muscovado sugar (dark) Where conventional brown sugar is composed of refined white sugar and molasses, muscovado is a coarse, raw sugar, from which the molasses was never removed. It has a deeper molasses flavor than conventional brown sugar. Find muscovado sugar in specialty grocery stores and from online sources; I use India Tree brand, which comes from the African island of Mauritius. If you can't find it, use conventional dark brown sugar in its place. Like brown sugar, lightly pack muscovado sugar when measuring. You can also find light brown muscovado sugar, which has a lighter color and lighter molasses flavor. If you use light brown muscovado sugar in place of dark brown muscovado sugar, your baked goods will turn out, but they won't have the same color or depth of flavor.

Powdered sugar Also called confectioners' sugar or icing sugar and referred to in professional kitchens as 10X sugar, powdered sugar is refined sugar that has been finely milled. It contains a very small amount of anticlumping agent, such as cornstarch. I use it in this book to make frostings and glazes, to coat Wedding Cookies (page 151), and to dust all sorts of things. A dusting of powdered sugar is the perfect finishing touch to many baked goods. I call for you to sift it in recipes where the lumps might be an issue. If your powdered sugar is clumpy or you want to be on the safe side, feel free to sift it through a mesh sieve or tamis.

Syrups

Lyle's Golden Syrup I didn't want to use corn syrup in these recipes since it's made with genetically modified corn, which negatively affects both farmers and the land they farm. Instead, I use Lyle's Golden Syrup, a British product made from sugar cane. Lyle's gives the same silky texture that corn syrup does to dessert sauces and other smooth desserts. It has a slight amber color, which I like; it doesn't look so artificial. It's readily available at supermarkets and from online sources. If you can't find Lyle's Golden Syrup, use an equal amount of corn syrup instead.

Maple syrup I recently discovered artisanal maple syrup, aged in wooden barrels. I've always been a fan of quality, pure Vermont maple syrup, but barrel-aging the syrup really takes it to another level. That's what I call for in these recipes.

Vanilla

Throughout my career, I've used vanilla beans whenever I wanted to infuse liquids with vanilla flavor. Back when I started, the only alternative to beans was vanilla extract, which didn't add the pretty specks of vanilla seeds, which you got when using vanilla beans. I was of the mind that vanilla beans were so superior to extract as to be worth their extra cost. But recently, that cost has gone crazy; it's just not justifiable anymore. In looking for an alternative, I discovered vanilla bean paste, a thick, spoonable product made of vanilla extract, sugar, and whole vanilla bean pods. It contains vanilla seeds, so you get pretty vanilla bean specks in whatever you add it to, whether it be a Vanilla Custard Tart with Raspberries (page 425), Shortbread Cookies (page 179), Bread Pudding (page 238), or any of the three cheesecakes in this book (pages 247, 250, and 252). There are a couple of recipes, such as Rugelach (page 155), in which I use pure vanilla extract instead of paste because the dough needs the thinner consistency of the extract.

Zante Currants

Zante currants are a small, sweet raisin variety. You can find them in grocery stores, sold in boxes alongside raisins. If you can't find them, use black raisins and chop them to the size of currants.

As both a baker and an eater, when I think of breakfast baked goods, I want there to be a healthy, or at least a substantial, component, and for them to not be too sweet. Bran muffins are the perfect example: The whole grains they're made with, along with the dried fruit you invariably find in them, make me feel like I'm eating, or feeding someone else, something that will help us get through the morning. The muffins in this book are scaled back to the size I grew up with, as opposed to the supersized versions you often see now. For me, that original, smaller size is the right size for a muffin. A muffin is *part* of a meal. It's not a meal, and it shouldn't be the size of one. Even though they are baked in the same tins, muffins are not cupcakes. A muffin shouldn't be frosted nor be as sweet as a cupcake, and the crumb, or texture, of the muffin should be a bit more substantial, not light and airy like a cupcake. Banana bread, though it's really a cake, is packed with bananas, so we can all convince ourselves it's a breakfast food. I have no healthy justification for scones, but they're quick and easy to make and delicious with coffee or tea, and I suppose that's justification enough. Same goes for Cinnamon Rolls and their cousin, Monkey Bread, which I'd file under special occasion foods. If you're creating a breakfast or brunch spread, along with one of those more indulgent items, make sure to include a savory item, such as Twice-Baked Ham and Cheese Croissants (page 75), and at least one thing that feels healthy, like those bran muffins. Your guests, especially if I am one of them, will appreciate it.

Baked Goods for Breakfast

Banana Bread

Back in my La Brea Bakery days, I used to top my banana bread loaf with sliced bananas to integrate more banana flavor into the loaf and for the visual impact. But because of the shape of the pan, you really didn't get much of that banana topping with each slice. In rethinking banana bread for this book, I traded in the typical loaf pan for a square cake pan, which provided more surface area, and thus room for more bananas on top of the cake. And since banana bread is really banana *cake,* baking it in a cake pan seemed like the honest thing to do. This bread/cake is made with the pureed bananas and yogurt, making it very moist. It's delicious at room temperature and even a day or two after it is made, but it is absolutely at its pinnacle when it's just cooling from the oven and the cinnamon-sugar sprinkled on top is still crunchy.

Makes one 10-inch square banana bread

What You Need—
The Essential Special Equipment

10-inch square cake pan

Cooking spray

Large disposable pastry bag

For the Banana Bread

226 grams (2 generous cups) walnut halves

1¼ pounds unpeeled very ripe (spotted or brown) bananas (5 to 7 bananas)

250 grams (1 cup) plain whole-milk yogurt (not Greek yogurt)

3 extra-large eggs

75 grams (¼ cup) artisanal maple syrup (preferably barrel-aged)

1 tablespoon pure vanilla bean paste or vanilla extract

170 grams (1½ sticks) cold unsalted butter, cubed

150 grams (¾ cup) granulated sugar

150 grams (¾ cup packed) dark brown sugar

1 tablespoon plus ¾ teaspoon baking powder

1½ tablespoons poppy seeds

1 tablespoon ground cinnamon

2 teaspoons baking soda

1½ teaspoons Diamond Crystal kosher salt

1 teaspoon grated nutmeg

½ teaspoon ground cloves

350 grams (2¼ cups) all-purpose flour

For the Topping

125 grams (½ cup plus 2 tablespoons) granulated sugar

2½ teaspoons ground cinnamon

4 large bananas (about 1 pound), not overripe, spotted, or bruised

1. To make the banana bread, adjust an oven rack to the center position and preheat the oven to 325°F.

2. Coat the bottom and sides of the cake pan with cooking spray. If you want to lift the banana bread out of the pan to cut and serve it, cut two 9 × 16-inch pieces of parchment paper. Lay one sheet of paper in the pan so it travels up and over two of the sides. Lay the other sheet perpendicular so it travels up and over the remaining two sides of the pan and spray the paper with cooking spray. →

3. Spread the walnuts on a baking sheet and toast them on the center rack of the oven until they're lightly browned and fragrant, 8 to 10 minutes, shaking the baking sheet and rotating it front to back halfway through the toasting time so the walnuts brown evenly. Remove the walnuts from the oven. (If you think the nuts are on the verge of being overtoasted, transfer them to a plate so they don't continue to cook from the residual heat of the pan.) Set the walnuts aside until they're cool enough to touch, then coarsely chop them.

4. Increase the oven temperature to 350°F.

5. Peel the bananas and break them up into the bowl of a stand mixer. Fit the mixer with the paddle and beat the bananas at medium speed for about 1 minute to make a chunky puree. Weigh out 517 grams (or measure 2¼ cups) of the banana puree and put it in a medium bowl. (Reserve any remaining banana puree for another use.) Add the yogurt, eggs, maple syrup, and vanilla to the bowl with the pureed bananas and stir with a whisk to combine.

6. If you don't have a second bowl for your stand mixer, transfer the banana mixture to a separate bowl and clean the mixer bowl, drying it thoroughly.

7. Put the butter in the clean mixer bowl. Return the paddle attachment to the mixer and beat the butter on medium speed until it is softened but still cold, 3 to 4 minutes, stopping to scrape down the sides and bottom of the bowl and the paddle with a rubber spatula whenever butter is accumulating. Add the granulated sugar and brown sugar and beat on medium speed until light and fluffy, 3 to 4 minutes, scraping down the bowl as needed. Add the baking powder, poppy seeds, cinnamon, baking soda, salt, nutmeg, and cloves and beat on medium speed for about 15 seconds to distribute the additions. Stop the mixer and scrape down the bowl and paddle. Add the flour and the banana mixture alternately in five additions for the flour and four for the banana mixture, starting and ending with the flour; mix on low speed until each addition is fully incorporated and stop to scrape down the bowl before the next addition. When all the ingredients are fully incorporated, stop the mixer, remove the paddle and bowl, and clean them with the rubber spatula. Add the walnuts and stir with a rubber spatula to distribute them. Scrape the bowl from the bottom up to release any ingredients from the bottom of the bowl.

8. Spoon the batter into the prepared pan and use a small offset spatula to smooth out the surface.

9. To make the topping, stir the granulated sugar and cinnamon together and sprinkle 50 grams (¼ cup) of the cinnamon-sugar evenly over the batter.

10. Peel the bananas and cut them in half lengthwise, following the contour of the banana. Lay the banana halves flat-side down on the cutting board. With your knife parallel to the cutting board, trim off the humps in the center part of the bananas, so you're left with flat slabs of banana that are of even thickness. (Reserve the trimmings for another use, such as to make a smoothie, or to snack on.) Sprinkle the sides of the banana slices that are facing up with the remaining cinnamon-sugar and gently pat the cinnamon-sugar into the bananas until the cinnamon-sugar looks wet. Pick up the banana slices with your hands and lay them in one direction, sugared-side up, to cover the banana bread.

11. Bake the banana bread on the center rack of the oven until a toothpick inserted into the center comes out clean and the bread is firm to the touch, 70 to 80 minutes, rotating the pan front to back halfway through the baking time so the bread bakes evenly. Remove the bread from the oven.

12. Cut the banana bread directly in the pan or lift on the parchment paper "wings" to remove the banana bread from the pan. Cut as desired.

Corn Muffins;
Bran Muffins;
Blueberry Millet Muffins

Corn Muffins

When developing this recipe, I wanted to create a corn muffin that tasted like corn. Is that too much to ask? These muffins are slightly sweeter than Corn Bread (page 458), but don't expect a corn cupcake. They're made with stoneground polenta, which gives them a slightly grainy texture. Whole corn kernels don't break down even when baked, so I start with fresh corn on the cob and grate it using a corn creamer, a handy tool that removes corn kernels from the cob and breaks them up, or "creams" the kernels, in the process, so they integrate into the batter. I then take the liquid released when the corn is creamed and cook it down until it's almost like a pudding, and intense with corn flavor, and then fold that into the batter.

The flavor of these muffins is dependent on sweet, summer corn. If you want to make this recipe when corn is not in season, the muffins will be delicious, but not earth-shattering. The muffins are topped with a mixture of sweetened cornflakes, which gives them a crispy, crunchy top. (You must use old-school style cornflakes for the topping; the "health food" varieties are thicker and not as crispy.) These muffins are best the day they're baked when the cornflake topping is at its crunchiest. If you're planning to keep them longer, skip the cornflake topping.

Makes about 18 muffins

What You Need—
The Essential Special Equipment

2 (12-cup) or 3 (6-cup) standard-size (½-cup capacity) muffin tins

Cooking spray

Corn creamer

For the Batter

225 grams (1½ cups) fine yellow stoneground polenta

5½ pounds summer corn (6 to 8 ears), husks and silks removed

374 grams (1⅔ cups) buttermilk (preferably whole-milk or low-fat), shaken

146 grams (⅔ cup) safflower oil, or another neutral-flavored oil, such as grapeseed

2 extra-large eggs

60 grams (2 tablespoons) mild-flavored honey, such as clover or wildflower

380 grams (3 cups) cake flour

180 grams (¾ cup plus 2 tablespoons plus 1 teaspoon) granulated sugar

1 tablespoon plus 1½ teaspoons baking powder

1 tablespoon Diamond Crystal kosher salt

1 teaspoon baking soda

For the Topping

1 extra-large egg white

75 grams (¼ cup plus 2 tablespoons) granulated sugar

¼ teaspoon ground cinnamon

60 grams (1⅔ cups) thin, crispy cornflakes →

Corn Muffins (continued)

1. To make the batter, adjust an oven rack to the center position and preheat the oven to 350°F. Coat the muffin cups with cooking spray. Line a baking sheet (or a quarter-sheet pan, if you have one) with parchment paper.

2. Spread the polenta in an even layer on the prepared baking sheet and toast it on the center rack of the oven until it is golden brown and fragrant, 8 to 10 minutes, rotating the baking sheet front to back and stirring the polenta halfway through that time so the polenta toasts evenly. Remove the baking sheet from the oven and set it aside to cool the polenta to room temperature.

3. Grate the corn on a corn creamer and discard the cobs. Drain the corn in a fine-mesh sieve set over a medium saucepan so the liquid falls into the pan, pressing on the corn with a spatula to squeeze out as much liquid as possible. Measure out 1 packed cup of the corn and set aside. (Reserve the remaining corn for another use, such as to toss in a salad.)

4. Set the pan of corn liquid over medium-high heat and cook, stirring constantly with a silicone spatula, until it thickens to the consistency of pudding, about 5 minutes. Remove from the heat. Weigh out 110 grams (or measure ½ cup) of the "pudding," transfer it to a medium bowl, and set aside to cool to room temperature (discard any remaining "pudding").

5. Add the buttermilk, oil, eggs, and honey to the bowl with the corn "pudding" and whisk to combine.

6. Transfer the polenta to a large wide bowl, using the parchment paper as a funnel. Add the flour, sugar, baking powder, salt, and baking soda and stir with a whisk to combine. Create a well in the center of the dry ingredients with your hands. Pour half of the buttermilk/egg mixture into the well and use a whisk to draw the flour mixture from the edges to the well to make a thick paste. Add the remaining wet ingredients and stir with the whisk to combine. Stir in the corn.

7. Use a measuring cup or scoop to fill each muffin cup with ⅓ cup of batter.

8. To make the topping, stir the egg white, sugar, and cinnamon together in a small bowl. Stir in the cornflakes.

9. Scoop the cornflakes out of the bowl with your hands, leaving any excess egg white in the bowl, and place the cornflakes on top of each muffin to cover the surface, leaving a ¼-inch border of batter around the edges visible. Discard the remaining egg white.

10. Bake the muffins on the center rack of the oven for 20 minutes. Rotate the muffin tins front to back and increase the oven temperature to 375°F. Bake the muffins until the tops are golden brown, the muffins are firm to the touch, and a toothpick inserted into the center of a muffin comes out clean, another 10 to 15 minutes. Remove the muffins from the oven.

11. To remove the muffins from the pans, run the tip of a paring knife around each cup to loosen them. One at a time, slide the knife under each muffin and pop it out.

Blueberry Millet Muffins

I became obsessed with millet muffins in the 1980s, when Alice Waters offered them at her wonderful Café Fanny (named for her daughter) in Berkeley, California. Millet is a small round seed often used in birdseed, with a mild, almost corn-like flavor. Alice's muffins contained whole millet. Eating them, you felt like you were having something healthy. For this recipe, I took the idea of Alice's millet muffins and added blueberries. The pop of acidity that the blueberries give to the millet muffins turns out to be a great addition. Plus, I knew for this book that I had to make a blueberry muffin because it's such a classic. But I am not a fan of typical blueberry muffins, with their white cake base, so with this recipe, I killed two birds with one stone: I included the recipe for millet muffins I've always loved, and I included the requisite blueberry muffin. If you want, you can make these without blueberries; note that they will take about 5 minutes less time to cook.

You process the millet for this recipe in a food processor, but only enough to crack it; you do not want to grind the millet into anything close to a flour or cornmeal texture. The point is simply to break down the outer walls of the millet so that it integrates into the batter. (See photo page 34.)

Makes about 9 muffins

**What You Need—
The Essential Special Equipment**

12-cup standard-size (½-cup capacity) muffin tin

Cooking spray

1½ teaspoons granulated sugar

⅛ teaspoon ground cinnamon

113 grams (1 stick) unsalted butter, cubed

196 grams (¾ cup plus 2 tablespoons) buttermilk (preferably whole-milk or low-fat), shaken

1½ teaspoons pure vanilla bean paste or vanilla extract

110 grams (½ cup plus 1 tablespoon) millet

192.5 grams (1¼ cups plus 2 tablespoons) unbleached all-purpose flour

1 teaspoon baking powder

1 teaspoon baking soda

137.5 grams (½ cup plus 3 tablespoons packed) dark brown sugar

1 extra-large egg

½ teaspoon Diamond Crystal kosher salt

144 grams (1 cup) blueberries

1. Adjust an oven rack to the center position and preheat the oven to 350°F. Coat the muffin cups with cooking spray.

2. Stir the granulated sugar and cinnamon together in a small bowl and set aside.

3. Warm the butter in a small saucepan or skillet with a light-colored bottom over medium heat until it melts and begins to bubble, swirling the pan

occasionally. Continue to cook the butter, swirling often so it cooks evenly, until it is golden and the milk solids are medium brown, 4 to 6 minutes. Remove from the heat. Working quickly so the butter doesn't continue to cook, weigh out 70 grams (or measure about 5 tablespoons) of the butter and transfer it to a large bowl to cool to room temperature. (Reserve the remaining butter for another use.)

4. When the butter has cooled, add the buttermilk and vanilla and whisk to combine.

5. Place the millet in a food processor, cover the feed tube with your hand and pulse for 30 seconds to crack the outer walls of the millet; the millet will look a little powdery but will not look cracked or broken.

6. Sift the flour, baking powder, and baking soda together into a large bowl. Sift the ingredients a second time.

7. Combine the brown sugar, egg, and salt in a stand mixer and fit with the whisk. Beat on medium speed until the mixture is pale yellow, thick, and falls from the whisk back into the bowl in a ribbon-like pattern that doesn't immediately melt into the surface, 2 to 3 minutes, stopping to scrape down the sides of the bowl with a rubber spatula whenever ingredients are accumulating. Remove the bowl from the mixer and add the flour mixture and buttermilk mixture alternately in three additions for the flour and two for the buttermilk, starting and ending with the flour mixture and stirring with a spatula to combine before the next addition. (Don't worry if the batter looks slightly lumpy; it will be fine.) Add the millet and blueberries and stir the batter with the rubber spatula, scraping the bowl from the bottom up to release any ingredients from the bottom of the bowl.

8. Using a measuring cup or scoop, fill each muffin cup with ⅓ cup of batter.

9. Sprinkle the cinnamon-sugar over the muffins, dividing it evenly.

10. Bake the muffins on the center rack of the oven until the tops are golden brown, the muffins are firm to the touch, and a toothpick inserted into the center of a muffin comes out clean, 28 to 32 minutes, rotating the pan front to back halfway through the baking time so the muffins bake evenly. Remove the muffins from the oven.

11. To remove the muffins from the pan, run the tip of a paring knife around each cup to loosen them. Slide the knife under each muffin and pop it out.

Bran Muffins

When you lose someone that you love, they come back to you in the most unexpected ways, and one way my dad comes to my mind is whenever I see or think about bran muffins. He loved anything bran: raisin bran cereal, oat bran, and most of all, bran muffins. I've made many versions over the decades, but they all have some qualities in common: They're dark, moist, and not too sweet. In the end, the ideal bran muffin leads you to believe that you are eating something nutritious. I think that's why my dad liked them. He, like all bran lovers I suspect, liked thinking he was making the better choice. (See photo page 34.)

Makes about 10 muffins

**What You Need—
The Essential Special Equipment**

12-cup standard-size (½-cup capacity) muffin tin

Cooking spray

For the Batter

130 grams (2 cups) wheat bran

244 grams (2 cups) Zante currants (or black raisins)

¾ cup brandy (or whiskey)

112 grams (½ cup) buttermilk (preferably whole-milk or low-fat), shaken

105 grams (½ cup) virgin coconut oil (melted if the oil is too hard to scoop)

42.5 grams (2 tablespoons) Lyle's Golden Syrup

1 extra-large egg

1 extra-large egg white

1 tablespoon pure vanilla bean paste or vanilla extract

100 grams (½ cup packed) dark muscovado sugar

1 teaspoon baking powder

1 teaspoon baking soda

½ teaspoon Diamond Crystal kosher salt

75 grams (½ cup) unbleached all-purpose flour

34 grams (¼ cup) whole wheat flour

For the Glaze

42.5 grams (2 tablespoons) Lyle's Golden Syrup

1. To make the batter, adjust an oven rack to the center position and preheat the oven to 350°F. Coat the muffin cups with cooking spray. Line a baking sheet (a quarter-sheet pan if you have one) with parchment paper.

2. Spread the bran in an even layer on the prepared baking sheet and toast it on the center rack of the oven until it is golden brown and fragrant, 6 to 8 minutes, rotating the baking sheet front to back and stirring the bran halfway through that time so it toasts evenly. Remove the baking sheet from the oven and set it aside for the bran to cool to room temperature.

3. Increase the oven temperature to 375°F.

4. Combine the currants with the brandy in a small saucepan and bring to a boil over high heat. Remove from the heat and set aside for 10 minutes for the currants to soften in the liquid. Reserving the soaking liquid, drain the currants. (If you're using raisins, chop them to about the size of currants.) Measure out 1 cup of the currants and set aside to fold into the batter. Place the remaining currants, along with ¼ cup of the reserved liquid, in a food processor and pulse for about 1 minute to a semismooth puree. Return the pureed currants to the saucepan and cook over medium heat, stirring constantly, for about 1 minute, to cook off any excess liquid and form a paste. Remove from the heat.

5. Transfer the puree to a medium bowl. Add the buttermilk, coconut oil, golden syrup, whole egg, egg white, and vanilla and whisk to combine.

6. Clean and dry the bowl of the food processor. Using the parchment paper as a funnel, transfer the bran to the food processor. Add the muscovado sugar, baking powder, baking soda, and salt and pulse to combine the ingredients and break up any lumps in the sugar. Transfer the contents of the food processor to a large bowl. Add the all-purpose flour and whole wheat flour and stir with a whisk to combine. Add the currant puree/buttermilk mixture and stir with a rubber spatula to combine. Add the reserved whole currants (or chopped raisins) and stir to distribute them.

7. Using a measuring cup or scoop, fill each muffin cup with ½ cup of batter.

8. Bake the muffins on the center rack of the oven until they are firm to the touch, and a toothpick inserted into the center of a muffin comes out clean, 22 to 26 minutes, rotating the tin front to back halfway through the baking time so the muffins bake evenly. Remove the muffins from the oven.

9. While the muffins are baking, to make the glaze, stir the golden syrup in a small bowl with 1 teaspoon of water.

10. Brush the glaze over the muffins while they're hot.

11. To remove the muffins from the pan, run the tip of a paring knife around each cup to loosen them. One at a time, slide the knife under each muffin and pop it out.

Apricot Thumbprint Scones (left);
Caramelized White Chocolate Scones with
Toasted Pecans and Cranberries (right)

Apricot Thumbprint Scones

I love scones with a jam-filled crater in the center—you get your scone and jam in the same bite. I like to imagine these scones offered among a selection of baked goods, with the colorful jam shimmering like jewels. The dough contains grated, hard-boiled egg yolk, a technique borrowed from traditional Linzer cookies that makes for a tender and crumbly scone. You need to plan in advance to make these, since I call for you to brown the butter and then to chill before using it. I fill the thumbprint with apricot jam, but if you wanted to use seedy raspberry or blackberry jam, those would be equally delicious— and pretty.

Makes about 9 scones

What You Need—
The Essential Special Equipment
2½-inch fluted round cutter

For the Dough
113 grams (1 stick) unsalted butter, cubed

2 extra-large eggs

52 grams (½ cup) walnut halves

120 grams (½ cup) heavy cream

1½ teaspoons pure vanilla bean paste or vanilla extract

37.5 grams (2 tablespoons) granulated sugar

2 teaspoons baking powder

1½ teaspoons Diamond Crystal kosher salt

175 grams (1¼ cups) unbleached all-purpose flour, plus more for dusting

44.5 grams (¼ cup) coarse yellow stoneground polenta

1½ teaspoons ground cardamom

½ teaspoon ground cinnamon

½ teaspoon grated nutmeg

For Finishing
12.5 grams (1 tablespoon) granulated sugar

12 grams (1 tablespoon) demerara sugar

⅛ teaspoon grated nutmeg

⅛ teaspoon ground cinnamon

30 grams (2 tablespoons) heavy cream

78 grams (¼ cup) apricot jam

1. To make the dough, place the butter in a small saucepan or skillet with a light-colored bottom to make brown butter. Warm the butter over medium heat until it melts and begins to bubble, swirling the pan occasionally. Cook the butter, swirling often so it cooks evenly, until the butter is caramel colored and the milk solids are the color of coffee grounds, 4 to 8 minutes. Remove from the heat. Working quickly so the butter doesn't continue to cook, weigh out 84 grams (or measure 6 tablespoons) of butter, making sure to include the milk solids, and place it in a bowl. Set aside to cool to room temperature. Cover the bowl and refrigerate until the butter is solid, at least several hours. (Reserve the remaining butter for another use.)

2. Bring a medium saucepan of water to a boil. Add the eggs and boil them for 11 minutes. While the eggs are cooking, fill a bowl with ice water. →

Remove the eggs from the boiling water with a slotted spoon and place them in the ice water to cool completely. Remove the eggs from the ice water and peel them. Separate the whites and yolks. (Reserve the whites for another use. I sprinkle them with salt to snack on.) Place the yolks in a small bowl and set aside.

3. Adjust an oven rack to the center position and preheat the oven to 325°F.

4. Spread the walnuts on a baking sheet and toast them on the center rack of the oven until they're lightly browned and fragrant, 10 to 12 minutes, shaking the baking sheet and rotating it front to back halfway through the toasting time so the walnuts brown evenly. Remove the walnuts from the oven and set aside to cool to room temperature. (If you think the nuts are on the verge of being overtoasted, transfer them to a plate so they don't continue to cook from the residual heat of the pan.)

5. Whisk the cream and vanilla together in a small bowl.

6. Transfer the walnuts to a food processor. Add the granulated sugar, baking powder, and salt and pulse until the walnuts are ground to a coarse meal, stopping to scrape down the corners of the food processor bowl to release any ingredients. Add the flour, polenta, cardamom, cinnamon, and nutmeg and pulse a few times to combine. Using a medium or fine Microplane (or on the small—but not the smallest—holes of a box grater), grate the egg yolks into the food processor. Pulse to combine the ingredients.

7. Remove the butter from the refrigerator and place the bowl in a large bowl of hot water to help release the butter. Dry off the bowl and invert it to release the butter onto a cutting board. (Alternatively, you may be able to wedge a knife under the butter and pop it out.) Cut the butter into roughly ½-inch cubes.

8. Add the butter to the food processor and pulse until the mixture is the texture of coarse meal. Transfer the mixture a large wide bowl. Create a well in the center of the butter/flour mixture with your hands. Pour the cream/vanilla mixture into the well and use your hands to draw the butter and flour mixture into the well to form a homogeneous dough.

9. Lightly dust a work surface with flour and place the dough on the floured surface. Lightly dust your hands with flour and pat the dough into a ¾-inch-thick disk. Fill a small bowl with flour.

10. Line a large baking sheet with parchment paper. Dip the cutter in the flour and use it to cut a round of the dough. With the dough still in the cutter, transfer the scone and cutter to the prepared baking sheet. Using your thumb, press on the center of the dough to make an indentation about 1 inch wide and three-quarters of the way to the bottom of the scone. Remove the cutter, dip it in flour again, and repeat with the remaining dough, leaving at least 1½ inches between the scones on the baking sheet. Gather the scraps, pat them out to ¾ inch thick, and cut as many rounds as you can from them. (Bake the remaining scraps to snack on or discard them.) Place the scones in the refrigerator to chill until the dough is firm, at least 1 hour.

11. Meanwhile, adjust an oven rack to the center position and preheat the oven to 375°F.

12. To finish the scones, stir the granulated sugar, demerara sugar, nutmeg, and cinnamon together in a small bowl.

13. Remove the scones from the refrigerator. Brush the tops and sides of the scones with cream and sprinkle the sugar and spice mixture over them, brushing and sprinkling around the craters. Spoon a generous teaspoon of jam into the crater of each scone.

14. Bake the scones on the center rack of the oven until they are golden brown and a toothpick inserted into the center of one comes out clean, 30 to 33 minutes, rotating the baking sheet front to back halfway through the baking time so the scones bake evenly. Remove the scones from the oven.

Caramelized White Chocolate Scones with Toasted Pecans and Cranberries

One day a few years ago, while filming a TV show in the town of Santa Rosa, north of San Francisco, I stumbled upon a wonderful food store called Miracle Plum. The store offered a selection of hand-chosen artisan items, sandwiches, and baked goods, including these eye-catching scones. Often, when you see scones on display, they look dry and pale, but these had a deep golden-brown crusty exterior, glittering with sugar—they just sparkled. I bought one and broke into it, and the inside was extremely moist and buttery. So moist, in fact, that I'm not sure how they qualify as scones . . . maybe because they're cut into triangles.

Lucky for us, the baker at Miracle Plum, Joni Davis, was nice enough to share her recipe with me to include here. The scones are baked first in a springform pan, and then cut into triangles and baked again. At Miracle Plum, they add various combinations of fruits, nuts, and chocolate to this base. But this combination was the one I tried, and the one I asked to publish: It contains toasted pecans, which give the scones a nice soft crunch; fresh cranberries, which add a pop of acidity; and chunks of caramelized white chocolate. Also called "roasted" or "blonde" white chocolate, the caramelized white chocolate has a deep, toasted flavor that makes it totally unlike plain white chocolate. I give you directions for caramelizing it in this recipe, but you can also buy it; Valrhona sells it in the shape of feves under the name Dulcey. (If you start with caramelized white chocolate, skip the directions for caramelizing the white chocolate.) (See photo page 42.)

Makes 8 scones

What You Need—
The Essential Special Equipment
9-inch springform pan

Cooking spray

Bench knife

Instant-read thermometer

For the Dough
150 grams (5 ounces) plain white chocolate, coarsely chopped (whole if you're using feves); or caramelized white chocolate (such as Valrhona Dulcey), coarsely chopped (halved if you're using feves; 1 heaping cup)

50 grams (½ cup) pecan halves

198 grams (1¼ cups plus 2 tablespoons) unbleached all-purpose flour, plus more for dusting

85 grams (½ cup plus 3 tablespoons plus 1 teaspoon) whole wheat pastry flour

62.5 grams (¼ cup plus 1 tablespoon) granulated sugar

1 tablespoon baking powder

1½ teaspoons Diamond Crystal kosher salt

113 grams (1 stick) cold unsalted butter, thinly sliced

50 grams (½ cup) fresh cranberries, halved

360 grams (1½ cups) heavy cream

For Finishing
15 grams (1 tablespoon) heavy cream

12.5 grams (1 tablespoon) granulated sugar

1. To make the dough, adjust an oven rack to the center position and preheat the oven to 300°F.

2. Spread the white chocolate pieces in a single layer in a large glass (or other nonreactive) baking dish and bake on the center rack, stirring and spreading the white chocolate out into a thin layer every 10 minutes, until it is a deep caramel color (about the color of peanut butter), 40 to 50 minutes. Remove the baking dish from the oven.

3. Line a large baking sheet with parchment paper and use a rubber spatula to scrape the white chocolate onto the paper. Place the parchment in the refrigerator to cool until the white chocolate is solid, about 1 hour. Remove the white chocolate from the refrigerator and roughly chop it. Place the chopped white chocolate in a bowl and return it to the refrigerator until you're ready to use it.

4. When ready to bake, adjust an oven rack to the center position and preheat the oven to 325°F.

5. Spread the pecans on a large baking sheet and toast them on the center rack of the oven until they're golden brown and fragrant, 15 to 20 minutes, shaking the baking sheet and rotating it front to back halfway through the toasting time so the pecans brown evenly. Remove the baking sheet from the oven. (If you think the nuts are on the verge of being overtoasted, transfer them to a plate so they don't continue to cook from the residual heat of the pan.) Set the pecans aside until they are cool enough to touch, then roughly chop them.

6. Increase the oven temperature to 425°F.

7. Separate the bottom and outer ring of the springform pan. Coat the bottom of the pan and the inside of the ring with cooking spray. Cut a piece of parchment paper to fit the bottom of the pan and lay it on the bottom. Cut 3-inch-wide strips of parchment and press them onto the inside of the ring to line it.

8. Place the all-purpose flour, whole wheat pastry flour, sugar, baking powder, and salt in a large wide bowl and stir with a whisk to combine. Add the butter pieces and toss to coat them with the flour. One by one, flatten each piece of butter between your fingertips. Work the butter and flour together between your fingers until some of the butter pieces are the size →

Caramelized White Chocolate Scones (continued)

of dimes and others are smaller, like peas. Place the bowl in the refrigerator to chill the butter until it is firm, about 20 minutes.

9. Remove the bowl with the flour and butter mixture from the refrigerator. Add the white chocolate pieces, chopped pecans, and cranberries and toss gently with your hands to distribute them evenly. Create a well in the center of the mixture with your hands. Pour the cream into the well and use your hands to draw the butter and flour mixture from the edges into the well to moisten the butter and flour mixture.

10. Dust your work surface generously with flour. Transfer the shaggy dough to the floured surface, dust it with flour, and use your hands to press it into a homogeneous dough. Pat the dough into a ¾-inch-thick block, dusting your hands with flour as needed. Slide the bench knife under the dough and use it to lift the dough off the work surface to fold the dough in half like a book. Use the bench knife to gather up any bits and place them on top of the dough. Dust the dough again with flour, flatten it out again to ¾ inch thick, and fold it again like a book.

11. Using your hands, shape the dough into a 9-inch round. Use a long sharp knife to cut it into 8 wedges. One by one, pick up the wedges and place them in the prepared bottom of the springform pan, putting them back together to form a complete round. Fit the ring onto the bottom and snap it closed.

12. To finish the scones, brush the tops with the cream and sprinkle with the sugar.

13. Bake the scones on the center rack of the oven until they are golden brown and a thermometer inserted into the center of the scones registers 190°F, 35 to 45 minutes, rotating the pan front to back halfway through the baking time so the scones bake evenly. Remove the pan from the oven and unhinge and remove the outer ring.

14. Line a large baking sheet with parchment paper. Use a large offset spatula (or another metal spatula) to separate the scones and slide the spatula under each scone to transfer them, evenly spaced, to the prepared baking sheet. Return the scones to the oven to bake until the tops are deep golden brown, 5 to 10 minutes longer. Remove the scones from the oven.

Parmesan and Pecorino Cheese Scones

Cheese scones, traditionally made with cheddar, are a classic. More recently, cheese scones made with Parmesan have made their way onto the scene. I make these with a combination of Parmesan and Pecorino Romano, a hard sheep's milk from Italy with a sharp, salty flavor. Both cheeses are quite pungent, so these scones are not shy in their cheese flavor. Sautéed scallions and coarsely ground black pepper put them firmly in the savory category. The threads of scallions peek out around the edges of the scones and burn slightly; I like the way they look. Serve these alongside eggs or as dinner rolls; or enjoy them by themselves as a breakfast or afternoon snack. While they don't satisfy a sweet tooth, they do satisfy one's craving for a delicious, buttery treat.

Makes about 12 scones

What You Need—
The Essential Special Equipment
2½-inch fluted round cutter

For the Scallions
2 ounces scallions (about 10)

56.5 grams (½ stick) unsalted butter

1½ teaspoons Diamond Crystal kosher salt

For the Dough
315 grams (2¼ cups) unbleached all-purpose flour, plus more for dusting

57 grams (½ cup plus 2 tablespoons) finely grated Parmesan cheese

57 grams (½ cup plus 2 tablespoons) finely grated Pecorino Romano cheese

1 tablespoon plus 1 teaspoon baking powder

2 teaspoons Diamond Crystal kosher salt

1 teaspoon coarse freshly ground black pepper

140 grams (1 stick plus 2 tablespoons) cold unsalted butter, cubed

232 grams (1 cup) crème fraîche (or 244 grams/1 cup sour cream)

For Finishing
28 grams (2 tablespoons) unsalted butter, melted

2 tablespoons fresh thyme leaves

Chunk of Parmesan

1. To prepare the scallions, trim off the unappealing outer layers. Starting at the green ends, cut the scallions on an extreme bias into slices ¼ inch thick until you reach the roots (discard the roots and trimmings).

2. Melt the butter in a medium sauté pan over medium heat. Add the scallions, sprinkle with the salt, and cook, stirring, until the scallions are soft but not browned, about 2 minutes. Remove from the heat and place the scallions in a fine-mesh sieve. Set the sieve on a plate and place the scallions in the refrigerator to cool to room temperature and continue draining. →

3. To make the dough, combine the flour, Parmesan, Pecorino, baking powder, salt, and pepper in a food processor and pulse to combine the ingredients. Add the butter and pulse until the mixture is the texture of coarse meal. Transfer the mixture a large wide bowl.

4. Remove the scallions from the refrigerator, add them to the butter and flour mixture, and stir to combine. Create a well in the center of the mixture with your hands. Add the crème fraîche to the well and use your hands to draw the butter and flour mixture into the well to form a shaggy dough.

5. Transfer the dough to a work surface and place any loose scraps on top. Roll the dough over itself with the heels of your hands a few times to form a smooth, homogeneous dough. Lightly dust your hands with flour and pat the dough into a ¾-inch-thick disk. Fill a small bowl with flour.

6. Line a large baking sheet with parchment paper. Dip the cutter in the flour and use it to cut one round of the dough. With the dough still in the cutter, transfer the scone and cutter to the prepared baking sheet. Remove the cutter, dip it in flour again, and repeat with the remaining dough, leaving at least 1½ inches between the scones on the baking sheet. Gather the scraps, pat them out to ¾ inch thick, and cut as many rounds as you can from them. (Bake the remaining scraps to snack on or discard them.) Place the scones in the refrigerator to chill until they are firm, at least 1 hour.

7. Adjust an oven rack to the center position and preheat the oven to 375°F.

8. To finish the scones, remove them from the refrigerator, brush the tops with the melted butter and sprinkle with the thyme leaves.

9. Place the baking sheet on the center rack and bake the scones until they are golden brown, about 25 minutes, rotating the baking sheet front to back halfway through the baking time so the scones bake evenly. Remove the scones from the oven. While the scones are still warm, use a fine microplane to grate a generous flurry of Parmesan over them.

British Scones (left);
Oat Currant Scones (right)

Oat Currant Scones

If you were to ask me to define the classic scone, without doing any research, an oat scone would be it. The oats, the currants, and the whiskey the currants are steeped in all bring to my mind visions of a cold, rainy, Scottish, or Irish landscape. I very untraditionally drop these scones in irregular blobs and top them with crunchy demerara sugar, resulting in a craggy, crunchy, appealing exterior.

The whiskey comes through more than you might imagine, so if you don't want that flavor in your morning or teatime pastry, skip the step of steeping the currants. This is such a simple recipe, with nothing that needs to be prepared in advance, so it's the ideal project to take on when you want something homey and delicious.

Makes 10 scones

175 grams (1¼ cups) Zante currants (or black raisins)

½ cup whiskey (or rum)

112 grams (½ cup) buttermilk (preferably whole-milk or low-fat), shaken

32 grams (2 tablespoons) clover honey (or another neutral honey)

1 tablespoon pure vanilla bean paste or vanilla extract

122.5 grams (¾ cup plus 2 tablespoons) all-purpose flour

108 grams (¾ cup) spelt flour

84 grams (½ cup) golden or brown flaxseeds

37.5 grams (3 tablespoons) granulated sugar

37.5 grams (3 tablespoons packed) dark brown sugar

2 tablespoons buttermilk powder (or milk powder; preferably whole-milk or low-fat)

2 teaspoons baking powder

1¼ teaspoons baking soda

1 teaspoon Diamond Crystal kosher salt

169.grams (1½ sticks) cold unsalted butter, cubed

150 grams (1½ cups) rolled oats

60 grams (¼ cup) heavy cream

35 grams (3 tablespoons) demerara sugar (or turbinado sugar)

1. Combine the currants with the whiskey in a small saucepan and bring to a boil over high heat. Remove from the heat and set aside for 10 minutes for the currants to soften in the liquid. Drain the currants and discard the alcohol or reserve it for another culinary use. (If you're using raisins, chop them to the size of currants.)

2. Line two large baking sheets with parchment paper.

3. Whisk the buttermilk, honey, and vanilla together in a small bowl.

4. Put the all-purpose flour, spelt flour, flaxseeds, granulated sugar, brown sugar, buttermilk powder, baking powder, baking soda, and salt in a large food processor and pulse to combine the ingredients. Add the butter →

and pulse until the mixture is the texture of coarse meal. Transfer the mixture a large wide bowl. Add the oats and currants and stir to combine.

5. Create a well in the center of the dry ingredients with your hands. Pour the buttermilk mixture into the well and use your hands to draw the dry ingredients into the well to form a homogeneous dough.

6. Scoop up an orange-size portion of dough with your hand and drop it in a high mound onto one of the prepared baking sheets. (I like to eyeball these scones and I don't mind that they're not all precisely the same size, but if you are aiming for consistency, you can weigh the dough; each will weigh approximately 100 grams.) Continue scooping and dropping the dough, placing 5 scones, evenly spaced apart, on each baking sheet. Place the scones in the refrigerator to chill until the dough is firm, about 1 hour.

7. Adjust the oven racks so one is in the top third and the other is in the bottom third of the oven and preheat the oven to 375°F.

8. To finish the scones, remove them from the refrigerator and brush the tops and sides of the scones with the cream. Sprinkle them with the demerara sugar.

9. Place one baking sheet on each oven rack and bake the scones until they are golden brown, 25 to 32 minutes, switching racks and rotating the baking sheets front to back halfway through the baking time so the scones bake evenly. Remove the scones from the oven.

British Scones

I have never really understood the appeal of traditional British-style scones; I find them to be dry, heavy, and lacking in flavor. I figured traditional scones were an acquired taste that I had not acquired. Maybe I am unsophisticated in terms of scones, but I've always preferred American-style ones, which are buttery and biscuit-like. I also have never been quite sure what qualifies as a traditional British scone, nor what distinguishes scones from biscuits. What I do know is that people who know British-style scones feel very passionately that they are the true and original scone. Purists love them, and I was determined to love them, too.

To understand British scones, and maybe even learn to like them, I tried several recipes from different British cookbooks. Some used lard in place of butter; some called for cream in the dough, others milk. (None called for buttermilk, yogurt, or crème fraîche, like American scones often do.) In the process, I embraced their denser, less-buttery quality, and grew to like them. But I will also say this: I completely understand why scones are traditionally served with clotted cream and jam—they are dry! Clotted cream is a thick, British cream sold in small glass jars in the dairy section of many grocery stores. If you can't find it, serve these with butter instead. And, in either case, serve them with jam.

I initially cut the scones into rounds, just like the British recipes instructed. Afterward, I gathered the scraps into scone-like shapes and baked them, and I found that I preferred the rugged, uneven look of those baked from scraps over the more polished look of the cut scones. To replicate the effect of the scrap scones, I call for you to cut the dough into random chunks and then put the chunks together to form the scones. If you want perfectly round scones, cut them out with a 3-inch fluted cutter. (See photo page 52.)

Makes about 9 scones

What You Need—
The Essential Special Equipment
Bench scraper (or large knife)

For the Dough
70 grams (½ cup) Zante currants
(or black raisins)

¼ cup whiskey (or rum)

1 extra-large egg

1 extra-large egg yolk

120 grams (½ cup) heavy cream

280 grams (2 cups) unbleached
all-purpose flour

50 grams (¼ cup) granulated sugar

2 teaspoons baking powder

1 teaspoon Diamond Crystal kosher salt

84 grams (6 tablespoons) cold unsalted
butter, cubed

For Finishing and Serving
1 extra-large egg

Clotted cream (or unsalted butter)

Jam →

1. To make the dough, combine the currants with the whiskey in a small saucepan and bring to a boil over high heat. Remove from the heat and set aside for 10 minutes for the currants to soften in the liquid. Drain the currants and discard the alcohol or reserve it for another culinary use. (If you're using raisins, chop them to the size of currants.)

2. Adjust an oven rack to the center position and preheat the oven to 425°F. Line a large baking sheet with parchment paper.

3. Whisk the whole egg, egg yolk, and cream together in a small bowl.

4. Combine the flour, sugar, baking powder, and salt in a large food processor and pulse to combine the ingredients. Add the butter and pulse until the mixture is the consistency of very coarse meal, with the pieces of butter about the size of peas. Transfer the mixture to a large wide bowl. Add the currants and stir to combine.

5. Create a well in the center of the flour and butter mixture with your hands. Pour the egg/cream mixture into the well and use your hands to draw the dry ingredients into the well to form a shaggy dough; stop mixing before the ingredients are fully combined.

6. Lightly dust a work surface with flour and place the dough on the surface. Bring the dough together with your hands and pat it into a 1-inch-thick round, dusting your hands with flour if needed. Using a bench scraper (or a large knife), cut the dough into roughly 2-inch chunks. Gently place 2 or 3 of the chunks together and press them together from the sides to form 9 scones; don't touch the tops, you want them to be uneven. Place the scones on the prepared baking sheet, leaving at least 1½ inches between them.

7. To finish the scones, whisk the egg in a small bowl to make an egg wash and brush the scones with the egg, making sure to get it into the nooks and crannies.

8. Bake the scones on the center rack of the oven until they are deep golden brown, 15 to 20 minutes, rotating the baking sheet front to back halfway through the baking time so they brown evenly. Remove the scones from the oven. Serve warm, with clotted cream or butter and jam.

Orange Cranberry Tea Loaf

A tea loaf is basically cake, baked in a loaf pan and sliced like bread. The fact that you slice it makes the loaf seem less like dessert and more substantial, like breakfast. This one also contains less sugar than a cake typically would. I really like the classic combination of orange and cranberry in this loaf. The orange zest complements the sweet yellow cake base, and the cranberries offer bursts of tartness throughout. The loaf is topped with a generous layer of toasted, sliced almonds, which get crunchy when the cake is baked; the crunchy almonds are a delicious contrast to the soft cake, and they also look pretty. This loaf is best the day it's baked, while the almonds are still crunchy.

Makes one 9-inch loaf

What You Need—
The Essential Special Equipment

9 × 5 × 2½-inch loaf pan

Cooking spray

For the Batter

168 grams (¾ cup) buttermilk (preferably whole-milk or low-fat), shaken

1 tablespoon pure vanilla bean paste or vanilla extract

4 extra-large egg yolks

160 grams (about 1½ sticks) cold unsalted butter, cubed

142 grams (about ¾ cup) granulated sugar

¼ cup buttermilk powder (or milk powder; preferably whole-milk)

½ teaspoon baking soda

1 teaspoon Diamond Crystal kosher salt

1 medium orange

210 grams (1½ cups) unbleached all-purpose flour

140 grams (1¼ cups) fresh or frozen cranberries

For the Topping

1 extra-large egg white

37 grams (3 tablespoons) granulated sugar

¼ teaspoon grated nutmeg

58 grams (½ cup plus 2 tablespoons) skin-on sliced almonds

1. Adjust an oven rack to the top third of the oven and preheat the oven to 350°F. Coat the bottom and sides of the loaf pan with cooking spray.

2. To make the batter, whisk the buttermilk and vanilla together in a small bowl. Whisk the egg yolks in a separate small bowl to break them up.

3. Put the butter in a stand mixer fitted with the paddle and beat until it is soft but still cold, 3 to 4 minutes, stopping to scrape down the sides and bottom of the bowl and the paddle with a rubber spatula whenever the butter is accumulating. Add the sugar and beat on medium speed until the mixture is light and fluffy, 3 to 4 minutes, scraping down the bowl as needed. Stop the mixer, add the buttermilk powder, baking soda, and salt. Use a fine Microplane to grate the zest (the orange-colored outer layer) of the orange →

Orange Cranberry Tea Loaf (continued)

directly into the bowl. (Reserve the orange for another use.) Beat on medium speed for about 15 seconds to distribute the additions. Stop the mixer and scrape down the bowl. With the mixer on low speed, drizzle the yolks into the bowl, making sure they are incorporated and stopping to scrape down the bowl before adding more. Once all the egg yolk is incorporated, stop the mixer and scrape down the bowl and paddle. Add the flour and the buttermilk/vanilla mixture alternately in three additions for the flour and two for the buttermilk/vanilla, starting and ending with the flour; mix on low speed until the additions are combined and stop to scrape down the bowl before the next addition. After the last addition of flour, mix until only a few streaks of flour are visible. Stop the mixer, remove the paddle and bowl from the stand, and clean them with the spatula. Add the cranberries and stir the batter with the rubber spatula to distribute the cranberries, scraping the bowl from the bottom up to release any ingredients. Scrape the batter into the prepared loaf pan and smooth the top with an offset spatula.

4. Bake the loaf on the top rack of the oven until it has just begun to rise, is starting to brown, and a thin skin has formed on top, about 30 minutes.

5. While the loaf is baking, to make the topping, whisk the egg white, sugar, and nutmeg together in a medium bowl. Stir in the almonds.

6. Remove the loaf from the oven. Scoop the almonds out of the bowl with your hands, leaving any excess egg white in the bowl, and distribute them in a single layer on top of the cake, leaving the edges of the cake visible and leaving some cake peeking through the almond topping (discard the remaining egg white).

7. Return the cake to the top rack of the oven, rotating it from front to back, and bake until a toothpick inserted into the center comes out clean, the center is firm to the touch, and the top is deep golden brown, 40 to 45 minutes longer. Remove the loaf from the oven and set aside to cool slightly.

8. To remove the loaf from the pan, run the tip of a paring knife around the inside edges of the pan and invert the loaf onto your hand, taking care not to knock off the almond topping. Tap the bottom and sides of the pan with a metal spoon (or another blunt object) to release any stuck bits. Invert the cake again onto a serving platter.

Yum-Yum Coffee Cake

In my book *Pastries from the La Brea Bakery,* I included a recipe for Summer Camp Coffee Cake, so named because it reminded me of the big squares of coffee cake, served directly out of the giant pan it was baked in, at my summer camp. I learned to make a version of that cake from Izzy Cohen, a Jewish baker from Philadelphia who found his way to Los Angeles. Izzy had that gruff, lovable, East Coast way about him. He loved to come in and bake with us at La Brea Bakery and tell how things should be done. They made a version of this coffee cake at the Philadelphia bakery where he had worked before coming west, and he passed what he knew on to me.

I've been tweaking this recipe for the last thirty-two years, ever since Izzy taught it to me, but I was never 100 percent happy with it; it had a weird color from the addition of baking soda. I found that using baking powder instead gave me the pretty, light golden cake that I was looking for. I also added more streusel, which I can never get enough of, both to the top, which becomes the bottom, and to the layer of streusel inside the cake. Now I believe I can say I have perfected this cake. I only wish Izzy were here to see it. He called it "Yum-Yum Cake." In memory of Izzy, I'm carrying on the name.

Makes 1 large Bundt cake

What You Need—
The Essential Special Equipment

10-cup capacity Bundt pan (I use a Nordic Ware Brilliance Bundt Pan)

Cooking spray

For the Streusel and the Pan

210 grams (2 generous cups) pecan halves (or walnut halves)

100 grams (½ cup) granulated sugar

1½ tablespoons ground cinnamon

100 grams (½ cup packed) dark brown sugar

¾ teaspoon grated nutmeg

For the Cake

2 extra-large eggs

1 tablespoon pure vanilla bean paste or vanilla extract

113 grams (1 stick) cold unsalted butter, cubed

250 grams (1¼ cups) granulated sugar

2 teaspoons baking powder

1 teaspoon Diamond Crystal kosher salt

280 grams (2 cups) unbleached all-purpose flour

232 grams (1 cup) crème fraîche (or 244 grams/1 cup sour cream)

1. To make the streusel and prepare the pan, adjust an oven rack to the center position and preheat the oven to 325°F.

2. Spread the pecans out on a baking sheet and toast them on the center rack of the oven until they're golden brown and fragrant, 15 to 20 minutes, shaking the pan and rotating it front to back halfway through the baking →

time so the pecans toast evenly. Remove the baking sheet from the oven. Leave the oven on and increase the oven temperature to 350°F. (If you think the nuts are on the verge of being overtoasted, transfer them to a plate so they don't continue to cook from the residual heat of the pan.) Set the pecans aside until they are cool enough to handle, then chop them to roughly the size of peas and put them in a medium bowl.

3. Stir the granulated sugar and cinnamon together in a small bowl. Measure out ¼ cup and set it aside.

4. Add the brown sugar and nutmeg to the bowl with the remaining sugar. Add the sugar mixture to the bowl with the chopped pecans and stir to combine. Set aside.

5. Coat the Bundt pan with cooking spray. Sprinkle the cinnamon-sugar in the pan and tilt the pan so the cinnamon-sugar coats it all over. Gently tap out the excess.

6. To make the cake, whisk the eggs and vanilla together in a small bowl.

7. Put the butter in a stand mixer fitted with the paddle and beat on medium speed until the butter is soft but still cold, 3 to 4 minutes, stopping to scrape down the sides and bottom of the bowl with a rubber spatula whenever the butter is accumulating. Add the granulated sugar and beat on medium speed until the mixture is light and fluffy, 3 to 4 minutes, scraping down the bowl as needed. Add the baking powder and salt and beat on medium speed for about 15 seconds to distribute them. Add the flour and the egg/vanilla mixture alternately in three additions for the flour and two for the egg/vanilla, starting and ending with the flour; mix on low speed until each addition is fully incorporated and stop to scrape down the bowl before the next addition. Stop the mixer, remove the bowl and paddle from the stand, and clean them with the spatula. Add the crème fraîche and stir the batter with the spatula to combine, scraping the bowl from the bottom up to release any ingredients that may be stuck there.

8. Scrape half of the batter into the Bundt pan with a rubber spatula and use the spatula to even out the surface. Reserve a heaping ⅓ cup of the streusel for the top of the cake. Sprinkle the remaining streusel over the batter. Scrape

the remaining batter on top of the streusel layer and smooth the surface. Sprinkle the reserved streusel on top of the cake and place the Bundt pan on a baking sheet.

9. Place the baking sheet with the Bundt pan on the center rack and bake until the coffee cake is firm to the touch and starts to pull away from the sides of the pan, the top is golden brown, and a toothpick inserted into the center comes out clean, 50 to 65 minutes, rotating the baking sheet front to back halfway through the baking time so the cake bakes evenly. Remove the cake from the oven and set it aside to cool slightly.

10. To remove the cake from the pan, run the tip of a paring knife around the inside edges of the pan and invert the cake onto a serving platter.

New York Crumb Cake

There are few things in this world that all New Yorkers agree on, but one of those things is that crumb cake should be equal parts cake to crumb. This crumb cake is just that. It's based on the crumb cake that you see in individual square servings, wrapped in plastic wrap, and sold at every corner deli in New York City. This recipe was inspired by the baker Sally McKenney, who has a blog called Sally's Baking Addiction that I am addicted to. Oftentimes while revisiting classics for this book, I would think: What does Sally do with this? And I'd go to her blog for ideas. This recipe is loosely inspired by two similar crumb cake recipes that Sally has on her blog.

The crumb topping is squeezed in your fist and dropped on the cake in chunks, like dirt clods. Biting into those sweet, buttery clods is such a delicious and decadent experience. I like to cut this cake and serve it directly from the pan it was baked in.

Makes one 9-inch square cake

What You Need—
The Essential Special Equipment

9-inch square baking dish (preferably deep-dish; I used a Le Creuset stoneware baking dish)

Cooking spray

For the Topping

310 grams (2 sticks plus 6 tablespoons) unsalted butter, cubed

137.5 grams (½ cup plus 3 tablespoons) granulated sugar

137.5 grams (½ cup plus 3 tablespoons packed) dark brown sugar

1 tablespoon pure vanilla bean paste or vanilla extract

1 tablespoon ground cinnamon

1 teaspoon grated nutmeg

1 teaspoon Diamond Crystal kosher salt

381.5 grams (2¾ cups) unbleached all-purpose flour

For the Cake

3 extra-large eggs

2 tablespoons pure vanilla bean paste or vanilla extract

170 grams (1½ sticks) cold unsalted butter, cubed

150 grams (¾ cup) granulated sugar

1½ teaspoons baking powder

½ teaspoon Diamond Crystal kosher salt

233.5 grams (1½ cups plus 2 tablespoons) unbleached all-purpose flour

116 grams (½ cup) crème fraîche (or 122 grams/½ cup sour cream)

1. Adjust an oven rack to the center position and preheat the oven to 350°F. Coat the bottom and sides of the baking dish with cooking spray.

2. To make the crumb topping, start by making the golden butter. Place the butter in a small saucepan or skillet with a light-colored bottom so you can better judge the color change in the butter. Warm the butter over medium heat until it melts and begins to bubble, swirling the pan occasionally. →

Cook the butter, swirling often so it cooks evenly, until it is golden and the milk solids are caramel colored, 3 to 6 minutes. Remove from the heat and transfer the butter to a bowl; set aside to cool to room temperature.

3. Add the granulated sugar, brown sugar, vanilla, cinnamon, nutmeg, and salt to the bowl with the butter and stir with a spatula to combine. Add the flour and stir to combine; the mixture will be the texture of dense, wet sand.

4. To make the cake, whisk the eggs and vanilla together in a medium bowl.

5. Put the butter in a stand mixer fitted with the paddle and beat on medium speed until the butter is soft but still cold, 3 to 4 minutes, stopping to scrape down the sides and bottom of the bowl with a rubber spatula whenever the butter is accumulating. Add the granulated sugar and beat on medium speed until the butter and sugar mixture is light and fluffy, 3 to 4 minutes, scraping down the bowl as needed. Add the baking powder and salt and mix on medium for about 15 seconds to distribute them. Stop the mixer and scrape down the sides and bottom of the bowl. Add the flour and the egg/vanilla mixture alternately in three additions for the flour and two for the egg/vanilla, starting and ending with the flour; mix on low speed until each addition is fully incorporated and stop to scrape down the bowl before the next addition. Stop the mixer, remove the bowl and paddle from the stand, and clean them with the spatula. Add the crème fraîche and stir the batter with the spatula to combine, scraping the bowl from the bottom up to release any ingredients that may be stuck there.

6. Scrape the batter into the prepared baking dish and smooth the top with an offset spatula. Dimple the surface of the batter with your fingers or a spoon to allow the crumb topping to sink down and melt into the cake. Pick up the crumb topping by the handful, press it together in your fist, and break it into small clumps over the cake.

7. Bake the cake on the center rack of the oven for 30 minutes. Check the cake, and if it appears the crumb is flattening, fluff it up with a fork. Rotate the pan front to back so the cake bakes evenly and bake until the top is golden brown, firm to the touch, and a toothpick inserted into the center of the cake comes out clean, 30 to 40 minutes longer, rotating the pan front to back halfway through the baking time so the cake bakes evenly. Remove the cake from the oven.

Granola

There are two schools of granola eaters, as far as I can tell: those who like clumpy granola, and those who like granola where the individual flakes of rolled oats stay separate. I'm all for clumpy, although I have one caveat: I don't like the clumps to be rock hard like they are in commercial granola. To achieve my granola ideal, I add ammonium bicarbonate (aka baker's ammonia), a leavening agent that works to make the granola clumps light and crispy.

Besides making the crucial decision between clumpy and flaky granola, the other big granola variables lie in the additions, and in how the granola is sweetened. I add a combination of pecans, coconut, and dates, which become chewy when baked. And I sweeten it with maple syrup, but not so much that you can't fool yourself into thinking that it's healthy. At my restaurant, The Barish, we use this granola in our yogurt parfaits. It also makes a great snack. It would also be good with milk, although I wonder: Does anyone still eat granola with milk?

You buy ammonium bicarbonate (not to be confused with baking soda) from online sources. It can be unpleasant if you inhale it, so avoid doing so. It can also give off an unpleasant smell the first time you open the door to check on the granola; don't worry, that unpleasantness goes away once the ammonium bicarbonate is baked.

Makes about 4 cups

250 grams (2½ cups) rolled oats

60 grams (generous ½ cup) pecans, coarsely chopped

75 grams (about ½ cup) unbleached all-purpose flour

100 grams (½ cup packed) dark brown sugar

40 grams (⅔ cup) unsweetened coconut chips

150 grams of large, fresh dates, pitted and roughly chopped (about 1 cup)

1 teaspoon Diamond Crystal kosher salt

1 teaspoon ground cinnamon

½ teaspoon grated nutmeg

113 grams (1 stick) unsalted butter

80 grams (¼ cup) artisanal maple syrup (preferably barrel-aged)

1 tablespoon pure vanilla bean paste or vanilla extract

¾ teaspoon ammonium bicarbonate (baker's ammonia)

1. Adjust an oven rack to the center position and preheat the oven to 350°F. Line a large baking sheet with parchment paper.

2. Combine the oats, pecans, flour, brown sugar, coconut, dates, salt, cinnamon, and nutmeg in a large bowl and mix with your hands to distribute the ingredients evenly and break apart any clusters of dates. →

3. Have your prepared baking sheet, a whisk, and a rubber spatula handy so you can work quickly for the following steps.

4. Melt the butter in a small saucepan over medium heat, taking care not to let it brown. Add the maple syrup and vanilla and bring to a boil. Remove from the heat, add the ammonium bicarbonate, and whisk quickly and vigorously to combine. Pour this mixture into the bowl with the oats and other ingredients and mix quickly with the rubber spatula to coat the ingredients with the liquid. (In order to reap the benefits of the ammonium bicarbonate, which results in a light and crispy granola, you need to coat the ingredients before the liquid stops bubbling. Try to avoid inhaling it while you are stirring; it is not dangerous, but it is unpleasant.)

5. Spread the granola evenly over the prepared baking sheet and bake it on the center rack of the oven for 25 minutes. Remove the baking sheet from the oven and gently stir the granola, taking care not to break up the clumps. Return the baking sheet to the oven, rotating it from front to back, and bake the granola until it is golden brown and crunchy, another 5 to 10 minutes. Remove the granola from the oven.

Granola Bar Bites

Growing up in the sixties, I missed the era of the granola bar as a school lunch snack, but it wouldn't have mattered; my mom was a health food nut, and you can be sure she would have seen through the marketing and recognized packaged granola bars as the cookies that they are. It wasn't until college that I had my first granola bar. (Ironically, this was at Sonoma State, which was nicknamed "Granola State," in reference to the hippie population and the large amounts of granola consumed there.) I was obsessed with those crunchy bars and kidded myself that they were healthy. It never occurred to me to make them until recently, after I became a grandmother. I keep a basket at my house of snack giveaways for my grandkids, Ike and Goldie—the same basket where the famous peanut butter cookie was found. The basket is filled with things that are put in my hotel rooms or on photo shoots that I bring home for them. Granola bars, it seems, are always among them. Seeing those bars inspired me to take on the challenge of creating one that my mom might have put in my snack basket, had I had one. It's packed with healthy ingredients, including dried fruit, almonds, flaxseeds, buckwheat flakes, and coconut oil—and contains just enough flour to bind them. Even though they contain far less sweetener than commercial granola bars (I use a combination of granulated sugar, brown sugar, honey, and Lyle's Golden Syrup), it's still more than my mom would have allowed. Although my mom would have recognized these as cookies, she would have approved of the size. I cut them into snack-size bites; you don't want a cookie to be too big, especially if you're giving it to your grandkids.

Makes about 36 granola bar bites

150 grams (1½ cups) skin-on thin-sliced almonds

80 grams (½ cup) dried sour cherries

75 grams (½ cup) raisins (preferably golden)

40 grams (¼ cup) golden or brown flaxseeds

244 grams (2 cups) Zante currants (or black raisins, chopped to the size of currants)

70 grams (½ cup) unbleached all-purpose flour

68 grams (½ cup) whole wheat flour

57 grams (¼ cup) virgin coconut oil (melted if the oil is too hard to scoop)

85 grams (¼ cup) mild-flavored honey, such as clover or wildflower

36 grams (2 tablespoons) Lyle's Golden Syrup

2 tablespoons pure vanilla bean paste or vanilla extract

2 teaspoons ground cinnamon

1 teaspoon baking soda

¾ teaspoon Diamond Crystal kosher salt

113 grams (1 stick) unsalted butter

141 grams (1¼ cups) rolled oats

37 grams (about ¼ cup) buckwheat flakes

50 grams (¼ cup packed) dark brown sugar

50 grams (¼ cup) granulated sugar →

1. Adjust an oven rack to the center position and preheat the oven to 325°F. Line a large baking sheet with parchment paper.

2. Spread the almonds on a baking sheet and toast them on the center rack of the oven until they are light golden brown, 8 to 10 minutes, rotating the baking sheet front to back and stirring the almonds halfway through the toasting time so they brown evenly. Remove the baking sheet from the oven. Transfer the almonds to a plate to prevent them from toasting further and set aside to cool. Turn off the oven.

3. Add the dried cherries, raisins, flaxseeds, and currants to the bowl with the toasted almonds and toss to combine.

4. Whisk together the all-purpose flour and whole wheat flour in a small bowl. Put the coconut oil, honey, golden syrup, vanilla, cinnamon, baking soda, and salt in a large bowl and stir with a whisk to combine.

5. Melt the butter in a medium saucepan over medium heat, stirring occasionally so it doesn't burn. Add the oats and buckwheat flakes, increase the heat to medium-high, and cook, stirring constantly with a silicone spatula, until the oats and buckwheat flakes are golden brown, 3 to 4 minutes. Remove from the heat. Add the brown sugar and granulated sugar and stir to combine. Add this mixture to the bowl with the wet ingredients and stir with a rubber spatula to combine. Stir in the dried fruit and nut mixture. Add the combined flours and stir until no flour is visible.

6. Scrape the granola bar mixture onto the center of the prepared baking sheet. Using your hands, form the dough into a 10 × 14-inch rectangle. Place the baking sheet in the refrigerator to chill until the mixture is firm, about 1 hour.

7. Adjust the oven racks so one is in the top third and the other is in the bottom third of the oven and preheat the oven to 325°F.

8. Remove the baking sheet from the refrigerator and slide the parchment with the granola bar mixture onto a work surface. Lay a sheet of parchment paper on top of the granola bar mixture, lining it up with the bottom sheet. Flip the parchment-sandwiched granola bars over onto the baking sheet. Peel off the top sheet of parchment paper and lay it clean-side up on the second baking sheet to line it.

9. The granola bars are now resting on the paper that you just used when you flipped them. The paper will keep the granola bars from sticking as you cut them. Using a ruler and a large knife, cut the granola bars into roughly 2½ × 1½-inch bars. Divide the granola bars evenly between the two baking sheets, spacing them evenly apart.

10. Place one baking sheet on each oven rack and bake the granola bars until they are deep brown and firm to the touch, 20 to 24 minutes, switching racks and rotating the baking sheets front to back halfway through the baking time so the granola bars brown evenly. Remove the granola bars from the oven.

Twice-Baked Almond Croissants (left);
Twice-Baked Ham and Cheese Croissants (right)

Twice-Baked Ham and Cheese Croissants

Typically, there are three ways to make a ham and cheese croissant. One is to add the ham and cheese to the croissant dough when you are shaping it, so the ham and cheese are integrated into the finished, baked croissants. The problem with this version is that the additions create moisture when baked, and you end up with gummy, raw dough around the ham and cheese. Another interpretation of a ham and cheese croissant is to take a plain croissant, cut it in half, and add ham and cheese, making a sandwich that is baked just long enough to warm the ham and melt the cheese. Not bad, but also not remarkable. The third way, which is the way these are made, is essentially a ham and cheese croissant prepared like a croque-monsieur: stuffed with ham and cheese, smothered in béchamel, topped with grated Gruyère, and baked into a gooey, melted, delicious masterpiece. I discovered this hybrid croque-croissant at the wonderful b. Patisserie in San Francisco, a creation of chef Belinda Leong. I adapted them slightly. I make them often when I need a breakfast or brunch option. People go wild for them. I think anytime you offer a nonsugary option for a morning meal, you're going to find it has a lot of fans.

I call for you to use store-bought croissants in this recipe (and also in the recipe that follows, Twice-Baked Almond Croissants, page 78). In the past, I never would have started a recipe with "buy a croissant." I would have given a croissant recipe. But making croissants is too time-consuming, too labor-intensive, and too technical for this book; I didn't want to ask you to make them since these days, you can get such good croissants in bakeries and even some grocery stores. You can also find unbaked croissants, frozen, which you bake at home; they're surprisingly good. Even if you were to start with less than stellar croissants, the way they're gussied up in these recipes and then rebaked, you wouldn't even notice. You can even use day-old croissants. The one thing you want to be sure of is that the croissants you start with are made with butter, not margarine or oil. The ones I used for the photo are from République, one of my favorite bakeries in Los Angeles, and the source of my Oatmeal Raisin Cookies (page 103).

The quantities in this recipe are based on starting with 7-inch-long croissants. →

Makes 8 croissant sandwiches

For the Béchamel

½ large Spanish onion, thinly sliced

42 grams (3 tablespoons) unsalted butter

1 bay leaf (preferably fresh)

1 árbol chile

35 grams (¼ cup) unbleached all-purpose flour

490 grams (2 cups) whole milk

2¼ teaspoons Diamond Crystal kosher salt

1 teaspoon freshly grated nutmeg (about ¼ of a whole nutmeg)

For the Croissants

8 large (about 7-inch-long) croissants (preferably day-old)

4 cups (about 340 grams/¾ pound) grated Gruyère cheese (grated on the largest holes of a box grater)

16 large paper-thin slices prosciutto or ham (about 113 grams/¼ pound)

3 tablespoons fresh thyme leaves

Fresh coarsely ground black pepper

Chunk of Parmesan

1. To make the béchamel, set a fine-mesh sieve over a bowl.

2. Put the onion slices, butter, bay leaf, and árbol chile in a medium saucepan and cook over medium-low heat until the onion is tender and translucent, 10 to 12 minutes, stirring often so it doesn't brown. Add the flour and cook for 3 minutes to cook off the flour flavor, stirring constantly with a whisk. Gradually add the milk, whisking constantly. Increase the heat to medium-high and bring the sauce to a boil, stirring constantly with the whisk. Reduce the heat to low and simmer, stirring constantly, until the sauce is thick enough to coat the back of a spoon, 3 to 4 minutes. Remove from the heat and strain the sauce into the bowl (discard the contents of the sieve). Stir in the salt and nutmeg and set aside to come to room temperature. Cover the bowl with plastic wrap and refrigerate until the sauce is chilled, at least 30 minutes.

3. Preheat the oven to 375°F. Line a large baking sheet with parchment paper.

4. To assemble and bake the croissants, using a serrated knife, cut a 4-inch-long slit along the top of each croissant, like you'd cut open a baked potato, stopping short of cutting all the way through to the bottom. Splay open the croissants.

5. Spoon 2 tablespoons of béchamel onto the inside of each croissant. Use the back of the spoon to spread it to the edges to cover the inside of the croissants in a thin layer, pushing the béchamel into the croissants so they absorb it. Sprinkle ¼ cup of grated Gruyère over the surface of the inside of each croissant. Tear each slice of prosciutto into two pieces and lay a total of 2 slices (4 pieces) inside each croissant, with some of the prosciutto flopping over the edges of the croissants. Push the croissants back together to close them. Spoon 1 tablespoon of béchamel on top of each croissant and use the back of the spoon to spread it over the surface. Sprinkle ¼ cup of Gruyère cheese over each croissant, pressing it into the béchamel so it adheres. Sprinkle the thyme over the croissants, dividing it evenly. Grind a few turns of coarsely ground black pepper over each croissant. Place the croissants on the prepared baking sheet, spacing them evenly.

6. Bake the croissants on the center rack of the oven until the cheese on top is golden brown, 18 to 25 minutes, rotating the baking sheet front to back halfway through the baking time so the croissants bake evenly. Remove the baking sheet from the oven and use a fine Microplane to grate Parmesan over the top of the croissants.

7. The croissants are best warm. Serve them fresh from the oven or place them in a 350°F oven for about 10 minutes to reheat them.

Twice-Baked Almond Croissants

The first time I tasted a *croissant aux amandes,* or almond croissant, was decades ago, when I was in culinary school at École Lenôtre, in Paris. I had never heard of them, and I expected a croissant with almonds; nothing more. Instead, what I got was a classic French pastry composed of a day-old croissant that had been sliced in half, drenched in a sugar syrup, filled with a rich, sweet almond cream, topped with thinly sliced almonds, baked, and dusted in a thick layer of powdered sugar. I was blown away. I'd ordered something that sounded so simple, and what I received was so complex and layered, literally. To distinguish this pastry from a plain croissant that has almonds inside or on top, it is often referred to as "twice-baked," the second baking referring to its transformation into this sophisticated, crowd-pleasing pastry.

The fact that we can make this wonderful pastry at home owes everything to the times in which we're living. Ten or twenty years ago, when there was no access to quality store-bought croissants, making this would have required that you start by making the croissants. It would have been a three-day project. But now that good croissants are readily available, making this very special, once very time-consuming confection is really manageable. I add orange blossom water to the sugar syrup, which adds another layer of complexity to the finished pastry. When I started out baking, you couldn't find orange blossom water easily, but today it is widely available in specialty food stores and from online sources. Look for quality, all-butter croissants in bakeries and even grocery stores; or unbaked croissants, frozen, which you bake at home.

The quantities in this recipe are based on 7-inch-long croissants. (See photo page 74.)

Makes 8 croissants

For the Almond Cream

2 extra-large eggs

2 tablespoons rum

1 teaspoon pure almond extract

150 grams (1½ cups) unblanched almond meal (or 150 grams/1 cup whole skin-on almonds)

50 grams (¼ cup) granulated sugar

113 grams (¼ cup plus 3½ tablespoons) almond paste (preferably unblanched)

141 grams (1 stick plus 2 tablespoons) cold unsalted butter, cubed

For the Syrup

600 grams (3 cups) granulated sugar

236 grams (1 cup) orange blossom water

2 tablespoons pure vanilla bean paste or vanilla extract

For the Croissants

200 grams (2 cups) skin-on thin-sliced almonds

8 large (about 7-inch-long) croissants (preferably day-old)

Powdered sugar for dusting

---

1. To make the almond cream, whisk the eggs, rum, and almond extract together in a small bowl.

2. Put the almond meal in a small bowl. (If you're using whole almonds instead of almond meal, put the almonds in a food processor with 2 tablespoons of the sugar and pulse to a fine meal, then add this mixture where the almond meal is added, below.)

3. Put the sugar in the bowl of a stand mixer (this will be only 2 tablespoons if you used some to grind whole almonds). Crumble the almond paste into the bowl. Fit the mixer with the paddle and beat on medium speed until the paste is combined with the sugar and the mixture is smooth, 3 to 4 minutes. Add the butter and beat on medium speed until the butter is combined with the almond paste mixture and no lumps remain, 4 to 5 minutes, stopping to scrape down the sides and bottom of the bowl and the paddle with a rubber spatula whenever the ingredients are accumulating. Add the almond meal (or the ground almond/sugar mixture) and mix on medium speed for about 30 seconds to combine. With the mixer on medium speed, gradually add the egg mixture and mix for about 1 minute, until the additions are incorporated. Stop the mixer, remove the bowl and paddle from the stand, and clean them with the spatula, scraping the bowl from the bottom up to release any ingredients that may be stuck there. Cover the bowl with plastic wrap and refrigerate the cream until it is firm but still spreadable, about 1 hour.

4. Meanwhile, to make the syrup, put the sugar in a small saucepan and add 2 cups water. Add the orange blossom water and vanilla and bring to a boil over medium-high heat, stirring so the sugar dissolves. Boil the syrup for 1 minute. Remove from the heat.

5. Adjust an oven rack to the center and preheat the oven to 375°F. Line a large baking sheet with parchment paper.

6. To assemble and bake the croissants, spread the sliced almonds on a baking sheet and toast them on the center rack of the oven until they're lightly browned and fragrant, 8 to 10 minutes, shaking the baking sheet and rotating it front to back halfway through the toasting time so the almonds brown evenly. Remove from the oven and set them aside to cool. (If you think the nuts are on the verge of being overtoasted, transfer them to a plate so they don't continue to cook from the residual heat of the pan.) →

7. Remove the almond cream from the refrigerator; if it is not a spreadable consistency, set it aside at room temperature for about 30 minutes. Line a large baking sheet with parchment paper.

8. Slice the croissants in half horizontally with a long serrated knife and lay the tops and bottoms together in pairs on your work surface. Dip a pastry brush in the syrup and use the brush to mop the syrup onto the croissant halves, paying attention to the tips of the croissant and mopping as much syrup on the croissants as they will absorb. (You may not use it all.) Spoon 2 tablespoons of the almond cream into the center of each croissant bottom and use an offset spatula to spread it to the edges. Set the croissant tops back onto the bottoms. Spoon 3 tablespoons of almond cream in the center of each croissant top, using the offset spatula to spread it unevenly over the surface, leaving the edges of the croissant visible. (You may have a small amount of almond cream left over.) Sprinkle ¼ cup of toasted sliced almonds over each croissant and use your fingertips to press the almonds into the cream so they adhere. Place the croissants on the prepared baking sheet, spacing them evenly.

9. Bake the croissants on the center rack of the oven until the almond cream on top is golden brown and the edges and bottoms of the croissants are deep brown, 20 to 25 minutes, rotating the baking sheet front to back halfway through the baking time so the croissants brown evenly. Remove the baking sheet from the oven and set aside to cool the croissants to room temperature.

10. Dust the croissants generously with powdered sugar before serving.

Monkey Bread

Monkey bread was not in my vocabulary until, on a recent family vacation to San Diego, I visited a lovely bakery there called Wayfarer Bread. The baker, Crystal White, was there when I came in and was nice enough to give me a tour. As we walked through the kitchen, the bakers were pulling loaf pans out of the oven with lumpy, golden chunks of buttery dough protruding irregularly. Lumpy and irregular is right up my alley, so I was intrigued. Crystal told me this was their cinnamon loaf, which they made with scraps of croissant dough left over from that morning's bake. The dough was thrown into the pan in chunks, baked, and then drenched in cinnamon-sugar syrup and covered in a thin glaze. She sent me home with a loaf, which it seemed weighed about five pounds. This type of loaf, often called "monkey bread," is meant to be a pull-apart bread, and pulling apart food, even when it's not meant to be pulled apart, is also very much my thing. At first, I thought: What am I going to do with five pounds of sugar, flour, and butter? I took it back to my hotel and proceeded to rip it apart—and devour almost the entire thing.

The next day, when I returned to Los Angeles, I walked into the pastry kitchen and, coincidentally, one of the pastry cooks, Adam Marca, was making none other than, you guessed it: Monkey bread! Where Crystal made her loaf with croissant dough, Adam was making his with scraps of brioche dough left over from making *bombolini* (doughnuts), one of our most popular desserts at the Osteria. I love seeing scraps and leftovers used in creative and delicious ways to treat our staff, rather than throwing them away, so I liked Adam's monkey bread, which he was making for staff meal, before I even tasted it. Of course, it was delicious. Adam showed me how to make it so I could include the recipe here. He drenches it in syrup but doesn't glaze it. If you want a more decadent, sweeter monkey bread, while it's in the oven, make the glaze in the recipe for Cinnamon Rolls (page 86) and pour it over the monkey bread when it comes out of the oven, while it is still warm. →

Makes one 9-inch loaf

**What You Need—
The Essential Special Equipment**

Cooking spray

9 × 5 × 2½-inch loaf pan

Instant-read thermometer

For the Dough

7 grams (1½ packed teaspoons) fresh cake yeast

41 grams (2 tablespoons plus 2 teaspoons) whole milk

315 grams (2¼ cups) unbleached all-purpose flour, plus more as needed and for dusting

3 extra-large eggs

75 grams (¼ cup plus 2 tablespoons) granulated sugar

1 tablespoon pure vanilla bean paste or vanilla extract

¼ of a whole nutmeg, grated on a fine Microplane

½ teaspoon Diamond Crystal kosher salt

113 grams European-style unsalted butter, cubed and left at room temperature until pliable but not greasy

For Baking the Bread

113 grams (1 stick) unsalted butter, melted

37.5 grams (3 tablespoons) granulated sugar

37.5 grams (3 tablespoons packed) dark brown sugar

1 tablespoon ground cinnamon

For the Cinnamon Syrup

100 grams (½ cup) granulated sugar

2 teaspoons pure vanilla bean paste or vanilla extract

1 teaspoon ground cinnamon

¼ teaspoon Diamond Crystal kosher salt

1. To make the dough, line a large baking sheet with parchment paper and coat the parchment with cooking spray.

2. Put the yeast in the bowl of a stand mixer.

3. Heat the milk in a small saucepan over medium heat until it is warm to the touch. Pour the milk into the bowl with the yeast. Add 70 grams (½ cup) of the flour and 1 of the eggs and stir with a rubber spatula to combine. Sprinkle 70 grams (½ cup) of the flour over the mixture; don't stir it in. Cover the bowl with a clean damp towel and set it aside in a warm place in your kitchen until the flour on the surface of the mixture has large cracks in it, 10 to 25 minutes. (The time will vary depending on the heat and humidity.) Uncover the bowl and add the granulated sugar, vanilla, nutmeg, salt, and the remaining 2 eggs and 175 grams (1¼ cups) flour.

4. Put the bowl on the mixer stand and fit the mixer with the dough hook. Mix the ingredients on low speed for 1 to 2 minutes to combine them. Increase the speed to medium-high and mix until the dough is smooth and shiny, slightly sticky, and leaves the sides of the bowl and wraps around the hook, about 5 minutes, adding 2 to 3 tablespoons of flour to the bowl as needed for the dough to wrap around the hook. Reduce the mixer speed to medium-low and add the butter a few cubes at a time, adding more only

after the added butter has been incorporated. After all the butter has been incorporated, increase the speed to medium-high and beat the dough until it pulls away from the sides of the bowl and wraps around the dough hook again, 2 to 3 more minutes. If the dough is not pulling away from the bowl and wrapping around the hook, sprinkle 2 to 3 tablespoons of flour into the bowl to encourage it to do so. Stop the mixer. Remove the bowl from the stand and remove the dough hook.

5. Lightly dust a work surface with flour and turn the dough out onto the floured surface. Knead the dough to bring it into a smooth ball.

6. Coat a large bowl generously with cooking spray and place the dough in the bowl. Cover the bowl with plastic wrap and set it aside in a warm place until the dough has doubled in size, 2 to 4 hours. Place the dough in the refrigerator overnight to allow it to rest.

7. To bake the bread, move the dough from the refrigerator to the freezer for 30 minutes, until it is cold but not frozen. Coat the bottom and sides of the loaf pan with cooking spray. Cut 2 pieces of parchment paper: one to 8 × 12 inches and another to 4 × 16 inches. Lay the longer sheet of paper lengthwise in the pan so it travels up and over two of the sides. Lay the other sheet perpendicular so it travels up and over the remaining two sides of the pan. Coat the paper with cooking spray.

8. Pour the melted butter into a large bowl. Add the granulated sugar, brown sugar, and cinnamon and stir to combine.

9. Remove the bowl of dough from the freezer and transfer the dough to a cutting board. Using a large knife, cut the dough into about 30 (roughly 1½-inch) chunks. Place the chunks in the bowl with the butter/sugar/cinnamon mixture and toss to coat on all sides. Place one piece of dough in each corner of the pan, then place enough pieces in the pan to form a single layer with the pieces close but not touching. Build the monkey bread in two more layers until you have used all the dough.

10. Coat a piece of plastic wrap with cooking spray and drape it, sprayed-side down, over the loaf pan. Place the pan in a warm place in your kitchen to proof until the dough looks puffy, has nearly doubled in size, and springs back slowly, leaving a small indent, when pressed with your finger, 1 to 3 hours.

11. Adjust an oven rack to the center position and preheat the oven to 350°F. →

12. Place the bread in the oven to bake until it is deep golden brown (an instant-read thermometer will register 90°C or 194°F when inserted into the center of the loaf), 50 minutes to 1 hour, rotating the loaf pan front to back halfway through the baking time so the bread browns evenly.

13. While the bread is baking, to make the cinnamon syrup, combine the granulated sugar, vanilla, cinnamon, salt, and 60 grams (¼ cup) water in a small saucepan and heat over medium heat until the sugar dissolves, stirring with a whisk to break up any lumps and to prevent the syrup from sticking to the pan. Remove from the heat and set aside until you're ready to use the syrup.

14. Remove the bread from the oven and immediately brush with half of the cinnamon syrup. Let the bread rest for about 10 minutes to absorb the syrup. Line a baking sheet with parchment paper. Lift up on the parchment paper "wings" to lift the bread out of the pan, leaving the paper in place. Place the bread on the lined baking sheet. Hold the side of the loaf with one hand while pulling the parchment gently with the other. Brush the sides with the remaining syrup. While the loaf is still warm and malleable, pick up any pieces of dough that have fallen off and gently press them onto the loaf, taking care not to burn your fingers in the process.

Cinnamon Rolls

I have never included a straight-up cinnamon roll recipe in any of my cookbooks. In fact, until recently, I'd only ever had a bite of one here and there. Cinnamon rolls didn't appeal to me. They always seemed pale and doughy and uninteresting. And then on the good old Internet, I saw a photo of the cinnamon rolls from the bakery Hart Bageri, in Copenhagen. I love absolutely everything they make, and they even managed to make cinnamon rolls look good. I contacted the baker, Talia Richard-Carvajal, who is a friend, and asked her what dough she used to make them. She told me she started with milk bread dough. Then she rolls cinnamon butter into them and tops them with a glaze, both typical of cinnamon rolls. What she does different is that before the glaze, while the rolls are still warm, she brushes them with cinnamon syrup. The resulting rolls are soft and squishy, wet and gooey, redolent of cinnamon—and totally addictive.

Milk bread, also called Hokkaido milk bread, starts with a roux "starter," made by cooking flour and milk together. The bread is light and airy, tender with a beautiful golden-brown exterior. I had never made milk bread before, so I borrowed the recipe from King Arthur Flour's website. These rolls require several steps and 2 to 3 hours to proof the dough. I call for you to make the dough and form the rolls one day, then bake them off the next, so you can enjoy them fresh from the oven. The dough will need to proof for up to 2½ hours before you bake them, so plan to wake up early. They're worth it.

Makes 8 rolls

What You Need—
The Essential Special Equipment
10-inch square baking pan

Cooking spray

For the Starter
46 grams (3 tablespoons) whole milk

17.5 grams (2 tablespoons) bread flour (or unbleached all-purpose flour)

For the Dough
32.5 grams (2½ packed tablespoons) fresh cake yeast

350 grams (2½ cups) bread flour (or unbleached all-purpose flour), plus more as needed and for dusting

122.5 grams (½ cup) whole milk, plus more for brushing

67 grams (½ stick plus generous 2 teaspoons) unsalted butter, melted and cooled slightly, plus more for greasing

50 grams (¼ cup) granulated sugar

2 tablespoons milk powder (preferably whole-milk)

1 extra-large egg

1 teaspoon Diamond Crystal kosher salt

For the Cinnamon Butter
113 grams (1 stick) cold unsalted butter, cubed

75 grams (¼ cup plus 2 tablespoons) granulated sugar

2 tablespoons ground cinnamon

1 teaspoon Diamond Crystal kosher salt

For the Cinnamon Syrup

50 grams (¼ cup) granulated sugar

1 tablespoon pure vanilla bean paste or vanilla extract

½ teaspoon ground cinnamon

⅛ teaspoon Diamond Crystal kosher salt

For the Glaze

105 grams (¾ cup plus 1 tablespoon) powdered sugar

28 grams (2 tablespoons) buttermilk (preferably full-fat or low-fat), shaken

9 grams (1 tablespoon) potato starch

21.25 grams (1 tablespoon) Lyle's Golden Syrup

¼ teaspoon Diamond Crystal kosher salt

1. To make the starter, combine the milk, flour, and 3 tablespoons water in a small saucepan and whisk to dissolve any lumps. Warm over low heat, stirring with the whisk, until the mixture is starchy and as thick as porridge, 3 to 5 minutes. Remove from the heat and set aside to cool to room temperature.

2. To make the dough, transfer the starter to the bowl of a stand mixer and crumble the cake yeast into the bowl. Add the flour, milk, melted butter, granulated sugar, milk powder, egg, and salt. Fit the mixer with the dough hook and mix on medium speed until the dough is smooth and elastic, 3 to 5 minutes. (If the dough is wet and sticky, add more flour, 1 tablespoon at a time, until the dough is the right consistency.) Stop the mixer and remove the bowl and hook from the stand.

3. Grease a large bowl with butter. Transfer the dough to the bowl, cover with a damp, clean cloth, and set aside in a warm place in the kitchen to proof, until the dough looks puffy and has roughly doubled in size, 1 to 1½ hours.

4. To make the cinnamon butter, when you're ready to shape the rolls, put the butter in a stand mixer fitted with the paddle and beat on medium speed until the butter is soft but still cold, 3 to 4 minutes, stopping to scrape down the sides and bottom of the bowl and the paddle whenever ingredients are accumulating. Add the granulated sugar, cinnamon, and salt and beat on medium speed until the butter is soft and spreadable, 3 to 4 minutes, scraping down the bowl and paddle as needed.

5. Lightly dust a work surface with flour. Coat the bottom and sides of the baking pan with cooking spray.

6. Remove the dough from the refrigerator. Place the dough on the floured surface and gently press on the dough with your fingertips to deflate it. Use your hands to form the dough into a rectangular block 1 or 2 inches thick. Lightly dust the work surface, the dough, and rolling pin with flour and roll the dough out into a 10 × 9-inch rectangle about ½ inch thick. →

7. Spoon the cinnamon butter on the dough and use an offset spatula to spread it in an even layer to the edges, leaving a ¾-inch border with no butter. Starting on a long side, roll the dough up, not too tightly, into a log.

8. Place the log on a cutting board with the seam facing down. Working quickly (before the dough gets too soft), use a large sharp knife to trim off the ends of the log. (Bake the trimmings to snack on or discard them.) Cut the log in half crosswise into 2 equal pieces. Cut each piece in half to make 4 segments. Cut each of the 4 segments in half again, giving you 8 1-inch-thick rolls. If the rolls are misshapen, gently round them out with your hands. Lay the rolls spiral-side up in the prepared pan. (If you are baking the cinnamon rolls the next day, wrap the pan in plastic wrap and place it in the refrigerator overnight. The next morning, remove from the refrigerator and continue with the next step.)

9. Cover the pan with a clean damp towel and set the rolls aside in a warm place to proof until the dough springs back slowly and leaves a small indent when you press on it, 40 to 60 minutes. (If the dough was refrigerated, proof for 2 to 2½ hours.)

10. While the rolls are proofing, adjust an oven rack to the center position and preheat the oven to 350°F.

11. Uncover the baking pan and brush the rolls with milk. Bake the rolls on the center rack of the oven until they're deep golden brown, 15 to 25 minutes, rotating the baking sheet front to back halfway through the baking time so the rolls brown evenly.

12. While the rolls are baking, to make the cinnamon syrup, combine the granulated sugar, vanilla, cinnamon, salt, and 2 tablespoons water in a small saucepan and heat over medium heat until the sugar dissolves, stirring with a whisk to break up any lumps and to prevent the syrup from sticking to the pan. Remove from the heat.

13. Remove the pan of rolls from the oven and brush them while they are still hot with the cinnamon syrup. Set aside to cool to room temperature.

14. While the rolls are cooling, to make the glaze, put the powdered sugar, buttermilk, potato starch, golden syrup, and salt in a medium bowl and whisk to combine and until no lumps remain.

15. Spoon the glaze over the rolls and use the back of the spoon to spread it over them, leaving about ¼ inch around the edges of each roll free of glaze.

Everyone loves cookies—making them and eating them. Many of us cut our baking teeth with cookies, either using a recipe on the back of a bag of Nestlé chocolate chips or the back of the canister of Quaker Oats. (I know I did!) Those two cookies fall under the heading "drop cookies," because the dough is traditionally dropped onto the baking sheet, and updated versions of those American favorites are here. In this chapter you'll also find cookies that are rolled out and cut into shapes, such as Shortbread Cookies (page 179) and Iced Animal Crackers (page 169); a selection of butter cookies that are rolled into logs and sliced into coins; and, the newest trend, cookie dough baked in flan rings, so they're like gooey, moist, individual cakes. Cookies make a great gift. One nice thing about giving them is that you can make the dough ahead of time, refrigerate or freeze it, and bake it off when you're ready. The other nice thing about making cookies to give to someone else is that when you bake them, you can save a few—or more than a few—for yourself.

Cookies

Peanut Butter Cookies

Yes, *the* peanut butter cookies!

I am happy to announce that the perfect peanut butter cookie has indeed been invented, but I also must admit that I am not the one who invented it. If you read the introduction, then you already know that these cookies—the base of which comes to you courtesy of Roxana Jullapat, a talented baker who owns the Los Angeles bakery-cafe Friends & Family—inspired this cookbook. After tasting Roxana's cookie and falling in love with it, I decided to make them, using a recipe from her cookbook, *Mother Grains*. I don't know if it was the addition of sorghum flour (which Roxana says makes the cookies chewier), or the fact that they're perfectly underbaked, but they were absolute peanut butter cookie perfection. They have a pretty crackle top and perfectly rounded edges, all hallmarks of success for this type of cookie. Most important, they really taste like peanut butter. I put a spoonful of peanut butter in the center and nestled a pile of salty, roasted Spanish peanuts on top to make them as peanutty as a peanut butter cookie can be. I also make mine smaller than Roxana's.

Use a supermarket variety of peanut butter, not health food or artisanal peanut butter; I use Skippy creamy peanut butter. These are best the day they're made and still delicious the next day; I don't recommend keeping them any longer than that.

Makes about 4 dozen cookies

For the Toasted Peanuts

375 grams (3 cups) skin-on Spanish peanuts

3 tablespoons grapeseed oil (or other neutral-flavored oil, such as safflower)

1½ tablespoons Diamond Crystal kosher salt

For the Dough

2 extra-large eggs

2 tablespoons pure vanilla bean paste or vanilla extract

140 grams (1 cup) unbleached all-purpose flour

130 grams (1 cup) sorghum flour

170 grams (1½ sticks) cold unsalted butter, cubed

270 grams (1 cup) creamy peanut butter

180 grams (about ¾ cup plus 2½ tablespoons) granulated sugar

110 grams (½ cup plus 2 teaspoons packed) dark brown sugar

1½ teaspoons baking soda

1 teaspoon Diamond Crystal kosher salt

½ teaspoon baking powder

For Finishing

100 grams (½ cup) granulated sugar

270 grams (1 cup) peanut butter (preferably creamy)

2 tablespoons flaky sea salt

1. To toast the peanuts, adjust an oven rack to the center position and preheat the oven to 350°F.

2. Put the peanuts on a large baking sheet, drizzle them with the oil, sprinkle with the salt, and toss to coat them. Spread the peanuts out in an even layer and toast them on the center rack of the oven until they are dark mahogany in color, 18 to 20 minutes, shaking the pan occasionally and rotating the pan front to back halfway through the toasting time so the peanuts brown evenly. Remove the baking sheet from the oven and set aside to cool the nuts to room temperature. (If you think they are on the verge of being overtoasted, transfer them to a plate so they don't continue to cook from the residual heat of the pan.)

3. Turn off the oven.

4. To make the dough, whisk the eggs and vanilla together in a small bowl. Combine the all-purpose and sorghum flours in a medium bowl and stir with a whisk to combine.

5. Put the butter in a stand mixer fitted with the paddle and beat at medium speed until the butter is softened but still cold, 3 to 4 minutes, stopping to scrape down the sides and bottom of the bowl and paddle with a rubber spatula whenever butter is accumulating. Add the peanut butter, granulated sugar, and brown sugar and beat on medium speed until the mixture is light and fluffy, 3 to 4 minutes, stopping to scrape down the sides and bottom of the bowl with a rubber spatula as needed. Add the baking soda, salt, and baking powder and beat on medium speed for about 15 seconds to incorporate the additions. Stop the mixer and scrape down the bowl and paddle. With the mixer on medium speed, gradually add the egg/vanilla mixture, mixing until the egg is completely incorporated. Stop the mixer and scrape down the bowl. Add the combined flours and mix on low speed for about 30 seconds until no flour is visible. Stop the mixer, remove the paddle and bowl, and clean them with the spatula, scraping from the bottom up to release any ingredients from the bottom of the bowl. Cover the bowl with plastic wrap and refrigerate until the dough is chilled and firm, at least 30 minutes.

6. Adjust the oven racks so one is in the top third and the other is in the bottom third of the oven and preheat the oven to 375°F. Line two large baking sheets with parchment paper. →

7. To finish the cookies, pour the granulated sugar into a small bowl. Remove the dough from the refrigerator. Remove the plastic wrap and reserve it. Scoop the dough into 21-gram (1½-tablespoon) portions and roll each portion into a ball. Roll the balls in the sugar to coat them and place 12 cookies on each of the prepared baking sheets, leaving at least 1½ inches between them. (Re-cover the remaining dough and return it to the refrigerator.)

8. Press your thumb in the center of each ball of dough and turn your thumb to expand the divot slightly and make it round. Spoon 1 teaspoon of peanut butter into each divot and sprinkle a generous pinch of flaky sea salt on top.

9. Place one baking sheet on each oven rack and bake the cookies for 4 minutes. Remove the baking sheets from the oven and pile a mound of peanuts (about 20) in the center of each cookie. Return the baking sheets to the oven, switching racks and rotating the sheets front to back, and bake the cookies until they are golden brown, have puffed up, and are just beginning to collapse, 4 to 5 minutes. (You want the cookies to be slightly underdone, so they will feel soft to the touch. They will firm up when they cool.) Remove the cookies from the oven.

10. If any of the cookies have become misshapen during baking, gently cup your hands around the edges to reshape them. If the cookies spread so much that there are gaps between the peanuts, add a few of the remaining peanuts to each cookie so you have a pretty, abundant nut cluster on each cookie. Allow the cookies to cool completely before removing them from the baking sheet.

11. Bake the remaining cookies in the same way.

Chocolate Chunk Cookies

In 2007, *The New York Times* published a recipe for chocolate chunk cookies that set a new standard for what a chocolate chip cookie should look and taste like. Until then, the average baker—professional or at home—made chocolate chip cookies that in some way resembled those from the Nestlé Toll House recipe; the cookies were often dry or cakey, not very flavorful, and dotted with little chips of waxy chocolate. Only the best bakeries used chunks instead of chips, and rarer still were those cookies that had the crackly top and gently rounded edges that are the tells of a moist, slightly chewy, drop cookie ideal. Then that recipe appeared in the paper of record: the Jacques Torres Chocolate Chunk cookie. Totally achievable to the home cook, it would forever alter the chocolate chip-turned-chunk cookie world.

I was on my way to Italy when the story broke, so I packed up the ingredients that I knew I couldn't get overseas (most notably, American flours and brown sugar). When I got to Italy and made them, I knew immediately that this was the ultimate chocolate chip cookie. They were moist and chewy, buttery and flavorful, with big chunks of molten chocolate strewn throughout, and large flakes of Maldon sea salt on top. Nowadays we take it for granted when we see those flakes of salt on a cookie, but that recipe started the trend.

In the years since, the *Times* cookie has been adopted by bakers all over the world, including me. We tweak this or that, substituting whole wheat flour for the white flours, or adding different kinds of chocolate or nuts. But they are all, at their core, the Jacques Torres cookie. Today, that recipe is so widely known that when I go to a bakery and see chocolate chip cookies that are clearly *not* the Jacques Torres cookie, I think: "Didn't you get the memo? Those dry chocolate chip cookie lumps are just not acceptable anymore. We've moved on." I have added my own touches to the original recipe to create the version you see here. I melt the butter and cook it until it is golden and I also add a touch of rye flour, which gives the cookies a hint of earthy flavor.

I offer you three totally distinct ways of forming and baking them. The first method, different from the original, is to bake the dough in flan rings; the ring holds the dough in a disk shape, creating a taller cookie that is almost like an individual cake or blondie. (See photo page 102.) The second method is to bake the dough in a free-form style, like a typical chocolate chip cookie. (That's what you see in the photo on page 99.) And third, you can roll the dough into a log and slice-and-bake the dough into thin, elegant rounds. →

Chocolate Chunk Cookies (continued)

All are topped with big flakes of sea salt, just like the original. (I give you instructions for the first two methods below. If you want to slice and bake the dough, refer to the instructions in the Cinnamon Walnut Slice-and-Bake Butter Cookies, page 124, and be sure to chop the chocolate into smaller pieces than this recipe calls for.)

It's important to use big chunks of chocolate that you chop from a block, or Valrhona feves. The chunks melt inside the cookies, which is an integral part of the experience. These cookies are best when the dough rests overnight, so plan ahead. (See photo page 102.)

Makes about 18 drop cookies, or about 12 cookies baked in rings

What You Need—
The Essential Special Equipment

8 (3-inch) flan rings (if you are baking the cookies in rings)

Cooking spray (if you are baking the cookies in rings)

For the Dough

226 grams (2 sticks) unsalted butter, cubed

124 grams (¾ cup plus 2 tablespoons) unbleached all-purpose flour

120 grams (1 cup) dark rye flour

1 extra-large egg

1 tablespoon pure vanilla bean paste or vanilla extract

142 grams (¾ cup packed) dark brown sugar

112.5 grams (½ cup plus 1 tablespoon) granulated sugar

1½ teaspoons Diamond Crystal kosher salt

¾ teaspoon baking powder

½ teaspoon baking soda

280 grams (9.8 ounces) bittersweet chocolate (70% cacao), coarsely chopped (about 2 cups); halved if you're using feves

For Finishing

226 grams (8 ounces) bittersweet chocolate (70% cacao), coarsely chopped (about 1½ cups); whole if you're using feves

Flaky sea salt

1. To make the dough, place the butter in a small saucepan or skillet with a light-colored bottom to make golden butter. Warm the butter over medium heat until it melts and begins to bubble, swirling the pan occasionally. Cook the butter, swirling often so it cooks evenly, until it is golden and the milk solids are caramel colored, 3 to 6 minutes. Remove from the heat. Working quickly so the butter doesn't continue to cook, weigh out 177.5 grams (or measure about ¾ cup plus 1 tablespoon) of the butter, making sure to include the milk solids, and transfer to a bowl. Set aside to cool to room temperature. Cover the bowl with plastic wrap and refrigerate until the butter is solid. (Reserve the remaining butter for another use.)

2. Stir the all-purpose flour and rye flour together in a medium bowl. Whisk the egg and vanilla together in a small bowl.

3. Remove the butter from the refrigerator and place the bowl in a large bowl of hot water to help release the butter. Dry off the bowl and invert it to release the butter onto a cutting board. (Alternatively, you may be able to wedge a knife under the butter and pop it out.) Cut the butter into roughly ½-inch cubes.

4. Put the butter in a stand mixer fitted with the paddle and beat on medium-high speed until the butter is soft and smooth but still cold, about 1 minute, stopping to scrape down the sides and bottom of the bowl and the paddle with a rubber spatula whenever butter is accumulating. Add the brown sugar and granulated sugar and beat on medium speed for about 1 minute, until the mixture is smooth, scraping down the bowl and paddle as needed. Add the salt, baking powder, and baking soda and mix on medium speed for about 1 minute to incorporate them. Stop the mixer and scrape down the bowl. Return the mixer to medium speed, drizzle in the egg/vanilla mixture, and beat until the egg is fully incorporated. Stop the mixer, add the combined flours, and mix on low speed for about 30 seconds until the flour is almost completely combined and just a little flour is still visible. Add the chocolate and mix on low speed for about 30 seconds to distribute the chocolate and fully incorporate the flour. Stop the mixer, remove the bowl and paddle from the stand, and clean them with the spatula, scraping the bowl from the bottom up to release any ingredients that may be stuck there.

5. Line a large baking sheet with parchment paper.

6. If you are baking the cookies in flan rings, scoop the dough into 85-gram (⅓-cup) portions, roll each portion between your palms into a ball, and place the balls on the prepared baking sheet, making sure they're not touching. If you are baking the cookies as traditional drop cookies, scoop the dough into 57-gram (¼-cup) portions, roll each portion between your palms into a ball, and place the balls on the prepared baking sheet, making sure they're not touching. Cover the baking sheet with plastic wrap and place it in the refrigerator overnight to allow the dough to rest.

7. Adjust the oven racks so one is in the top third and the other is in the bottom third of the oven and preheat the oven to 350°F. Line two large baking sheets with parchment paper. If you are baking the dough in rings, coat the insides of the flan rings with cooking spray and place 4 rings on each baking sheet, spaced evenly apart. →

Chocolate Chunk Cookies (continued)

8. If baking in rings: To finish the cookies, remove the dough from the refrigerator and remove and reserve the plastic wrap. Place 1 ball of dough in the center of each ring. Place 1 chunk of chocolate (or 2 whole feves) on each ball of dough. Sprinkle with a generous pinch of flaky salt. (Re-cover the dough and return it to the refrigerator.)

9. Place one baking sheet on each oven rack and bake the cookies until they are golden brown and the cookies look set around the edges but still slightly wet in the centers, 18 to 22 minutes, switching racks and rotating the baking sheets front to back halfway through the baking time so the cookies bake evenly. (You want the cookies to be slightly underdone, so they will feel soft to the touch. They will firm up when they cool.)

10. Remove the cookies from the oven and set aside for a few minutes, just until they are cool enough to touch. While the cookies are still warm, run the tip of a paring knife around the inside edge of the rings and lift off the rings. Then allow the cookies to cool completely before removing them from the baking sheet.

11. Bake the remaining cookies in the same way, spraying the rings before baking each batch. (You may not use all the chocolate for finishing; reserve it for another use or snack on it.)

12. If baking as drop cookies: To finish the cookies, remove the dough from the refrigerator and place 6 of the balls on each baking sheet, leaving at least 2 inches between them. Place 1 chunk of chocolate or 2 feves on each ball and sprinkle each ball with a big pinch of flaky salt. (Re-cover the dough and return it to the refrigerator.)

13. Place one baking sheet on each oven rack and bake the cookies until they are golden brown and set around the edges and slightly wet looking in the center, 14 to 16 minutes, switching racks and rotating the baking sheets front to back halfway through the baking time so the cookies bake evenly. (You want the cookies to be slightly underdone, so they will feel soft to the touch. They will firm up when they cool.) Remove the cookies from the oven. If any of the cookies have misshapen during baking, gently cup your hands around the edges to reshape them. Allow the cookies to cool completely before removing them from the baking sheet.

14. Bake the remaining cookies in the same way. (You may not use all the chocolate for finishing; reserve it for another use or snack on it.)

Black Sesame White Chocolate Cookies

Most of the recipes in this book are my takes on old favorites, but this is neither my take nor an old favorite. I'm betting on the fact that they are good enough to stand the test of time, and that kids growing up today will one day say, oh, these remind me of the black sesame cookies of my youth. Everything about them is very of-the-moment. They're made with black tahini—tahini (sesame seed paste) made from black as opposed to golden sesame seeds—and rolled in black sesame seeds. Tahini is a hipster ingredient, and black sesame seeds are undoubtedly the hipster seed of the moment. The cookies are baked in flan rings, which is also in fashion. They are the brainchild of baker Talia Richard-Carvajal, from my favorite bakery in all the world, Hart Bageri, in Copenhagen. Black tahini is made from unhulled black sesame seeds, which have a slightly bitter taste. These cookies have an intense, nutty, almost burnt flavor, and they are not terribly sweet. The cookies have of chunks of white chocolate in them; the sweetness is welcome here. (See photo page 102.)

Makes about 24 cookies

What You Need—
The Essential Special Equipment

8 (3⅛- or 3-inch) flan rings

Cooking spray

For the Dough

2 extra-large eggs

250 grams (2 sticks plus about 2 tablespoons) cold unsalted butter, cubed

158 grams (¾ cup plus ½ tablespoon) granulated sugar

142 grams (½ cup plus ½ tablespoon) black tahini (black sesame paste)

175 grams (¾ cup plus 2 tablespoons packed) dark brown sugar

1¼ teaspoons baking powder

¾ teaspoon baking soda

1 teaspoon flaky sea salt

355 grams (2½ cups) bread flour (or unbleached all-purpose flour)

142 grams (about 5 ounces) white chocolate, coarsely chopped (halved if you're using feves); about 1 cup

For Finishing

142 grams (about 5 ounces) white chocolate, coarsely chopped (whole if you're using feves); about 1 cup

140 grams (about 1¾ cups) toasted (Japanese style) black sesame seeds

1. To make the dough, whisk the eggs in a small bowl to break up the yolks.

2. Put the butter in a stand mixer fitted with the paddle and beat on medium speed until the butter is soft but still cold, 3 to 4 minutes, stopping to scrape down the sides and bottom of the bowl and the paddle with a rubber spatula whenever ingredients have accumulated there. Add the granulated sugar, tahini, and brown sugar and beat until the mixture is light and fluffy, 3 to 4 minutes, scraping down the bowl as needed. Add the baking powder, baking soda, and salt and beat on medium speed for about 15 seconds to

distribute them. Stop the mixer and scrape down the bowl. With the mixer on medium speed, drizzle in the eggs a little at a time, making sure the egg is fully incorporated before adding more. Stop the mixer, add the flour, and mix on low speed for about 30 seconds until almost all the flour is incorporated. Add the white chocolate and mix for about 30 seconds until no flour is visible and the white chocolate is distributed throughout. Stop the mixer, remove the bowl and paddle from the stand, and clean them with the spatula, scraping the bowl from the bottom up to release any ingredients that may be stuck there. Cover the bowl with plastic wrap and refrigerate until the dough is chilled and firm, at least 1 hour.

3. Adjust the oven racks so one is in the top third and the other is in the bottom third of the oven and preheat the oven to 350°F. Line two large baking sheets with parchment paper. Coat the insides of the flan rings with cooking spray and place 4 rings on each baking sheet, spaced evenly apart.

4. To finish the cookies, remove the bowl from the refrigerator and remove and reserve the plastic wrap. Place the sesame seeds in a small bowl. Scoop a 57-gram (¼-cup) portion of dough and roll it between the palms of your hands into a ball. Gently press the ball into a 1½-inch-thick puck and roll in the sesame seeds, pressing gently to evenly coat it with the seeds. Place the puck inside one of the rings and repeat to fill all the rings. Place 1 chunk of white chocolate (or 2 feves) on each puck. (Re-cover the dough and return it to the refrigerator.)

5. Place one baking sheet on each oven rack and bake the cookies for 7 minutes. Remove the baking sheets from the oven and use the bottom of a measuring cup to gently press on the dough to flatten it slightly. Return the baking sheets to the oven, switching racks and rotating the baking sheets front to back, and bake the cookies until they have puffed up and the edges are set, 7 to 8 minutes. (The centers will look slightly shiny and underbaked and will feel soft to the touch. They will firm up when they cool.)

6. Remove the cookies from the oven and set aside for a few minutes, until they are cool enough to touch. While the cookies are still warm, run the tip of a paring knife around the inside edge of the rings, and lift off the rings. Cool the cookies on the baking sheets.

7. Bake the remaining cookies in the same way, spraying the rings before baking each batch. (You may not use all the chocolate for finishing; reserve it for another use or snack on it.)

Chocolate Chunk Cookies (baked in ring molds;
top and center); Oatmeal Raisin Cookies (left and right);
Black Sesame White Chocolate Cookies (foreground)

Oatmeal Raisin Cookies

In Los Angeles, when the subject of République Bakery comes up, the first thing people are likely to talk about are the oatmeal raisin cookies. République is located in the space where I launched La Brea Bakery decades ago, and I couldn't have asked for a better person than baker Marge Manzke and her husband, the chef Walter Manzke (who has the restaurant adjacent to the bakery, where Campanile was), to honor that space that is so dear to my heart. Marge is one of those rare bakers who truly has her own way of doing things, a unique style that comes through in everything she bakes. When you enter République B and see the long display, you can't help but be awed by the rustic beauty of it all, including that of these cookies. They're so different from the oatmeal cookies we're used to because they're baked in a ring. There is so much butter in the dough that without the ring, I imagine they would flatten out into pancakes. Baked in a ring, the cookies turn out chewy, gooey, and, yes, incredibly buttery. The butter in them is brown butter, and its nutty flavor is front and center. This recipe is not in Marge's cookbook, *Baking at République,* so it's an honor to put it in mine.

These cookies are made with unblanched almond meal (finely ground almonds with skins) in place of flour, so they're gluten-free. Seek out golden raisins that are plump, fresh, and large; farmers' markets are a great place to start.

Makes about 24 cookies

What You Need—
The Essential Special Equipment

8 (4-inch) flan rings

Cooking spray

452 grams (4 sticks) unsalted butter, cubed

2 extra-large eggs

2 teaspoons pure vanilla bean paste or vanilla extract

212 grams (2 cups plus 2 tablespoons) rolled oats

218 grams (about 1 cup plus 1½ tablespoons packed) dark brown sugar

218 grams (about 1 cup plus 1½ tablespoons) granulated sugar

204 grams (2 cups plus 2 tablespoons) unblanched almond meal

1 teaspoon baking powder

1 teaspoon baking soda

1 tablespoon Diamond Crystal kosher salt

150 grams (1 cup) golden raisins (halved if large) →

Oatmeal Raisin Cookies (continued)

1. Place the butter in a small saucepan or skillet with a light-colored bottom to make brown butter. Warm the butter over medium heat until it melts and begins to bubble, swirling the pan occasionally. Cook the butter, swirling often so it cooks evenly, until the butter is caramel colored and the milk solids are the color of coffee grounds, 4 to 8 minutes. Remove from the heat. Working quickly so the butter doesn't continue to cook, weigh out 340 grams (or measure 1½ cups plus 1 tablespoon) of the butter, making sure to include the milk solids, and transfer to a bowl. Set aside to cool to room temperature. (Reserve the remaining butter for another use; you can use it to grease the rings instead of cooking spray.)

2. Whisk the eggs and vanilla together in a small bowl.

3. Put the oats, brown sugar, granulated sugar, almond meal, baking powder, baking soda, and salt in a stand mixer fitted with the paddle. Mix on low speed to combine the ingredients and distribute the leavenings and salt. With the mixer on low speed, gradually add the egg/vanilla mixture and mix on low speed to combine. With the mixer on low speed, gradually add the brown butter. Increase the speed to medium and beat until combined, stopping to scrape down the bowl as needed. (If the mixture appears to be separating, refrigerate it for about 30 minutes to chill the butter. Remove it from the refrigerator and beat the dough on low speed for about 30 seconds before proceeding with the recipe.) Add the raisins and mix on low speed for about 30 seconds to distribute them. Stop the mixer, remove the bowl and paddle from the stand, and clean them with the spatula, scraping the bowl from the bottom up to release any ingredients that may be stuck there. Cover the bowl with plastic wrap and refrigerate until the dough is firm enough to scoop, at least 1 hour.

4. Arrange the oven racks so one is in the top third and the other is in the bottom third of the oven and preheat the oven to 350°F. Line two large baking sheets with parchment paper. Coat the insides of the flan rings with cooking spray and place 4 rings on each baking sheet, spaced evenly.

5. Remove the cookie dough from the refrigerator and remove the plastic wrap but reserve it. Use a 2-ounce scoop or a large spoon to scoop 57 grams (¼ cup) of the dough and roll it between the palms of your hands into a ball. Place it in the center of one ring and repeat, placing one dough ball in each ring. (Re-cover the remaining dough and return it to the refrigerator.)

6. Place one baking sheet on each oven rack and bake the cookies until the edges are golden brown and the centers are just beginning to turn brown, 13 to 15 minutes, switching racks and rotating the baking sheets front to back halfway through the baking time so the cookies bake evenly. (You want the cookies to be slightly underdone, so they will feel soft to the touch. They will firm up when they cool.) Remove the cookies from the oven and set aside for a few minutes until they are cool enough to touch. While the cookies are still warm, run the tip of a paring knife around the inside edge of the rings, and lift off the rings. Allow the cookies to cool completely before removing them from the baking sheet.

7. Bake the remaining cookies in the same way, coating the rings before the next batch.

Snickerdoodles (foreground);
Chewy Ginger Cookies (background)

Snickerdoodles

During the pandemic, when I was just beginning to develop the recipes for this book, I opened a small counter-service restaurant called Pizzette in a boutique food court in the Culver City neighborhood of Los Angeles. In the same food court is a coffee shop/bakery that I frequented often called goodboybob Coffee Roasters, named for the owner's dog, Bob. Before I go further, I must say that in all my years as a baker and eater of cookies, I have never understood the attraction of snickerdoodles. What exactly were they anyway—sugar cookies with cinnamon on them? Why did recipes for snickerdoodles always contain cream of tartar? Were they supposed to be flavorless and dry, or had I never tasted a good one? And why the unusual (and not particularly appetizing) name? All this is to say that I was a snickerdoodle-skeptic when I walked into goodboybob one day and spotted, among their display, a platter of snickerdoodles looking (if I do admit) extremely appealing.

I bought one, and with the first bite, I thought: Yes, I get it! It wasn't just the moist and chewy texture, but also the flavor that won me over. The baker, Robyn Collins, gave me her recipe. There is nothing unusual in the ingredients, but at every turn, she did something special. She uses demerara sugar, a coarse brown sugar that imparts molasses flavor to the dough and a wonderful crunchy texture to the outsides of the cookies. And she starts with brown butter, which gives a nutty, buttery flavor to an otherwise fairly plain flavor profile. The result is one of my favorite types of victory, even when it's not mine: taking something simple, with an unremarkable list of ingredients, and making it remarkable.

For optimum results, bake these cookies in a convection oven. A convection oven is ideal for many baked goods, but in the case of these cookies, I found it was almost mandatory to achieve the rounded edge and crackly top that I was aiming for. As much as I hate to ask you to buy yogurt only to use 1 tablespoon in this recipe, it really does contribute to the finished product. These are best the day they're made and still delicious the next day, but I don't recommend keeping them any longer than that. →

Makes about 30 cookies

For the Dough

452 grams (4 sticks) unsalted butter, cubed

1 extra-large egg

1 extra-large egg yolk

1 tablespoon plain whole-milk yogurt

1 teaspoon pure vanilla bean paste or vanilla extract

425 grams (2¼ cups) demerara sugar

170 grams (¾ cup plus 1 tablespoon) granulated sugar

2 teaspoons cream of tartar

1 teaspoon baking soda

1 teaspoon ground cinnamon

1 teaspoon Diamond Crystal kosher salt

320 grams (2¼ cups plus 2 tablespoons) unbleached all-purpose flour

For Finishing

50 grams (¼ cup) demerara sugar

35 grams (3 tablespoons) granulated sugar

2 teaspoons ground cinnamon

½ teaspoon Diamond Crystal kosher salt

1. To make the dough, fill a large bowl with ice and place the bowl of a stand mixer on the ice.

2. Place the butter in a small saucepan or skillet with a light-colored bottom to make brown butter. Warm the butter over medium heat until it melts and begins to bubble, swirling the pan occasionally. Cook the butter, swirling often so it cooks evenly, until the butter is caramel colored and the milk solids are the color of coffee grounds, 4 to 8 minutes. Remove from the heat. Working quickly so the butter doesn't continue to cook, weigh out 340 grams (or measure 1½ cups plus 1 tablespoon) of the butter, making sure to include the milk solids, and transfer to the stand mixer bowl set on ice. (Reserve the remaining butter for another use.) Cool the butter on the ice, stirring often so it cools evenly, until it is thick and creamy, about 10 minutes. (Alternatively, place the butter in the refrigerator to chill for about 1 hour, stirring often, until it is thick and creamy looking, about 30 minutes.)

3. Line a large baking sheet with parchment paper.

4. Whisk the whole egg, egg yolk, yogurt, and vanilla together in a small bowl.

5. Remove the mixer bowl from the ice and dry off the bottom. Add the demerara and granulated sugars to the mixer bowl and set the bowl on the mixer stand. Fit the mixer with the paddle and beat the butter and sugars together on medium speed until the mixture lightens slightly in color, about 1 minute, stopping to scrape down the sides and bottom of the bowl and the paddle with a rubber spatula whenever ingredients are accumulating. Add

the cream of tartar, baking soda, cinnamon, and salt and mix on medium speed for about 15 seconds to distribute them. Stop the mixer and scrape down the bowl and paddle. Return the mixer to medium speed and gradually add the egg mixture, making sure it is incorporated before adding more. When all of the egg is incorporated, stop the mixer and scrape down the sides of the bowl. Add the flour and mix on low speed for about 30 seconds until no flour is visible. Stop the mixer, remove the bowl and paddle from the stand, and clean them with the spatula, scraping the bowl from the bottom up to release any ingredients that may be stuck there.

6. Scoop the dough into 43-gram (3-tablespoon) portions and drop them side by side onto the prepared baking sheet, making sure they are not touching. Place the dough in the refrigerator to chill until firm, at least 1 hour.

7. Adjust the oven racks so one is in the top third and the other is in the bottom third of the oven and preheat the oven to 350°F. Line two large baking sheets with parchment paper.

8. To finish the cookies, stir the demerara sugar, granulated sugar, cinnamon, and salt together in a medium bowl.

9. Remove the dough from the refrigerator. Working with 6 at a time, roll each portion of dough between your palms into a perfect ball. Roll them in the cinnamon-sugar, making sure they are generously covered all over. Place them on one of the prepared baking sheets, spacing them evenly, leaving at least 1½ inches between them. Roll 6 more balls in the cinnamon-sugar and place them, evenly spaced, on the second baking sheet. (Re-cover the remaining dough and return it to the refrigerator.)

10. Place one baking sheet on each oven rack and bake the cookies until they are light golden brown with a slight dome in the center, 9 to 13 minutes, switching racks and rotating the baking sheets front to back halfway through the baking time so the cookies bake evenly. (You want the cookies to be slightly underdone, so they will feel soft to the touch. They will firm up when they cool.) Remove the cookies from the oven and let them cool on the baking sheets. If any of the cookies have misshapen during baking, gently cup your hands around the edges to reshape them.

11. Bake the remaining cookies in the same way.

Chewy Ginger Cookies

This recipe by the pastry chef Brad Ray was featured, alongside a photograph of the cookies, in the *Los Angeles Times*. It was love at first sight. The picture showed these enormous, flat, obviously chewy cookies with a beautiful crackly top: just the way I like them. I was looking for the ultimate ginger cookie for this book, so I tried the recipe. Brad calls for you to rest the dough in the freezer overnight before baking. I did as I was told, and the cookies turned out just as good as I'd hoped they would: moist and chewy, with intense molasses and ginger flavor. My feeling is that if you're eating a ginger cookie, you should really taste the ginger. Otherwise, eat a snickerdoodle. I didn't change a thing, other than to bake them at half the size of his. (See photo page 106.)

Makes about 30 cookies

3 extra-large eggs

2 tablespoons plus ½ teaspoon baking soda

1 tablespoon plus 1 teaspoon ground ginger

2 teaspoons ground cardamom

2 teaspoons ground cinnamon

2 teaspoons Diamond Crystal kosher salt

1½ teaspoons ground cloves

227 grams (2 sticks) cold unsalted butter, cubed

725 grams (3½ cups plus 2 tablespoons) granulated sugar

360 grams (1 cup plus 2 tablespoons) unsulphured molasses

57 grams (¼ cup plus 2 tablespoons) grated peeled fresh ginger (grated on a fine Microplane; include the juices extracted when you grate the ginger)

2 tablespoons distilled white vinegar

980 grams (7 cups) bread flour (or unbleached all-purpose flour)

200 grams (1 cup) turbinado sugar (or demerara sugar)

1. Line a large baking sheet with parchment paper.

2. Whisk the eggs together in a small bowl. Stir the baking soda, ground ginger, cardamom, cinnamon, salt, and cloves together in a separate small bowl.

3. Put the butter in a stand mixer fitted with the paddle and beat on medium speed until the butter is soft but still cool, 3 to 4 minutes, stopping to scrape down the sides and bottom of the bowl with a large rubber spatula whenever butter is accumulating. Stop the mixer, add the granulated sugar, molasses, and fresh ginger, and beat on medium speed until fluffy and creamy, 3 to 4 minutes, scraping down the bowl as needed. Add the baking soda/spice mixture and beat for about 15 seconds to incorporate them. With the mixer on medium speed, drizzle in the eggs, making sure they are incorporated and stopping to scrape down the bowl before adding more. Once all the eggs

are incorporated into the batter, stop the mixer and scrape down the bowl and paddle. Add the vinegar and mix on low speed to combine. Add the flour and mix on low speed until no flour is visible. Stop the mixer, remove the bowl and paddle from the stand, and clean them with the spatula, scraping the bowl from the bottom up to release any ingredients that may be stuck there.

4. Scoop the dough into 57-gram (¼-cup) portions and roll each portion between the palms of your hands into a ball. Place the balls on the prepared baking sheet and gently flatten to a disk ½ to ¾ inch thick. As you add and flatten the balls of dough on the baking sheet, make sure they are not touching. Wrap the baking sheet in plastic wrap and place it in the freezer overnight.

5. Arrange the oven racks so one is in the top third and the other is in the bottom third of the oven and preheat the oven to 350°F. Line two large baking sheets with parchment paper.

6. Pour the turbinado sugar into a shallow bowl. Remove the dough from the freezer and remove and reserve the plastic wrap. Add one disk at a time to the bowl with the sugar and turn to coat the top, bottom, and sides, pressing so the sugar adheres to the dough. Place the dough on one of the prepared baking sheets and repeat, placing 6 disks of dough on each baking sheet, spacing them out evenly and making sure there are at least 2 inches between them. (Re-cover the remaining dough and return it to the freezer.)

7. Place one baking sheet on each oven rack and bake the cookies until they have spread out and the edges are deep golden brown, 12 to 15 minutes, switching racks and rotating the baking sheets front to back halfway through the baking time so the cookies bake evenly. (You want the cookies to be slightly underdone, so they will feel soft to the touch. They will firm up when they cool.) Remove the baking sheets from the oven and firmly tap them against the counter to deflate the cookies. Let the cookies cool on the baking sheets. If any of the cookies have misshapen during baking, gently cup your hands around them to reshape them.

8. Bake the remaining cookies in the same way.

Alaska Cookies with Chocolate Chunks, Dulce de Leche, and Marshmallows

Everything about this cookie is anathema to what I would claim to like. The cookies consist of a chocolatey cookie base, with other sweet, rich ingredients, including chunks of bittersweet and milk chocolate, chopped marshmallows, and swirls of dulce de leche or caramel strewn throughout. I tasted them at Winterlake Lodge, a rustic lodge outside of Anchorage, Alaska, where I was hosting an event for my gelato brand, Nancy's Fancy. With the marshmallow and dulce de leche, they sounded like they'd be too sweet and gooey for my taste. I tried one to be polite, and I was shocked at my response: I devoured the entire cookie—and then reached for another one! They are indeed gooey, but with the dark chocolate base and a hint of salt, it all just worked. The chef and owner of the lodge, Kristen Dixon, was nice enough to share the recipe with me.

I give you a recipe for making dulce de leche (caramel sauce) from a can of sweetened condensed milk; alternatively, skip that step and use store-bought dulce de leche. (Note that it is called for both in the dough and on top of each cookie before it's baked.) I added a dusting of cocoa powder to the cookies after they come out of the oven. The cocoa powder melts into the cookies and turns the already-dark cookies almost black. They're unexpectedly beautiful. They are so gooey that they need to be baked on a silicone baking mat to prevent them from sticking.

Makes about 30 cookies

**What You Need—
The Essential Special Equipment**

Silicone baking mat

For the Dough

1 (14-ounce) can sweetened condensed milk (or 74 grams/¼ cup dulce de leche)

350 grams (2½ cups) unbleached all-purpose flour

76 grams (¾ cup) natural cocoa powder, plus more for dusting

2 extra-large eggs

1 teaspoon pure vanilla bean paste or vanilla extract

226 grams (2 sticks) cold unsalted butter, cubed

200 grams (1 cup) granulated sugar

200 grams (1 cup packed) dark brown sugar

1½ teaspoons Diamond Crystal kosher salt

1 teaspoon baking soda

250 grams (9 ounces) bittersweet chocolate (70% cacao), coarsely chopped (heaping 1½ cups); halved if you're using feves

70 grams large marshmallows (about 10 whole marshmallows), cut into thirds (about 1½ cups)

For Finishing

100 grams (¼ cup plus 1 tablespoon) dulce de leche (store-bought, or made from the sweetened condensed milk in the ingredients list)

10 to 12 marshmallows, cut into thirds

Natural cocoa powder for dusting

1 heaping tablespoon flaky sea salt →

Alaska Cookies with Chocolate Chunks (continued)

1. If you're making dulce de leche, place the unopened can of sweetened condensed milk on its side in a large pot. Fill the pot with enough water to cover by at least 3 inches and bring the water to a boil over high heat. Reduce the heat until the water is simmering and simmer for 3 hours, adding more boiling water as needed to cover the can. Remove from the heat and use tongs to remove the can from the water to cool to room temperature. (Do not open the can before it has completely cooled.)

2. Line a large baking sheet with parchment paper.

3. Combine the flour and cocoa powder in a medium bowl and stir with a whisk to combine. Whisk the eggs and vanilla together in a small bowl.

4. Put the butter in a stand mixer fitted with the paddle and beat on medium speed until the butter is soft but still cold, 3 to 4 minutes, stopping to scrape down the sides and bottom of the bowl with a rubber spatula whenever butter is accumulating. Stop the mixer and scrape down the bowl. Add the granulated sugar and brown sugar and beat on medium speed until the mixture is light and fluffy, 3 to 4 minutes, stopping to scrape down the bowl as needed. Add the salt and baking soda and beat on medium speed for about 15 seconds to distribute them. Stop the mixer and scrape down the bowl and paddle. Return the mixer to medium speed and gradually add the egg/vanilla mixture, making sure the addition is incorporated and stopping to scrape down the bowl before adding more. Add the flour/cocoa powder mixture and mix on low speed for about 1 minute until no flour or cocoa is visible. Add the chocolate and marshmallows and mix for about 30 seconds to distribute them. Stop the mixer, remove the bowl and paddle from the stand, and clean them with the spatula.

5. Scrape the dough onto the prepared baking sheet and use your hands to spread it evenly over the surface. Spoon 2 tablespoons of the dulce de leche over the dough. Lightly fold the dough in half like a book with your hands. Spoon all but a few spoonfuls of the remaining dulce de leche over the dough and fold it in half again in the opposite direction. Spoon the 2 additional tablespoons of dulce de leche over the dough and fold it in half a third time. (Adding the dulce de leche in this way ensures you will have streaks of caramel in your cookies rather than blending the caramel into the dough.) Refrigerate the dough until it is chilled and firm, at least 1 hour. Reserve the remaining dulce de leche to use after the dough is chilled.

6. Adjust the oven racks so one is in the top third and the other is in the bottom third of the oven and preheat the oven to 350°F. Line two large baking sheets with parchment paper.

7. To finish the cookies, remove the dough from the refrigerator. Scoop the dough into 57-gram (¼-cup) portions and roll each portion between the palms of your hands into a ball. Place the balls on the prepared baking sheets, leaving 1½ inches between the cookies. Spoon ½ teaspoon of the remaining dulce de leche and place one piece (one-third) of marshmallow atop each cookie. (Cover the remaining dough in plastic wrap and return it to the refrigerator. Save the remaining dulce de leche for another use, such as to spoon over ice cream.) Sprinkle a pinch of flaky sea salt on each cookie.

8. Place one baking sheet on each oven rack and bake the cookies until they are firm around the edges, 10 to 12 minutes, switching racks and rotating the baking sheets front to back halfway through the baking time so they bake evenly. (You want the cookies to be slightly underdone, so they will feel soft to the touch. They will firm up when they cool.) Remove the cookies from the oven.

9. If any of the cookies are misshapen due to the caramel or marshmallow oozing out, use a spoon to push the edges of the cookie back into shape. While the cookies are still warm, dust them lightly with cocoa powder. Cool the cookies on the baking sheets.

10. Repeat, forming and baking the remaining cookies in the same way.

Brownies and Blondies

Brownies

If you're a chocolate lover, proceed with caution: These brownies are extremely addictive. The recipe is based on one from Alice Medrich, which I learned about from the New York baker Melissa Weller, who included the recipe in her book, *A Good Bake.* When I baked them from Melissa's book, I thought: Brownies truly cannot get any better. They have three subtly different textures: chewy edges and corners, like the ends of a loaf of bread; a thin, crackly top; and beneath that, a moist and fudgy middle. I add chunks of chocolate, which give them yet a fourth texture, and more chocolate flavor. They had so much salt in them that I wondered if it was a typo; it's not! That salt works with the chocolate to make it so that you just can't stop eating them. It also confirms that these are adult brownies. These are so fudgy that I refrigerate them to firm them up; I like to eat them cold, straight from the refrigerator.

Makes one 10-inch square pan of brownies

What You Need—
The Essential Special Equipment

10-inch square cake pan

Cooking spray

200 grams (2 cups) walnut halves (optional)

227 grams (8 ounces) unsweetened chocolate, cut into large chunks; about 1½ cups

226 grams (2 sticks) cold unsalted butter, cubed

1 tablespoon plus 1 teaspoon Diamond Crystal kosher salt

500 grams (2½ cups) granulated sugar

2 tablespoons pure vanilla bean paste or vanilla extract

4 extra-large eggs

120 grams (¾ cup plus 2 tablespoons) unbleached all-purpose flour

227 grams (8 ounces) bittersweet chocolate (70% cacao), coarsely chopped (about 1½ cups); if you're using feves, cut most of them in half and leave a handful whole

1 teaspoon flaky sea salt

1. Adjust an oven rack to the center position. If you are adding walnuts to the brownies, preheat the oven to 325°F; if not, preheat the oven to 400°F.

2. If you are adding walnuts, spread them on a baking sheet and toast them on the center rack of the oven until they're toasted and fragrant, 16 to 20 minutes, shaking the baking sheet and rotating it halfway through the toasting time so the walnuts brown evenly. Remove the baking sheet from the oven and set aside until the walnuts are cool enough to touch. If you think the nuts are on the verge of being overtoasted, transfer them to a plate so they don't continue to cook from the residual heat of the pan. Coarsely chop the toasted walnuts and put them in a bowl. →

3. Coat the bottom and sides of the cake pan with cooking spray. Cut two pieces of parchment paper to 9 × 16 inches. Lay one sheet of paper in the pan so it travels up and over two of the sides. Lay the other sheet perpendicular so it travels up and over the remaining two sides of the pan. Coat the paper with cooking spray.

4. Adjust an oven rack to the center position and preheat the oven to 400°F.

5. Fill a small saucepan with 1½ to 2 inches of water and set a small stainless steel bowl atop the saucepan to make a double boiler, making sure the water doesn't touch the bottom of the bowl. Bring the water to a simmer over medium heat. Put the unsweetened chocolate, butter, and kosher salt in the bowl and heat until the chocolate and butter melt, stirring and scraping the bowl with a silicone spatula to prevent the chocolate from burning. Turn off the heat and remove the bowl from the double boiler; dry the bottom of the bowl. Add the granulated sugar and vanilla and whisk them in. (The batter will look broken, but don't worry; it will come back together when you add the eggs.) Add the eggs one at a time, whisking until each egg is combined before adding the next egg. Add the flour and stir with a rubber spatula until no flour is visible. Add the bittersweet chocolate chunks and the chopped toasted walnuts, if you are using them, and stir to combine.

6. Pour the batter into the prepared pan and use the spatula to smooth out the top of the batter.

7. Place the brownies on the center rack of the oven and reduce the oven temperature to 375°F. Bake the brownies for 10 minutes. Slide the oven rack out and sprinkle the flaky salt over the brownies, rotate the pan front to back, and slide the rack back in. Bake the brownies for another 20 minutes. It's hard to overbake these, so if you're questioning whether the brownies are done, err on the side of overbaking, not underbaking. Remove the brownies from the oven and set them aside to cool to room temperature. Cover the pan with plastic wrap and refrigerate the brownies until they're chilled, at least 2 hours.

8. Remove the brownies from the refrigerator. Uncover and lift up on the parchment paper wings to lift the brownies out of the pan; peel off the paper. Serve the brownies chilled or at room temperature.

Blondies

Blondies were never in my repertoire, or even in my vocabulary, until fairly recently. My mom didn't make them, and they weren't available in my school cafeteria. I guess I lived a sheltered life. It wasn't until 2010, when my late friend, the baker Amy Pressman, opened her bakery, Short Order, that I tasted my first blondie. My instinct was not to like them: they seemed a bit one-dimensional. That wasn't the case at all. Amy's blondies, which she called Brunettes, were made with muscovado sugar, a grainy dark brown sugar heavy in molasses flavor. I could never stop eating them when I went to her bakery. I carry on that tradition in these blondies. I also cook the butter until it's golden and add a lot of vanilla. When baked, the outsides get crusty and chewy, and the insides moist and caramelly and loaded with toasted pecans and chunks of milk chocolate, both friends of caramel. They are sweet, but with the complexity of the sugars and the pecans, they don't feel overwhelming. They're totally addictive. If you're anything like me, you'll just keep slicing away, just to even out the cut, of course. (If you want your blondies less sweet, use bittersweet instead of milk chocolate.) (See photo page 116.)

Makes one 10-inch square pan of blondies

**What You Need—
The Essential Special Equipment**

10-inch square cake pan

Cooking spray

300 grams (3 cups) pecan halves

3 extra-large eggs

2 tablespoons pure vanilla bean paste or vanilla extract

508 grams (4½ sticks) unsalted butter

425 grams (2 cups plus 2 tablespoons packed) dark brown sugar

175 grams (¾ cup plus 2 tablespoons) granulated sugar

65 grams (¼ cup plus 1 heaping tablespoon packed) muscovado sugar (or dark brown sugar)

1½ teaspoons Diamond Crystal kosher salt

¾ teaspoon baking powder

½ teaspoon baking soda

490 grams (3½ cups) unbleached all-purpose flour

114 grams (4 ounces) milk chocolate (40% cacao), cut into ¾-inch pieces (about ¾ cup); halved if you're using feves

1 teaspoon flaky sea salt

1. Adjust an oven rack to the center position and preheat the oven to 325°F. Coat the bottom and sides the baking pan with cooking spray. Cut two pieces of parchment paper to 9 × 16 inches. Lay one sheet of paper in the pan so it travels up and over two of the sides. Lay the other sheet perpendicular so it travels up and over the remaining two sides of the pan. Coat the paper with cooking spray. →

2. Spread 200 grams (2 cups) of the pecans on a baking sheet and toast them on the center rack of the oven until they're toasted and fragrant, 16 to 20 minutes, shaking the baking sheet and rotating it halfway through the toasting time so the pecans brown evenly. Remove the baking sheet from the oven and set aside until the pecans cool enough to touch. (If you think the nuts are on the verge of being overtoasted, transfer them to a plate so they don't continue to cook from the residual heat of the pan.) Coarsely chop the toasted pecans and place them in a bowl.

3. Increase the oven temperature to 350°F.

4. Cut the raw pecans in thirds lengthwise and place them in a separate bowl. Whisk the eggs and vanilla together in a small bowl.

5. Place the butter in a small saucepan or skillet with a light-colored bottom to make brown butter. Warm the butter over medium heat until it melts and begins to bubble, swirling the pan occasionally so the butter cooks evenly. Continue to cook the butter, swirling often, until the melted butter is caramel colored and the solids are the color of coffee grounds, 5 to 8 minutes. Remove from the heat. Working quickly so the butter doesn't continue to cook, weigh out 397 grams (or measure 1¾ cups plus 2 tablespoons) of the butter, making sure to include the milk solids, and transfer it to the bowl of a stand mixer. Let the butter cool to room temperature. (Reserve the remaining butter for another use.)

6. Add the brown sugar, granulated sugar, and muscovado sugar to the bowl with the brown butter. Set the bowl on the mixer, fit with the paddle, and beat on medium speed until the butter and sugars lighten in both texture and color, about 1 minute, stopping to scrape down the sides and bottom of the bowl with a rubber spatula whenever ingredients are accumulating. Add the salt, baking powder, and baking soda and mix on medium speed for about 15 seconds to distribute them. With the mixer on medium speed, slowly add the egg/vanilla mixture and mix until it is fully incorporated, making sure each addition is incorporated before adding more. Add the flour and mix on low speed for about 30 seconds, until almost no flour is visible. Add the chopped toasted pecans and 85 grams (½ cup plus 2 tablespoons) of the chocolate and mix on low speed for about 15 seconds to distribute the

additions and fully combine the flour. Stop the mixer, remove the bowl and paddle from the stand, and clean them with the spatula, scraping the bowl from the bottom up to release any ingredients that may be stuck there.

7. Scrape the batter into the prepared baking pan and use the spatula to spread the batter to the edges, maintaining a natural rustic look. Sprinkle the raw pecans over the top.

8. Bake the blondies on the center rack of the oven for 10 minutes. Slide the oven rack out and sprinkle the flaky sea salt over the blondies. Slide the rack back in and bake the blondies until they are golden brown and have pulled away from the sides of the pan, for another 1 hour 15 minutes to 1 hour 30 minutes, rotating the pan front to back halfway through the baking time so the blondies brown evenly. Remove the blondies from the oven and set them aside to cool slightly.

9. Lift the parchment paper wings to lift the blondies out of the pan and peel off the paper.

A plate of cookies is such a simple and elegant dessert offering, but there is some artistry to it. When I create a cookie plate, I like to focus on one style of cookies, with different variations on that style. I wouldn't want to serve giant gooey chocolate chip cookies, for example, on a platter along with tiny Chewy Almond Cookies (page 189). The shape, scale, and style of each cookie should be complementary.

The five butter cookie recipes that follow are an assorted cookie platter waiting to happen. They're the same size and shape as one another, but the flavor of each one is distinct. And because each one is finished differently—the toasted sesame butter cookies (page 126) are rolled in sesame seeds, whereas the coconut almond cookies (page 132) have a tuft of toasted coconut on top—they each have a distinct look. In a perfect world, I would tell you to make a batch of each and keep the logs in your freezer. This way, an assorted cookie platter is always at your fingertips. (Freeze the dough for up to 3 months. Move the log to the refrigerator the day before you want to slice it and bake the cookies.)

Slice-and-Bake Butter Cookies (clockwise from top):
Toasted Sesame; Cinnamon Walnut; Coconut Almond;
Maple Pecan; Chocolate Chunk Hazelnut

Cinnamon Walnut Slice-and-Bake Butter Cookies

I've been making these since the 1980s, at my first pastry job, at Michael's restaurant in Santa Monica. This recipe is the base for all the combinations that follow (except the coconut version). (See photo page 123.)

Makes about 28 cookies

For the Dough

190 grams (scant 2 cups) walnut halves

1 extra-large egg yolk

1 tablespoon pure vanilla bean paste or vanilla extract

226 grams (2 sticks) cold unsalted butter, cubed

75 grams (¼ cup plus 2 tablespoons packed) dark brown sugar

50 grams (¼ cup) granulated sugar

2 teaspoons ground cinnamon

1 teaspoon Diamond Crystal kosher salt

226 grams (1½ cups plus 2 tablespoons) all-purpose flour

For Coating

1 extra-large egg white

37.5 grams (3 tablespoons) granulated sugar

2 teaspoons ground cinnamon

1. To make the dough, adjust an oven rack to the center position and preheat the oven to 325°F.

2. Spread the walnuts on a baking sheet and toast them on the center rack of the oven until they're lightly browned and fragrant, 8 to 10 minutes, shaking the baking sheet and rotating it front to back halfway through the baking time so the walnuts brown evenly. Remove the walnuts from the oven. (If you think the nuts are on the verge of being overtoasted, transfer them to a plate so they don't continue to cook from the residual heat of the pan.) Set the walnuts aside until they're cool enough to touch. Weigh out 113 grams (or measure a heaping cup) of the toasted walnut halves and set them aside to add to the dough. Finely chop the remaining toasted walnuts and set them aside for coating the cookie dough log.

3. Turn off the oven.

4. Whisk the egg yolk and vanilla together in a small bowl.

5. Put the butter in a stand mixer fitted with the paddle attachment and beat on medium speed, until the butter is soft but still cold, 3 to 4 minutes, stopping to scrape down the bottom and sides of the bowl and the paddle with a rubber spatula whenever butter is accumulating. Add the brown sugar and granulated sugar and beat on medium speed until the mixture is light and fluffy, 3 to 4 minutes, scraping down the bowl as needed. Add

the cinnamon and salt and beat for about 15 seconds to incorporate the additions. With the mixer on medium speed, and the egg yolk/vanilla mixture and beat until the egg is fully incorporated. Stop the mixer and scrape down the bowl. Add the flour and mix on low speed for about 30 seconds, until almost no flour is visible. Add the toasted walnut halves and mix on low speed for about 30 seconds to distribute them and fully incorporate the flour. Stop the mixer, remove the bowl and paddle from the stand, and clean them with the spatula, scraping the bowl from the bottom up to release any ingredients that may be stuck there.

6. Lay a sheet of plastic wrap on your work surface. Divide the dough in half. Place one portion of dough on the plastic wrap and shape it into a log 2 inches in diameter. Wrap the log in the plastic, twisting the ends like a candy wrapper. Repeat, shaping and wrapping the remaining dough into a second log. Place the logs in the refrigerator to chill until firm, at least 1 hour.

7. Adjust the oven racks so one is in the top third and the other is in the bottom third of the oven and preheat the oven to 350°F. Line two large baking sheets with parchment paper.

8. To coat the cookies, put the egg white in a small bowl. Add the granulated sugar and cinnamon to the bowl with the finely chopped toasted walnuts and stir to combine. Spread half of the walnut mixture out on a sheet of parchment paper or a baking sheet.

9. Remove a log from the refrigerator and unwrap. Brush the egg white on the log to coat it. (Do not brush the ends.) Roll the log in the walnut mixture, pressing gently so it sticks to the dough and coats the log evenly.

10. Place the log on a cutting board and use a long sharp knife to slice it into ⅜-inch-thick rounds. Place the rounds on the prepared baking sheets, leaving 1 inch between them. (If the cookies become misshapen when you transfer them, one at a time, gently turn the cookies in your hand to reshape them.)

11. Place one baking sheet on each oven rack and bake the cookies until the edges are golden brown, 17 to 20 minutes, switching racks and rotating the baking sheets front to back halfway through the baking time so the cookies bake evenly. Remove the cookies from the oven and cool them on the baking sheets.

12. Repeat, coating, slicing, and baking the second log as you did the first.

Toasted Sesame Slice-and-Bake Butter Cookies

These cookies get their flavor from the pungent nutty flavor of toasted sesame seeds and sesame seed oil. You will find the oil in the Asian section of supermarkets; be sure to refrigerate it after opening it to prevent it from going rancid. (See photo page 123.)

Makes about 30 cookies

For the Dough

226 grams (2 sticks) cold unsalted butter, cubed

20 grams (2 tablespoons) toasted sesame oil

100 grams (½ cup) granulated sugar

1 teaspoon Diamond Crystal kosher salt

1 extra-large egg yolk

300 grams (about 2 cups plus 2 tablespoons) unbleached all-purpose flour

106 grams (1¼ cups plus 1 tablespoon) toasted golden sesame seeds (or unhulled sesame seeds)

For Coating

1 extra-large egg white

20 grams (¼ cup) toasted golden sesame seeds (or unhulled sesame seeds)

1. To make the dough, combine the butter and sesame oil in a stand mixer fitted with the paddle and beat on medium speed until the butter is soft but still cold, 3 to 4 minutes, stopping to scrape down the sides and bottom of the bowl and the paddle with a rubber spatula whenever butter is accumulating. Add the granulated sugar and beat on medium speed until the mixture is light and fluffy, 3 to 4 minutes, scraping down the bowl as needed. Add the salt and beat on medium speed for about 15 seconds to incorporate it. With the mixer on medium speed, add the egg yolk and beat until it is fully incorporated. Stop the mixer and scrape down the bowl. Add the flour and mix on low speed for about 30 seconds, until almost no flour is visible. Add the sesame seeds and beat on low speed for about 30 seconds to distribute them and until no flour is visible. Stop the mixer, remove the bowl and paddle from the stand, and clean them with the spatula, scraping the bowl from the bottom up to release any ingredients that may be stuck there.

2. Lay a sheet of plastic wrap on your work surface. Divide the dough in half. Place one portion of dough on the plastic wrap and shape it into a log 2 inches in diameter. Wrap the log in the plastic, twisting the ends like a candy wrapper. Repeat, shaping and wrapping the remaining dough into a second log. Place the logs in the refrigerator to chill until firm, at least 1 hour.

3. Adjust the oven racks so one is in the top third and the other is in the bottom third of the oven and preheat the oven to 350°F. Line two large baking sheets with parchment paper.

4. To coat the cookies, place the egg white in a small bowl. Spread 2 tablespoons of the sesame seeds out on a sheet of parchment paper or a baking sheet.

5. Remove a log from the refrigerator and unwrap. Brush the egg white on the log to coat it. (Do not coat the ends.) Roll the log in the sesame seeds, pressing gently so they stick to the dough and coat the log evenly.

6. Place the log on a cutting board and use a long sharp knife to slice the log into ⅜-inch-thick rounds. Place the rounds on the prepared baking sheets, leaving 1 inch between them. (If the cookies become misshapen when you transfer them, one at a time, gently turn the cookies in your hand to reshape them.)

7. Place one baking sheet on each oven rack and bake the cookies until the edges are golden brown, 17 to 20 minutes, switching racks and rotating the baking sheets front to back halfway through the baking time so the cookies bake evenly. Remove the cookies from the oven and let them cook on the baking sheets.

8. Repeat, coating, slicing, and baking the second log as you did the first.

Chocolate Chunk Hazelnut Slice-and-Bake Butter Cookies

Hazelnut and chocolate are a classic pairing. If you ever decide you want to taste the world's best hazelnut, try those from Trufflebert Farm in Oregon, available by mail order. Your hazelnut world will be forever changed. (See photo page 123.)

Makes about 30 cookies

For the Dough

240 grams (1¾ cups) hazelnuts (preferably skinless)

1 extra-large egg yolk

1 tablespoon pure vanilla bean paste or vanilla extract

226 grams (2 sticks) cold unsalted butter, cubed

100 grams (½ cup) granulated sugar

1 teaspoon Diamond Crystal kosher salt

300 grams (2 cups plus 2 tablespoons) unbleached all-purpose flour

170 grams (6 ounces) bittersweet chocolate (70% cacao), coarsely chopped (about 1¼ cups); halved if you're using feves

For Coating

1 extra-large egg white

Flaky sea salt

1. To make the dough, adjust an oven rack to the center position and preheat the oven to 325°F.

2. Spread the hazelnuts on a baking sheet and place them on the center rack of the oven to toast until they are fragrant and golden brown, 15 to 18 minutes, shaking the baking sheet and rotating it front to back halfway through the toasting time so the hazelnuts brown evenly. Remove the baking sheet from the oven. (If you think the nuts are on the verge of being overtoasted, transfer them to a plate so they don't continue to cook from the residual heat of the pan.) Turn off the oven.

3. Set the nuts aside until they are cool enough to touch. If the hazelnuts have skins, place them in the center of a clean dish towel; close the towel into a bundle and rub the nuts together inside the towel to remove the skins. Discard the skins. Set aside to cool to room temperature.

4. Weigh out 170 grams (or measure 1¼ cups) of the hazelnuts, very coarsely chop them, and set them aside to add to the dough. Finely chop the remaining hazelnuts and set them aside for coating the cookie dough log.

5. Whisk the egg yolk and vanilla together in a small bowl.

6. Put the butter in a stand mixer fitted with the paddle and beat on medium speed until the butter is soft but still cold, 3 to 4 minutes, stopping to scrape

down the sides and bottom of the bowl and the paddle with a rubber spatula whenever butter is accumulating. Add the granulated sugar and salt and beat on medium speed until the mixture is light and fluffy, 3 to 4 minutes, scraping down the bowl as needed. With the mixer on medium speed, add the egg yolk/vanilla mixture and beat until the egg is fully incorporated. Stop the mixer and scrape down the bowl. Add the flour and mix on low speed for about 30 seconds, until almost no flour is visible. Add the chocolate and coarsely chopped hazelnuts and mix on low speed to distribute them and fully incorporate the flour. Stop the mixer, remove the bowl and paddle from the stand, and clean them with the spatula, scraping the bowl from the bottom up to release any ingredients that may be stuck there.

7. Lay a sheet of plastic wrap on your work surface. Divide the dough in half. Place one portion of dough on the plastic wrap and shape it into a log 2 inches in diameter. Wrap the log in the plastic, twisting the ends like a candy wrapper. Repeat, shaping and wrapping the remaining dough into a second log. Place the logs in the refrigerator to chill until firm, at least 1 hour.

8. Adjust the oven racks so one is in the top third and the other is in the bottom third of the oven and preheat the oven to 350°F. Line two large baking sheets with parchment paper.

9. To coat the cookies, put the egg white in a small bowl. Spread half of the finely chopped toasted hazelnuts on a sheet of parchment paper or a baking sheet.

10. Remove a log from the refrigerator and unwrap. Brush the egg white on the log to coat it. (Don't coat the ends.) Roll the log in the hazelnuts, pressing gently so they stick to the dough and coat it evenly.

11. Place the log on a cutting board and use a long sharp knife to slice the log into ⅜-inch-thick rounds. Place the rounds on the prepared baking sheets, leaving 1 inch between them. (If the cookies become misshapen when you transfer them, one at a time, gently turn the cookies in your hand to reshape them.) Sprinkle a pinch of flaky salt in the center of each cookie.

12. Place one baking sheet on each oven rack and bake the cookies until the edges are golden brown, 17 to 20 minutes, switching racks and rotating the baking sheets front to back halfway through the baking time so the cookies bake evenly. Remove the cookies from the oven.

13. Repeat, coating, slicing, and baking the second log as you did the first one.

Maple Pecan Slice-and-Bake Butter Cookies

Of all the butter cookies in this book, this is my favorite. They're delicious made with any pure maple syrup, but using an artisanal variety, aged in oak, takes them to yet another level. (See photo page 123.)

Makes about 30 cookies

For the Dough

210 grams (heaping 2 cups) pecan halves

1 extra-large egg yolk

37.5 grams (2 tablespoons) artisanal maple syrup (preferably barrel-aged)

1 tablespoon pure vanilla bean paste or vanilla extract

226 grams (2 sticks) cold unsalted butter, cubed

100 grams (½ cup) granulated sugar

1 teaspoon Diamond Crystal kosher salt

298 grams (2 cups plus 2 tablespoons) unbleached all-purpose flour

For Coating

1 extra-large egg white

1. Adjust an oven rack to the center position and preheat the oven to 325°F.

2. Spread the pecans on a baking sheet and toast them on the center rack of the oven until they're lightly browned and fragrant, 8 to 10 minutes, shaking the baking sheet and rotating it front to back halfway through the toasting time so the pecans brown evenly. Remove the baking sheet from the oven and set aside until the pecans cool enough to touch. (If you think the nuts are on the verge of being overtoasted, transfer them to a plate so they don't continue to cook from the residual heat of the pan.)

3. Turn off the oven.

4. Weigh out 131 grams (or measure 1¼ cups) of the pecan halves and set them aside to add to the dough. Finely chop the remaining pecans and set them aside to coat the cookie dough in.

5. Whisk the egg yolk, maple syrup, and vanilla together in a small bowl.

6. Put the butter in a stand mixer fitted with the paddle and beat on medium speed until the butter is soft but still cold, 3 to 4 minutes, stopping to scrape down the sides and bottom of the bowl and the paddle with a rubber spatula whenever butter is accumulating. Add the granulated sugar and salt and beat on medium speed until the mixture is light and fluffy, 3 to 4 minutes, scraping down the bowl as needed. With the mixer on medium speed, add the egg yolk mixture and beat until it is incorporated. Stop the mixer and scrape down the bowl. Add the flour and mix on low speed for about

30 seconds, until almost no flour is visible. Add the pecan halves and mix on low speed to distribute the pecans and fully incorporate the flour. Stop the mixer, remove the bowl and paddle from the stand, and clean them with the spatula, scraping the bowl from the bottom up to release any ingredients that may be stuck there.

7. Lay a sheet of plastic wrap on your work surface. Divide the dough in half. Place one portion of dough on the plastic wrap and shape it into a log 2 inches in diameter. Wrap the log in the plastic, twisting the ends like a candy wrapper. Repeat, shaping and wrapping the remaining dough into a second log. Place the logs in the refrigerator to chill until firm, at least 1 hour.

8. Adjust the oven racks so one is in the top third and the other is in the bottom third of the oven and preheat the oven to 350°F. Line two large baking sheets with parchment paper.

9. To coat the cookies, put the egg white in a small bowl. Spread half of the finely chopped pecans on a sheet of parchment paper or a baking sheet.

10. Brush the egg white on the log to coat it. (Don't coat the ends.) Roll the log in the pecans, pressing gently so they stick to the dough and coat it evenly.

11. Place the log on a cutting board and use a long sharp knife to slice it into ⅜-inch-thick rounds. Place the rounds on the prepared baking sheets, leaving 1 inch between them. (If the cookies become misshapen in this process, one at a time, gently turn the cookies in your hand to reshape them.)

12. Place one baking sheet on each oven rack and bake the cookies until they are golden brown around the edges, 20 to 26 minutes, switching racks and rotating the baking sheets front to back halfway through the baking time so the cookies bake evenly. Remove the cookies from the oven.

13. Repeat, coating, slicing, and baking the second log as you did the first.

Coconut Almond Slice-and-Bake Butter Cookies

This recipe originated with Fred Chino, an avid baker and member of the famous Chino Farm family in Del Mar, near San Diego. Where the other butter cookies in this collection are decorated on the edges, this is decorated with a tuft of coconut chips on top. They're really pretty. (See photo page 123.)

Makes about 42 cookies

For the Dough

133 grams (1 heaping cup) slivered almonds

2 extra-large eggs

1 teaspoon pure vanilla bean paste or vanilla extract

1 teaspoon pure almond extract

300 grams (2 cups plus 2 tablespoons) unbleached all-purpose flour

60 grams (¼ cup plus 2½ tablespoons) potato starch

280 grams (2½ sticks) cold unsalted butter, cubed

140 grams (½ cup plus 3½ tablespoons) granulated sugar

1¾ teaspoons Diamond Crystal kosher salt

120 grams (1½ cups) unsweetened shredded coconut

For Finishing

2 extra-large egg whites

160 grams (2⅔ cups) unsweetened coconut flakes

Powdered sugar for dusting

1. Adjust an oven rack to the center position and preheat the oven to 325°F.

2. Spread the almonds on a baking sheet and toast them on the center rack of the oven until they're lightly browned and fragrant, 10 to 15 minutes, shaking the baking sheet and rotating it front to back halfway through the toasting time so the almonds brown evenly. Remove the almonds from the oven and set them aside until they're cool enough to touch. (If you think the nuts are on the verge of being overtoasted, transfer them to a plate so they don't continue to cook from the residual heat of the pan.) Coarsely chop the almonds.

3. Turn off the oven.

4. Whisk the eggs, vanilla, and almond extract together in a small bowl. Stir the flour and potato starch together in a medium bowl.

5. Put the butter in a stand mixer fitted with the paddle and beat on medium speed until the butter is soft but still cold, 3 to 4 minutes, stopping to scrape down the sides and bottom of the bowl and the paddle with a rubber spatula whenever butter is accumulating. Add the granulated sugar and salt and beat on medium speed until the mixture is light and fluffy, 3 to 4 minutes, scraping down the bowl as needed. Add the egg yolk mixture and beat on medium speed until the egg is fully incorporated. Stop the

mixer and scrape down the bowl. Add the flour and mix on low speed for about 30 seconds, until almost no flour is visible. Add the almonds and shredded coconut and mix on low speed to distribute the additions and fully incorporate the flour. Stop the mixer, remove the bowl and paddle from the stand, and clean them with the spatula, scraping the bowl from the bottom up to release any ingredients that may be stuck there.

6. Lay a sheet of plastic wrap on your work surface. Divide the dough in half and place one portion on the plastic wrap. Shape the dough into a log 2 inches in diameter. Tightly wrap the log in the plastic, twisting the ends like a candy wrapper. Repeat, wrapping the second log of dough. Place the logs in the refrigerator to chill until firm, at least 1 hour.

7. Adjust the oven racks so one is in the top third and the other is in the bottom third of the oven and preheat the oven to 350°F. Line two large baking sheets with parchment paper.

8. To finish the cookies, put the egg whites in a small bowl.

9. Remove a log from the refrigerator and unwrap.

10. Place the log on a cutting board and use a long sharp knife to slice the log into ⅜-inch-thick rounds. Place the rounds on the prepared baking sheets, leaving at least 1 inch between them. (If the cookies become misshapen when you transfer them, one by one, gently turn the cookies in your hand to reshape them.)

11. Brush the top of each cookie with egg white and, using your fingers, place enough coconut flakes to cover each cookie (1½ to 2 teaspoons), pressing gently so the flakes adhere to the cookie. (Any pieces not touching the egg white will fall off when the cookies are baked.)

12. Place one baking sheet on each oven rack and bake the cookies until the edges of the cookies and the coconut on top are golden brown, 12 to 16 minutes, switching racks and rotating the baking sheets front to back halfway through the baking time so the cookies bake evenly. Remove the cookies from the oven and set them aside to cool to room temperature. Dust the cookies with powdered sugar.

13. Repeat, slicing, finishing baking, and dusting the second log as you did the first.

Ultimate Chocolate Cookies

My goal with this recipe was to create the definitive chocolate cookie, one that was as chocolatey as a cookie could possibly be. It consists of a crisp cookie bottom—borrowed from the recipe for "Oreos" that I published in *Nancy Silverton's Sandwich Book*—and a chewy, fudgy topping, studded with toasted walnuts and cocoa nibs, that becomes shiny and crackly when baked. Cocoa nibs are cracked bits of cacao beans, which is what chocolate is made of. They have a hard, crunchy texture and slightly bitter flavor. They make a great addition when you really want an intense chocolate flavor.

Between the two components of this cookie, this recipe contains two kinds of cocoa powder (natural and black, or nonalkalized), cocoa nibs, and a *lot* of bittersweet chocolate. The black cocoa powder makes the crisp bottoms black and almost bitter, which tones down the sweetness of the fudgy topping. It's a chocolate lover's dream, and I think destined to become a classic.

The dough for the bottoms is very sticky and it needs to be rolled very thin, so I roll it out between sheets of parchment paper. Rolling dough this way may seem intimidating if you've never done it, but it makes the task easier.

Makes about 24 cookies

What You Need—
The Essential Special Equipment

2½-inch round cutter (preferably fluted)

For the Fudgy Topping

75 grams (¾ cup) walnut halves

180 grams (1½ cups) powdered sugar

51 grams (½ cup) natural cocoa powder

½ teaspoon Diamond Crystal kosher salt

1 extra-large egg

1 extra-large egg white

57 grams (2 ounces) bittersweet chocolate (70% cacao), coarsely chopped (scant ½ cup); halved if you're using feves

8 grams (1 tablespoon) cocoa nibs

For the Cookie Bottoms

85 grams (3 ounces) bittersweet chocolate (70% cacao), coarsely chopped (about ¾ cup); halved if you're using feves

16 grams (2 tablespoons) cocoa nibs

84 grams (6 tablespoons) cold unsalted butter, cubed

69 grams (¼ cup plus 1½ tablespoons) granulated sugar

69 grams (¼ cup plus 1½ tablespoons) packed dark brown sugar

16 grams (about 2½ tablespoons) black (nonalkalized) cocoa powder

½ teaspoon baking soda

½ teaspoon Diamond Crystal kosher salt

1 tablespoon pure vanilla bean paste or vanilla extract

122.5 grams (¾ cup plus 2 tablespoons) unbleached all-purpose flour

Flaky sea salt →

1. To make the fudgy topping, adjust an oven rack to the center position and preheat the oven to 325°F.

2. Spread the walnuts on a baking sheet and place them on the center rack of the oven to toast until they're lightly browned and fragrant, 8 to 10 minutes, shaking the baking sheet and rotating it front to back halfway through the toasting time so the walnuts brown evenly. Remove the walnuts from the oven and set them aside until they're cool enough to touch. (If you think the nuts are on the verge of being overtoasted, transfer them to a plate so they don't continue to cook from the residual heat of the pan.) Coarsely chop the walnuts.

3. Turn off the oven.

4. Sift the powdered sugar and cocoa powder into the bowl of a stand mixer, put the bowl on the stand, and fit it with the paddle. Add the salt and mix on low speed for a few seconds to distribute it. Add the whole egg and egg white and mix on low speed until combined, stopping to scrape down the sides and bottom of the bowl with a rubber spatula as needed. Add the chocolate, cocoa nibs, and walnuts and mix on low speed for about 30 seconds to distribute the additions. Take the bowl and paddle off the stand and clean them with the spatula, scraping from the bottom up to release any ingredients from the bottom of the bowl. Cover the bowl with plastic wrap and refrigerate until the topping is chilled, at least 1 hour.

5. To make the cookie bottoms, fill a small saucepan with 1½ to 2 inches of water and set a small stainless steel bowl atop the saucepan to make a double boiler, making sure the water doesn't touch the bottom of the bowl. Bring the water to a simmer over medium heat. Put the chocolate in the bowl and melt it, stirring and scraping the bowl with a silicone spatula to prevent the chocolate from burning. Turn off the heat and take the bowl off the double boiler.

6. Put the cocoa nibs in a spice grinder or a mini food processor and pulse to chop them to the size of grains of rice. Transfer the nibs to a small bowl.

7. Put the butter in a stand mixer fitted with the paddle and beat on medium speed until the butter is soft but still cold, 3 to 4 minutes, stopping to scrape down the sides and bottom of the bowl and the paddle with a rubber spatula whenever butter is accumulating. Add the granulated sugar, brown sugar,

and cocoa powder and beat on medium speed until the mixture is light and fluffy, 3 to 4 minutes, scraping down the bowl as needed. Add the baking soda and salt and beat on medium speed for about 15 seconds to incorporate them. Stop the mixer, add the melted chocolate and vanilla and mix on medium-low speed for about 30 seconds to combine. Stop the mixer and scrape down the bowl. Add the flour and cocoa nibs and mix on low speed for about 30 seconds until no flour is visible. Remove the bowl and paddle from the stand, and clean them with the spatula, scraping from the bottom up to release any ingredients from the bottom of the bowl.

8. Lay a large sheet of parchment paper on a work surface. Divide the dough in half. Form one portion of the dough into a disk and place it in the center of the parchment. Lay another sheet of parchment paper on top of the dough, lining it up with the bottom sheet. Applying firm steady pressure with the rolling pin, roll the dough between the parchment to ⅛ inch thick. Place the parchment-sandwiched dough on a baking sheet and place it in the refrigerator. Repeat, rolling out the second half of the dough in the same way, between two fresh sheets of parchment paper. Add it to the baking sheet in the refrigerator, laying it on top of the first sheet of dough. Chill the dough until it is firm, at least 1 hour.

9. Remove one sheet of dough from the refrigerator and lay it on your work surface. Peel the top sheet of parchment off the dough and lay it back down on the dough. (This loosens the parchment so after you cut the cookie rounds, you will be able to lift them easily off the parchment without them sticking.) Flip the sheet of dough over. Peel off the top sheet of parchment paper and lay it clean-side up on a large baking sheet to line it.

10. Using the round cutter, cut rounds from the dough, cutting them as close together as possible to get as many as you can from one sheet of dough. (If the dough is so stiff that it cracks when you cut the cookies, lay the parchment paper back on the dough, let it rest for about 5 minutes, running the palms of your hands over the dough during that time to soften it slightly; remove the parchment and resume cutting the cookies.) Use a thin metal spatula to lift the dough rounds and place them on the prepared baking sheet, leaving at least ½ inch between them. Gather the scraps and set aside. Use the bottom sheet of parchment paper to line a second baking sheet. →

11. Remove the second sheet of dough from the refrigerator and repeat, peeling off the parchment paper, cutting the cookie rounds, and placing the rounds on the prepared baking sheet, leaving at least ½ inch between them. Gather all the scraps and form them into a 1-inch-thick disk, refrigerate until the dough is firm, then roll out between two sheets of parchment. (You can reuse sheets that were removed from the dough, with the clean sides facing out.) Cut the scraps into rounds and add them to the baking sheets. Wrap the dough in plastic wrap and refrigerate until it is chilled and firm, at least 30 minutes.

12. Adjust the oven racks so one is in the top third and the other is in the bottom third of the oven and preheat the oven to 300°F.

13. Remove the baking sheets from the refrigerator and remove and discard the plastic wrap. Place one baking sheet on each oven rack and bake the cookies until they are firm around the edges, about 25 minutes, switching racks and rotating the baking sheets front to back halfway through the baking time so the cookies bake evenly. Remove the cookies from the oven and set aside to cool to room temperature.

14. Increase the oven temperature to 350°F.

15. Remove the fudgy cookie topping from the refrigerator. Using 2 tablespoons, one to scoop the fudgy topping and one to scrape if off the spoon, spoon about 16 grams (1 tablespoon) of the fudgy topping onto the center of each cookie bottom, leaving the edges of the bottoms visible. Sprinkle each cookie with flaky salt.

16. Place one baking sheet on each oven rack and bake the cookies until the fudge is set around the edges and beginning to crackle on top, 10 to 12 minutes, switching racks and rotating the baking sheets front to back halfway through the baking time. Remove the cookies from the oven.

Linzer Cookies

Linzer cookies are European sandwich cookies with a layer of jam sandwiched between butter cookies made with ground hazelnuts or almonds and dusted with a thick layer of powdered sugar. They're basically little jam-filled tartlets. I've always liked the idea of Linzers more than the reality of them; with all that powdered sugar, they tend to be too sweet for me, and I don't like the way, with traditional Linzers, the tops of the sandwich cookies slide around on the jam, making the jam seem like an afterthought. I bake the jam in the cookies, so it caramelizes. I love the taste and the chewy texture of the baked jam, and I like that when constructed this way, the cookies stay sandwiched together, and the jam feels integral to the cookie and not like an afterthought. The small round cut-outs from the cookie tops are baked on the side and used to cover the jam circles so the jam doesn't get powdered sugar on it when the cookies are dusted. (This also gives you the added benefit of having the dusted little cookie rounds to snack on.)

I make this dough with ground hazelnuts and almond paste, so the cookies have the flavor of both. I use raspberry jam with seeds because I like the look and the texture of the seeds. You may be surprised to see that there is grated egg yolk in this dough; many Linzer cookie recipes include this detail. The egg yolk makes for a very delicate, tender cookie.

Makes about 24 cookies

**What You Need—
The Essential Special Equipment**

2⅝-inch round cutter (preferably fluted)

1-inch round cutter
(preferably straight-sided)

3 or more large baking sheets

4 extra-large eggs

114 grams (scant 1 cup) hazelnuts
(preferably skinless)

125 grams (½ cup plus 2 tablespoons)
granulated sugar

1 tablespoon ground cinnamon

1 teaspoon grated nutmeg

1 teaspoon Diamond Crystal kosher salt

315 grams (2¼ cups) all-purpose flour,
plus more for dusting

85 grams (¼ cup plus 1 tablespoon
plus 2 teaspoons) almond paste
(preferably unblanched)

226 grams (2 sticks) cold unsalted
butter, cubed

1 large lemon

1 tablespoon pure vanilla bean paste
or vanilla extract

2 teaspoons pure almond extract

213 grams (⅔ cup) seedy raspberry jam
(or apricot jam)

37 grams (3 tablespoons) demerara
sugar (or turbinado sugar)

Powdered sugar for dusting →

1. Bring a medium saucepan of water to a boil over high heat. Lower the eggs into the water with a slotted spoon to prevent them from cracking and cook them for 11 minutes. While the eggs are cooking, fill a bowl with ice water. Remove the eggs with the slotted spoon and transfer them to the ice water to cool completely. Remove the eggs from the ice water and peel them. Separate the whites and yolks. (Reserve the whites for another use. I sprinkle them with salt to snack on.)

2. Meanwhile, adjust an oven rack to the center position and preheat the oven to 325°F.

3. Spread the hazelnuts on a large baking sheet and place them on the center rack of the oven to toast until they are fragrant and golden brown, 15 to 18 minutes, shaking the baking sheet and rotating it front to back halfway through the toasting time so the hazelnuts brown evenly. Remove the baking sheet from the oven and turn off the oven. (If you think the nuts are on the verge of being overtoasted, transfer them to a plate so they don't continue to cook from the residual heat of the pan.) Set the hazelnuts aside until they are cool enough to touch. If the hazelnuts have skins, place them in the center of a clean dish towel; close the towel into a bundle, and rub the nuts together inside the towel to remove the skins. Discard the skins. Set aside to cool to room temperature.

4. Transfer the hazelnuts to a food processor. Add 100 grams (½ cup) of the granulated sugar, the cinnamon, nutmeg, and salt and pulse until the hazelnuts are ground to a coarse meal, stopping to scrape down the sides of the bowl to release any nuts that are stuck there. Add the flour and pulse a few times to combine. Transfer the hazelnut/sugar mixture to a large bowl.

5. Put the remaining 25 grams (2 tablespoons) granulated sugar in the bowl of a stand mixer and crumble the almond paste into the bowl. Fit the mixer with the paddle and beat on medium speed until the paste is combined with the sugars and the mixture is smooth, 3 to 4 minutes. Add the butter and beat on medium speed until the butter is combined with the almond paste mixture and no lumps remain, 4 to 5 minutes, stopping to scrape down the sides and bottom of the bowl and the paddle with a rubber spatula whenever ingredients are accumulating.

6. Using a fine Microplane, grate the zest (the bright-yellow outer layer) of the lemon into the mixer bowl. (Reserve the lemon for another use.) Using a

medium or fine Microplane (or on the small—but not the smallest—holes of a box grater), grate the egg yolks into the bowl. Add the vanilla and the almond extract and mix on medium speed for about 30 seconds to combine. Stop the mixer, add the hazelnut/sugar mixture, and mix on low speed for about 30 seconds until combined. Stop the mixer, remove the bowl and paddle from the stand, and clean them with the spatula, scraping the bowl from the bottom up to release any ingredients that may be stuck there.

7. Divide the dough into 4 equal portions and form each into a 1-inch-thick disk. Lay a large sheet of parchment paper on your work surface and place 1 disk on the parchment. Lay another sheet of parchment paper on top of the dough, lining it up with the bottom sheet. Applying firm, steady pressure with a rolling pin, roll the dough out between the parchment paper to ¼ inch thick. Lay the parchment-sandwiched dough on a large baking sheet and place it in the refrigerator. Repeat, rolling each of the remaining portions of dough between two sheets of parchment, and laying them on top of the first sheet of dough in the refrigerator. Refrigerate the dough until firm, at least 1 hour.

8. Remove one sheet of dough from the refrigerator and lay it on your work surface. Peel the top sheet of parchment off the dough and lay it back down on the dough. (This loosens the parchment so after cutting the cookie rounds, you will be able to lift them easily off the parchment without them sticking.) Flip the sheet of dough over. Peel off the top sheet of parchment paper and lay it clean-side up on a large baking sheet to line it.

9. Using the 2⅝-inch cutter, cut rounds from the dough, making the cuts as close together as possible to get as many rounds as you can from the sheet. (If the dough is so stiff that it cracks when you cut the cookies, lay the parchment paper back on the dough and let it rest for about 5 minutes, running the palms of your hands over the dough during that time to soften it slightly; remove the parchment and resume cutting the cookies.) Use a metal spatula to transfer the rounds to the prepared baking sheet, placing them side by side without touching. Set the scraps aside. Remove a second sheet of dough from the refrigerator and repeat, cutting rounds out of the sheet of dough. Add them to the baking sheet and set the scraps aside. After you have filled the baking sheet in a single layer, lay a sheet of parchment on the rounds and add the remaining rounds in a second layer. Repeat until you have cut all 4 sheets of dough. Gather the scraps, pat them into a 1-inch-thick disk, and roll them out between parchment. Cut the scraps as you →

did the other sheets of dough and add the rounds to the baking sheets. Discard the remaining scraps. Place the dough in the refrigerator until the rounds are chilled and firm, at least 1 hour.

10. Adjust the oven racks so one is in the center position and the other is in the bottom third of the oven and preheat the oven to 350°F. Line two large baking sheets with parchment paper.

11. Remove the baking sheet from the refrigerator.

12. Slide one sheet of parchment paper with the cut rounds onto the counter. Use the 1-inch round cutter to cut the centers out of half of the total number of rounds. Use a metal spatula to transfer the tiny centers to one of the prepared baking sheets. (These will be placed on the baked cookies before they are dusted with powdered sugar to prevent the powdered sugar from getting on the jam and discoloring it.)

13. Place the baking sheet with the tiny rounds on the lower rack of the oven and the larger cookies on the center rack and bake until they are light golden brown, 12 to 15 minutes, switching racks and rotating the baking sheets front to back halfway through the baking time. Remove the cookies from the oven. Leave the oven on.

14. To assemble the cookies, place the cookie bottoms (the whole rounds) on your work surface and spoon 1 teaspoon of jam into the center of each. Use the back of the spoon to spread the jam toward the edges, leaving a ¼-inch border around the edges free of jam. Place the tops on the cookies (those with the holes cut out) on the rounds, lining them up, and press gently to seal the cookies.

15. Divide the cookies between the two baking sheets, leaving at least 1 inch between them. Sprinkle the cookies generously with demerara sugar.

16. Place one baking sheet on the upper and one on the lower rack of the oven and bake until the cookies are light golden around the edges, 18 to 24 minutes, switching racks and rotating the baking sheets front to back halfway through the baking time so they bake evenly. Remove the cookies from the oven and set aside to cool to room temperature.

17. Place a tiny round in the center of each cookie to cover the jam. Generously dust the cookies with powdered sugar. Remove the tiny rounds from the cookies and set them aside to snack on.

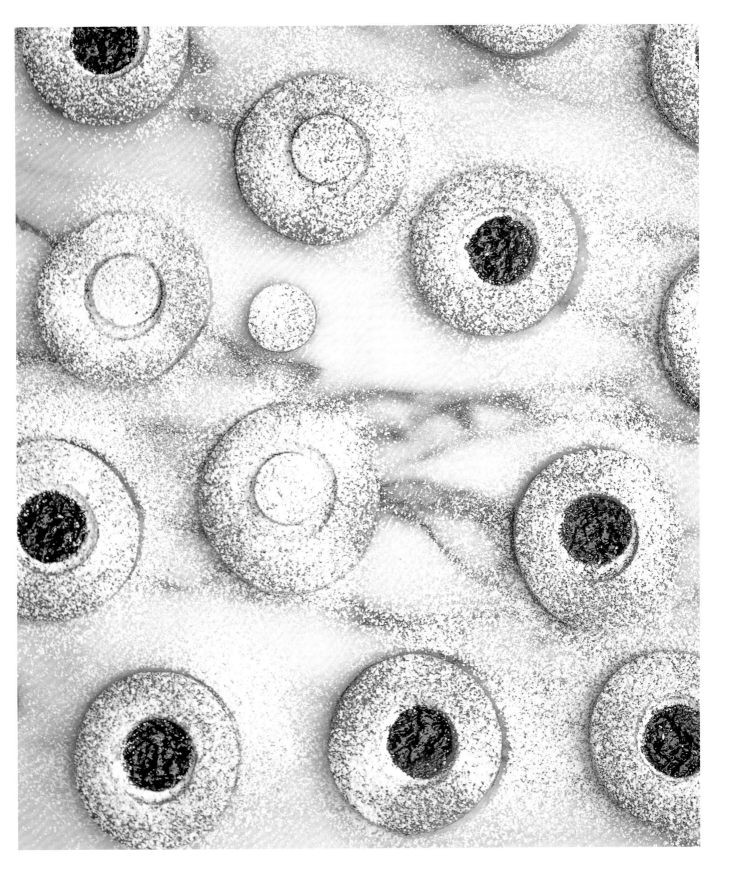

Walnut Sandies

"Sandie" is the American term for a *sablée,* a crumbly, very buttery cookie that gets its name because of its sand-like (*sablée* means "sandy" in French) texture. This version is made with ground walnuts and walnut oil to intensify the walnut flavor. After they're baked, they're tossed in sugar, which makes them look sandy.

Walnut oil, once relegated to specialty food stores, is easy to find now; you can often even find it in conventional grocery stores. After opening it, store the oil in the refrigerator; like all nut oils, it turns rancid quickly.

These cookies are patted into a disk inside a round cutter, and then the cutter is removed, eliminating the steps of rolling, chilling, and cutting the dough. It makes for perfectly round cookies; they're thicker than many rolled-out cookies. I really like the way they look.

Makes about 24 cookies

**What You Need—
The Essential Special Equipment**

2-inch round cutter

For the Dough

113 grams (1 heaping cup) walnut halves, plus 2 dozen walnut halves

113 grams (1 stick) unsalted butter

75 grams (¼ cup plus 2 tablespoons) walnut oil

14 grams (2 tablespoons) rum (or whiskey)

1 tablespoon pure vanilla bean paste or vanilla extract

75 grams (¼ cup plus 2 tablespoons) granulated sugar

1½ teaspoons Diamond Crystal kosher salt

300 grams (about 2 cups plus 2 tablespoons) unbleached all-purpose flour

For Coating

125 grams (½ cup plus 2 tablespoons) granulated sugar

1 tablespoon ground cinnamon

1. To make the dough, adjust the oven racks so one is in the top third and the other is in the bottom third of the oven and preheat the oven to 325°F.

2. Spread the 113 grams (or 1 heaping cup) walnuts on a baking sheet and toast them on the center rack of the oven until they're lightly browned and fragrant, 8 to 10 minutes, shaking the baking sheet and rotating it front to back halfway through the baking time so the walnuts brown evenly. Remove the walnuts from the oven and set aside until they're cool enough to touch. (If you think the nuts are on the verge of being overtoasted, transfer them to a plate so they don't continue to cook from the residual heat of the pan.)

3. Increase the oven temperature to 350°F. Line two large baking sheets with parchment paper. →

4. Place the butter in a small saucepan or skillet with a light-colored bottom to make brown butter. Warm the butter over medium heat until it melts and begins to bubble, swirling the pan occasionally. Cook the butter, swirling often so it cooks evenly, until the butter is caramel colored and the milk solids are the color of coffee grounds, 4 to 8 minutes. Remove from the heat. Working quickly so the butter doesn't continue to cook, weigh out 113 grams (or measure about ½ cup) of the butter, making sure to include the milk solids. (Reserve the remaining butter for another use.) Transfer the butter to a medium bowl. Add the walnut oil, rum, and vanilla and stir to combine.

5. Transfer the walnuts to a food processor. Add the granulated sugar and salt and pulse until the walnuts are ground to a coarse meal, stopping to scrape down the sides of the bowl to release any nuts that are stuck there. Add the flour and pulse a few times to combine. Transfer the flour mixture to a large wide bowl.

6. Create a well in the center of the flour mixture with your hands. Pour the butter mixture into the well. Draw the wet and dry ingredients together with your hands to form a homogeneous dough. Gather the dough into a smooth ball.

7. Place the round cutter on one of the prepared baking sheets. Scoop up 30 grams (about 2 tablespoons) of dough and place it in the cutter. Pat the dough toward the edges of the cutter to fill it in an even layer. Lift off the cutter and use it to form another cookie, leaving at least 1 inch between the cookies. Form 12 cookies on each baking sheet. Press one walnut half into the center of each cookie.

8. Place one baking sheet on each oven rack and bake the cookies until the edges and bottoms are golden brown and the cookies are firm to the touch, 22 to 25 minutes, switching racks and rotating the baking sheets front to back halfway through the baking time so the cookies bake evenly.

9. While the cookies are baking, to coat the cookies, stir the granulated sugar and cinnamon together in a small bowl.

10. Remove the baking sheets from the oven and set aside for about 3 minutes, until the cookies are cool enough to handle but still warm. One at a time, toss the warm cookies in the cinnamon-sugar to coat them.

Chinese Restaurant Almond Cookies

These crumbly, delicious cookies have two incarnations with the same distinct flavor: One is a Jewish deli staple with a giant chocolate drop in the center. In their other life, the cookies, with a blanched almond pressed into their center, are often served after the meal alongside fortune cookies at many Chinese restaurants. Even though those two lives would seem to be only distantly related, the cookies are almost identical. I learned this and more about them from my longtime friend Izzy Cohen. Izzy taught me to make a lot of traditional Jewish baked goods including Rugelach (page 155), Yum-Yum Coffee Cake (page 61), and these cookies. Long after Izzy left us, I learned that the secret to the crumbly quality of the Chinese version is none other than lard.

These are made with baker's ammonia (also known as ammonium bicarbonate), a leavening agent that imparts a distinct crunchy texture to the cookies. You can buy ammonium bicarbonate (not to be confused with baking soda) from online sources. It can be unpleasant if you inhale it, so avoid doing so. It can also give off an unpleasant smell the first time you open the oven door to check on the cookies; don't worry, that unpleasantness goes away once the ammonium bicarbonate is baked.

Makes about 60 cookies

For the Dough

1 extra-large egg

3 tablespoons pure almond extract

1 tablespoon pure vanilla bean paste or vanilla extract

230 grams (1 cup plus 2 tablespoons) cold lard

287.5 grams (1¼ cups plus 3 tablespoons) granulated sugar

2 teaspoons ammonium bicarbonate (baker's ammonia)

1½ teaspoons Diamond Crystal kosher salt

½ teaspoon baking soda

481 grams (3¼ cups plus 2 tablespoons) unbleached all-purpose flour

For Coating and Topping

4 extra-large egg yolks

100 grams (½ cup) demerara sugar

70 grams (heaping ½ cup) salted Marcona almonds (the largest you can find)

1. To make the dough, whisk the egg, almond extract, and vanilla together in a small bowl.

2. Put the lard in a stand mixer fitted with the paddle and mix on medium speed until it is soft but still cold, about 1 minute, stopping to scrape down the sides and bottom of the bowl and the paddle with a rubber spatula whenever lard is accumulating. Add the granulated sugar and beat on medium speed until the mixture is light and fluffy, about 1 minute, →

scraping down the bowl as needed. Add the ammonium bicarbonate, salt, and baking soda and beat on medium speed for about 30 seconds to combine. With the mixer on low speed, gradually add the egg mixture, making sure it is incorporated before adding more. Stop the mixer and scrape down the bowl. Add the flour and mix on low speed for about 30 seconds until it is combined. Stop the mixer, remove the bowl and paddle from the stand, and clean them with the spatula, scraping the bowl from the bottom up to release any ingredients that may be stuck there.

3. Lay a sheet of plastic wrap on your work surface. Divide the dough in half. Place one portion of dough on the plastic wrap and shape it into a log 2 inches in diameter. Tightly wrap the log in the plastic, twisting the ends like a candy wrapper. Repeat, making a second log with the remaining dough. Place the logs in the refrigerator to chill until firm, at least 1 hour.

4. Adjust the oven racks so one is in the top third and the other is in the bottom third of the oven and preheat the oven to 300°F. Line two large baking sheets with parchment paper.

5. To coat the cookies, whisk the egg yolks together in a small bowl. Sprinkle half of the demerara sugar on a sheet of parchment paper or a baking sheet.

6. Remove a dough log from the refrigerator and unwrap. Brush the log with egg yolk to coat it. (Don't coat the ends.) Roll the log in the demerara sugar, pressing gently to coat the log with the sugar.

7. Place the log on a cutting board and use a long sharp knife to slice it into ½-inch-thick rounds. Place the rounds on the prepared baking sheets, leaving 2 inches between them. (If the cookies become misshapen when you transfer them, one by one, gently turn the cookies in your hand to reshape them.) Brush the tops of the cookies with egg yolk and firmly press an almond into the center of each cookie.

8. Place one baking sheet on each oven rack and bake the cookies until they are light golden brown, 20 to 25 minutes, switching racks and rotating the baking sheets front to back halfway through the baking time so the cookies bake evenly. Remove the cookies from the oven and cool them on the baking sheet.

9. Repeat, coating, slicing, and baking the second log as you did the first.

Wedding Cookies

These were the only cookie my mom made, and she was so proud of them. They're essentially a shortbread cookie (meaning they don't contain eggs) made from ground walnuts or pecans, butter, and powdered sugar, and coated in powdered sugar after they're baked. There are many names for this type of cookie, but I know them as Mexican wedding cookies. In Mexico, they call them *"polvorones."* *Polvo* means "dust," so I assume the name comes from the little dust storm of powdered sugar that occurs when you bite into one.

I've made these cookies throughout my career, and over the years I've tweaked them in more ways than I can remember—changing the type of nuts, the texture the nuts were ground to, the amount of sugar, the blend of spices. The one thing I never changed before was the shape. I always formed them into smooth balls, as they are traditionally done. But for this recipe, I let loose and bake them in organic-shaped lumps. These are made with toasted pecans, ground (but not too finely!), and golden butter (which adds a warmth to the buttery flavor) and then tossed in powdered sugar mixed with cinnamon and nutmeg. Mom, yours were no doubt great. But I think you might like these even better!

These cookies must be coated while they're still warm to ensure that the sugar adheres to them. They're best eaten if you wait an hour or so after they're coated; the cookie absorbs the sugar and they become even more tender and crumbly. When you bite into them, they completely implode in your mouth, the sign of a perfect *polvorone*. If by the time you serve them the sugar has completely absorbed into the cookies and is no longer visible, reroll them in the spiced powdered sugar.

Makes about 24 cookies

For the Dough

226 grams (2 sticks) unsalted butter

141 grams (scant 1½ cups) pecan halves

60 grams (½ cup) powdered sugar

½ teaspoon Diamond Crystal kosher salt

1½ teaspoons baking powder

245 grams (1¾ cups) unbleached all-purpose flour

1 tablespoon rum (or whiskey)

1 tablespoon pure vanilla extract

For Rolling

180 grams (1½ cups) powdered sugar

1 tablespoon ground cinnamon

½ teaspoon grated nutmeg →

1. For the dough, place the butter in a small saucepan or skillet with a light-colored bottom to make golden butter. Warm the butter over medium heat until it melts and begins to bubble, swirling the pan occasionally. Cook the butter, swirling often so it cooks evenly, until it is golden and the milk solids are caramel colored, 3 to 6 minutes. Remove from the heat. Working quickly so the butter doesn't continue to cook, weigh out 170 grams (or measure about ¾ cup plus 1 tablespoon) of butter, making sure to include the milk solids. (Reserve the remaining butter for another use.) Transfer the butter to a bowl and set it aside to cool to room temperature. Cover the bowl with plastic wrap and place it in the refrigerator to chill until the butter is solid.

2. Adjust an oven rack to the center position and preheat the oven to 325°F.

3. Spread the pecans on a baking sheet and toast them on the center rack of the oven until they're lightly browned and fragrant, 15 to 20 minutes, shaking the baking sheet and rotating it front to back halfway through the toasting time so the pecans brown evenly. Remove the baking sheet from the oven and set the pecans aside to cool to room temperature. (If you think the nuts are on the verge of being overtoasted, transfer them to a plate so they don't continue to cook from the residual heat of the pan.)

4. Increase the oven temperature to 350°F.

5. Remove the butter from the refrigerator and place the bowl in a large bowl of hot water to help release the butter. Dry off the bowl and invert it to release the butter onto a cutting board. (Alternatively, you may be able to wedge a knife under the butter and pop it out.) Cut the butter into roughly ½-inch cubes.

6. Set aside a handful of the pecans. Place the remaining pecans in a food processor. Add the powdered sugar, salt, and baking powder and pulse a few times to coarsely chop the nuts. Add the flour and the reserved pecans and pulse several times until the mixture is ground to an irregular meal with some pieces of nuts ground to a coarse meal and others as big as peas. Add the butter and pulse to incorporate it with the dry ingredients and nuts. Add the rum and vanilla and pulse to combine into a crumbly dough. Transfer the dough to a large bowl and knead to bring it together.

7. Scoop 28 grams (or 2 tablespoons) of dough, pinch it into a lumpy mound, and place it on the prepared baking sheet. Repeat with the remaining dough, adding the mounds to the baking sheet, leaving at least 1 inch between them.

8. Place one baking sheet on each oven rack and bake the cookies until the peaks, edges, and bottoms of the cookies are golden brown, 15 to 18 minutes, switching racks and rotating the baking sheets front to back halfway through the baking time so the cookies bake evenly.

9. While the cookies are baking, to roll the cookies, sift the powdered sugar, cinnamon, and nutmeg into a medium bowl.

10. Remove the cookies from the oven and set aside until the cookies are cool enough to handle but still warm. Roll the warm cookies, a few at a time, in the spiced powdered sugar. If you like things on the sweet side, roll them in the sugar a second time.

Rugelach

I learned to make rugelach from my baker friend Izzy Cohen, who taught me many tricks of the Jewish baking trade. This dough is made with equal parts butter and cream cheese and then laminated, meaning the dough is rolled out, folded, and then rolled out and folded again—and again. It's rolled and folded a total of three times, creating a light layered dough when baked. I laminate it with sugar, meaning I sprinkle sugar on the dough each time I roll it out. The resulting rugelach are light and tender, with a flaky and crispy exterior. They're not at all heavy and doughy, as rugelach can be. If you don't already love rugelach, these will make you a convert. I got the idea to laminate with sugar from the New York–based baker Melissa Weller. She got the idea to laminate rugelach dough at all from me. And I, in turn, learned it from Izzy. That's a beautiful example of how bakers learn and grow from each other. And you, the home baker and eater of baked goods, are the winner.

I give you two choices of fillings: raspberry jam or fresh date puree. Both have their virtues. Raspberry is the more traditional filling; it also looks pretty and saves you the step of pureeing the dates. The date puree, on the other hand, is more unusual, and the dates are delicious with the toasted walnuts that are layered throughout. If you opt for the date filling, buy soft, fresh dates. In Los Angeles, I get them at farmers' markets. If all you can find are hard dates from a grocery store, make the raspberry. These need to be baked on a silicone baking mat. The filling melts out of the rugelach and gets very sticky. Without the baking mat, it's nearly impossible to get the rugelach off the baking sheet without them sticking.

Makes 32 rugelach

What You Need—
The Essential Special Equipment

12-inch pie plate or cake pan
(to use as a stencil)

2 silicone baking mats

For the Dough

226 grams (2 sticks) cold unsalted butter, cubed

½ teaspoon Diamond Crystal kosher salt

226 grams (one 8-ounce package) cold cream cheese, cubed

280 grams (2 cups) unbleached all-purpose flour, plus more for dusting

75 grams (¼ cup plus 2 tablespoons) granulated sugar

1½ teaspoons ground cinnamon

For the Filling

170 grams (1½ cups) walnut halves

200 grams (7 ounces) soft, fresh dates (about 14 large), pitted (about ¾ cup)

2½ tablespoons pure vanilla extract

OR

240 grams (¾ cup) seedy raspberry jam

For Finishing

1 extra-large egg

50 grams (¼ cup) granulated sugar

1 teaspoon ground cinnamon →

Rugelach (continued)

1. To make the dough, place the butter, salt, and cream cheese in a stand mixer fitted with the paddle and beat on low speed until the butter and cream cheese are combined, about 2 minutes, stopping to scrape down the sides and bottom of the bowl and the paddle with a rubber spatula whenever ingredients are accumulating. Turn the mixer off, add the flour, then mix on low speed for about 1 minute until no flour is visible. Stop the mixer, remove the bowl and paddle from the stand, and clean them with the spatula, scraping the bowl from the bottom up to release any ingredients that may be stuck there.

2. Lightly dust a work surface with flour and turn the dough out onto the floured surface. Knead the dough to bring it together and pat it into a 1-inch-thick block. Wrap the dough in plastic wrap and refrigerate it until it is firm, at least 2 hours.

3. Stir the sugar and cinnamon together in a small bowl.

4. Lightly dust a work surface with flour. Place the dough on the floured surface and pound the dough with a rolling pin to soften it until it is malleable and as flat as possible. (The more you flatten it by pounding it, the easier it will be to roll out.) Dust the dough and rolling pin lightly with flour. Using firm, steady pressure, roll the dough into an 8 × 15-inch rectangle with a short side facing you, dusting with flour as needed. Sprinkle 2 tablespoons of the cinnamon-sugar over the dough and run your hands over the dough to evenly distribute the cinnamon-sugar and spread it to the edges and corners of the dough.

5. Fold the top edge of the dough down by two-thirds and the bottom edge up to meet the top edge so the dough is folded in thirds, like a letter. Rotate the dough 90 degrees clockwise so an open edge is facing you. This completes the first of three turns.

6. Roll the dough out again to 8 × 15 inches. Sprinkle it with 2 tablespoons of the cinnamon-sugar again and make another letter fold again. Turn the dough clockwise again and roll it out to 8 × 15 inches a third time. Sprinkle with the remaining 2 tablespoons cinnamon-sugar and make a third letter fold. Wrap the dough in plastic wrap and refrigerate until the dough is chilled and firm, at least 1 hour.

7. Lightly dust your work surface with flour. Remove the block of dough from the refrigerator. Cut the block in half through the middle so you have two squarish blocks of dough.

8. Lightly dust the dough and rolling pin with flour and, applying firm, steady pressure, roll the dough out so it's just big enough that you can cut out a 12-inch round from it. Place the dough on a baking sheet and cover it with a sheet of parchment paper. Repeat, rolling out the second block of dough in the same way. Add the second to the baking sheet on top of the first round of dough. Place the dough in the refrigerator to chill and relax, at least 30 minutes.

9. To make the filling, adjust an oven rack to the center position and preheat the oven to 325°F.

10. Spread the walnuts on a baking sheet and toast them on the center rack of the oven until they're lightly browned and fragrant, 8 to 10 minutes, shaking the baking sheet and rotating it front to back halfway through the toasting time so the walnuts brown evenly. Remove the walnuts from the oven and set them aside until they're cool enough to touch. (If you think the nuts are on the verge of being overtoasted, transfer them to a plate so they don't continue to cook from the residual heat of the pan.) Finely chop the walnuts, measure out 1 cup and set aside. (Reserve any remaining walnuts for another use.)

11. If you are making date rugelach, place the dates and vanilla in a mini food processor and puree. Scrape the puree out into a small bowl.

12. Line two large baking sheets with silicone baking mats.

13. Remove one round of dough from the refrigerator. Using a paring knife and the pie plate or cake pan as a stencil, cut out a 12-inch round.

14. Spoon half of the date puree or raspberry jam into the center of the round and use the back of the spoon or an offset spatula to spread it toward the edges, leaving a ¼-inch border free of puree or jam. Sprinkle ½ cup of the chopped walnuts evenly over the date puree or jam.

15. Using a ruler and a large knife, cut the round of dough into quarters. Cut each quarter into quarters again, resulting in 16 pie-shaped wedges. →

Rugelach (continued)

Slide a wedge out of the round. Pull on the outer corners of the wedge to widen it slightly. Use the palms of your hands to roll the wedge from the wide side toward the tip to form the rugelach into a crescent shape. Place the rugelach on one of the prepared baking sheets. Continue rolling and forming the rugelach, making sure they are not touching when you add them to the baking sheet. Repeat with the second sheet of dough and remaining filling to fill, cut, and shape more rugelach, placing them on the second baking sheet. Place the baking sheets in the refrigerator until the rugelach are chilled and firm, at least 30 minutes.

16. Adjust the oven racks so one is in the top third and the other is in the bottom third of the oven and preheat the oven to 350°F.

17. To finish the rugelach, whisk the egg in a small bowl. Stir the sugar and cinnamon together in a separate small bowl. One at a time, pick up the rugelach and brush them generously all over with the egg, making sure to get the egg into the nooks and crannies. Hold the rugelach over the bowl of cinnamon-sugar and dust the tops and sides with the cinnamon-sugar, turning the rugelach to coat on all sides. (Discard the remaining cinnamon-sugar.) Put the rugelach back on the baking sheets, leaving 1 inch between them.

18. Place one baking sheet on each oven rack and bake the rugelach until they are golden brown, 25 to 35 minutes (the raspberry-filled rugelach will be on the shorter end of the range, while the date-filled rugelach will be on the longer end). Switch racks and rotate the baking sheets front to back halfway through the baking time so the rugelach bake evenly. Remove the rugelach from the oven and let them cool on the baking sheets.

Almond Biscotti

These cookies were inspired by those from a bakery called Il Cantuccio di San Lorenzo, in Florence, that my friend, the food writer and editor Laurie Ochoa, happened upon in the summer of 2021. She was coming to dinner at my house in nearby Umbria that night and wanted to bring something. When she saw the line out the door to this bakery, she figured it had to be good. They sold a variety of *cantucci,* the real name for the cookies that we Americans refer to as biscotti, including these *cantucci morbidi,* or soft *cantucci.* I had never heard of soft *cantucci,* and I just loved them. They had a subtle give to them; they weren't rock hard like biscotti often are. The next chapter in this cookie story came that fall, when I was leading a group of food lovers on a tour of Italy. I suggested to a few people from the tour that they go to this bakery. One of them, a woman named Pauline Godfrey, was just as smitten with the cookies as I was, and when she returned to the States, she was determined to figure out how to make them. And she succeeded! This is her recipe, with the exception of the sugar crystals on top. Late in the book-writing game, we made these at Mozza and discovered that, as good as Pauline's were, they were even better with a sprinkling of sugar on top. I use extra-coarse sugar crystals (aka Con AA Confectioners Sugar), which adds a pretty sparkling touch, and a nice crunchy texture. It's available at baking stores or from online sources. If you can't find it, use demerara or turbinado sugar instead; the sugar won't be quite as crunchy. I also swapped out pastry flour for the all-purpose flour she used. The softer pastry flour made the cookies spread more, and also made them chewier and more tender, reflecting the texture of the *cantucci morbidi* that we discovered in Florence. I made these changes after the cookies were photographed, so you will be happy to know that your cookies will look even better than mine in the picture. I think they're the best biscotti, *cantucci*— whatever you call them!—I've ever had.

Makes about 24 cookies

150 grams (1 cup) skin-on whole almonds

2 extra-large eggs

16 grams (1 tablespoon) mild-flavored honey, such as clover or wildflower

1 teaspoon pure almond extract

1 medium orange

165 grams (¾ cup plus 1 tablespoon) granulated sugar

150 grams (1 cup plus 1 tablespoon) pastry flour, plus more for dusting

150 grams (1½ cups) unblanched almond meal (or 150 grams/1 cup skin-on whole almonds)

1 teaspoon Italian leavening (or ½ teaspoon baking powder and ½ teaspoon baking soda)

1 teaspoon Diamond Crystal kosher salt

2 tablespoons (24 grams) extra-coarse sugar crystals (or demerara or turbinado sugar) →

Almond Biscotti (continued)

1. Adjust an oven rack to the center position and preheat the oven to 325°F.

2. Spread the almonds on a baking sheet and toast them on the center rack of the oven until they're lightly browned and fragrant, 8 to 10 minutes, shaking the baking sheet and rotating it halfway through the toasting time. Remove the almonds from the oven. (If they are on the verge of being overtoasted, transfer them to a plate so they don't continue to cook from the residual heat of the pan.) Set aside to cool to room temperature.

3. Line a large baking sheet with parchment paper.

4. Put the eggs, honey, and almond extract in a medium bowl. Use a fine Microplane to grate the zest (the orange-colored outer layer) of the orange. (Reserve the orange for another use.) Whisk to combine the ingredients.

5. Combine the granulated sugar, flour, almond meal, Italian leavening (or baking powder and baking soda), and salt in a large bowl and stir with a whisk to combine. Add the wet ingredients and stir with a rubber spatula until no flour is visible; the mixture will be crumbly. Add the almonds and stir with the spatula or your hands to form a smooth dough.

6. Place half of the dough on the prepared baking sheet and use damp hands to form it into a flat log 14 inches long, 1¾ inches wide, and 1 inch tall. Repeat with the second half of the dough, forming another log alongside the first one, with at least 4 inches between them. Sprinkle both logs with the sugar crystals (or demerara or turbinado sugar), dividing it evenly, and gently pat the sugar so it sticks.

7. Bake the logs on the center rack of the oven until golden brown, 25 to 30 minutes, rotating the baking sheet front to back halfway through. Remove the logs from the oven and reduce the oven temperature to 300°F. Set the logs aside until they're cool enough to touch, about 15 minutes.

8. Transfer the logs to a cutting board and use a long serrated knife to slice them at a slight diagonal ¾ inch thick. Lay the slices cut-side down on the same baking sheet you baked the logs on.

9. Return the biscotti to the center rack of the oven and bake until they are slightly firm to the touch and the edges are golden brown, about 10 minutes, rotating the baking sheet front to back halfway through the baking time so they brown evenly. Remove the biscotti from the oven and let them cool on the baking sheet.

Chocolate Salami (left);
Almond Biscotti (right)

Chocolate Salami

Italians are masters at giving ingredients delicious and creative second lives. Chocolate salami, a dense chocolate log that utilizes the crumbs of leftover biscotti, is the perfect example. The "salami" is not baked—it's almost like a giant chocolate truffle—so it's a stretch to include it in this book. I snuck it in because it contains biscotti, which are baked.

This makes a great gift. It's dusted in powdered sugar to mimic the moldy exterior of salami. In Italy, fancier versions go so far as to wrap the salami artfully in butcher's twine to give it the full salami look. (If you want that look, you can find instructions online, which is how Mozza's executive chef Liz Hong learned to tie the salami for this photo.) If you don't have leftover biscotti, use quality store-bought biscotti or other crunchy cookies; don't use any cookies in this salami that you wouldn't want to eat on their own.

This recipe is very versatile, so experiment with it according to your taste. Use whatever combination of nuts, including almonds, walnuts, and pecans, you want. (Toast the nuts at 325°F until they are fragrant and light golden before adding them.) You could also add dried fruit, chopped to the size of your added nuts. (See photo page 161.)

Makes two 14-inch salami

150 grams (1 heaping cup) pistachios

300 grams (10½ ounces) biscotti, homemade (page 159) or store-bought (or another crunchy cookie)

200 grams (7 ounces) bittersweet chocolate (70% cacao), coarsely chopped (about 1¼ cups); halved if you're using feves

150 grams (about 1 stick plus 3 tablespoons) unsalted butter

42.5 grams (2 tablespoons) Lyle's Golden Syrup

2 tablespoons brandy (or whiskey)

1 tablespoon pure vanilla bean paste or vanilla extract

3 extra-large egg yolks

100 grams (½ cup) granulated sugar

1 teaspoon flaky sea salt

Powdered sugar for dusting

1. Adjust an oven rack to the center position and preheat the oven to 325°F.

2. Spread the pistachios on a baking sheet and toast them on the center rack of the oven until they are light golden brown, 8 to 9 minutes, rotating the baking sheet front to back and stirring the pistachios halfway through the toasting time so they brown evenly. Transfer the pistachios to a plate to prevent them from toasting further and set aside to cool.

3. Coarsely chop the biscotti into roughly ½-inch pieces.

4. Fill a small saucepan with 1½ to 2 inches of water and set a small stainless steel bowl atop the saucepan to make a double boiler, making sure the water doesn't touch the bottom of the bowl. Bring the water to a simmer over medium heat. Put the chocolate, butter, golden syrup, brandy, and vanilla in the bowl of the double boiler and heat until the butter and chocolate melt, stirring the mixture and scraping the bowl with a silicone spatula to prevent the ingredients from burning. Turn off the heat, remove the bowl from the double boiler, and set aside to cool slightly.

5. Put the egg yolks, granulated sugar, and flaky salt together in a medium bowl and whisk to combine. Fill a medium saucepan with water. Place the bowl on top of the saucepan. (The weighted saucepan anchors the bowl, so it remains stable when you whisk ingredients in it.) Drizzle the chocolate mixture into the bowl with the egg yolk mixture, whisking constantly. Add the biscotti crumbs and pistachios and stir with a rubber spatula to combine. Clean the bowl with the spatula, scraping from the bottom up to release any ingredients from the bottom of the bowl.

6. Lay two sheets of plastic wrap on your work surface. Dividing the mixture evenly, use your hands to scrape the chocolate mixture onto the pieces of plastic wrap. Shape the chocolate into logs 2 inches thick. Wash and dry your hands and tightly wrap the logs in the plastic, twisting the ends closed like a candy wrapper. Refrigerate the salami until they are firm, at least several hours.

7. Before serving the salami, lay a sheet of parchment paper on your work surface. Unwrap the salami and place it on the parchment paper. Sift the powdered sugar over the log and roll the log in the sugar that falls on the parchment paper to coat it evenly. Serve the salami with a sharp knife for people to slice it themselves.

8. Store the leftover salami in the refrigerator.

Spiced Graham Crackers

Recently I learned the Urban Dictionary definition of a graham cracker: "a person who seems great but once you get to know them, they're boring." This perfectly describes my experience with actual graham crackers—my own included. For years I thought that I made the best graham crackers, and I was very proud to put my recipe for them in my book *Pastries from the La Brea Bakery*. But when I revisited that recipe recently, I thought: "Wow. These are bland. They could really use a makeover." For inspiration, I went back to the source: the original boxed graham crackers that I grew up eating. They were the definition of bland and boring. That got me thinking: What *is* a graham cracker? And what flavor is it supposed to have?

During my research and development process, I learned that the distinguishing feature of graham crackers is that they're made with whole wheat flour, which at one time was called "graham" flour. In developing these, my goal was to utilize the flavor of whole wheat flour to make something uniquely delicious. I sweeten these with a combination of maple syrup and honey to give them a more nuanced flavor. And I enhance the flavor with a lot of sweet spices: nutmeg and cloves in the crackers and a generous coating of cinnamon-sugar on the finished crackers. Today, if I were to define graham crackers, I'd say they're like a crunchy, whole wheat spiced biscuit. That's what these are. And they're nothing you're going to get bored of.

Makes about 15 graham crackers

What You Need—
The Essential Special Equipment
Ruler

Rolling pastry cutter (or large knife)

For the Dough
120 grams (½ cup) heavy cream

37.5 grams (2 tablespoons) artisanal maple syrup (preferably barrel-aged)

32 grams (2 tablespoons) mild-flavored honey, such as clover or wildflower

2 tablespoons pure vanilla bean paste or vanilla extract

238 grams (1¾ cups) whole wheat flour

122.5 grams (¾ cup plus 2 tablespoons) unbleached all-purpose flour, plus more for dusting

125 grams (½ cup plus 2 tablespoons) granulated sugar

1 teaspoon baking soda

1 teaspoon Diamond Crystal kosher salt

¼ teaspoon ground cloves

¼ teaspoon grated nutmeg

113 grams (1 stick) cold unsalted butter, cubed

For Finishing
62.5 grams (¼ cup plus 1 tablespoon) granulated sugar

1½ teaspoon ground cinnamon →

Spiced Graham Crackers (continued)

1. To make the dough, whisk the cream, maple syrup, honey, and vanilla together in a small bowl to combine.

2. Put the whole wheat flour, all-purpose flour, sugar, baking soda, salt, cloves, and nutmeg in a food processor and pulse to combine. Add the butter and pulse until it is the texture of a fine meal. Add the wet ingredients and pulse until the dough just comes together.

3. Lightly flour your work surface and turn the dough out onto it. Divide the dough in half and pat each half into a 1-inch-thick block. Wrap each block tightly in plastic wrap and refrigerate until the dough is firm, at least 2 hours.

4. Lay a sheet of parchment paper on your work surface. Remove one block of dough from the refrigerator, unwrap, and place in the center of the parchment paper. Pound the dough with a rolling pin to soften it until it is malleable and flatten it as much as possible. (The more you flatten the dough by pounding it, the easier it will be to roll out, and the less you will need to roll since it's already flat.) Place a second sheet of parchment paper on top of the dough, lining it up with the bottom sheet. Applying firm, steady pressure with the rolling pin, roll the dough out between the parchment paper to $3/16$ inch thick. Lay the parchment-sandwiched dough on a large baking sheet and place it in the refrigerator. Repeat, pounding and rolling out the second block of dough between two sheets of parchment paper. Lay it on top of the first sheet of dough in the refrigerator. Chill until the dough is firm, at least 1 hour.

5. Remove one sheet of dough from the refrigerator and lay it on your work surface. Peel the top sheet of parchment off the dough and lay it back down on the dough. (This loosens the parchment so after you cut the graham crackers, you will be able to lift them off the parchment without them sticking.) Flip the sheet of dough over. Peel off the top sheet of parchment paper and lay it clean-side up on a baking sheet to line it.

6. Using a ruler and a rolling pastry cutter (or a large knife), trim the edges of the dough to square off the sheet of dough. Make cuts every 4½ inches in one direction and 4 inches in the other direction to create 4½ × 4-inch graham crackers. Slide a wide metal spatula underneath each cracker and transfer them side by side to the prepared baking sheet. Repeat with the

second sheet of dough and add the cut graham crackers to the baking sheet. Once you have filled the baking sheet with a single layer of graham crackers, lay one of the sheets of parchment paper the dough was rolled between on top of the crackers and lay more graham crackers in a second layer. Gather the scraps, pat them into a 1-inch-thick block, and reroll them between two sheets of parchment paper. Cut the sheet of scraps as you did the other sheets and add the graham crackers to the baking sheet. Refrigerate until the graham crackers are chilled and firm, at least 1 hour.

7. Arrange the oven racks so one is in the top third and the other is in the bottom third of the oven and preheat the oven to 350°F. Line two large baking sheets with parchment paper.

8. To finish the graham crackers, stir the sugar and cinnamon together in a small bowl.

9. Remove the baking sheet with the graham crackers from the refrigerator and transfer the graham crackers to the prepared baking sheets, leaving at least 1 inch between them.

10. Using the ruler and a paring knife, score a line down the center of the 4-inch side of each cracker, to mark into 2 × 4½-inch rectangles. Use a skewer (or the sharp point of an instant-read thermometer) to prick two rows of dots on each side of the dividing line. (Alternatively, you can also use a toothpick, but rotate it in a circle to widen the dots.) Sprinkle about 1 teaspoon of cinnamon-sugar over each cracker.

11. Place one baking sheet on each oven rack and bake the graham crackers until they are lightly browned and firm to the touch, 15 to 17 minutes, switching racks and rotating the baking sheets front to back halfway through the baking time so the graham crackers bake evenly. Remove the graham crackers from the oven.

Iced Animal Crackers

I developed this recipe years ago to taste like the animal crackers that I grew up on, the ones that came in the little box that was meant to look like a circus cage. They are not terribly sweet, so for this version, I decorate them with a thin powdered sugar icing. When I added the icing and sprinkles, I realized that I had created a hybrid between those plain, circus-box crackers and the pink and white iced animal cookies that I was never allowed to eat. I shake the canister of sprinkles directly over the cookies, which results in an uneven sprinkling that I like. I start by making golden butter, which is butter that is melted and cooked just shy of brown butter, to bring out the butter flavor in these simple cookies.

I bake these into animal shapes, but you can cut them into whatever shape you like. Make sure to bake similar-size cookies on the same baking sheets so they bake for the same length of time.

Makes as many as 96 cookies (the number will vary with the size of the cutters you use)

**What You Need—
The Essential Special Equipment**

Cookie cutters (whatever size and shape you like)

For the Dough

340 grams (3 sticks) unsalted butter, cubed

3 extra-large eggs

1 extra-large egg yolk

60 grams (¼ cup) heavy cream

3 tablespoons pure vanilla bean paste or vanilla extract

300 grams (1½ cups) granulated sugar

2 teaspoons baking powder

1 teaspoon Diamond Crystal kosher salt

560 grams (4 cups) unbleached all-purpose flour, plus more for dusting

For the Icing

180 grams (1½ cups) powdered sugar, plus more as needed

45 grams (3 tablespoons) whole milk

Colored sprinkles

1. To make the dough, place the butter in a small saucepan or skillet with a light-colored bottom to make golden butter. Warm the butter over medium heat until it melts and begins to bubble, swirling the pan occasionally. Cook the butter, swirling often so it cooks evenly, until it is golden and the milk solids are caramel colored, 3 to 6 minutes. Remove from the heat. Working quickly so the butter doesn't continue to cook, weigh out 227 grams (or measure 1 cup plus 2 teaspoons) of butter, making sure to include the milk solids. (Reserve the remaining butter for another use.) Transfer the butter to a bowl and set it aside to cool to room temperature. Cover the bowl with plastic wrap and place it in the refrigerator to chill until the butter is solid. →

2. Whisk the whole eggs, egg yolk, cream, and vanilla together in a medium bowl.

3. Remove the butter from the refrigerator and place the bowl in a large bowl of hot water to help release the butter. Dry off the bowl and invert it to release the butter onto a cutting board. (Alternatively, you may be able to wedge a knife under the butter and pop it out.) Cut the butter into roughly ½-inch cubes.

4. Put the butter in a stand mixer fitted with the paddle and beat on medium-high speed until the butter is soft and smooth but still cold, about 1 minute, stopping to scrape down the sides and bottom of the bowl and the paddle with a rubber spatula whenever butter is accumulating. Add the granulated sugar and beat on medium-high speed until the mixture is smooth, about 1 minute, scraping down the bowl as needed. Add the baking powder and salt and beat on low speed for about 15 seconds to distribute them. Add the flour alternately with the egg mixture in five additions for the flour and four for the egg mixture, starting and ending with the flour, beating on low speed until the additions are incorporated and stopping to scrape down the bowl before the next addition. Stop the mixer, remove the bowl and paddle from the stand, and clean them with the spatula, scraping the bowl from the bottom up to release any ingredients that may be stuck there.

5. Lightly dust a work surface with flour, transfer the dough to the floured surface, and bring it together into a ball. Divide the dough into 4 equal portions and pat each portion into a 1-inch-thick disk. Wrap each disk of dough in plastic wrap and refrigerate until the dough is firm, at least 2 hours.

6. Lay a sheet of parchment paper on a work surface. Working with one portion at a time, remove the dough from the refrigerator, unwrap, and place in the center of the parchment paper. Pound the dough with a rolling pin to soften it until it is malleable and flatten it as much as possible. (The more you flatten it by pounding it, the easier it will be to roll out, and the less you will need to roll it out.) Lay another sheet of parchment paper on top of the first, lining them up. Applying firm, steady pressure to the rolling pin, roll the dough between the parchment to ¼ inch thick. Lay the parchment-sandwiched dough on a baking sheet and place it in the refrigerator. Repeat, rolling out the remaining disks of dough in the same way and stacking them

on top of the first sheet in the refrigerator. Chill the dough until it is firm, at least 1 hour.

7. Remove one sheet of dough from the refrigerator and lay it on your work surface. Peel the top sheet of parchment off the dough and lay it back down on the dough. (This loosens the parchment so after you cut the shapes, you will be able to lift them off the parchment without them sticking.) Flip the sheet of dough over. Peel off the top sheet of parchment paper and lay it clean-side up on a baking sheet to line it.

8. Fill a small bowl with flour to dust the cookie cutters.

9. Using cookie cutters of whatever sizes and shapes you want, cut shapes from the dough, dipping the cutters in flour to keep them from sticking to the dough, and cutting the shapes as close together as possible to get as many cookies as you can from one sheet of dough. Use a metal spatula to lift the shapes off the parchment paper and place them side by side but not touching on the prepared baking sheet. When you have filled the baking sheet with a single layer of shapes, lay a sheet of parchment on top and lay another layer of shapes on it. Set the scraps aside. Repeat, cutting the remaining sheets of dough in the same way and adding them to the baking sheet, dividing the layers with parchment paper and setting the scraps aside. When you have cut all the sheets of dough, gather the scraps, pat them into a disk, and reroll them between two sheets of parchment paper. Cut the sheet of scraps as you did the other sheets and add the shapes to the baking sheet. Refrigerate until the shapes are chilled and firm, at least 1 hour.

10. Adjust the oven racks so one is in the top third and the other is in the bottom third of the oven and preheat the oven to 325°F. Line two large baking sheets with parchment paper.

11. Remove the baking sheet with the stacks of dough from the refrigerator. Transfer as many of the shapes to the prepared baking sheets as will fit, leaving ½ inch between them. Cover the cookies that you are not baking with plastic wrap and return them to the refrigerator.

12. Place one baking sheet on each oven rack and bake the cookies until the tops are dark golden brown, 15 to 25 minutes (the time varies depending on the size of the cookies you cut), switching racks and rotating the baking →

sheets front to back halfway through the baking time so the cookies bake evenly. Remove the cookies from the oven and set them aside to cool to room temperature on the baking sheets. Bake the remaining cookies in the same way.

13. To make the icing, sift the powdered sugar into a medium bowl. Add the milk and whisk until no lumps remain, adding more powdered sugar if necessary to obtain the consistency of a thick glaze.

14. One at a time, dip the top side of the cookies into the icing so the center of the cookie barely touches the icing, leaving the edges of the cookie visible. (Don't dip the cookies so deep into the icing that the icing covers the cookie.) Lift the cookies out of the icing and gently tip them back and forth over the bowl of icing so the excess icing drips back into the bowl. Place the cookies iced-side up on a flat surface. Shake the sprinkles over the cookies while the icing is still wet.

Iced Raisin Bars

When I was growing up, the only cookies my mother would buy for my sister and me were those she found wholesome, like Fig Newtons or raisin bars, long flat cookies scored in zigzag lines into individual bars that fit together like a jigsaw puzzle.

You never see these cookies anymore, but recently, I found a different kind of raisin cookies in Italy. That's when I really fell in love with them. The fact that they make raisin cookies in Italy (albeit not iced and not flat) legitimized them for me; I realized my mom's choice wasn't just a health food compromise, but also delicious. I put almond paste in this dough as a nod to the Italian version, since Italians often bake with almond paste.

I usually recommend you use plump raisins from a farmers' market or another quality source. In this case, because the raisins are simmered and then pureed, even boxed grocery store raisins will do. If you want to use currants instead of raisins, substitute an equal amount by weight.

Makes 16 cookies

What You Need—
The Essential Special Equipment

Rolling pastry cutter (preferably fluted)

For the Dough

5 extra-large eggs

37.5 grams (3 tablespoons) granulated sugar

25 grams (2 tablespoons packed) dark brown sugar

113 grams (¼ cup plus 2 tablespoons) almond paste (preferably unblanched)

113 grams (1 stick) cold unsalted butter, cubed

2 tablespoons pure vanilla bean paste or vanilla extract

1 teaspoon ground cinnamon

½ teaspoon Diamond Crystal kosher salt

⅛ teaspoon ground cloves

175 grams (1¼ cups) unbleached all-purpose flour, plus more for dusting

200 grams (1¼ cups) raisins

For the Glaze

60 grams (½ cup) powdered sugar

15 grams (1 tablespoon) whole milk

1. To make the dough, bring a medium saucepan of water to a boil over high heat. Lower the eggs into the water with a slotted spoon to prevent them from cracking and cook them for 11 minutes. While the eggs are cooking, fill a bowl with ice water. Remove the eggs with the slotted spoon and transfer them to the ice water to cool. Remove the eggs from the ice water and peel them. Separate the whites and yolks. (Reserve the whites for another use. I sprinkle them with salt to snack on.) Pass the egg yolks through a fine-mesh sieve into a small bowl. →

2. Put the granulated sugar and brown sugar in the bowl of a stand mixer. Crumble the almond paste into the bowl, fit the mixer with the paddle, and beat on medium speed until the paste is combined with the sugars and the mixture is smooth, 3 to 4 minutes. Stop the mixer, add the butter and vanilla, and beat on medium speed until the butter is combined with the almond paste mixture and no lumps remain, 4 to 5 minutes, stopping to scrape down the sides and bottom of the bowl and the paddle with a rubber spatula whenever ingredients are accumulating. Stop the mixer, add the cinnamon, salt, and cloves, and beat on medium speed for about 15 seconds to incorporate the additions. Stop the mixer, scrape down the bowl, and add the flour. Using a medium or fine Microplane (or on the small—but not the smallest—holes of a box grater), grate the egg yolks into the mixer bowl. Mix on low speed for about 30 seconds until no flour is visible. Stop the mixer, remove the bowl and paddle from the stand, and clean them with the spatula, scraping the bowl from the bottom up to release any ingredients that may be stuck there.

3. Lightly flour your work surface and turn the dough out onto it. Divide the dough in half and pat each half into a 1-inch-thick block. Wrap each block in plastic wrap and refrigerate until the dough is firm enough to roll, about 1 hour, but not so long that it is solid, as it will be too hard to roll. (If you refrigerate the dough for so long that it is too hard to roll, set it out at room temperature for about 30 minutes to soften slightly before rolling it.)

4. While the dough is chilling, put the raisins in a small saucepan with 180 grams (¾ cup) water. Bring to a boil over high heat and boil, shaking the pan occasionally to prevent the raisins from sticking, until the liquid has evaporated, about 5 minutes. Remove from the heat and let the raisins cool to room temperature. Transfer the raisins to a food processor and puree them. Return the pureed raisins to the saucepan and cook over medium heat, stirring constantly, for about 1 minute, to cook off any excess liquid and form a paste. Remove from the heat.

5. Lay a sheet of parchment paper on a work surface. Pound one portion of the dough with a rolling pin to soften it until it is malleable and flatten it as much as possible. (The more you flatten it, the easier it will be to roll out.) Place a second sheet of parchment paper on top of the dough, lining it up with the bottom sheet. Applying firm, steady pressure with the rolling pin, roll the dough out between the parchment paper to an 8 × 16-inch rectangle about ⅛ inch thick. Put the parchment-sandwiched dough on a large baking sheet and place it in the refrigerator. Repeat, rolling the second block of dough between two sheets of parchment paper to the same dimensions. Lay it on top of the first sheet of dough in the refrigerator. Chill until the dough is firm, at least 1 hour.

6. To assemble the cookies, remove one sheet of dough from the refrigerator and lay it on a work surface. Peel the top sheet of parchment off the dough and lay it back down on the dough. (This loosens the parchment so after you cut the cookies, you will be able to lift them off the parchment without them sticking.) Flip the sheet of dough over. Peel off the top sheet of parchment paper and lay it clean-side up on a baking sheet to line it. Set the baking sheet aside.

7. Spoon the raisin puree onto the dough and use an offset spatula or the back of the spoon to spread the puree to the edges of the dough in an even layer.

8. Remove the baking sheet with the second sheet of dough from the refrigerator. Lay the sheet of dough on your work surface. Peel off the top sheet of parchment paper. Invert the sheet of dough onto the raisin-covered dough so the side with the parchment paper is facing up, lining up the two sheets of dough. Transfer the sandwiched sheets of dough to the baking sheet and refrigerate until the dough is firm, at least 30 minutes.

9. Adjust an oven rack to the center position and preheat the oven to 350°F.

10. Remove the baking sheet with dough from the refrigerator. Peel off the top sheet of parchment paper and lay it back down on the dough. Flip the sandwiched dough onto the baking sheet so the loosened parchment is on the bottom. Remove the top sheet of parchment paper and discard it.

11. Using a ruler and a fluted pastry cutter, trim the dough to a 6 × 16-inch rectangle. (Bake the trimmings to snack on or discard them.) Cut the dough down the middle lengthwise to make two long rows. Slide the rows apart so they're evenly spaced on the parchment paper. (You'll bake them on this parchment.) Use the fluted pastry cutter to cut across the rows every 2 inches to get 8 (2 × 3-inch) bars from each row; cut through both sheets of dough but don't separate the bars. Use a skewer (or the sharp end of an →

instant-read thermometer) to prick about 6 dots on each bar. (Alternatively, you can also use a toothpick, but rotate it in a circle to widen the dots.)

12. Bake the bars on the center rack of the oven until they are lightly browned and firm to the touch, 15 to 20 minutes, rotating the baking sheet front to back halfway through the baking time so the bars bake evenly. Remove the baking sheet from the oven and set aside to cool to room temperature on the baking sheet. Break the slabs into individual bars along the fluted cuts.

13. To make the glaze, while the cookies are cooling, sift the powdered sugar into a medium bowl. Add the milk and whisk until no lumps remain. Brush the glaze over the bars.

Shortbread Cookies

Classic butter shortbread is probably my favorite type of cookie. It's buttery, salty, and simple: all things that I love. That said, not all shortbread cookies are created equal. Some are so white and pale that they look floury and unappealing to me. Shortbread is all about butter, but the flavor of the butter needs to be coaxed out, which happens only if you bake them long enough. For me, the gold standard for shortbread is Walkers shortbread. Yes, they're mass-produced, but they're made with pure butter, and they are baked to a perfect light golden color. To achieve the same pretty tone and optimum buttery flavor, these are baked at a high enough temperature and long enough that the butter browns slightly inside the cookie, which gives it a delicious, nutty flavor. The word "confit" (something cooked in its own fat) comes to mind.

I use a decorative rolling pin to emboss the top of these cookies. I love the old-fashioned look. Because this dough is so buttery, it doesn't hold the indentation as some other doughs would, but it still leaves a pretty pattern on the cookies; I like the subtlety. You could also use a handheld cookie stamp to create the same effect or press the dough into an embossed shortbread pan, such as a Nordic Ware English Shortbread Pan. Or skip the stamping altogether.

Makes about 40 cookies

**What You Need—
The Essential Special Equipment**
Embossed rolling pin (optional)
Ruler

565 grams unsalted European-style butter, cubed
100 grams (½ cup) granulated sugar
60 grams (½ cup) powdered sugar
2 teaspoons Diamond Crystal kosher salt

2 tablespoons pure vanilla bean paste or vanilla extract
560 grams (4 cups) unbleached all-purpose flour, plus more for dusting
Flaky sea salt

1. Place the butter in a small saucepan or skillet with a light-colored bottom to make golden butter. Warm the butter over medium heat until it melts and begins to bubble, swirling the pan occasionally. Cook the butter, swirling often so it cooks evenly, until it is golden and the milk solids are caramel colored, 3 to 6 minutes. Remove from the heat. Working quickly so the butter doesn't continue to cook, weigh out 453 grams (or measure about 2 cups plus 2 tablespoons) of butter, making sure to include the milk solids. →

Shortbread Cookies (continued)

(Reserve the remaining butter for another use.) Transfer the butter to a bowl and set it aside to cool to room temperature. Cover the bowl with plastic wrap and place it in the refrigerator to chill until the butter is solid.

2. Remove the butter from the refrigerator and place the bowl in a large bowl of hot water to help release the butter. Dry off the bowl and invert it to release the butter onto a cutting board. (Alternatively, you may be able to wedge a knife under the butter and pop it out.) Cut the butter into roughly ½-inch cubes.

3. Put the butter in a stand mixer fitted with the paddle and beat on medium-high speed until the butter is soft and smooth but still cold, about 1 minute, stopping to scrape down the sides and bottom of the bowl and the paddle with a rubber spatula whenever butter is accumulating. Add the granulated sugar and powdered sugar and beat for about 1 minute on medium-high speed, until the mixture is smooth, scraping down the bowl as needed. Add the kosher salt and vanilla and beat on low speed for about 15 seconds to distribute them. Add the flour in three additions, beating on low speed until the flour is combined and stopping to scrape down the bowl before the next addition. When all the ingredients have been added, stop the mixer, remove the paddle and bowl from the stand, and clean them with the spatula, scraping the bowl from the bottom up to release any ingredients that may be stuck there.

4. Lightly flour a work surface and transfer the dough to the floured surface. Gather the dough with your hands and form it into a 1-inch-thick block.

5. Lay a sheet of parchment paper on your work surface. Place the dough in the center of the parchment paper and lay another sheet of parchment paper on top of the dough, lining it up with the lower sheet. Using a standard rolling pin (not the embossed pin), roll the dough between the parchment to a ½-inch-thick rectangle. If you're using an embossed rolling pin, make sure the rectangle is wider than the embossed rolling pin. (Alternatively, you can skip the parchment paper and roll out this dough on a flour-dusted work surface.) Lay the parchment-sandwiched dough on a baking sheet and place it in the refrigerator to chill until the dough is firm, at least 1 hour.

6. Remove the dough from the refrigerator and lay it on your work surface. Peel the top sheet of parchment off the dough and lay it back down on the dough. (This loosens the parchment so after you cut the shapes, you will be able to lift them off the parchment without them sticking.) Flip the sheet of dough over. Peel off the top sheet of parchment paper and lay it clean-side up on the baking sheet to line it.

7. If using the embossed rolling pin to make patterns in the dough, lightly dust the sheet of dough and also the rolling pin with flour. Starting from the edge closest to you, line the rolling pin up with the edge of the dough and, applying firm pressure, roll the pin away from you to create an embossed pattern on the surface of the dough.

8. If you did not use the embossed rolling pin, use a ruler and a large sharp knife to cut the cookies into 1½-inch squares. If you embossed the dough, you will use the marks from the embossed pin as a guide for cutting the dough.

9. Gently transfer the cookies to the prepared baking sheet, placing them side by side in a single layer. Place the baking sheet in the freezer until the dough is firm, at least 30 minutes.

10. Adjust an oven rack to the top third of the oven and preheat the oven to 350°F. Line a large baking sheet with parchment paper.

11. Remove the shortbread from the freezer. Transfer half of the cookies to the prepared baking sheet and spread out the cookies that remain on the original baking sheet, leaving at least 1 inch between them. Sprinkle a generous pinch of flaky salt on each cookie. Return one baking sheet to the refrigerator.

12. Place one baking sheet in the top third of the oven and bake until the cookies just begin to get color on them, about 15 minutes. Reduce the oven temperature to 300°F and bake until the cookies are light golden brown and firm to the touch, another 15 minutes. Remove the cookies from the oven and let them cool on the baking sheets.

Giant Toasted Almond Cookie

Deb Michail is one of the all-star cooks who came out of the Mozza kitchens. Every summer, when Deb goes to Italy to visit her sister, who lives near Milan, she makes the trip to visit me at my house in Umbria. The first year she came, she surprised me with a gift from a bakery in her sister's town—a big flat disk wrapped beautifully, as Italian baked goods are. Deb said it was called a *torta di almendra*. *Almendra* means "almond," and *torta* can refer to a cake, a pie, or a tart, but this was none of those things. What it resembled more than anything else was a giant, crunchy, almond-studded cookie. I put it on the dining table, and throughout the day, we all broke off pieces to eat with our coffee or snack on. (Cutting it is out of the question; it's too hard and it would crumble.) The fact that you eat it that way makes me like it even more. Although this is not a classic like the other items in this book, once the world gets wind of the idea of a giant, cake-size crunchy communal cookie, it will be.

Makes one 12-inch cookie

**What You Need—
The Essential Special Equipment**

12-inch flan ring

Cooking spray

2 cups (210 grams) skin-on whole almonds

182 grams (1½ sticks plus 1 tablespoon) cold unsalted butter, cubed

150 grams (¾ cup) granulated sugar

1 tablespoon pure vanilla bean paste or vanilla extract

1½ teaspoons Diamond Crystal kosher salt

1 teaspoon Italian leavening (or ½ teaspoon baking powder and ½ teaspoon baking soda)

1 large lemon

225 grams (1¾ cups) unbleached pastry flour (or unbleached all-purpose flour)

Powdered sugar for dusting

1. Adjust an oven rack to the center position and preheat the oven to 325°F. Line a large baking sheet with parchment paper. Spray the insides of the flan ring with cooking spray and place it on the baking sheet.

2. Spread the almonds on a baking sheet and toast them on the center rack of the oven until they're lightly browned and fragrant, 8 to 10 minutes, shaking the baking sheet and rotating it front to back halfway through the toasting time so the almonds brown evenly. Remove the almonds from the oven. (If you think the nuts are on the verge of being overtoasted, transfer them to a plate so they don't continue to cook from the residual heat of the pan.) Set the almonds aside to cool to room temperature. →

3. Transfer the almonds to a food processor and pulse about 5 times; some of the pieces will be medium ground, others coarsely ground.

4. Put the butter in a stand mixer fitted with the paddle and beat on medium speed until the butter is soft but still cold, 3 to 4 minutes, stopping to scrape down the sides and bottom of the bowl with a rubber spatula whenever the butter is accumulating. Stop the mixer and scrape down the bowl. Add the granulated sugar and beat on medium speed until the mixture is light and fluffy, 3 to 4 minutes, stopping to scrape down the bowl as needed. Add the vanilla, salt, and leavening. Using a fine Microplane, grate the zest (the bright-yellow outer layer) of the lemon into the bowl. (Reserve the lemon for another use.) Beat on medium speed for about 15 seconds to distribute the additions. Stop the mixer, scrape down the bowl, and add the almonds. Mix on low speed for about 15 seconds to incorporate them. Stop the mixer, add the flour, and mix on low speed until no flour is visible. Stop the mixer, remove the bowl and paddle from the stand, and clean them with the spatula, scraping the bowl from the bottom up to release any ingredients that may be stuck there.

5. Scoop the dough into the prepared ring. Using your fingers, press the dough to fill the ring in an even layer. Smooth out the top with an offset spatula. Run the tines of a fork down the center of the cookie to create decorative lines on the top. Then use the fork to create another set of lines on either side of the first lines. Make another set of lines at a 45-degree angle to the first lines to create a diamond pattern on top of the cookie.

6. Bake the cookie on the center rack of the oven until golden brown all over but not firm to the touch (it will harden as it cools), 35 to 40 minutes, rotating the baking sheet front to back halfway through the baking time so it bakes evenly. Remove the baking sheet from the oven.

7. To remove the cookie from the ring, run the tip of a paring knife around the inside edge of the ring to loosen any stuck bits. Slide the cookie onto a serving platter or board.

8. Dust with powdered sugar before serving.

Nut Clusters

These are not really cookies; they're crunchy, shaped clusters of nuts with just enough egg white to bind them. They're on the healthy side since they contain very little sugar and no flour. They remind me of cornflake clusters, but with nuts in place of the cornflakes. If you like snacking on nuts (which I do), you will love these. The addition of orange blossom water to the egg white binder gives them an exotic touch.

Makes about 24 nut clusters

210 grams (1¾ cups) slivered almonds

238 grams (1¾ cups) hazelnuts (preferably skinless)

100 grams (½ cup) granulated sugar

37 grams (2 tablespoons plus 1 teaspoon) mild-flavored honey, such as clover or wildflower

1 tablespoon pure vanilla bean paste or vanilla extract

1 teaspoon orange flower water

1 extra-large egg white

¼ teaspoon baking powder

½ teaspoon Diamond Crystal kosher salt

Powdered sugar for dusting

1. Adjust the oven racks so one is in the top third and the other is in the bottom third of the oven and preheat the oven to 325°F.

2. Spread the almonds on a small baking sheet and spread the hazelnuts on a separate small baking sheet. (Quarter-sheet pans if you have them.) Place one baking sheet on each oven rack. Toast the nuts until they are light golden and fragrant, 10 to 14 minutes for the almonds and 15 to 18 minutes for the hazelnuts, gently shaking the pans, switching racks, and rotating the baking sheets front to back halfway through the toasting time so the nuts brown evenly. Remove the nuts from the oven. (If you think they are on the verge of being overtoasted, transfer them to a plate so they don't continue to cook from the residual heat of the pan.) Set the hazelnuts aside until they are cool enough to touch. If they have skins, gather them into a clean dish towel and rub them together inside the towel to remove the skins; discard the skins. Transfer the almonds and hazelnuts to a medium bowl.

3. Increase the oven temperature to 350°F. Line two large baking sheets with parchment paper.

4. Put the granulated sugar, honey, vanilla, orange flower water, egg white, baking powder, and salt in a medium bowl and stir with a rubber spatula to combine. Add the almonds and hazelnuts and stir to coat the nuts in the syrup. →

5. Scoop up 30 grams (about 2 tablespoons) of the cluster mixture, letting any excess syrup drain back into the bowl, and drop the cluster onto the prepared baking sheets. Repeat, leaving at least 1½ inches between the clusters. Discard the excess syrup.

6. Place one baking sheet on each oven rack and bake the clusters until the tops are golden brown, 20 to 23 minutes, switching racks and rotating the baking sheets front to back halfway through the baking time so the clusters bake evenly.

7. Remove the nut clusters from the oven. While they are still warm, pinch the clusters with your fingers to make them taller, and give them a more irregular shape. Let the cookies cool completely on the baking sheet.

8. Dust the nut clusters with powdered sugar.

Chewy Almond Cookies (top right);
Coconut Macaroons (bottom left)

Chewy Almond Cookies

These simple three-ingredient cookies are my attempt to re-create the meringue cookies at Wil Wright's, a San Fernando Valley ice cream shop where my parents took my sister and me on special family outings. The cookies, which came in a glassine envelope alongside ice cream dishes, were barely bigger than a quarter. I made mine a bit bigger, about the size of a silver dollar, but just like those of my youth, they are light, chewy, and intensely almond flavored.

With only three ingredients, it's one of the simplest and quickest recipes in this book. The key to success is to use the exact right amount of egg white. Too little and the cookies won't spread, which is what creates the signature crackle top; too much and they will flatten like pancakes. For this reason, I give you the amount of egg white by weight and not by the number of eggs.

These need to be baked on a silicone baking mat to prevent them from sticking.

Makes about 24 cookies

**What You Need—
The Essential Special Equipment**

2 silicone baking mats

50 grams (½ cup) granulated sugar

227 grams (1 cup minus 1 tablespoon) blanched almond paste

40 grams egg whites
(from about 1½ extra-large eggs)

1. Put the sugar in the bowl of a stand mixer. Crumble the almond paste into the bowl, fit the mixer with the paddle, and beat on medium speed until the paste is combined with the sugar and the mixture is smooth, 3 to 4 minutes. With the mixer on medium speed, gradually add the egg white and mix until it is incorporated and the dough is smooth, about 1 minute. Stop the mixer, remove the paddle and bowl from the stand, and clean them with the spatula, scraping the bowl from the bottom up to release any ingredients that may be stuck there. Cover the bowl in plastic wrap and place it in the refrigerator until the dough is firm, at least 1 hour.

2. Adjust the oven racks so one is in the top third and the other is in the bottom third of the oven and preheat the oven to 350°F. Line two large baking sheets with silicone baking mats. →

Chewy Almond Cookies (continued)

3. Remove the dough from the refrigerator and unwrap. Scoop up 15 grams (about 1 tablespoon) of the dough and roll it between your palms into a ball. Place the ball on one of the prepared baking sheets. Press lightly with the palm of your hand to flatten the ball slightly. Repeat, rolling the rest of the dough into balls and placing them on the baking sheets, leaving at least 1 inch between them.

4. Place one baking sheet on each oven rack and bake the cookies until they are lightly browned and springy to the touch, about 15 minutes, switching racks and rotating the baking sheets front to back halfway through the baking time so the cookies bake evenly. Remove the cookies from the oven and set them aside to cool to room temperature on the baking sheets before peeling them off the baking mat.

Coconut Macaroons

Coconut macaroons, aka "haystacks" (and not to be confused with the Crayola-colored cotton candy–like sandwich cookie that is all the rage), are one of my favorites. I learned to make them while in pastry school in France, where they are called *roches*. These are crunchy on the outside, moist and chewy on the inside, not too sweet, and have a touch of acidity from the addition of applesauce. They're far superior to the coconut macaroons I had as a kid, which came out of a Manischewitz can, at Passover. I pinch the haystack shapes so they have lots of nooks and crannies.

This batter is very sticky, so you need to bake them on a silicone baking mat. (See photo page 188.)

Makes about 14 cookies

What You Need—
The Essential Special Equipment
Silicone baking mat

For the Cookies
250 grams (1 cup) unsweetened applesauce

100 grams (½ cup) granulated sugar

32 grams (2 tablespoons) mild-flavored honey, such as clover or wildflower

2 extra-large egg whites

1 tablespoon pure vanilla bean paste or vanilla extract

1 teaspoon pure almond extract

¼ teaspoon Diamond Crystal kosher salt

⅛ teaspoon grated nutmeg

87.5 grams (1¾ cups) unsweetened shredded coconut

Powdered sugar for dusting

---

1. Set a fine-mesh sieve over a bowl and spoon the applesauce into the sieve. Let it sit for 1 hour to drain off as much liquid as possible. Weigh out 125 grams (or measure ½ cup) of applesauce. (Drink the juice and enjoy any extra applesauce.)

2. Adjust an oven rack to the center position and preheat the oven to 300°F. Line a large baking sheet with a silicone baking mat.

3. Combine the granulated sugar, honey, egg whites, vanilla, almond extract, salt, and nutmeg in a large bowl and stir with a rubber spatula to combine. Add the coconut and drained applesauce and stir with the spatula to combine.

4. Scoop up 30 grams (about 2 tablespoons) of the dough and place on the prepared baking sheet. Pinch it with your fingers to make a lumpy, pyramid-like shape. Repeat, forming the remaining dough in the same way, leaving at least 1 inch between each cookie. →

5. Bake the macaroons on the center rack of the oven until the tips and the bottoms are crispy and almost black in places, 60 to 70 minutes, rotating the baking sheet front to back halfway through the baking time so they bake evenly. Remove the macaroons from the oven and set aside to cool to room temperature. Use a metal spatula to peel the macaroons from the baking mat. Dust them generously with powdered sugar.

6. The macaroons are best the day they're made while they're still crunchy. If you are serving them later, reheat them for 5 to 10 minutes in a 300°F oven to revive their crunchy exterior. Let them cool to room temperature and dust them again with powdered sugar before serving.

These are simple, not-too-sweet, unadorned cakes, the kind that you put on the counter for everyone who walks by to sneak a slice or a sliver (to even out the edge, of course!), and by the end of the day, the cake is gone. I absolutely love this category of dessert, though until recently, I'd never heard the term "casual cakes." Some of the cakes in this chapter are coated with a glaze and others are poked to allow a sweet soaking liquid or glaze to seep inside the cake. But there are no layers here, no frosting, and no decoration. In this chapter, I took advantage of the variety of cake pans that are available these days. Using baking pans in different shapes and sizes, with various decorative details, appeals to my sensibility as a baker, making the cakes beautiful but in an unfussy way. The pound cake is baked in a loaf pan with a pretty starburst pattern on top. I use a decorative Bundt pan to give a traditional lemon Bundt cake new life. The Kentucky Butter Cake (page 197), an American classic, is baked in a wide, low gelatin mold, providing lots of surface area for its sweet glaze. And the Canelés (page 230), Financiers (page 228), Madeleines (page 225), and Olive Oil Cakes (page 232) are baked in individual molds of different shapes and sizes. I like to imagine all of them presented as part of a bakery window display. If you are a novice baker, this chapter is an excellent place to start.

Casual Cakes

Kentucky Butter Cake

To know me is to know that this is a very "Nancy" cake, and my co-author, Carolynn, knows me well. So, when she saw a picture of it online for the first time, knowing I would be drawn to how plain and straightforward it is, she sent it to me. I immediately thought: "Oh, my God! A butter cake with a simple glaze. What could be more perfect?" It seemed so obvious, and yet I had never made one, and had never heard of this cake. It turns out, Kentucky Butter Cake is a thing. It first appeared in 1963 when a woman named Nell Lewis entered the cake into a Pillsbury Bake-Off—and won. In recent years, just about every blogger out there has published a recipe for it, as has *The New York Times.* And what's incredible is this: All these years later, all the recipes are identical. Nobody has touched a thing.

The cake is like a cross between a pound cake and a yellow cake, with different ratios of flour, butter, and sugar. It's moist and flavorful, with a tender, delicate crumb. But what makes it really stand out is the glaze. When the cake comes out of the oven, you poke it all over with a skewer, so the glaze seeps down into the cake. Then you invert the cake and glaze the top side as well. Some of the glaze stays on the cake instead of going *in* the cake, hardening into a thin exterior glaze with a discernible, delicate crunch. The result is like everything you want in a glazed old-fashioned doughnut, without it being fried. I added bourbon to the glaze, otherwise this is the classic. If you don't want to make it with bourbon, just eliminate it.

This cake is best the day after it's made.

Makes one 12-inch cake

What You Need— The Essential Special Equipment

12-inch-wide decorative cake mold (or another 12-cup capacity baking mold or pan)

Cooking spray

Pastry brush

For the Cake

224 grams (1 cup) buttermilk (preferably whole-milk or low-fat), shaken

4 extra-large eggs

1 tablespoon pure vanilla bean paste or vanilla extract

420 grams (3 cups) unbleached all-purpose flour

400 grams (2 cups) granulated sugar

1½ teaspoons Diamond Crystal kosher salt

1 teaspoon baking powder

½ teaspoon baking soda

226 grams (2 sticks) unsalted butter, cubed and left at room temperature until pliable but not greasy

For the Glaze

141 grams (1 stick plus 2 tablespoons) unsalted butter, cubed

300 grams (1½ cups) granulated sugar

¼ cup Kentucky bourbon (or another bourbon; optional)

1 tablespoon plus 1 teaspoon pure vanilla bean paste or vanilla extract →

Kentucky Butter Cake (continued)

1. To make the cake, adjust an oven rack to the center position and preheat the oven to 325°F. Coat the baking mold (or pan) with cooking spray.

2. Whisk the buttermilk, eggs, and vanilla together in a medium bowl.

3. Put the flour, sugar, salt, baking powder, and baking soda in a stand mixer fitted with the paddle and mix on low speed for about 15 seconds to combine the ingredients. Add the butter and half of the buttermilk mixture and mix on low speed until no flour is visible, about 30 seconds. With the mixer on low speed, slowly add the remaining buttermilk mixture. Increase the speed to medium and beat until the batter is pale, smooth, and creamy, 2 to 3 minutes, stopping to scrape down the bowl and paddle whenever ingredients are accumulating. Stop the mixer, remove the bowl and paddle from the stand, and clean them with the spatula, scraping the bowl from the bottom up to release any ingredients that may be stuck there.

4. Scrape the batter into the prepared mold (or pan) and smooth out the top with an offset spatula. Place the mold (or pan) on a large baking sheet.

5. Place the baking sheet with the cake on it on the center rack of the oven and bake until the cake is golden brown and begins to pull away from the sides of the pan, and a toothpick inserted into the center comes out clean, 60 to 75 minutes, rotating the pan front to back halfway through the baking time so it bakes evenly. Remove the cake from the oven.

6. To make the glaze, when the cake comes out of the oven, combine the butter, sugar, bourbon, vanilla, and 60 grams (¼ cup) water in a medium saucepan and bring to a boil over medium-high heat. Reduce the heat and gently simmer until the glaze is slightly thickened and sticky, about 2 minutes. Remove from the heat.

7. While the cake is still warm, use a skewer or toothpick to poke about 40 holes in it, penetrating about three-fourths of the way to the bottom. Dip a pastry brush into the glaze and, using about one-third of the glaze, dab a generous amount of glaze over the surface of the cake, going back over the cake two or three times to create a thick, even layer.

8. To remove the cake from the pan, run the tip of a paring knife around the top edge of the pan to loosen any stuck bits. Place a cake round or large platter on top of the cake pan, invert the cake, and lift off the pan. Generously dab about half of the remaining glaze evenly over the surface of the cake, going back over the cake two or three times. Set the cake aside for about 1 hour for the glaze to set. Warm the remaining glaze over low heat and serve it on the side for people to drizzle over their portion of cake.

Poppy Seed Cake

Poppy seed cake, usually baked in a loaf or Bundt pan, is a bakeshop classic. This version doesn't contain egg yolks, only whites. The whites give the cake a wonderful white hue, which looks so pretty in contrast with the black poppy seeds. I bake it in a fluted tart pan, so it has a low profile and pretty, scalloped edges. It's the perfect treat when you want something plain, simple, and satisfying.

Makes one 10-inch cake

**What You Need—
The Essential Special Equipment**

10-inch fluted tart pan with a removable bottom

Cooking spray

For the Cake

40 grams (¼ cup) poppy seeds

210 grams (1½ cups) unbleached all-purpose flour

149 grams (⅔ cup) buttermilk (preferably whole-milk or low-fat), shaken

1 tablespoon pure vanilla bean paste or vanilla extract

226 grams (2 sticks) cold unsalted butter, cubed

150 grams (¾ cup) granulated sugar

¾ teaspoon Diamond Crystal kosher salt

¾ teaspoon baking soda

¼ teaspoon cream of tartar

2 large lemons

4 extra-large egg whites

For the Glaze and Topping

120 grams (1 cup) powdered sugar, plus more as needed

25 grams (1 tablespoon plus 2 teaspoons) whole milk

1 teaspoon fresh lemon juice

Poppy seeds for sprinkling

1. To make the cake, adjust an oven rack to the center position and preheat the oven to 350°F. Coat the bottom and sides of the tart pan with cooking spray. Sprinkle 20 grams (2 tablespoons) of the poppy seeds inside the tart pan and tilt the pan to distribute the seeds over the surface.

2. Combine the flour and the remaining 20 grams (2 tablespoons) of poppy seeds in a large bowl and stir with a whisk to combine. Whisk the buttermilk and vanilla together in a small bowl.

3. Put the butter in a stand mixer fitted with the paddle and beat at medium speed until the butter is softened but still cold, 3 to 4 minutes, stopping to scrape down the sides and bottom of the bowl and paddle with a rubber spatula whenever butter is accumulating. Add 100 grams (½ cup) of the granulated sugar and beat on medium speed until light and fluffy, 3 to 4 minutes, scraping down the bowl as needed. Add the salt, baking soda, and cream of tartar. Using a fine Microplane, grate the zest (the bright-yellow →

outer layer) of the lemons into the bowl. (Reserve the lemons to juice for the soaking liquid and for another use.) Beat on low speed for about 30 seconds to incorporate the additions. Stop the mixer and scrape down the bowl and paddle. Add the flour mixture and the buttermilk mixture alternately in three additions for the flour mixture and two for the buttermilk mixture, starting and ending with the flour mixture; mix on low speed until the additions are combined and stop to scrape down the bowl before each addition. Stop the mixer, remove the bowl and paddle from the stand, and clean them with the spatula, scraping the bowl from the bottom up to release any ingredients that may be stuck there. Transfer the batter to a separate, large bowl.

4. If you have only one bowl for your stand mixer, clean and dry the mixer bowl. Place the egg whites in the clean stand mixer bowl and fit the mixer with the whisk. Beat the whites on medium speed until they are foamy, 1½ to 2 minutes. Increase the speed to medium-high and mix until soft peaks form, 1½ to 2 minutes. Increase the speed to high, and with the mixer running, gradually add the remaining 50 grams (¼ cup) granulated sugar and mix until the peaks are stiff and shiny but not dry, 1½ to 2 minutes. Stop the mixer and remove the whisk and bowl from the stand. Tap the whisk against the bowl to remove the egg whites.

5. Using the rubber spatula, scoop two-thirds of the egg whites into the bowl with the batter and vigorously stir them into the batter, turning the bowl with one hand while quickly and aggressively stirring the whites into the batter with the other. Add the lightened batter to the bowl of the stand mixer with the remaining egg whites and fold them into the batter until no streaks of egg whites remain.

6. Scrape the batter into the prepared pan and smooth the top with an offset spatula.

7. Bake the cake on the center rack of the oven until the top is golden brown, the center is firm to the touch, and a toothpick inserted in the center comes out clean, 28 to 35 minutes, rotating the pan front to back halfway through the baking time so the cake bakes evenly. Remove the cake from the oven and set it aside to cool.

8. To remove the cake from the pan, press up on the bottom of the pan to remove the outer ring. Invert the cake onto a serving platter and gently pry the bottom of the pan off the top of the cake.

9. To make the glaze, combine the powdered sugar, milk, and lemon juice in a small bowl and whisk until no lumps remain.

10. Spoon about two-thirds of the glaze onto the center of the cake and use the back of a spoon to spread it in a circular motion to cover the cake, leaving about 1 inch of cake visible around the edges. Lightly sprinkle poppy seeds over the glaze. Reserve the remaining glaze for people to spoon over their individual slices.

Angel Food Cake

I've never been a fan of traditional angel food cake; I don't like the spongy texture, to say nothing of the lack of flavor. I've always assumed that the only reason angel food cake had any fans at all was because it's made with egg whites and no butter or oil, so people viewed it as a "healthy" or "low-fat" choice. Typical angel food cake, in my view, is like the commercial white bread of cakes: Where commercial bread is the neutral vehicle for sandwich fillings, angel food cake is the neutral vehicle for berries and whipped cream. But with a sandwich, as we now know, the bread, not just the filling, should have flavor. Likewise, angel food cake shouldn't be overlooked. I decided to go back to the angel food cake drawing board, and accomplished something I never thought I would: a version of angel food cake that I would want to eat. It took me no fewer than ten tries, a lot of research, a lot of tinkering, and a lot of brainstorming with others, but I knew I had succeeded after Shiri, my recipe tester, made it and told me, "You know . . . I don't hate it."

What makes this version so inviting? First, I coat the inside of the cake pan with cinnamon-sugar, which adds flavor and gives the exterior an appealing, crunchy texture. I add almond extract in addition to the traditional vanilla. I also swirl melted bittersweet chocolate into the batter to break up the whiteness and to add another dimension of flavor. The final difference lies in how I remove the cake from the pan. With traditional angel food cake, the inside of the pan isn't greased. When the cake comes out of the oven, you invert the pan, so it stands on the stilts that are the hallmark of a traditional angel food cake pan. The stilts elevate the pan, so the cake slowly slides down, out of the pan, contributing to the cake's perfectly smooth texture and squared-off shape. I don't do this. Instead, I lift the cake out of the pan. I like the craggy, uneven surface and the crusty texture of the top of the cake; I didn't have the heart to invert it. The result is an inviting white cake with a sandy exterior, dark swirls throughout, and a craggy, uneven top. While these details enhance the cake and give it a lot more character, I assure you, it's still plain enough to enjoy with berries and whipped cream.

The most challenging part of making angel food cake is whipping the egg whites just right. I borrowed the technique for the whites from the website Serious Eats; their directions were so specific, it removed all the guesswork and made this recipe foolproof. (For a full tutorial on making angel food cake, refer to their website.) →

Angel Food Cake (continued)

Makes 1 angel food cake

**What You Need—
The Essential Special Equipment**

Aluminum angel food cake pan with removable bottom

Cooking spray

For the Cinnamon-Sugar

62.5 grams (¼ cup plus 1 tablespoon) granulated sugar

1½ teaspoons ground cinnamon

For the Cake

147 grams (1 cup) cake flour

85 grams (3 ounces) bittersweet chocolate (70% cacao), coarsely chopped (about ¼ cup); whole if you're using feves

370 grams egg whites from about 10 extra-large eggs, cold

250 grams (1¼ cups) granulated sugar

1 tablespoon pure vanilla bean paste or vanilla extract

1 teaspoon pure almond extract

½ teaspoon cream of tartar

½ teaspoon Diamond Crystal kosher salt

1. To make the cinnamon-sugar, mix the sugar and cinnamon together in a small bowl. Measure out 2 tablespoons of the cinnamon-sugar to sprinkle over the top of the cake and set it aside.

2. To make the cake, adjust an oven rack to the center position and preheat the oven to 350°F.

3. Coat the walls and the inner ring of the pan with cooking spray. Sprinkle the remaining cinnamon-sugar into the pan and tilt the pan to coat it with an even layer of cinnamon-sugar.

4. Sift the flour into a small bowl.

5. Fill a small saucepan with 1½ to 2 inches of water and set a small stainless steel bowl atop the saucepan to make a double boiler, making sure the water doesn't touch the bottom of the bowl. Bring the water to a simmer over medium heat. Put the chocolate in the bowl and melt it, stirring and scraping the bowl with a silicone spatula to prevent the chocolate from burning. Remove from the heat, leaving the bowl on the double boiler.

6. Combine the egg whites, sugar, vanilla, almond extract, cream of tartar, and salt in a stand mixer fitted with the whisk and beat on low speed for 1 minute. Increase the speed to medium-low and beat until the whites are dense and dark, about 3 minutes. Increase the speed to medium and beat until the whites are thin and foamy, about 3 minutes. Increase the speed to medium-high and beat until the whites are smooth, shiny, white, and thick

enough that the whisk will leave traces while it's mixing, 2 to 4 minutes. (The whites will be soft enough at this point to run off the wires when the whisk is lifted out, but thick enough to mound up on itself like soft serve in the bowl.) Stop the mixer, remove the whisk and bowl from the stand, and tap the whisk to remove the excess egg whites.

7. Sprinkle half the flour over the beaten egg whites and fold the flour in with a rubber spatula. Add the remaining flour and fold it in. Transfer the mixture to a large wide bowl. Drizzle half of the melted chocolate over the batter and run a skewer through it in large zigzag motions to create streaks of chocolate throughout the top layer of the batter.

8. Using the rubber spatula, gently lift out the top half of the batter (with the chocolate streaks) and scoop it unevenly into the prepared pan. Drizzle the remaining melted chocolate over the plain batter in the bowl and run the skewer through it in large zigzag motions to create streaks of chocolate. Use the spatula to scoop the remaining batter unevenly into the pan. Sprinkle the reserved 2 tablespoons cinnamon-sugar on top of the batter.

9. Bake the cake on the center rack of the oven until it is firm to the touch and the top is crusty, 45 to 50 minutes, rotating the pan front to back halfway through the baking time. Remove the cake from the oven and set it aside for about 10 minutes, until it is cool enough to handle.

10. To remove the cake from the pan, run the tip of a paring knife around the inside of the pan and central tube to release any stuck bits. Push up on the bottom of the pan to remove the outer ring. Slide an offset spatula (or the paring knife) between the cake and the bottom of the pan and around the inner circle to release any stuck bits. Use both hands to lift the cake off the center ring and onto a serving platter, with the sugared side up.

Lemon Bundt Cake (right);
Meyer Lemon Polenta Cake (left)

Lemon Bundt Cake

Sometimes you just want something simple, familiar, and delicious. This all-American lemon Bundt cake is exactly that. I didn't do anything groundbreaking with this recipe, but I did manage to make a lemon cake that tastes like lemon. Where with many lemon cakes, the only lemon flavor is in the glaze, in this cake, the cake is drenched in lemon juice, which gives it a true, intense lemon flavor, and also makes it moist. I eliminated the glaze to show off the beauty of the mold.

Makes one 10-inch decorative Bundt cake

**What You Need—
The Essential Special Equipment**

10-inch (10-cup) Bundt pan (I used a Nordic Ware Blossom Bundt Pan)

Cooking spray

Pastry brush

For the Cake

224 grams (1 cup) buttermilk (preferably whole-milk or low-fat), shaken

2 extra-large eggs

113 grams (1 stick) cold unsalted butter, cubed

200 grams (1 cup) granulated sugar

4 large lemons

1 teaspoon baking soda

½ teaspoon Diamond Crystal kosher salt

280 grams (2 cups) unbleached all-purpose flour

For the Soaking Liquid

½ cup fresh lemon juice

50 grams (¼ cup) granulated sugar

1. Adjust an oven rack to the center position and preheat the oven to 350°F. Coat the Bundt pan with cooking spray.

2. To make the cake, whisk the buttermilk and eggs together in a medium bowl.

3. Put the butter in a stand mixer fitted with the paddle and beat on medium speed until the butter is soft but still cold, 3 to 4 minutes, stopping to scrape down the sides and bottom of the bowl with a rubber spatula whenever butter is accumulating. Add the sugar and beat on medium speed until the mixture is light and fluffy, 3 to 4 minutes, scraping down the bowl as needed. Stop the mixer. Using a fine Microplane, grate the zest (the bright-yellow outer layer) of the lemons into the bowl. (Juice the lemons to use for the soaking liquid.) Add the baking soda and salt and mix on low speed for about 15 seconds to incorporate the additions. Stop the mixer and scrape down the bowl and paddle. Add the flour and the buttermilk/egg mixture alternately in five additions for the flour and four for the buttermilk/egg mixture, →

starting and ending with the flour; mix on low speed until the additions are combined and stop to scrape down the bowl before each addition. Stop the mixer, remove the bowl and paddle from the stand, and clean them with the spatula, scraping the bowl from the bottom up to release any ingredients that may be stuck there.

4. Scrape the batter into the prepared pan and use an offset spatula to smooth out the surface.

5. Place the Bundt pan on a baking sheet and place it on the center rack of the oven to bake until the cake is golden brown and starts to pull away from the sides of the pan, and a toothpick inserted into the center comes out clean, 35 to 45 minutes, rotating the cake front to back halfway through the baking time so it bakes evenly. Remove the cake from the oven and set aside to cool slightly.

6. While the cake is baking, to make the soaking liquid, combine the lemon juice and sugar in a small saucepan and heat over medium heat just to dissolve the sugar, about 2 minutes, wiping the edges of the pot once or twice with a pastry brush so sugar doesn't stick to the sides and burn. Remove from the heat.

7. Use a skewer or toothpick to poke holes in the cake, spacing the holes about 1 inch apart. Use the pastry brush to generously dab half of the soaking liquid over the surface of the cake. Let the cake sit for about 30 minutes to absorb the liquid and cool slightly.

8. To remove the cake from the pan, run the tip of a paring knife around the inside edges of the pan to loosen any stuck bits. Invert the cake onto a serving platter and lift off the pan. Use the pastry brush to dab the top side of the cake with the remaining soaking liquid.

Marzipan Cake

Of all the recipes in this book, this is the item I would choose to have with my morning cappuccino. Although it is not a classic, it is composed of classic components: a sweet, buttery crust, a marzipan cake, a little raspberry jam, and a simple glaze, this one with brown butter and toasted almonds. Sneaking a thin layer of jam into cakes was a big thing in the '90s. You'd cut into a cake innocently thinking it was a white or lemon or even chocolate cake, only to discover that there was this pretty, glistening streak of ruby-colored jam running through it. I took that idea and spread a layer of raspberry jam on the bottom of the tart crust before I put the batter in. It may be dated, but I like it. It adds a hint of color and a burst of fruit flavor; one that is available year-round. The cake is baked in a giant brioche pan and topped with salted brown butter and toasted almonds. I honestly can't tell you how I thought of putting a cake inside a tart crust, but the crispy crust is the perfect textural contrast to the creamy cake. You could call it a cake disguised as a tart, or a tart disguised as a cake.

Makes one 9-inch cake

**What You Need—
The Essential Special Equipment**

9-inch brioche mold

Cooking spray

For the Crust

½ recipe Sweet Tart Dough (page 329)

Unbleached all-purpose flour for dusting (optional)

For the Cake

93 grams (⅔ cup) unbleached all-purpose flour

25 grams (¼ cup) unblanched almond meal

5 extra-large eggs

60 grams (¼ cup) light or dark rum (or whiskey)

1 teaspoon pure almond extract

62.5 grams (¼ cup plus 1 tablespoon) granulated sugar

227 grams (1 cup plus 2 tablespoons) almond paste (preferably unblanched)

226 grams (2 sticks) cold unsalted butter, cubed

1½ teaspoons baking powder

1 teaspoon Crystal Diamond kosher salt

2 large lemons

40 grams (2 tablespoons) seedy raspberry jam

For the Glaze

25 grams (¼ cup) skin-on thin-sliced almonds

112.5 grams (¾ cup plus 3 tablespoons) powdered sugar

37.5 grams (2½ tablespoons) buttermilk (preferably whole-milk or low-fat), shaken

½ tablespoon pure vanilla bean paste or vanilla extract

¾ teaspoon Diamond Crystal kosher salt

26 grams (2 tablespoons) unsalted butter, cubed →

1. To prepare the crust, coat the brioche mold with cooking spray.

2. Lay a sheet of parchment paper on a work surface. Remove the dough from the refrigerator, unwrap, and place in the center of the parchment paper. Pound the dough with a rolling pin to soften it until it is malleable and as flat as possible. (The more you flatten it, the easier it will be to roll out.) Lay another sheet of parchment paper on top of the dough, lining it up with the lower sheet. Applying firm steady pressure to the rolling pin, roll the dough between the parchment to ³⁄₁₆ inch thick. Lay the parchment-sandwiched dough on a baking sheet and refrigerate for at least 30 minutes, until the dough is firm. (Alternatively, you can skip the parchment paper and roll the dough on a flour-dusted work surface, dusting the surface, the dough, or the pin with flour as needed.)

3. Remove the sheet of dough from the refrigerator and lay it on your work surface. Peel the top sheet of parchment off the dough and lay it back down on the dough. (This loosens the parchment so you will be able to lift it off without it sticking.) Flip the sheet of dough over. Peel off and discard the top sheet of parchment paper. Place the brioche mold bottom-side down on the dough (toward the edge, not centered, as you'll be cutting pieces from the remaining dough) and trace around it with a paring knife to cut out a round. Place the round of dough in the bottom of the mold. Using a ruler and a large knife, cut the dough into nine fan-shaped strips 4½ inches long and 2 inches wide at one end and 5 inches wide at the other.

4. One at a time, gently ease the strips of dough with the 2-inch end toward the bottom of the mold, and gently press the dough into the scalloped sides of the mold. Repeat with the remaining strips of dough until you have lined the mold. (Discard the scraps.) Place the mold in the refrigerator to chill until the dough is firm, at least 1 hour.

5. To make the cake, adjust an oven rack to the center position with no racks above it. Preheat the oven to 350°F.

6. Stir the flour and almond meal together in a medium bowl. Whisk the eggs, rum, and almond extract together in a separate medium bowl.

7. Put the granulated sugar in the bowl of a stand mixer and crumble the almond paste into the bowl. Fit the mixer with the paddle and beat on medium speed until the paste is combined with the sugars and the mixture

is smooth, 3 to 4 minutes. Add the butter and beat on medium speed until the butter is combined with the almond paste mixture and no lumps remain, 4 to 5 minutes, stopping to scrape down the sides and bottom of the bowl and the paddle with a rubber spatula whenever the ingredients are accumulating. Stop the mixer and add the baking powder and salt. Using a fine Microplane, grate the zest (the bright-yellow outer layer) of the lemon into the bowl. (Reserve the lemon for another use.) Beat on medium speed for about 15 seconds to distribute the additions. Stop the mixer, scrape down the bowl, and add the flour and almond meal mixture. Mix on low speed for about 1 minute to combine, stopping to scrape down the bowl and paddle as needed. Add the dry ingredients and the egg mixture alternately in five additions for the flour mixture and four for the egg mixture, starting and ending with the flour mixture; mix on low speed until the additions are incorporated and stop to scrape down the bowl before each addition. Stop the mixer, remove the bowl and paddle from the stand, and clean them with the spatula, scraping the bowl from the bottom up to release any ingredients that may be stuck there.

8. Remove the mold from the refrigerator. Spoon the jam into the bottom of the mold and use the spoon or your fingers to spread it to cover the bottom. Scrape the batter into the mold and smooth the top with an offset spatula.

9. Bake the cake in the center rack of the oven until the top is golden brown and a toothpick inserted in the center comes out clean, 50 to 65 minutes, rotating the cake front to back halfway through the baking time so it bakes evenly. Remove the cake from the oven and set it aside to cool.

10. Reduce the oven temperature to 325°F.

11. To make the glaze, spread the almonds on a baking sheet and toast them on the center rack of the oven until they are light golden brown, 8 to 10 minutes, rotating the baking sheet front to back and stirring the almonds halfway through the toasting time so they brown evenly. Remove the baking sheet from the oven. Transfer the almonds to a plate to prevent them from browning further and set aside to cool.

12. Put the powdered sugar, buttermilk, vanilla, and salt in a medium bowl and whisk to combine them. →

13. Place the butter in a small saucepan or skillet with a light-colored bottom to make brown butter. Warm the butter over medium heat until it melts and begins to bubble, swirling the pan occasionally so the butter cooks evenly. Continue to cook the butter, swirling often, until the melted butter is caramel colored and the solids are the color of coffee grounds, 5 to 8 minutes. Remove from the heat. Working quickly so the butter doesn't continue to cook, weigh out 27 grams (or measure 2 tablespoons) of the butter, making sure to get the brown milk solids, and add it to the bowl with the powdered sugar and buttermilk, whisking until no lumps remain. (Reserve the remaining butter for another use.)

14. To remove the cake from the mold, hold the cake with one hand and invert it onto the other. Lift off the mold. Turn the cake right-side up and slide it onto a platter. Spoon the glaze over the cake and pile the toasted almonds on top.

Pineapple Upside-Down Cake

Yet another "I've never been a fan of until now" recipe, along with those for Lemon Bars (page 349) and Angel Food Cake (page 205). I couldn't *not* include pineapple upside-down cake here; it's such a classic, and it has so many fans. So I had no choice but to tinker with it until I made a version that I liked, which is what you see here. I added polenta to the batter, which gives texture to the cake, and even makes it feel vaguely Italian. In sticking with tradition, I used canned pineapple for the top, albeit an organic version. I normally don't like using canned ingredients, but in this case, using canned pineapple ensures that you're getting a ripe pineapple, whereas fresh pineapple is very often unripe. Also, side by side, I didn't taste the difference between the cakes made with fresh or canned pineapple. It also works out nicely that the size of the organic canned pineapple rings fit perfectly in the pan.

In old-school versions, this cake always includes a glow-in-the-dark cheap imitation "maraschino" cherry in the center of each pineapple ring. I replaced those with imported Italian cherries. Use either Amarena cherries, wild dark cherries from the Emilia-Romagna region of Italy, bottled in sweet syrup, or Luxardo maraschino cherries, which are from an Italian variety of cherry called *marasca* and entirely different from the so-called maraschino cherries we grew up with garnishing our Shirley Temples. You can find either variety of cherry at Italian specialty markets and from online sources.

Makes one 10-inch cake

What You Need—
The Essential Special Equipment

10-inch round cake pan

Cooking spray

For the Pineapple Topping

1 (15-ounce) can organic pineapple rings

226 grams (2 sticks) unsalted butter, cubed

50 grams (¼ cup) dark muscovado sugar (or dark brown sugar)

1 tablespoon pure vanilla bean paste or vanilla extract

1 tablespoon dark rum (or bourbon)

¼ teaspoon Diamond Crystal kosher salt

7 Amarena cherries or Luxardo maraschino cherries

For the Cake

112 grams (½ cup) buttermilk (preferably whole-milk or low-fat), shaken

3 extra-large eggs

2 tablespoons pure vanilla bean paste or vanilla extract

140 grams (1 cup) unbleached all-purpose flour

122 grams (¾ cup plus 1 tablespoon) fine yellow stoneground polenta

113 grams (1 stick) cold unsalted butter, cubed

150 grams (¾ cup) granulated sugar

50 grams (¼ cup) packed dark muscovado sugar (or dark brown sugar)

2 teaspoons baking powder

1 teaspoon ground cardamom

½ teaspoon Diamond Crystal kosher salt

¼ teaspoon baking soda

1 tablespoon grated peeled fresh ginger (grated on a fine Microplane), including the ginger juices →

1. To prepare the pineapple topping, coat the bottom and sides of the cake pan with cooking spray.

2. Drain the pineapple slices, reserving 1 tablespoon of the juice.

3. Place the butter in a small saucepan or skillet with a light-colored bottom to make golden butter. Warm the butter over medium heat until it melts and begins to bubble, swirling the pan occasionally. Cook the butter, swirling often so it cooks evenly, until it is golden, and the milk solids are caramel colored, 3 to 6 minutes. Remove from the heat. Working quickly so the butter doesn't continue to cook, weigh out 29 grams (or measure out 2 tablespoons) of butter, making sure to include the milk solids, and return it to the saucepan. (Reserve the remaining butter for another use.)

4. Add the muscovado sugar, vanilla, rum, salt, and the reserved 1 tablespoon pineapple juice to the saucepan with the butter and bring to a boil over medium-high heat. Reduce the heat and gently simmer until the sugar is dissolved, about 1 minute. Pour the mixture into the prepared cake pan and place the pan in the refrigerator to chill until the sauce is firm, about 45 minutes.

5. Remove the cake pan from the refrigerator. Lay 6 pineapple slices around the edges of the pan and place one in the center. (Reserve the remaining pineapple slices to snack on.) Put a cherry in the center of each pineapple ring and return the pan to the refrigerator.

6. To make the cake, adjust an oven rack to the center position and preheat the oven to 350°F.

7. Whisk the buttermilk, eggs, and vanilla together in a small bowl. Whisk the flour and polenta together in a medium bowl.

8. Put the butter in a stand mixer fitted with the paddle and beat on medium speed until it is soft but still cold, 3 to 4 minutes, stopping to scrape down the sides and bottom of the bowl and the paddle with a rubber spatula whenever butter is accumulating. Add the granulated sugar and muscovado sugar and beat on low speed for about 30 seconds. Increase the speed to medium and beat until the mixture is light and fluffy, 3 to 4 minutes, scraping down the bowl as needed. Add the baking powder, cardamom, salt, and baking soda and beat on medium speed for about 30 seconds to distribute the additions. Stop the mixer and scrape down the bowl and paddle.

9. Add the flour mixture and the buttermilk mixture alternately in five additions for the flour/polenta mixture and four for the buttermilk mixture, starting and ending with the flour/polenta mixture. Mix on low speed until the additions are combined and stop to scrape down the bowl before each addition. After the last addition, mix until only a few streaks of dry ingredients are visible. Add the grated ginger (and juices) and mix on low speed for about 15 seconds to incorporate. Stop the mixer, remove the bowl and paddle from the stand, and clean them with the spatula, scraping the bowl from the bottom up to release any ingredients in the bottom of the bowl.

10. Remove the cake pan from the refrigerator. Pour the batter into the prepared pan and smooth out the top with an offset spatula.

11. Bake the cake on the center rack of the oven until it is golden brown and a toothpick inserted into the center comes out clean, 40 to 50 minutes, rotating the cake front to back halfway through the baking time so it bakes evenly. Remove the cake from the oven and set it aside for 10 minutes until it is cool enough to handle.

12. To remove the cake from the pan, run the tip of a paring knife around the top inside edge of the pan to loosen any stuck bits. Place a serving platter on top of the pan, quickly invert the cake onto the platter, and lift off the pan.

Pound Cake

Pound cake gets its name from the fact that it's made with equal parts sugar, flour, butter, and eggs, traditionally a pound each. Four ingredients in equal amounts. That's it. This recipe stays within that promise when it comes to the basic ingredients, but then, naturally, I meander a bit off that path. My biggest departure is that I start with golden butter (butter that is cooked just shy of brown butter, which enhances the butter's flavor). I also add baking powder to lighten the cake up, vanilla because I love the flavor, and milk powder to give the cake a dense, moist, creamy texture. This recipe also calls for you to whip the egg whites before mixing them with the batter. This technique is used in the French version of pound cake, called *quatre quarts*.

Because this cake is so simple, I thought it could use some dressing up, so I traded in the traditional loaf pan for a decorative loaf pan with a fluted, starburst pattern on top. The fluted surface of the pan I used gave the cake a beautiful, thick, brown crust. The contrast between that toothsome crust and the moist, tender crumb is what distinguishes pound cake from, say, a butter cake or a yellow cake. It's what good pound cake is all about, and what makes this pound cake addictive.

This cake is best the day after it's made; the cake softens, in a good way.

Makes one 8½-inch loaf cake

**What You Need—
The Essential Special Equipment**

8½ x 4½-inch loaf pan (or another 6-cup capacity pan; I used a Nordic Ware Classic Fluted Loaf Pan)

Cooking spray

350 grams cold unsalted European-style butter, cubed

250 grams (1¾ cups plus 2 teaspoons) unbleached all-purpose flour

1½ tablespoons milk powder (preferably whole-milk)

1 tablespoon baking powder

1 teaspoon Diamond Crystal kosher salt

5 extra-large eggs

1 tablespoon pure vanilla bean paste or vanilla extract

250 grams (1¼ cups) granulated sugar

---

1. Adjust an oven rack to the center position and preheat the oven to 350°F. Coat the bottom and sides of the loaf pan with cooking spray.

2. Place the butter in a small saucepan or skillet with a light-colored bottom to make golden butter. Warm the butter over medium heat until it melts and begins to bubble, swirling the pan occasionally. Cook the butter, swirling often so it cooks evenly, until it is golden and the milk solids are caramel colored, 3 to 6 minutes. Remove from the heat. Working quickly so the →

butter doesn't continue to cook, weigh out 250 grams (or measure about 1 cup plus 3 tablespoons) of the butter and transfer it to a bowl; set aside to cool to room temperature. (Reserve the remaining butter for another use.)

3. Stir the flour, milk powder, baking powder, and salt together in a medium bowl.

4. Separate the eggs, dropping the yolks into the bowl of a stand mixer and the whites into a small bowl. Set the whites aside.

5. Add the vanilla and 200 grams (1 cup) of the sugar to the bowl with the egg yolks. Place the bowl on the stand, fit with the whisk, and beat on medium speed until the mixture is pale yellow and thick enough so that it creates a ribbon-like pattern that doesn't immediately melt into the surface, 3 to 5 minutes, stopping to scrape down the sides of the bowl with a rubber spatula whenever ingredients are accumulating. With the mixer on medium-low speed, drizzle in the butter, making sure each addition is incorporated before adding more. (At this point, the mixture will look goopy and wrong; it's not. Forge ahead!) Stop the mixer, remove the whisk and bowl from the stand, and wash and dry the whisk. Scrape the batter into a large wide bowl and wash and thoroughly dry the bowl of the stand mixer. Add one-third of the flour to the bowl with the batter and stir with a rubber spatula to combine. Add another third of the flour and fold it in. Add the remaining flour and stir with the rubber spatula until no flour is visible, scraping down the sides and bottom of the bowl.

6. Place the egg whites in the clean stand mixer bowl and fit the mixer with the whisk. Beat the whites on medium speed until they are foamy, 1½ to 2 minutes. Increase the speed to medium-high and mix until soft peaks form, 1½ to 2 minutes. Increase the speed to high, and with the mixer running, gradually add the remaining 50 grams (¼ cup) sugar and mix until the peaks are stiff and shiny but not dry, 1½ to 2 minutes. Stop the mixer, remove the whisk and bowl from the stand, and tap the whisk against the bowl to remove the egg whites.

7. Using the rubber spatula, scoop two-thirds of the egg whites into the bowl with the batter and vigorously stir them into the batter, turning the bowl with one hand while quickly and aggressively stirring the whites into the batter with the other. Add the batter back to the stand mixer bowl with the remaining egg whites and fold them into the batter until no streaks of egg whites remain. Scrape the batter into the prepared pan and smooth the top with an offset spatula.

8. Bake the cake on the center rack of the oven until the top is golden brown and a toothpick inserted into the center comes out clean, 60 to 70 minutes, rotating the cake from front to back halfway through the baking time. Remove the cake from the oven and set it aside to cool slightly.

9. To remove the cake from the pan, place a cake round on top of the pan. Invert the cake onto the round and set aside to cool completely. Wrap the pound cake in plastic wrap and let it rest at room temperature until you're ready to serve it, ideally until the following day. (You can serve the pound cake immediately, but I think it is at its best after it's rested overnight wrapped in plastic wrap.)

Clockwise from the top:
Financiers; Canelés; Madeleines;
Olive Oil Cakes

Madeleines

Madeleines are small, two-bite cakes, baked in scalloped molds. I learned to make madeleines at my first pastry job, at Michael's restaurant in Santa Monica, working under pastry chef Jimmy Brinkley. Jimmy's madeleines had all the tells of a perfect madeleine: a golden, slightly crunchy exterior; a moist interior; the lovely, mild flavors of honey and vanilla; and, most important, a big hump on the top (nonscalloped) side of each madeleine. But I decided that in the pursuit of perfection, I owed it to myself and to my readers to make the little cakes even richer than they already were, and I did. (Thank you, Michel Suas, for all your madeleine expertise.) These are best served warm, straight from the oven. They begin to stale immediately. The batter keeps, refrigerated, for a few days, so you can bake it off in batches to enjoy them fresh from the oven over that period.

You will need a madeleine mold, preferably one made of stainless steel, and not nonstick or silicone, which won't give you the color or crust on the exterior that you want. Using a convection oven is the only surefire way to achieve the desired hump on each madeleine that is the telltale sign of success. I've given you baking instructions for both convection and conventional ovens.

Makes about 48 madeleines

**What You Need—
The Essential Special Equipment**

Stainless steel madeleine mold

Large disposable piping bag (optional)

Cooking spray

452 grams (4 sticks) cold unsalted butter, cubed

255 grams (2 cups plus 2 tablespoons) unbleached pastry flour

2 tablespoons milk powder (preferably whole milk)

1½ teaspoons baking powder

¾ teaspoon Diamond Crystal kosher salt

5 extra-large eggs

1 extra-large egg yolk

48 grams (3 tablespoons) mild-flavored honey, such as clover or wildflower

2 tablespoons pure vanilla bean paste or vanilla extract

1 large lemon

212.5 grams (1 cup plus 1 tablespoon) granulated sugar

42 grams (3 tablespoons plus 1 teaspoon packed) dark brown sugar

---

1. Place the butter in a small saucepan or skillet with a light-colored bottom to make golden butter. Warm the butter over medium heat until it melts and begins to bubble, swirling the pan occasionally. Cook the butter, swirling often so it cooks evenly, until it is golden and the milk solids are caramel colored, 3 to 6 minutes. Remove from the heat. Working quickly so the butter doesn't continue to cook, weigh out 283 grams (or measure 1⅓ cups) of →

butter, making sure to include the milk solids; transfer to a bowl and set aside to cool. (Reserve the remaining butter for another use.)

2. Sift the flour, milk powder, baking powder, and salt together in a medium bowl. Sift the ingredients a second time into another bowl or onto a sheet of parchment paper.

3. Combine the whole eggs, egg yolk, honey, and vanilla in a medium bowl. Use a fine Microplane to grate the zest (the bright-yellow outer layer) of half of the lemon into the bowl and whisk to combine. (Reserve the lemon for another use.)

4. Combine the granulated sugar and brown sugar in a large bowl and stir with a whisk to combine. Add the egg mixture and stir with the whisk to combine. Add the flour mixture and stir with a rubber spatula until almost no flour is visible. Add the golden butter and stir with the spatula to combine, scraping down the sides and bottom of the bowl. Cover the bowl with plastic wrap and refrigerate until it is chilled, at least 3 hours and up to 3 days. (Chilling the batter allows you to pipe it into the molds and contributes to the desired hump in the finished madeleines.)

5. Adjust an oven rack to the top third of the oven and preheat the oven to 425°F (for both convection and conventional ovens). Coat the madeleine mold with cooking spray.

6. Remove the bowl of batter from the refrigerator; uncover but reserve the plastic wrap. If you're using a piping bag to fill the molds, place the bag in a tall container or glass so that the bag flops over the top of the container (this makes it easier to fill the piping bag). Spoon the batter into the bag and cut a ⅝-inch hole in the tip of the bag. Pipe or spoon the batter into the prepared mold, filling each one three-quarters full. Re-cover the bowl and return it to the refrigerator.

7. Place the madeleine mold on a baking sheet and place it in the center rack of the oven.

8. **If using a convection oven,** bake for 3 minutes. Reduce the oven temperature to 350°F and bake until the edges are deep golden brown and the tops are no longer wet looking, 5 to 7 minutes, rotating the baking sheet from front to back halfway through the baking time so the madeleines bake evenly.

9. **If using a conventional oven,** immediately reduce the oven temperature to 350°F and bake until the edges are deep golden brown and the tops are no longer wet looking, 8 to 10 minutes, rotating the baking sheet from front to back halfway through the baking time so the madeleines bake evenly.

10. Remove the madeleines from the oven. Run a small knife around the edges of each madeleine to loosen them and flip the pan to release them. Place the madeleines scalloped-side down on a serving platter. Serve warm.

11. Return the oven temperature to 425°F.

12. Wash and dry the madeleine mold and place it in the refrigerator to cool to room temperature. Repeat with the remaining batter, spraying the molds with cooking spray and filling in the same way. Bake according to the instructions above for convection or conventional oven. (How many batches you make will depend on the molds you use.)

Financiers

If I were on the proverbial desert island with only one sweet treat for the rest of my life, I think *financiers,* small French almond cakes, might be my first choice. They have a delicate outer crust, contrasted with insides that are soft and chewy, made with egg whites and ground almonds, and redolent of brown butter. Traditionally, *financiers* are baked in a three-bite rectangular mold that resembles a gold bar, thus the name. I left that mold behind, so I guess I should have left the name behind, too. But for me, a light, chewy, French almond cake will always be a *financier.*

Financiers are traditionally made with ground almonds, as they are here; you can also make them with hazelnuts. I infuse the brown butter in this recipe with fresh rosemary, which is a delicious addition to these classic little cakes. I borrowed the idea from Anna Higham, the pastry chef at one of my favorite London restaurants, the Lyle. (See photo page 224.)

Makes eight 4-inch round financiers

**What You Need—
The Essential Special Equipment**

8 (4-inch) fluted tart pans with removable bottoms (or flan rings)

Cooking spray

3 extra-large egg whites

1 teaspoon pure vanilla bean paste or vanilla extract

1 teaspoon pure almond extract

150 grams unblanched almond meal (150 grams/1½ cups meal or 1 cup skin-on whole almonds)

75 grams (⅔ cup) powdered sugar

75 grams (⅓ cup) demerara sugar

3 tablespoons potato starch

¾ teaspoon Diamond Crystal kosher salt

150 grams (1 stick plus about 3 tablespoons) unsalted butter, cubed

10 grams fresh rosemary sprigs (about 3 medium sprigs)

---

1. Adjust an oven rack to the center position and preheat the oven to 350°F. Line a large baking sheet with parchment paper. Spray the insides of the tart pans (or flan rings) with cooking spray and place them on the baking sheet.

2. Whisk the egg whites, vanilla, and almond extract in a small bowl.

3. Combine the almond meal, powdered sugar, flour, and salt in the bowl of a stand mixer. (If you're using almonds instead of almond meal, grind them in a food processor along with 2 tablespoons of the total powdered sugar to a fine meal. Then combine that mixture with the remaining powdered sugar and flour in the bowl of the stand mixer.) Put the bowl on the stand, fit the mixer with the paddle, and mix on low speed for about 15 seconds to combine the ingredients. With the mixer on low speed, slowly drizzle in the egg white mixture and mix until the ingredients are combined. Turn off the mixer.

4. Place the butter in a small saucepan or skillet with a light-colored bottom to make brown butter. Add the rosemary and warm the butter with the rosemary over medium heat until the butter melts and begins to bubble, swirling the pan occasionally. Cook the butter and rosemary, swirling often so it cooks evenly, until the butter is caramel colored and the milk solids are the color of coffee grounds, 4 to 8 minutes. Remove from the heat, and remove and discard the rosemary. Working quickly so the butter doesn't continue to brown, turn the mixer on medium speed and add the butter, including the browned bits, to the mixer bowl, pouring it down the side of the bowl so the warm butter doesn't hit the paddle. Continue to mix for about 1 minute until the butter is combined. Stop the mixer, remove the paddle and bowl, and clean them with the rubber spatula.

5. Using a measuring cup or scoop, fill each mold with 61 grams (¼ cup) of batter, filling them to within ⅜ inch of the top.

6. Place the baking sheet on the center rack of the oven and bake the financiers until the outer edges are golden brown and the centers are firm to the touch and no longer wet looking, for 25 to 30 minutes, rotating the baking sheet front to back halfway through baking time so the financiers brown evenly. Remove the financiers from the oven and set aside for about 5 minutes until they are cool enough to handle.

7. To remove the financiers from the tart pans, run the tip of a paring knife around the inside of the tart pans (or flan rings) to release any stuck bits. One at a time, push up on the bottoms of the pans to release them from the pans. (If you used flan rings, lift off the rings.)

Canelés

Canelé means "fluted" in French, and these pastries, from the Bordeaux region, are named for the deep fluted molds, shaped almost like a giant thimble or mini-Bundt cake, in which they're baked. They are essentially a custard, flavored with rum and vanilla, baked just about forever (2 hours!) so that the outside forms a thick, chewy, caramelized crust, while the inside remains moist and custardy. Traditionally, the molds were coated with beeswax to prevent the custard from sticking and to promote a shiny, crunchy exterior. I have fine results with cooking spray.

I recommend you use classic copper molds, which ensure the *canelés* will have the proper mahogany-like exterior. These molds are not inexpensive, but once you start making canelés, I'm sure you'll want to make them again and again. The batter for these pastries is as easy to make as crepe or pancake batter. I suggest you invest in at least 12 molds, to bake off this recipe in two batches. The batter needs to be prepared a day in advance to allow the flour in the batter to absorb the milk. (See photo page 224.)

Makes about 24 canelés

What You Need—
The Essential Special Equipment

12 or 24 copper canelé molds

Cooking spray

1.04 kilograms (4¼ cups) whole milk

57 grams (4 tablespoons) unsalted butter, cubed

5 extra-large egg yolks

1 extra-large egg

400 grams (2 cups) granulated sugar

280 grams (2 cups) unbleached all-purpose flour

1 tablespoon pure vanilla bean paste or vanilla extract

2 tablespoons rum (or brandy)

½ teaspoon Diamond Crystal kosher salt

1. Combine 612 grams (2½ cups) of the milk and the butter in a medium saucepan and warm over medium-high heat, stirring occasionally to prevent the milk from scalding, until the butter is melted and the mixture comes to a boil. Remove from the heat and set aside to cool slightly.

2. Combine the egg yolks and whole egg in a large bowl and whisk to break up the yolks. Add the sugar and stir with the whisk to combine. Add the flour and stir with a spatula to combine. Add 184 grams (¾ cup) of the remaining milk and stir with the whisk until no lumps remain. Add the remaining 245 grams (1 cup) milk, the vanilla, rum, and salt and stir with the whisk to combine.

3. Fill a medium saucepan with water. Place the bowl on top of the saucepan. (The weighted saucepan anchors the bowl, so it remains stable when you whisk ingredients in it.) Add the warm milk and butter mixture in a slow, steady stream, whisking constantly to prevent the warm liquid from cooking the eggs. Place a fine-mesh sieve over a large pitcher or bowl and strain the batter into the container. Set aside to cool to room temperature. Cover the pitcher or bowl and let the batter rest in the refrigerator for 24 to 48 hours.

4. When you're ready to bake the canelés, adjust an oven rack to the center position and preheat the oven to 500°F.

5. Coat the molds with cooking spray and place them on your work surface. Remove the batter from the refrigerator and stir thoroughly with a rubber spatula to reincorporate the ingredients.

6. Pour 70 grams (about ¼ cup) of the batter into the molds, filling them to about ¼ inch from the top. (Alternatively, use a ¼-cup measuring cup to scoop the batter into the molds.) Place the molds on a large baking sheet, leaving at least 1½ inches between them.

7. Place the baking sheet with the canelés on the center rack of the oven and bake for 10 minutes. Reduce the oven temperature to 375°F and bake until the tops are very dark brown, for another 55 to 65 minutes, rotating the baking sheet front to back halfway through the baking time so the canelés bake evenly. The best way to test for doneness is to sacrifice a canelé; remove it from the oven and set it aside for about 5 minutes until it's cool enough to handle. Invert the mold to remove the canelé. If it is deep brown all over, remove the remaining molds. Otherwise, cook the canelés for another 5 to 10 minutes. Remove the baking sheet from the oven and set aside for the canelés to cool for 5 or 10 minutes before inverting the molds to release them. Cool the canelés for at least 30 minutes before serving.

8. Repeat, baking the remaining canelés in the same way.

Olive Oil Cakes

Olive oil cake, a simple sponge cake made with olive oil instead of butter, is a Tuscan classic. I first had it about thirty years ago, while visiting a Tuscan olive oil estate with my friend Rolando Beramendi, whose import company Manicaretti is my source for many of my favorite Italian products. At this estate, where we were staying, they served olive oil cake for breakfast. I had never heard of such a thing, but it was love at first bite: so delicate and simple, and the flavor of the olive oil really came through. I must have eaten the entire cake, one little sliver at a time. It's that kind of cake.

As a home baker, you're going to love making this as much as eating it, because the batter is just so easy and forgiving. I bake it in decorative tea cake molds. For me, the best part of these is the delicate, golden, crunchy crust, and by making them small I get more of that crust. You can use a mold as small as 2-tablespoon capacity or as large as a 4-inch removable-bottom tart pan. (See photo page 224.)

Makes 24 to 36 small cakes

**What You Need—
The Essential Special Equipment**

Small decorative molds (2-tablespoon to ¼-cup capacity) or tart pans with removable bottoms (I used Nordic Ware Bundt Charms, which have a 2-tablespoon capacity)

Cooking spray

247.5 grams (2 cups plus 2 tablespoons) unbleached pastry flour (or all-purpose flour)

300 grams (1½ cups) granulated sugar

1 teaspoon Diamond Crystal kosher salt

½ teaspoon baking soda

½ teaspoon baking powder

367.5 grams (1½ cups) whole milk

337.5 grams (1½ cups) extra-virgin olive oil

3 extra-large eggs

1 medium orange

2 tablespoons chopped fresh rosemary

1. Sift the flour, sugar, salt, baking soda, and baking powder together into a large wide bowl. Whisk the milk, olive oil, and eggs together in a separate large bowl.

2. Create a well in the center of the dry ingredients with your hands. Pour half of the wet ingredients into the well and use a whisk to draw the dry ingredients from the edges to the center into a thick paste. Add the remaining wet ingredients and whisk to combine. (If the batter is lumpy, pour it through a fine-mesh sieve to strain out the lumps.) Using a fine Microplane, grate the zest (the bright-orange outer layer) of the orange into

the bowl. (Reserve the orange for another use.) Add the rosemary and stir to incorporate it. Transfer the batter to a pitcher or another vessel that is easy to pour from.

3. Adjust an oven rack to the center position. Put the molds on a large baking sheet. Place the baking sheet in the oven and preheat the molds and the oven to 350°F for at least 20 minutes.

4. Remove the baking sheet from the oven. Working quickly so they don't cool and taking care not to burn yourself, coat the molds with cooking spray. Pour the batter into the molds. (Alternatively, use a measuring cup or scoop to fill the molds to the rim with batter.)

5. Return the baking sheet with the molds to the center rack of the oven and bake the cakes until they are deep golden brown and firm to the touch, 25 to 35 minutes, rotating the baking sheet front to back halfway through the baking time so the cakes brown evenly.

6. Remove the baking sheet from the oven and gently bang the molds on the countertop to loosen the cakes. Invert the cakes onto the cold baking sheet and turn them upright.

7. Repeat to bake more batches.

Sticky Toffee Pudding

This is not a pudding in the American sense of the word; it's a dark, moist, and sticky cake drenched in molasses-sweetened toffee sauce—but it's English, and English desserts are referred to as pudding. The cake contains relatively little sugar; it gets most of its sweetness from the toffee sauce that is poured over it. It is the creation of Mozza's former, longtime executive pastry chef Dahlia Narvaez, who put it on the menu at Chi Spacca, topped with a scoop of vanilla ice cream and candied pecans. Dahlia referenced several sticky toffee pudding recipes, including one of my old recipes, and applied different elements of each to come up with this ultimate version. The cake gets its signature stickiness from dates, which Dahlia poaches in tea, and is sweetened with a combination of molasses and dark muscovado sugar, all of which add some complexity to this sweet dessert. While the classic version is drenched in the toffee sauce, it's too sweet for my taste, so I pour a touch of the sauce over the cake and serve the rest on the side for people to spoon over their portion.

Makes one 6-inch Bundt cake

What You Need—
The Essential Special Equipment

6-cup capacity Bundt pan (I used a Nordic Ware Heritage Bundt Pan)

Cooking spray

For the Cake

25 grams (¼ cup) walnut halves

225 grams Medjool dates (about 15)

1 teaspoon baking soda

1 tablespoon black tea leaves or 1 tea bag (English breakfast or another black tea)

2 extra-large eggs

1 tablespoon pure vanilla bean paste or vanilla extract

149 grams (1 cup plus 1 tablespoon) unbleached all-purpose flour

84 grams (6 tablespoons) unsalted butter

50 grams (¼ cup packed) dark muscovado sugar (or dark brown sugar)

37.5 grams (3 tablespoons) granulated sugar

40 grams (2 tablespoons) unsulphured molasses

2 teaspoons baking powder

1 teaspoon Diamond Crystal kosher salt

1 teaspoon ground cinnamon

¼ teaspoon ground cloves

For the Sauce

300 grams (1½ cups packed) dark muscovado sugar (or dark brown sugar)

210 grams (¾ cup plus 2 tablespoons) heavy cream

154 grams (1 stick plus 3 tablespoons) cold unsalted butter, cubed

20 grams (1 tablespoon) unsulphured molasses

¼ teaspoon Diamond Crystal kosher salt

3 tablespoons whiskey

For the Whipped Cream

360 grams (1½ cups) heavy cream

116 grams (½ cup) crème fraîche (or 122 grams/½ cup sour cream) →

Sticky Toffee Pudding (continued)

1. To make the cake, adjust an oven rack to the center position and preheat the oven to 325°F.

2. Spread the walnuts on a baking sheet and toast them on the center rack of the oven until they're lightly browned and fragrant, 8 to 10 minutes, shaking the baking sheet and rotating it front to back halfway through the baking time so the walnuts toast evenly. Remove the walnuts from the oven. (If you think the nuts are on the verge of being overtoasted, transfer them to a plate so they don't continue to cook from the residual heat of the pan.) Set the walnuts aside until they're cool enough to touch, then coarsely chop them.

3. Increase the oven temperature to 350°F.

4. Coat the Bundt pan with cooking spray.

5. Make 1 cup of strong black tea and discard the tea bag or tea leaves. Pour the tea into a small heatproof bowl. Add the dates and set aside to soak until the tea cools to room temperature or for at least 15 minutes. Remove the dates (reserving the tea). Remove and discard the pits and chop the dates.

6. Whisk the eggs and vanilla together in a small bowl. Sift the flour into a large bowl.

7. Put the butter in a stand mixer fitted with the paddle and beat on medium speed until it is soft but still cold, 3 to 4 minutes, stopping to scrape down the sides and bottom of the bowl with a rubber spatula whenever butter is accumulating. Add the muscovado sugar, granulated sugar, and molasses and beat on medium speed until the mixture lightens in color, 3 to 4 minutes, scraping down the bowl as needed. Add the baking powder, salt, cinnamon, and cloves and beat on low speed for about 15 seconds to distribute the additions. With the mixer on low speed, drizzle the egg/vanilla mixture into the bowl, making sure the addition is incorporated and stopping to scrape down the bowl before adding more. Once all the eggs are incorporated, stop the mixer and scrape down the bowl and paddle. Add the flour and mix on low speed until very little flour is visible, about 15 seconds. Add the toasted walnuts and mix on low speed for about 15 seconds to distribute them. Stop the mixer, remove the bowl and paddle from the stand, and clean them with the spatula. Add the dates and the tea they were poached in (you may want to add the tea gradually to make it easier to integrate into the batter) and stir with a rubber spatula to combine, scraping

the bowl from the bottom up to release any ingredients from the bottom of the bowl. (Don't be discouraged that this batter looks broken. That's the nature of it; the cake will be fine.)

8. Scrape the batter into the prepared Bundt pan and smooth out the top with an offset spatula.

9. Bake the cake on the center rack of the oven until it begins to pull away from the sides of the pan and springs back when touched, and a toothpick inserted into the center comes out clean, 40 to 50 minutes.

10. While the cake is baking, to make the sauce, combine the muscovado sugar, cream, butter, molasses, and salt in a medium saucepan and heat over low heat, stirring with a silicone spatula until the butter is melted. Remove from the heat and stir in the whiskey.

11. Remove the cake from the oven. Use a skewer or toothpick to poke holes in the cake, spacing the holes about 1 inch apart. Spoon ¼ cup of the sauce over the cake and let it sit for 15 minutes to absorb the liquid.

12. Meanwhile, to make the whipped cream, pour the cream into a stand mixer fitted with the whisk and whip the cream on low speed for about 1 minute until it thickens enough not to spatter. Increase the speed to medium-high and whip until soft peaks form, 2 to 3 minutes. Add the crème fraîche and whip on medium-low speed until medium peaks form, about 1 minute.

13. Invert the cake onto a plate and drizzle ¼ cup of the remaining sauce over the top. Serve the cake with the whipped cream and the remaining sauce on the side.

Bread Pudding

This is obviously not a simple cake like the others in this chapter, but it had to go in the book somewhere, and this seemed as good a place as any since, though not a cake, it is a simple (or at least homey) dessert. There are several steps involved, but none of them is technically challenging. I assume that bread pudding came about to use up leftover bread, but that's not the case with this recipe, which calls for so much bread (3 pounds) that unless you own or work at a bread bakery, you are very unlikely to have it lying around. Unlike many bread puddings, which are mushy and one-dimensional, this one has a variety of textures and components. The most striking textural component comes from the bread itself. The loaves are cut in half and then the insides pulled out in large, irregularly shaped hunks.

This is not a "use any kind of bread" recipe. You must start with quality, crusty, country-style bread. It's okay if the bread is day-old, if it's soft enough that you can pull the insides out from the crust. The hunks are toasted in the oven until they're golden brown and crisp, then tossed in butter and cinnamon-sugar, creating what are essentially cinnamon toast croutons. Because the hunks are torn in irregular shapes, they crisp up differently, and some protrude from the surface of the pudding and get crunchy. I added another layer of flavor to the pudding by putting caramel on the bottom of the dish.

You can eat this still warm from the oven, but I like it best chilled overnight and reheated the next day. This gives the caramel on the bottom a chance to thicken up. It's important that you use a baking dish similar in size and volume to the one used here to give you the correct surface area, and thus the correct proportions of caramel to bread and custard. Look for plump, moist raisins, ideally from a farmers' market. Because of the custard, this needs to be stored in the refrigerator.

Makes one 12-inch oval bread pudding

**What You Need—
The Essential Special Equipment**

8½ x 12¾-inch oval baking dish (or another shallow 10-cup capacity baking dish)

Pastry brush

For the Raisins and Caramel

160 grams (1 cup) golden raisins

¾ cup rum (or whiskey)

300 grams (1½ cups) granulated sugar

For the Bread

1.35 kilograms (3 pounds) crusty country-style bread

565 grams (5 sticks) unsalted butter, cubed

100 grams (½ cup) granulated sugar

2 teaspoons ground cinnamon

For the Custard

2 extra-large eggs

2 extra-large egg yolks

75 grams (¼ cup plus 2 tablespoons) granulated sugar

2 tablespoons pure vanilla bean paste or vanilla extract

1 teaspoon Diamond Crystal kosher salt

735 grams (3 cups) whole milk

720 grams (3 cups) heavy cream

2 cinnamon sticks

For the Finishing

½ teaspoon ground cinnamon

¼ teaspoon grated nutmeg

¼ teaspoon anise seed

1. To prepare the raisins, combine them with the rum in a small saucepan and bring to a boil over high heat. Remove from the heat, cover the pan, and set aside to absorb the liquid and come to room temperature. Drain the raisins and discard the alcohol (or reserve it for another culinary use).

2. To make the caramel layer, have your baking dish handy.

3. Put the sugar in a heavy-bottomed, light-colored medium saucepan. Add 120 grams (½ cup) water and stir with your finger to combine. Bring to a boil over medium-high heat without stirring, using a wet pastry brush to remove any sugar granules that may be stuck to the sides. Continue boiling, tilting, and swirling the pan so the sugar cooks evenly, until it is a dark mahogany color and is just beginning to smoke, 9 to 12 minutes. Remove the pan from the heat and pour the caramel into the baking dish. Tilt the dish so the caramel coats about 1 inch up the sides. Set aside for the caramel to set while you prepare the rest of the bread pudding.

4. To prepare the bread, adjust the oven racks so one is in the top third and the other is in the bottom third of the oven and preheat the oven to 350°F. Line two large baking sheets with parchment paper. Locate a roasting pan that the baking dish will fit inside of with at least a few inches of space around the dish and set both aside.

5. Cut the bread loaves in half through the top and pull the bread out of the crust in 2- to 3-inch chunks. You want the bread chunks to be consistent in size but not in shape; their beauty is in their irregularity. (Reserve the crusts for another use, such as to make bread crumbs.)

6. Lay the bread chunks in an even layer on the baking sheets and put a baking sheet on each rack in the oven and bake until they are crunchy (but not hard) in places and soft in others, 12 to 15 minutes, switching racks and →

rotating the baking sheets front to back halfway through the baking time so the bread toasts evenly. Remove the bread from the oven. Leave the oven on.

7. Place the butter in a small saucepan or skillet with a light-colored bottom to make golden butter. Warm the butter over medium heat until it melts and begins to bubble, swirling the pan occasionally. Cook the butter, swirling often so it cooks evenly, until it is golden and the milk solids are caramel colored, 3 to 6 minutes. Remove from the heat and pour the butter into a large wide bowl. Add the sugar and cinnamon and stir to combine.

8. Add the toasted bread chunks to the bowl with the butter and toss with your hands for 1 or 2 minutes to coat the bread with the butter and cinnamon-sugar. (The bread will not absorb all the butter; excess butter will pool at the bottom of the bowl.) Lift the bread chunks from the bowl and place them on a large baking sheet. Clean the bowl, reserving the leftover butter for another use where cinnamon and sugar are welcome or discarding it. Return the bread to the bowl.

9. To make the custard, whisk the whole eggs, egg yolks, sugar, vanilla, and salt together in a large bowl. Fill a medium saucepan with water. Place the bowl on top of the saucepan. (The weighted saucepan anchors the bowl, so it remains stable when you whisk ingredients in it.)

10. Combine the milk, cream, and cinnamon sticks in a large saucepan and bring to a simmer over medium heat. Remove from the heat and discard the cinnamon sticks.

11. Slowly add the hot milk and cream to the bowl with the egg mixture, stirring constantly with a whisk and adding it gradually to prevent the hot cream and milk from cooking the eggs. Set aside for about 20 minutes to infuse the custard with the cinnamon. Pass the custard through a fine-mesh sieve to strain out any remaining bits of cinnamon sticks and any lumps that may have formed in the custard.

12. Pour 3 cups of the custard over the bread, toss gently, and set aside for about 5 minutes, tossing occasionally so the bread absorbs the custard evenly.

13. To finish the bread pudding, stir the cinnamon, nutmeg, and anise seed together in a small bowl. Bring a kettle of water to a boil to fill a roasting pan and make a bain-marie, or water bath. →

Bread Pudding (continued)

14. Place the baking dish with the caramel in front of you; pour in 1 cup of the custard and scatter ¼ cup of the raisins over the caramel. Building the bread pudding in three layers, lay one-third of the bread chunks in the dish, pour in one-third of the remaining custard, and scatter ¼ cup of raisins over the bread. Build a second layer using half of the remaining bread chunks and half of the remaining custard and scatter ¼ cup of raisins over the top. Add the remaining bread chunks, mounding them so the center of the pudding has a slightly domed shape, and pour over the bread as much of the remaining custard to fill the baking dish to ¼ inch from the top (discard any remaining custard). Scatter the remaining raisins and the spice mixture over the top of the pudding and place the bread pudding in the roasting pan.

15. Pull out the center rack of the oven and place the roasting pan on it. Carefully pour enough boiling water into the roasting pan to come halfway up the sides of the baking dish, taking care not to get any water on the bread pudding. Gently slide the oven rack back in and bake the bread pudding until it is set around the edges but is still slightly runny in the center, 1 hour 20 minutes to 1 hour 30 minutes. To test for doneness, squeeze on a chunk of bread; if liquid comes out, it needs more time.

16. Increase the oven temperature to 450°F and bake the pudding until the top is well browned and crispy, another 10 to 15 minutes.

17. Remove the roasting pan from the oven and let the bread pudding cool to room temperature in the bain-marie. Remove the bread pudding from the bain-marie and dry the bottom of the baking dish. Refrigerate the bread pudding overnight, uncovered, to chill. (You can serve the bread pudding still slightly warm from the oven, but I think it is at its best reheated after it has been chilled.)

18. To serve, adjust an oven rack to the center position and preheat the oven to 350°F.

19. Remove the bread pudding from the refrigerator and place it in the oven until it is warmed through but not piping hot, 30 to 45 minutes. Remove from the oven and serve slightly warm.

Ginger Stout Cake

If you were to put a bunch of American bakers in a room and ask them to talk about gingerbread (or ginger cake), they would agree unanimously that Claudia Fleming's ginger cake is the one to beat. Claudia is one of the great bakers of our time; she made her mark as the pastry chef at Gramercy Tavern in New York City in the 1990s. Everything she bakes is great, but this ginger cake is exceptional: It's super moist, dark in color, with a strong ginger flavor—everything I want in a ginger cake. I've made it for years. For this book, I knew the best I could do as far as a ginger cake recipe was to pick up the phone and ask Claudia for hers. I did, and thankfully, she shared it with us here.

This recipe calls for a lot of fresh ginger; there's no replacement for that flavor but it's a pain to grate. To grate fresh ginger, use the side of an ordinary spoon to peel it, then grate it on a fine Microplane. When it becomes so fibrous that it's difficult to grate, stop grating, chop off and discard the fibrous end, and resume grating. I like to serve this with vanilla ice cream or whipped cream to complement the intense flavor of the cake. I bake it in a tall decorative pudding mold. If you bake it in a shallower mold or pan, the baking time will be shorter, so pay attention to the indicators for doneness.

Makes 1 tall 5-inch round cake

What You Need—
The Essential Special Equipment

5-inch-wide (8-inch-tall) decorative pudding mold (or another 10-cup capacity baking mold or pan)

Cooking spray

For the Cake

315 grams (1⅓ cups) Guinness stout

427 grams (1⅓ cups) unsulphured molasses

2 teaspoons baking soda

373 grams (2⅔ cups) unbleached all-purpose flour

2 tablespoons plus 2 teaspoons ground ginger

2 teaspoons baking powder

1 teaspoon ground cinnamon

1 teaspoon Diamond Crystal kosher salt

¼ teaspoon ground cloves

¼ teaspoon freshly grated nutmeg

¼ teaspoon freshly ground cardamom

4 extra-large eggs

137.5 grams (½ cup plus 3 tablespoons) granulated sugar

137.5 grams (½ cup plus 3 tablespoons packed) dark brown sugar

1 tablespoon plus 1 teaspoon pure vanilla bean paste or vanilla extract

225 grams (1 cup) olive oil

36 grams (¼ cup) grated peeled fresh ginger (grated on a fine Microplane), including the ginger juices

For the Whipped Cream (optional)

360 grams (1½ cups) heavy cream

116 grams (½ cup) crème fraîche (or 122 grams/½ cup sour cream) →

1. To make the cake, adjust an oven rack to the center position and preheat the oven to 350°F. Coat the mold (or pan) generously with cooking spray.

2. Combine the stout and molasses in a large saucepan and bring to a boil over high heat, stirring occasionally with a whisk to combine. Remove from the heat, add the baking soda, and whisk to combine. (The liquid will foam up when you add the baking soda, but the foam will subside as it cools.) Set aside to cool to room temperature.

3. Put the flour, ground ginger, baking powder, cinnamon, salt, cloves, nutmeg, and cardamom in a large wide bowl and stir with a whisk to combine.

4. Put the eggs, granulated sugar, brown sugar, and vanilla in a medium bowl and stir with a whisk to combine. Gradually add the olive oil, whisking to combine. Add the stout mixture and whisk to combine.

5. Create a well in the center of the flour mixture with your hands. Pour half of the stout/egg mixture into the well and use a whisk to draw the flour from the edges to the center into a thick paste. Add the remaining stout/egg mixture and the grated fresh ginger (and juices) and stir with the whisk to combine.

6. Pour the batter into the prepared mold (or pan) and place on a baking sheet.

7. Place the baking sheet on the center rack of the oven and bake until the cake springs back when pressed gently with your finger, 1 hour to 1 hour 40 minutes (the time will vary depending on the pan you use), rotating the cake front to back halfway through the baking time so it bakes evenly. (Do not open the oven before 50 minutes, or it may cause the cake to cave in.) Remove the cake from the oven and set aside to cool.

8. If you are serving this with whipped cream, pour the cream into a stand mixer fitted with the whisk and whip on low speed for about 1 minute until it thickens enough not to spatter. Increase the speed to medium-high and whip until soft peaks form, 2 to 3 minutes. Add the crème fraîche and whip on medium-low speed until medium peaks form, about 1 minute.

9. To remove the cake from the mold, run the tip of a paring knife around the inside edge of the mold, sliding it down as deep as possible to help to release the cake. Invert the cake onto a serving platter. Serve warm or at room temperature by itself, or with vanilla ice cream or whipped cream.

Clockwise from the top:
Basque Cheesecake;
Cheesecake with
Graham Cracker Crust;
New York Cheesecake

Cheesecake with Graham Cracker Crust

I've included three recipes for cheesecake in this book: New York Cheesecake (page 250), Basque Cheesecake (page 252), and this classic cheesecake with graham cracker crust. This is the cheesecake that I grew up eating, and baking: smooth and creamy, topped with a bright white layer of sour cream. I give you a recipe for homemade graham crackers to make the crust, but if you want to skip that step, you have my permission to use store-bought graham crackers instead. Professional bakers and home bakers alike are always tinkering with this classic, trying to tweak this or that to make the ultimate version, while still staying within the pretty simple boundaries of what a cheesecake is. I'm guilty of the same. I added mascarpone, which is a fresh creamy Italian cheese, like a softer, more flavorful version of cream cheese. And I top the cheesecake with crème fraîche, the more flavorful French version of sour cream.

You need to use Philadelphia brand cream cheese (or something similar) for this, one that comes in a block, wrapped in foil, not an artisanal product that comes in a tub or from a cheese shop. I'm sure those are delicious, but they're not what you want for baking.

Makes one 9-inch cheesecake

**What You Need—
The Essential Special Equipment**

9-inch springform pan

Cooking spray

Heavy-duty aluminum foil

Roasting pan large enough to hold the springform pan with a few inches around it

For the Crust

125 grams Spiced Graham Crackers (page 165; or quality store-bought graham crackers)

25 grams (2 tablespoons) granulated sugar

¼ teaspoon Diamond Crystal kosher salt

¼ teaspoon ground cinnamon (if you are using store-bought graham crackers)

42 grams (3 tablespoons) unsalted butter, melted

For the Filling

4 extra-large egg yolks

700 grams (24 ounces) cream cheese, cubed, at room temperature

200 grams (1 cup) granulated sugar

200 grams (¾ cup plus 2 heaping tablespoons) mascarpone cheese, at room temperature

1 teaspoon pure vanilla bean paste or vanilla extract

½ teaspoon Diamond Crystal kosher salt

348 grams (1½ cups) crème fraîche (or 336 grams/1½ cups sour cream) →

1. To make the crust, adjust an oven rack to the center position and preheat the oven to 350°F. Spray the bottom and sides of the springform pan with cooking spray and line a large baking sheet with parchment paper.

2. Break the graham crackers into pieces, place them in a food processor, and grind the crackers to fine crumbs. Turn the crumbs out into a large bowl. Add the sugar, salt, and cinnamon (if using) and stir to combine. Add the melted butter and stir with your hands to combine and break up any lumps.

3. Transfer the crumbs to the prepared pan and spread them over the bottom. Use the bottom of a measuring cup to gently press the crumbs in an even layer to line the bottom of the pan. Place the pan on the prepared baking sheet and bake the crust on the center rack of the oven until it is firm to the touch, 12 to 15 minutes, rotating it front to back halfway through the baking time so it bakes evenly. Remove the crust from the oven and set it aside to cool to room temperature.

4. Reduce the oven temperature to 300°F.

5. When the pan is cool, wrap the bottom tightly in a doubled sheet of heavy-duty aluminum foil. Locate a roasting pan that the springform will fit inside with at least 2 inches of space around. Place the springform pan inside the roasting pan. Bring a kettle of water to a boil to fill the roasting pan and make a bain-marie, or water bath.

6. To prepare the filling, whisk the egg yolks together in a small bowl.

7. Put the cream cheese in a stand mixer fitted with the paddle and beat on medium-high speed until the cream cheese is soft, 2 to 3 minutes, stopping to scrape down the bottom and sides of the bowl and the paddle as needed. Add the sugar and beat until the mixture is light and fluffy, about 1 minute. Add the mascarpone, vanilla, and salt and beat for about 30 seconds to combine the ingredients. With the mixer on medium speed, drizzle in the egg yolks, stopping to scrape down the bowl and making sure the addition is incorporated before adding more. Stop the mixer, remove the paddle and bowl, and clean them with the rubber spatula.

8. Pour the batter into the crust and smooth out the top with an offset spatula. Set the springform pan inside the roasting pan. Pull out the center oven rack and place the roasting pan on it. Carefully pour enough boiling

water into the roasting pan to come halfway up the sides of the springform pan, taking care not to get any water on the cheesecake. Cover the roasting pan tightly with aluminum foil and pierce the foil in several places with a sharp knife for steam to escape.

9. Gently slide the oven rack back in and bake the cheesecake for 1 hour. Gently pull out the oven rack and carefully lift a corner of the foil to release steam. Put the foil back down on the roasting pan. Rotate the roasting pan front to back and slide the oven rack back in. Bake the cheesecake for another 30 to 60 minutes. To check for doneness, peel back the foil, being mindful of the steam that will arise, and gently shake the springform pan; if it is done, the edges will be set, and the center will jiggle slightly. Remove the roasting pan from the oven and set aside for about 15 minutes for the cheesecake to cool slightly in the bain-marie. Leave the oven on.

10. While the cheesecake is cooling, put the crème fraîche in a small bowl and whisk to thin it slightly.

11. With the cheesecake still in the bain-marie, remove the foil. Pour the crème fraîche on top. Gently smooth it out with an offset spatula. Return the roasting pan with the cheesecake to the oven, uncovered, to bake for 10 minutes to set the crème fraîche.

12. Remove the roasting pan from the oven and let the cheesecake cool to room temperature in the bain-marie. Remove the cheesecake from the bain-marie and dry the bottom of the springform pan. Remove the foil. Cup your hands around the sides of the pan to confirm that the cheesecake has completely cooled, then cover the pan with plastic wrap and refrigerate the cheesecake overnight or for at least several hours.

13. When you're ready to serve the cheesecake, unlatch the springform pan and carefully remove the sides. Place the base with the cheesecake on a platter. Slice the cake with a large knife, wiping the knife clean with a warm wet towel between cuts.

New York Cheesecake

I was perfectly happy with the classic rendition of cheesecake I grew up with, until 1985, when I moved to New York City and tasted New York cheesecake for the first time. I remember walking around the city, seeing these cheesecakes in deli and bakery windows with what seemed to be no crust and a beautifully browned top. The unadorned, organic look of those cakes with their mottled tops really appealed to me. They looked almost like wheels of baked cheese. After I tasted one, I discovered that not only did it look like cheese, it also tasted more like cheese. It's less creamy and drier than the classic cheesecake I grew up with, and I liked that. I assigned the task of re-creating my memory of a New York cheesecake to Adam Marca, who worked in our pastry kitchen at the time. Soon after perfecting this recipe, ironically, he left us to move to New York.

As with the previous cheesecake recipe, you need to use Philadelphia brand cream cheese (or something similar) for this, one that comes in a block, wrapped in foil. Traditional New York cheesecake is very tall, but I don't like tall cakes. If you do, increase this batter by one-third and bake for an additional 20 to 30 minutes. To achieve the golden-brown top that I love in a New York Cheesecake, I bake the cake twice: once in a bain-marie (water bath) to set the filling; then the cake is chilled and baked again to brown the top. (See photo page 246.)

Makes one 9-inch cake

**What You Need—
The Essential Special Equipment**

9-inch springform pan

Cooking spray

Heavy-duty aluminum foil

Roasting pan large enough to hold the springform pan with a few inches around it

2 extra-large eggs

2 extra-large egg yolks

907 grams (21 ounces) cream cheese, cubed, at room temperature

75 grams (about 5 tablespoons) unsalted butter, left at room temperature until pliable but not greasy

309 grams (1⅓ cups) crème fraîche (or 325 grams/1⅓ cups sour cream)

200 grams (1 cup) granulated sugar

1 tablespoon plus 1 teaspoon potato starch

1 tablespoon pure vanilla bean paste or vanilla extract

½ teaspoon Diamond Crystal kosher salt

---

1. Adjust an oven rack to the center position and preheat the oven to 325°F.

2. Coat the bottom and sides of the springform pan with cooking spray and wrap the bottom tightly in a doubled sheet of heavy-duty aluminum foil.

Find a roasting pan that the springform will fit inside of with at least 2 inches of space around it and set both pans aside. Bring a kettle of water to a boil to fill the roasting pan and make a bain-marie, or water bath. Line a large baking sheet with parchment paper.

3. Whisk the whole eggs and egg yolks together in a small bowl.

4. Put the cream cheese and butter in a stand mixer fitted with the paddle and beat on medium-high speed until they are soft, 3 to 4 minutes, stopping to scrape down the bottom and sides of the bowl and the paddle as needed. With the mixer on medium-low speed, drizzle in the eggs and egg yolks, stopping to scrape down the bowl and making sure the egg is incorporated before adding more. Add the crème fraîche and beat on low speed for about 10 seconds, until the mixture is smooth. Add the sugar, potato starch, vanilla, and salt and beat for about 30 seconds to combine.

5. Pour the batter into the prepared pan. Use an offset spatula to smooth out the top and place the springform pan inside the roasting pan.

6. Pull out the center oven rack and place the roasting pan on it. Carefully pour enough boiling water into the roasting pan to come halfway up the sides of the springform pan, taking care not to get any water on the cheesecake. Gently slide the oven rack back in and bake the cheesecake until the edges of the cake are set and the surface moves as one when you gently jiggle the pan, 1 hour 30 minutes to 1 hour 45 minutes. Remove the roasting pan from the oven and turn off the oven.

7. Let the cheesecake cool to room temperature in the bain-marie. Remove the cheesecake from the bain-marie and dry the bottom of the springform pan. Remove the foil. Cup your hands around the sides of the pan to confirm that the cheesecake has completely cooled, then cover the pan tightly with plastic wrap and refrigerate the cheesecake overnight or for at least several hours.

8. Preheat the oven to 350°F.

9. Remove the cheesecake from the refrigerator and unwrap. Place the cheesecake on the center rack of the oven and bake until the top is golden brown, 20 to 30 minutes. Remove the cheesecake from the oven and set it aside to cool completely. Unlatch the springform pan and carefully remove the sides. Place the base with the cheesecake on a platter. Slice the cake with a large knife, wiping the knife clean with a warm wet towel between cuts.

Basque Cheesecake

Decades after my mind was opened when I saw New York cheesecake for the first time, my whole cheesecake world was turned upside down with the international debut of Basque cheesecake. What distinguishes a Basque cheesecake from any other is that the cake is burnt; and I mean really *charred*. And the cheesecake itself is so soft and creamy that it almost caves in when baked. The result is very rustic and beautiful, like something precious that was salvaged from a fire.

I first saw Basque cheesecakes in London at a restaurant called Brat, which is totally centered on wood-fire cooking. When you walk into Brat, you go past an open kitchen with flames roaring, and there, on a wooden shelf at the side of the kitchen, are these Basque cheesecakes lined up, still in their parchment-paper casings, all burnt and so, so beautiful! It really sets the tone for what's to come. I was like, what is *that!?* "Cheesecake" was the last answer I expected to hear. Little did I know, within a few weeks' time, back in Los Angeles, every single newspaper and magazine would be talking about Basque cheesecake, and many restaurants were trying their hand at it. Dave Beran, the owner and chef of a restaurant called Dialogue, made the best version and was kind enough to share his recipe with me. (Dialogue has since closed but he serves the cheesecake now at Pasjoli in Santa Monica.) Basque cheesecake, the creation of a restaurant called La Vina, is new on the cheesecake scene, but I believe it's here to stay.

In a perfect world, your Basque cheesecake will be creamy and loose. It will not be firmly set. If it turns out that you did not achieve this perfect middle ground, it will still be delicious. And it just gives you a reason to make it again. I like to present the cake with the parchment paper intact, like they do at Brat. For best results, bake this cheesecake in a convection oven. Once again, you need to use Philadelphia brand cream cheese (or something similar) for this. (See photo page 246.)

Makes one 9-inch cake

**What You Need—
The Essential Special Equipment**

9-inch springform pan

Cooking spray

Heavy-duty aluminum foil

1 kilogram (35 ounces) cream cheese, cubed, at room temperature

300 grams (1½ cups) granulated sugar

185 grams egg yolks (about 10 extra-large yolks)

1½ teaspoons Diamond Crystal kosher salt

400 grams (about 1¾ cups) crème fraîche (or 427 grams/1¾ cups sour cream)

---

1. Adjust an oven rack to the center position. Preheat the oven to 500°F if you're using a convection oven, 525°F if you're using a conventional oven. Coat the bottom and sides of the springform pan with cooking spray. Line the bottom and sides of the pan with parchment paper so the paper extends over the edges of the pan. Coat the parchment with cooking spray. Line a large baking sheet with parchment paper.

2. Working in 2 batches, put half of the cream cheese, half of the sugar, half of the egg yolks, and half of the salt in a food processor and pulse until the mixture is smooth, stopping to scrape down the sides of the bowl occasionally. Scrape the mixture into a large bowl. Repeat, mixing the remaining cream cheese, sugar, egg yolks, salt, and the crème fraîche in the same way. Add this to the bowl with the first batch and stir with the spatula to combine. (If you have a mixer with a very large bowl, you may be able to do this in one batch.)

3. Pour the batter into the prepared pan and use an offset spatula to smooth out the top. Tap the pan against a work surface a few times to smooth the top and eliminate air bubbles.

4. Place the springform pan on the prepared baking sheet and place it on the center rack of the oven to bake until the top is dark brown, the edges start to pull away from the sides of the pan, and the center is very loose and jiggly when you gently shake the pan, 20 to 28 minutes.

5. Remove the cheesecake from the oven and set it aside to cool to room temperature. Cup your hands around the sides of the pan to confirm that the cheesecake has completely cooled, then cover the pan tightly with plastic wrap and refrigerate it overnight or for at least several hours. (If you did not achieve the black exterior that you were hoping for, after chilling the cheesecake overnight, place it under a hot broiler until the top is burnt, 5 to 10 minutes. Let it cool to room temperature before serving.)

6. Remove the cheesecake from the refrigerator. Unlatch the springform pan and carefully remove the sides. Leaving the parchment paper intact, gently peel it back just enough to cut into the cake. Slice the cake with a large knife, wiping the knife clean with a warm wet towel between cuts.

Chocolate Brandy Cake

I included this recipe in my first cookbook, *Mark Peel and Nancy Silverton at Home*. That book didn't exactly fly off the shelves, and I love the cake, so I decided to give it another chance at life here. The cake is easy to put together: It's not decorated, and it manages to be super chocolatey without being overly rich, like a crusty loaf of bread meets a fudgy chocolate cake. It's not a chocolate decadence dessert; there's something almost subdued about it. You wouldn't feel guilty having a slice with your morning coffee, except that you do taste the alcohol in the cake; if you don't want that flavor, replace the brandy with strong brewed coffee. For me, this is the perfect chocolate cake: not too sweet, really chocolate, a little boozy, and totally unadorned. I want to thank Kerry Caloyannidis, who gave me this recipe more than 100 years ago.

This is baked in a cake ring. It is like a cake pan with no bottom; the baking sheet acts as the bottom. You can find the rings at baking supply stores or from online sources.

Makes one 8-inch cake

**What You Need—
The Essential Special Equipment**

8 × 3-inch cake ring

Cooking spray

312 grams (11 ounces) bittersweet chocolate (70% cacao), coarsely chopped (about 2¼ cups); whole if you're using feves

⅓ cup brandy (or strong brewed coffee, at room temperature)

4 extra-large eggs

1 tablespoon pure vanilla bean paste or vanilla extract

170 grams (1½ sticks) cold unsalted butter, cubed

300 grams (1½ cups) granulated sugar

1 teaspoon baking soda

½ teaspoon Diamond Crystal kosher salt

175 grams (1¼ cups) unbleached all-purpose flour

1. Adjust an oven rack to the top third of the oven and preheat the oven to 350°F. Line a large baking sheet with parchment paper. Coat the inside of the cake ring with cooking spray and place it on the baking sheet.

2. Fill a small saucepan with 1½ to 2 inches of water and set a small stainless steel bowl atop the saucepan to make a double boiler, making sure the water doesn't touch the bottom of the bowl. Bring the water to a simmer over medium heat. Put the chocolate in the bowl and melt it, stirring and scraping the bowl with a silicone spatula to prevent the chocolate from burning. Turn off the heat and take the bowl off the double boiler. Add the brandy and whisk to combine. Set aside to cool to room temperature. →

3. Separate the egg whites and yolks into 2 small bowls. Add the vanilla to the bowl with the yolks and whisk to combine. Set the egg whites aside.

4. Put the butter in a stand mixer fitted with the paddle and mix at medium speed until it is softened but still cold, 2 to 3 minutes, stopping to scrape down the sides and bottom of the bowl and the paddle with a rubber spatula whenever the butter is accumulating. Add 250 grams (1¼ cups) of the sugar and beat on medium speed until the mixture is light and fluffy, 3 to 4 minutes, scraping down the bowl as needed. Add the baking soda and salt and beat on medium speed for about 15 seconds to distribute them. Stop the mixer and scrape down the sides and bottom of the bowl. Return the mixer to medium speed and slowly drizzle in the egg yolk/vanilla mixture, stopping to scrape down the bowl and making sure the egg is incorporated before adding more. Add the melted chocolate mixture and beat on medium speed for about 1 minute to combine. Stop the mixer and scrape down the bowl. Add the flour and beat on low speed for about 30 seconds until no flour is visible. Stop the mixer, remove the bowl and paddle from the stand, and clean them with the spatula, scraping the bowl from the bottom up to release any ingredients that may be stuck there.

5. Transfer the batter to a large wide bowl. If you don't have a second bowl for your stand mixer, clean the bowl of the mixer and dry it thoroughly.

6. Place the egg whites in the clean bowl of the stand mixer fitted with the whisk and beat the whites on medium speed until they are foamy, 1½ to 2 minutes. Increase the speed to medium-high and mix until soft peaks form, 1½ to 2 minutes. Increase the speed to high, and with the mixer running, gradually add the remaining 50 grams (¼ cup) sugar and mix until the peaks are stiff and shiny but not dry, 1½ to 2 minutes. Stop the mixer, remove the whisk and bowl from the stand, and tap the whisk against the bowl to remove the egg whites.

7. Using the rubber spatula, scoop two-thirds of the egg whites into the bowl with the batter and vigorously stir them into the batter with the spatula, turning the bowl with one hand while quickly and aggressively stirring the whites into the batter with the other. Add the remaining egg whites, quickly stirring and folding them, until no streaks of egg whites remain, noting that it is more important to work quickly here than gently, since the whites lose their volume with time.

8. Scrape the batter into the prepared cake ring and smooth the top with an offset spatula.

9. Place the baking sheet in the top third of the oven and bake the cake until the top is golden brown, the cake is pulling away from the sides of the ring, and a toothpick inserted into the center comes out clean, 50 minutes to 1 hour, rotating the baking sheet front to back halfway through the baking time so it bakes evenly. (Do not open the oven door during the first 20 minutes of baking time or the cake may fall.) Remove the cake from the oven.

10. To remove the cake from the ring, run the tip of a paring knife around the inside edge of the cake ring to loosen any stuck bits. Slide the cake onto a cardboard cake round or a platter and lift off the ring. Set the cake aside to cool to room temperature. If the cake is on a round, slide it off the round onto a platter.

When you look at the selection of cakes in this chapter, my guess is that each and every one will evoke some kind of memory. They are all American classics. My work in creating these recipes was not to tinker too much, but to find a way to make each cake just a little better. There are cakes in this chapter for every occasion. Some are kid-friendly, like the Yellow Layer Cake or the Original Chocolate Birthday Cake with White Mountain Frosting. The Devil's Food Cake, on the other hand, and the Chocolate Decadence Cake are most definitely for grown-ups. And for those for whom chocolate is not the be-all, end-all, you'll find a nostalgic Spice Cake and Carrot Cake. Professional and home bakers alike know that when making a layer cake, things start to get difficult when you go to frost the sides. The enchanting Bay Area bakery Miette solved that problem when they debuted their beautiful layer cakes devoid of frosting on the sides. Somehow they managed to make the cakes look elevated, like an unfrosted side was the more elegant choice, forever giving permission to bakers everywhere (or at least to me!) to frost between the layers and forget the sides altogether. While not difficult, decorated cakes, even when done as simply as these are, do take time. Give yourself that time and enjoy the process. The act of making a cake from scratch, and the satisfaction of having made it, being able to say, "I made this for you!" This is the point. Otherwise just buy the cake.

Dressed-Up Cakes and Cupcakes

Yellow Layer Cake with Chocolate Frosting

I've long known that people have strong opinions about yellow cake, but, until I approached this recipe for this book, nothing could have prepared me for just how strong these opinions were. I finally got the cake to where I thought it was superb, and I thought I was finished with yellow cake, but evidently Shiri, who tested these recipes, thought differently. She never let on that she wasn't sold on my version, but when I went to Italy for the summer, she went about trying to improve on my cake. In the end, she came up with a cake, which borrows inspiration from a recipe of *Bon Appétit* magazine's Claire Saffitz, that is soft, moist, and not at all dense, as yellow cake can be. It was more to her liking than the one I had created, and it turned out to be more to my liking as well.

What I love about this fudge frosting, which we kept from my original yellow cake, is that it doesn't get hard when refrigerated, as many chocolate frostings do. This means you can sneak into the kitchen in the middle of the night and eat a slice of cake straight from the refrigerator. If you have golden butter (butter cooked just shy of brown butter) left over from another recipe, use it in place of the butter to make the frosting.

I know how challenging it can be for the home baker to frost a tall cake without it looking lopsided, and to frost the sides of a cake, so I made this friendly to the home baker in that it's constructed of only two layers, and it doesn't call for frosting the sides. To turn this into a three-layer cake, divide the batter among three cake pans and decrease the baking time (bake the cakes until you reach the indicators in the recipe). Double the frosting recipe, which will give you enough to frost between three layers and the sides. The batter also makes delicious cupcakes. Ask my grandchildren. Just don't forget the most important part—the sprinkles! To make the cake extra yellow, seek out Japanese eggs. These eggs come from chickens that are fed a particular diet to provide bright almost orange-colored eggs. I use them whenever the color of the yolk is important. →

Makes one 8-inch two-layer cake

What You Need—
The Essential Special Equipment

2 (8-inch) round cake pans

Cooking spray

12-inch cardboard cake round (optional)

For the Cake

140 grams (½ cup plus 2 tablespoons) buttermilk (preferably whole-milk or low-fat), shaken

27 grams (2 tablespoons) grapeseed oil (or other neutral-flavored oil, such as safflower)

3 extra-large egg yolks

1 extra-large egg (preferably farm-fresh)

1 tablespoon pure vanilla bean paste or vanilla extract

227.5 grams (1½ cups plus 2 tablespoons) unbleached all-purpose flour

200 grams (1 cup) granulated sugar

1½ teaspoons baking powder

¼ teaspoon baking soda

1 teaspoon Diamond Crystal kosher salt

113 grams (1 stick) unsalted butter, cubed and left at room temperature until pliable but not greasy

For the Frosting

45 grams (¼ cup plus 2 tablespoons) powdered sugar

227 grams (8 ounces) bittersweet chocolate (70% cacao), coarsely chopped (heaping 1½ cups); whole if you're using feves

42.5 grams (2 tablespoons) Lyle's Golden Syrup

184 grams (¾ cup) whole milk

14 grams (1 tablespoon) unsalted butter, left at room temperature until pliable but not greasy

1 teaspoon Diamond Crystal kosher salt

1. To make the cake, adjust an oven rack to the center position and preheat the oven to 350°F. Coat the bottom and sides of the cake pans with cooking spray. Cut two pieces of parchment paper to fit the bottom of the pans and place them in the pans. Coat the parchment with cooking spray.

2. Whisk the buttermilk, oil, egg yolks, whole egg, and vanilla together in a medium bowl.

3. Put the flour, sugar, baking powder, baking soda, and salt in a stand mixer fitted with the paddle and mix on low speed for about 15 seconds to combine. Add the butter and beat on low speed until the butter and dry ingredients mix to form a coarse meal, 2 to 3 minutes. Stop the mixer, add half of the buttermilk/egg mixture, and mix on low speed for about 15 seconds to moisten the dry ingredients. Stop the mixer and scrape down the sides of the bowl with a rubber spatula. Add the remaining buttermilk/egg mixture and mix on medium speed until the batter is pale, smooth, and creamy, 2 to 3 minutes, stopping to scrape down the bowl and paddle with the spatula whenever ingredients accumulate.

4. Scrape the batter into the prepared pans, dividing it evenly. Smooth out the tops of the cakes with an offset spatula.

5. Bake the cakes on the center rack of the oven until they are lightly browned and have begun to pull away from the sides of the pan, and a toothpick inserted into the center comes out clean, 30 to 35 minutes. Remove the cakes from the oven and set aside until they are cool enough to handle.

6. To remove the cakes from the pans, run the tip of a paring knife around the inside edges of each pan to loosen any stuck bits. One at a time, invert the cakes onto a cake round or plate, lift off the cake pan, and invert the cake again onto a cake round or your work surface. Set aside to cool to room temperature.

7. To make the frosting, while the cakes are cooling, sift the powdered sugar into a small bowl.

8. Put the chocolate and golden syrup in a heatproof medium bowl.

9. Bring the milk to a boil in a small saucepan over medium-high heat. Remove from the heat and pour the milk over the chocolate and syrup. Stir with a whisk until the chocolate is melted and the ingredients are combined. Add the butter and salt and whisk to combine. Add the powdered sugar and whisk until no lumps remain.

10. Using a long serrated knife, with the blade held parallel to the work surface, trim each cake to 1 inch high. (Reserve the trimmings to snack on or discard them.) Place one cake cut-side up on a serving platter. Spoon half of the frosting onto the center of the cake layer and use an offset spatula to spread it to the edges. Invert the second cake layer onto a cake round or plate so the bottom side is facing up. Spoon the remaining frosting onto the center of the cake layer and spread it toward the edges, leaving ½ inch of cake visible, with no frosting, around the edges. Use the spatula to create natural-looking swishes and waves in the frosting. Place the cake layer on top of the first, aligning them.

The Original Chocolate Birthday Cake with White Mountain Frosting

The cooks and bakers who come through my kitchens leave their legacies in the form of recipes. This one is the mark of Michelle Rizzolo, who worked with me at Campanile and went on to open the wonderful Big Sur Bakery. I use this recipe for birthdays, and every baker who has worked in my kitchens has carried on that tradition. I've changed Michelle's recipe, adding melted chocolate and increasing the salt and vanilla, but to me, it will always be Michelle's cake. I don't frost the sides, but if you want to, double the frosting recipe and use half of it for the sides. This and the German Chocolate Cake are the only three-layer cakes in the book. I tried to avoid making three-layer cakes because it can be challenging to get the third cake layer to sit on the cake evenly, and so often you end up with a lopsided cake. In both cases, I felt that the third layer was important to the balance of frosting and cake layers.

Makes one 8-inch three-layer cake

What You Need—
The Essential Special Equipment

3 (8-inch) round cake pans

Cooking spray

3 (12-inch) cardboard cake rounds (optional)

Candy thermometer

Pastry brush

For the Cake

113 grams (4 ounces) bittersweet chocolate (70% cacao), coarsely chopped (heaping ¾ cup); whole if you're using feves

255 grams (1 cup plus 2 tablespoons) boiling water

425 grams (2 cups plus 2 tablespoons) granulated sugar

227 grams (1½ cups plus 2 tablespoons) unbleached all-purpose flour

127.5 grams (1¼ cups) natural cocoa powder

2 teaspoons baking soda

2 teaspoons Diamond Crystal kosher salt

255 grams (1 cup plus 2 tablespoons) buttermilk (preferably whole-milk or low-fat), shaken

170 grams (¾ cup) grapeseed oil (or other neutral-flavored oil, such as safflower)

2 extra-large eggs

2 tablespoons pure vanilla bean paste or vanilla extract

For the Frosting

3 extra-large egg whites

127.5 grams (¼ cup plus 2 tablespoons) Lyle's Golden Syrup

150 grams (¾ cup) granulated sugar

1½ tablespoons pure vanilla bean paste or vanilla extract →

1. Adjust an oven rack to the center position and preheat the oven to 350°F. Coat the bottom and sides of the cake pans with cooking spray. Cut three pieces of parchment paper to fit the bottom of the pans and place them in the pans. Coat the parchment with cooking spray.

2. To make the cake, put the chocolate in a heatproof medium bowl and pour the boiling water over it. Stir with a whisk until the chocolate is melted and combined with the water. Set aside to cool to room temperature.

3. Sift the sugar, flour, cocoa powder, baking soda, and salt into a large bowl. Sift it a second time into a large wide bowl.

4. Combine the buttermilk, oil, eggs, and vanilla in a medium bowl and stir with a whisk to combine. Add the melted chocolate and stir it in.

5. Create a well in the center of the dry ingredients with your hands. Pour half of the buttermilk/chocolate mixture into the well and use a whisk to draw the dry ingredients from the edges to the center to form a thick paste. Add the remaining buttermilk/chocolate mixture and stir with the whisk to combine.

6. Pour the batter into the prepared pans, dividing it evenly. Smooth out the tops with an offset spatula.

7. Bake the cakes on the center rack of the oven until they pull away from the sides of the pans and feel firm to the touch, and a toothpick inserted into the center of the cakes comes out clean, 30 to 35 minutes, rotating them front to back halfway through the baking time so they bake evenly. Remove the cakes from the oven and set them aside until they are cool enough to handle.

8. To remove the cakes from the pans, run the tip of a paring knife around the inside edges of each pan to loosen any stuck bits. One at a time, invert one cake onto a cake round or plate and lift off the cake pan. Set aside to cool to room temperature.

9. To make the frosting, put the egg whites in a stand mixer fitted with the whisk.

10. Fasten a candy thermometer to the side of a small saucepan and add the syrup, sugar, vanilla, and 2 tablespoons water and stir to combine. Bring the liquid to a boil over high heat without stirring and boil until the temperature reaches 235°F, about 5 minutes, using a wet pastry brush to clean any sugar granules from the sides of the pan if there is sugar crystallization there. Remove from the heat.

11. Beat the whites on medium speed until they are foamy, 1½ to 2 minutes. With the mixer running, slowly add the hot sugar syrup, pouring it down the side of the bowl and taking care not to pour it onto the whisk. Beat until the frosting has cooled to room temperature, about 5 minutes; to check the temperature of the frosting, stop the mixer and cup your hands around the bottom of the bowl. Remove the whisk and bowl from the stand and tap the whisk against the bowl to remove the frosting.

12. Invert the cakes again onto your work surface or additional cake rounds so the rounded sides are facing up. Using a long serrated knife with the blade parallel to the work surface, trim each cake to 1 inch high. (Reserve the trimmings to snack on or discard them.)

13. Place the first cake layer cut-side up on a cake round or serving platter. Spoon one-third of the frosting onto the center of the cake and use an offset spatula to spread it evenly to the edges. Place the second cake layer on your work surface cut-side up. Spoon another third of the frosting onto the center of the cake and spread it to the edges. Place this cake layer on top of the first cake layer, aligning them. Invert the third cake layer onto a cake round or your work surface so the bottom side is facing up. Spoon the remaining frosting onto the center of the cake layer and use the offset spatula to spread the frosting to the edges, leaving ½ inch of the cake visible, free of frosting. Use the spatula to create pretty swooshes and waves in the frosting. Place the cake layer on top of the other two layers, aligning them.

Devil's Food Cake with Fudge Frosting

A classic chocolate cake, this devil's food cake is slightly denser, with a tighter crumb, than the Original Chocolate Birthday Cake (page 265). The name devil's food comes from the fact that the baking soda reacts with the melted chocolate in the batter, giving the dark chocolate cake a slightly red hue. The frosting is dense and fudgy and chocolatey. I'd choose this for an adult birthday party and the Original Chocolate Birthday Cake for kids.

This is the only cake recipe where I call for you to frost the sides. Since it's a single layer cake, I felt that it would be easy enough to do. If you have golden butter (butter that is cooked just shy of brown butter) left over from another recipe, use it in place of the softened butter in the frosting recipe.

Makes one 8-inch cake

What You Need—
The Essential Special Equipment

8-inch round cake pan

Cooking spray

12-inch cardboard cake round (optional)

Large disposable piping bag (optional)

Large star tip (optional)

For the Cake

5 extra-large egg yolks

85 grams (3 ounces) bittersweet chocolate (70% cacao), coarsely chopped (scant ⅔ cup); whole if you're using feves

25.5 grams (½ cup) natural cocoa powder

1½ teaspoons baking soda

43.5 grams (3 tablespoons) crème fraîche (or 45.75 grams/3 tablespoons sour cream)

2 tablespoons grapeseed oil (or other neutral-flavored oil, such as safflower)

2 teaspoons pure vanilla bean paste or vanilla extract

113 grams (1 stick) cold unsalted butter, cubed

100 grams (½ cup packed) dark brown sugar

½ teaspoon Diamond Crystal kosher salt

148.75 grams (1 cup plus 1 tablespoon) unbleached all-purpose flour

4 extra-large egg whites

50 grams (¼ cup) granulated sugar

For the Frosting

3 extra-large egg yolks

510 grams (1 pound 2 ounces) bittersweet chocolate (70% cacao), coarsely chopped (about 3¼ cups); whole if you're using feves

490 grams (2 cups) whole milk, plus 1 tablespoon warm milk as needed

57.5 grams (½ cup plus 1 tablespoon) natural cocoa powder

191 grams (½ cup plus 1 tablespoon) Lyle's Golden Syrup

¼ cup pure vanilla bean paste or vanilla extract

2¼ teaspoons Diamond Crystal kosher salt

70 grams (5 tablespoons) unsalted butter, cubed and left at room temperature until pliable but not greasy →

1. To make the cake, adjust an oven rack to the center position and preheat the oven to 350°F. Coat the bottom and sides of the cake pan with cooking spray.

2. Put the egg yolks in a medium bowl and whisk them to break them up.

3. Fill a medium saucepan with 1½ to 2 inches of water and set a medium stainless steel bowl atop the saucepan to make a double boiler, making sure the water doesn't touch the bottom of the bowl. Bring the water to a simmer over medium heat. Put the chocolate in the bowl and melt it, stirring and scraping the bowl with a silicone spatula to prevent the chocolate from burning. Turn off the heat and take the bowl off the double boiler.

4. Combine the cocoa powder, baking soda, and 120 grams (½ cup) water in a medium saucepan and bring to a simmer over medium heat, stirring constantly with a whisk. Continue to simmer, stirring constantly, until it is thick enough that the whisk leaves a trail when you draw it across the bottom of the pan, about 1 minute. Pour this mixture into the bowl with the melted chocolate and stir with the whisk to combine. Set aside to cool to room temperature. Add the crème fraîche, oil, and vanilla and stir with the whisk to combine.

5. Put the butter in a stand mixer fitted with the paddle and beat at medium speed until it is softened but still cold, 3 to 4 minutes, stopping to scrape down the sides and bottom of the bowl and the paddle with a rubber spatula whenever butter is accumulating. Add the brown sugar and beat on medium speed until the mixture is light and fluffy, 3 to 4 minutes, scraping down the bowl and paddle as needed. Add the salt and beat on low speed for about 15 seconds to distribute it. With the mixer on low speed, drizzle the egg yolks into the bowl, making sure they are incorporated and stopping to scrape down the bowl before adding more. Stop the mixer and scrape down the bowl and paddle. Add the chocolate mixture and beat on medium speed for about 30 seconds to combine. Stop the mixer, scrape down the bowl, and add the flour. Beat on low speed for about 30 seconds, until no flour is visible. Stop the mixer, remove the paddle and bowl, and clean them with the spatula, scraping the bowl from the bottom up to release any ingredients from the bottom of the bowl.

6. Transfer the batter to a large wide bowl. If you don't have a second bowl for your stand mixer, clean the bowl of the mixer and dry it thoroughly.

7. Place the egg whites in the clean bowl of a stand mixer and fit the mixer with the whisk. Beat the whites on medium speed until they are foamy, 1½ to 2 minutes. Increase the speed to medium-high and mix until soft peaks form, 1½ to 2 minutes. Increase the speed to high, and with the mixer running, gradually add the granulated sugar and mix until the peaks are stiff and shiny but not dry, 1½ to 2 minutes. Stop the mixer, remove the whisk and bowl from the stand, and tap the whisk against the bowl to remove the egg whites.

8. Scoop two-thirds of the egg whites into the bowl with the batter and vigorously stir them into the batter with a rubber spatula, turning the bowl with one hand while quickly and aggressively stirring the whites into the batter with the other. Add the batter back to the bowl of the stand mixer with the remaining egg whites and fold them into the batter until no streaks of egg whites remain.

9. Pour the batter into the prepared pan and smooth the top with an offset spatula.

10. Bake the cake on the center rack of the oven until it begins to pull away from the sides of the pan and springs back when touched, and a toothpick inserted into the center comes out clean, for about 1 hour, rotating the pan front to back halfway through the baking time so it bakes evenly.

11. Remove the cake from the oven and set aside until it is cool enough to handle. With a long serrated knife resting on the edge of the cake pan, slice off the top of the cake to create an even surface. Set the cake aside to cool to room temperature.

12. While the cake is baking, to make the frosting, whisk the egg yolks together in a small bowl. Place the chopped chocolate in a large heatproof bowl.

13. Combine the milk and cocoa powder in a medium saucepan and bring to a boil over low heat, whisking constantly. Remove from the heat, pour the hot milk mixture over the chopped chocolate, and stir with the whisk until the chocolate melts. Add the egg yolks and whisk to combine. Add →

the golden syrup, vanilla, and salt and stir with the whisk to combine. Add the butter and stir with the whisk until the frosting is a smooth, homogeneous consistency. Cover the bowl and refrigerate the frosting to chill until it is thick enough to spread, at least 30 minutes.

14. To remove the cake from the pan, run the tip of a paring knife around the inside edges of the pan to loosen any stuck bits. Invert the cake onto a cake round or plate, lift off the pan, and place the cake cut-side down on your work surface.

15. Remove the frosting from the refrigerator. If the frosting is too thick to spread, stir in a tablespoon of warm milk to loosen it to a spreadable consistency. Spoon half of the frosting on top of the cake and use an offset spatula to spread it over the top and down the sides of the cake. Use the remaining frosting to decorate the cake as you wish. Pipe it on the cake in rosettes or spoon it on the cake and then use an offset spatula to create natural-looking swishes and waves.

16. Transfer the cake to a serving platter.

Chocolate Cupcakes with Fudge Frosting

I make these cupcakes using the same batter as for my Original Chocolate Birthday Cake (page 265). It's the most delicious, soft, moist chocolate cake I know, and it works wonderfully for cupcakes. I top the cupcakes with a fudgy chocolate frosting. Nothing sophisticated or creative—just simple and delicious. This recipe makes 1½ dozen cupcakes, perfect for a party.

This frosting doesn't harden in the refrigerator the way some frostings do, so you can make it a day in advance, refrigerate it, and then just whisk it up before piping it onto the cupcakes. You can even frost the cupcakes and then refrigerate them. They're delicious cold, or bring them to room temperature before serving. If you have golden butter left over from another recipe, use that in place of the softened butter in the frosting recipe.

Makes about 18 cupcakes

**What You Need—
The Essential Special Equipment**

2 (12-cup) or 3 (6-cup) standard-size (½-cup capacity) muffin tins

Cooking spray

Large disposable piping bag

For the Cupcakes

113 grams (4 ounces) bittersweet chocolate (70% cacao), coarsely chopped (heaping ¾ cup); whole if you're using feves

255 grams (1 cup plus 2 tablespoons) boiling water

425 grams (2 cups plus 2 tablespoons) granulated sugar

227 grams (1½ cups plus 2 tablespoons) unbleached all-purpose flour

127.5 grams (1¼ cups) natural cocoa powder

2 teaspoons baking soda

2 teaspoons Diamond Crystal kosher salt

255 grams (1 cup plus 2 tablespoons) buttermilk (preferably whole-milk or low-fat), shaken

170 grams (¾ cup) grapeseed oil (or other neutral-flavored oil, such as safflower)

2 extra-large eggs

2 tablespoons pure vanilla bean paste or vanilla extract

For the Frosting

3 extra-large egg yolks

510 grams (1 pound 2 ounces) bittersweet chocolate (70% cacao), coarsely chopped (about 3¼ cups); whole if you're using feves

490 grams (2 cups) whole milk, plus 1 tablespoon warm milk as needed

57.5 grams (½ cup plus 1 tablespoon) natural cocoa powder

191 grams (½ cup plus 1 tablespoon) Lyle's Golden Syrup

¼ cup pure vanilla bean paste or vanilla extract

2¼ teaspoons Diamond Crystal kosher salt

70 grams (5 tablespoons) unsalted butter, cubed and left at room temperature until pliable but not greasy →

1. To make the cupcakes, adjust an oven rack to the center position and preheat the oven to 350°F. Coat the muffin cups with cooking spray.

2. Put the chocolate in a heatproof medium bowl and pour the boiling water over it. Stir with a whisk until the chocolate is melted and combined with the water. Set aside to cool to room temperature.

3. Sift the sugar, flour, cocoa powder, baking soda, and salt into a large bowl. Sift it a second time into a large wide bowl.

4. Put the buttermilk, oil, eggs, and vanilla in a medium bowl and stir with a whisk to combine. Add the melted chocolate and stir it in.

5. Create a well in the center of the dry ingredients with your hands. Pour half of the buttermilk/chocolate mixture into the well and use a whisk to draw the dry ingredients from the edges to the center to form a thick paste. Add the remaining buttermilk/chocolate mixture and stir with the whisk to combine.

6. Using a measuring cup or scoop, fill each muffin cup with ⅓ cup of batter.

7. Bake the cupcakes on the center rack of the oven until they feel firm to the touch and a toothpick inserted into the center of a cupcake comes out clean, 20 to 25 minutes, rotating the pan front to back halfway through the baking time so the cupcakes bake evenly. Remove the cupcakes from the oven and set them aside to cool to room temperature.

8. While the cupcakes are baking, to make the frosting, whisk the egg yolks together in a small bowl.

9. Place the chopped chocolate in a large heatproof bowl.

10. Combine the milk and cocoa powder in a medium saucepan and bring to a boil over low heat, whisking constantly. Pour the hot milk mixture over the chopped chocolate and stir with the whisk until the chocolate melts. Add the egg yolks and whisk to combine. Add the golden syrup, vanilla, and salt and stir with the whisk to combine. Add the butter and stir with the whisk until the frosting is a smooth, homogeneous consistency. Cover the bowl and refrigerate the frosting until it is thick enough to pipe, at least 30 minutes. →

Chocolate Cupcakes with Fudge Frosting and
Coconut Cupcakes with Cream Cheese Frosting

11. To remove the cupcakes from the pan, run the tip of a paring knife around each cup to loosen them. One at a time, slide the knife under each cupcake and pop it out. Place the cupcakes right-side up on your work surface.

12. Remove the frosting from the refrigerator. If the frosting is too thick to pipe easily, stir in a tablespoon of warm milk to loosen it to a spreadable consistency.

13. Put the piping bag in a tall container or glass so the bag flops over the top of the container. (This makes it easier to fill the bag.) Spoon the frosting into the bag and push it down toward the tip. Twist the top of the bag until it puts enough pressure on the frosting that it will squeeze out of the bottom of the bag, and cut a ½-inch hole in the tip of the bag. Starting ½ inch from the edge of the cupcakes, hold the top of the bag with one hand and steer the tip with the other. Spiraling toward the center, pipe the frosting onto each cupcake, ending with an upward motion to create a peak and leaving the edges of the cupcakes visible; refill the piping bag as needed.

Coconut Cupcakes with Cream Cheese Frosting

A classic three-layer coconut cake is a very "not Nancy" dessert, and yet a favorite of many. Traditionally, coconut layer cake consists of white cake with raw coconut flakes stuck to the bland frosting. In fact, given a piece with my eyes closed, I wouldn't even know what flavor of cake I was eating. I don't know what the appeal is other than maybe the way it looks. For this book, I took on the challenge of making a coconut cake that I would like, and I was pleased when I did so—in the form of a cupcake. I found this recipe in the archives of notebooks that I have dating back to 1972, the beginning of my cooking career. I don't think I'd ever made it before, but when I came across it recently, intrigued by the fact that the recipe for the batter called for coconut cream and coconut powder, I decided to try it. And lo and behold, it was exactly what I was looking for in a coconut cake; it was moist, delicious, and it tasted like coconut. By reducing the cake size to a small cupcake, the ratio of frosting to cake works better for me. And by packing the cupcake with everything coconut—coconut milk powder, coconut cream, shredded coconut, and coconut chips—it really earns its name.

Coconut cream and coconut milk powder can be found in Thai markets or from online sources. This recipe calls for self-rising flour, since that's what the original recipe called for. Self-rising flour is a premixture of all-purpose flour, baking powder, and salt. You can find it in many grocery stores and online. You can also make your own using a ratio of 1 cup flour, 1½ teaspoons baking powder, and ¼ teaspoon Diamond Crystal kosher salt. You need to use Philadelphia brand cream cheese (or something similar) for the frosting, one that comes in a block, wrapped in foil, not an artisanal product that comes in a tub or from a cheese shop. I'm sure those are delicious, but they won't give the frosting the right consistency. (See photo page 275.)

Makes 12 cupcakes

What You Need—
The Essential Special Equipment

12-cup (standard-size; ½-cup capacity) muffin tin

Cooking spray

Large disposable piping bag

Star tip

For the Topping

1 extra-large egg white

15 grams (1 heaping tablespoon) granulated sugar

30 grams (½ cup) unsweetened coconut chips

For the Nutmeg-Sugar

25 grams (2 tablespoons) granulated sugar

½ teaspoon freshly grated nutmeg

For the Cupcakes

178.5 grams (¾ cup) canned coconut cream, plus more for the frosting as needed →

1½ teaspoons pure almond extract

113 grams (1 stick) cold unsalted butter, cubed

20 grams (¼ cup) coconut milk powder

150 grams (¾ cup) granulated sugar

½ teaspoon Diamond Crystal kosher salt

210 grams (1½ cups) self-rising flour

100 grams (1¼ cups) sweetened shredded coconut

4 extra-large egg whites

For the Frosting

45 grams (¼ cup plus 2 tablespoons) powdered sugar

227 grams (one 8-ounce package) cold cream cheese, cubed

57 grams (½ stick) cold unsalted butter, cubed

½ teaspoon Diamond Crystal kosher salt

½ teaspoon pure almond extract

30 grams (¼ cup plus 2 tablespoons) sweetened shredded coconut

1. Adjust an oven rack to the center position and preheat the oven to 350°F. Coat the muffin cups with cooking spray.

2. To make the topping, stir the egg white and granulated sugar together in a small bowl. Stir in the coconut chips to combine. Set aside.

3. To make the nutmeg-sugar, stir the sugar and nutmeg together in a small bowl and set aside.

4. To make the cupcakes, stir the coconut cream and almond extract together in a separate small bowl.

5. Put the butter in a stand mixer fitted with the paddle and beat on medium speed until it is soft but still cold, 3 to 4 minutes, stopping to scrape down the sides and bottom of the bowl and the paddle with a rubber spatula whenever butter is accumulating. Add the coconut milk powder, 100 grams (½ cup) of the sugar, and the salt and beat on low speed for about 30 seconds. Increase the speed to medium and beat until the mixture is light and fluffy, 4 to 5 minutes, stopping to scrape down the paddle and bowl as needed. Stop the mixer and scrape down the bowl and paddle. Add the flour and the coconut cream/almond mixture alternately in four additions for the flour and three for the coconut cream/almond mixture, starting and ending with the flour; mix on low speed until the additions are combined and stop to scrape down the bowl before the next addition. Stop the mixer, remove the bowl and paddle from the stand, and clean them with the spatula. Add the shredded coconut and stir to combine, scraping the bowl from the bottom up to release any ingredients that may be stuck there.

6. If you have only one bowl for your stand mixer, transfer the batter to a separate large wide bowl and clean and dry the mixer bowl. If you have a second mixer bowl, set the bowl with the batter aside.

7. Place the egg whites in the clean bowl of a stand mixer and fit the mixer with the whisk. Beat the whites on medium speed until they are foamy, 1½ to 2 minutes. Increase the speed to medium-high and mix until soft peaks form, 1½ to 2 minutes. Increase the speed to high and with the mixer running, gradually add the remaining 50 grams (¼ cup) granulated sugar and mix until the peaks are stiff and shiny but not dry, 1½ to 2 minutes. Stop the mixer, remove the whisk and bowl from the stand, and tap the whisk against the bowl to remove the egg whites.

8. Using the rubber spatula, scoop two-thirds of the egg whites into the bowl with the batter and vigorously stir them into the batter, turning the bowl with one hand while quickly and aggressively stirring the whites into the batter with the other. Add the batter back to the bowl of the stand mixer with the remaining egg whites and fold them into the batter until no streaks of egg whites remain.

9. Using a measuring cup or scoop, fill each muffin cup with ¼ cup of batter. Sprinkle the nutmeg-sugar over the surface of the cupcakes, dividing it evenly. Scoop the coconut topping out of the bowl with your hands, leaving the excess egg white in the bowl, and distribute it over the cupcakes, leaving a ¼-inch border of cupcake visible around the edges. Discard any remaining egg white.

10. Bake the cupcakes on the center rack of the oven until they are golden brown, firm to the touch, and a toothpick inserted in the center of one comes out clean, 25 to 30 minutes, rotating the pan front to back halfway through the baking time so the cupcakes bake evenly. Remove the cupcakes from the oven and set them aside to cool to room temperature.

11. While the cupcakes are cooling, to make the frosting, sift the powdered sugar into a bowl or onto a sheet of parchment paper.

12. Put the cream cheese and butter in a stand mixer fitted with the paddle and beat on medium speed until they're combined and smooth, 3 to 4 minutes, stopping to scrape down the sides and bottom of the bowl with a rubber spatula as needed; don't mix longer than necessary or the mixture will separate. Reduce the speed to low, add the powdered sugar and salt, and beat until no lumps remain, 1 to 2 minutes, stopping to scrape down the bowl as needed. With the mixer on low speed, add the almond extract and beat on low for about 10 seconds to combine. Stop the mixer, remove the →

paddle and bowl, and clean them with the rubber spatula. Add the shredded coconut and stir with a rubber spatula to distribute it. Scrape the bowl from the bottom up to release any ingredients from the bottom of the bowl.

13. To remove the cupcakes from the pan, run the tip of a paring knife around each cup to loosen them. One at a time, slide the knife under each cupcake and pop it out. Place the cupcakes right-side up on your work surface.

14. To frost the cupcakes, fit the piping bag with a large star tip. Put the piping bag in a tall container or glass so the bag flops over the top of the container. (This makes it easier to fill the bag.) Spoon the frosting into the bag and push it down toward the tip. Twist the top of the bag until it puts enough pressure on the frosting that it will squeeze out of the bottom of the bag. Hold the top of the bag with one hand and steer the tip with the other. Pipe the icing onto the cupcakes starting about ½ inch from the edge of the cupcakes and spiraling toward the center; end with an upward motion to create a peak. Refill the piping bag as needed. Top each cupcake with a tuft of shredded coconut, dividing it evenly.

Carrot Cake with Brown Butter Cream Cheese Frosting

Everyone likes to put their spin on carrot cake, but at their essence, all carrot cakes are created equal. There are a few variables: nuts or no nuts? And, if nuts, walnuts or pecans? Raisins or no raisins? And what combination of spices? But the basic batter, right down to the addition of canned pineapple, remains the same. I've been making carrot cake since the 1970s, and each time I include it in a cookbook, I have the urge to change it. With this version, I wanted to eliminate the canned pineapple, which seems so out of place in this pseudohealthy, hippieish cake. I threw the challenge out to the pastry department to see if anyone had any ideas as to what to replace it with. Diana Leal, a quiet, shy cook in the pastry kitchen, piped up and said she'd just tried a carrot cake that contained roasted carrot puree. What a great idea! I tried it and found that indeed the carrot puree added the moisture and sweetness that canned pineapple did, and also added carrot flavor. Finally, a carrot cake where a hint of carrot flavor shone through.

There's no better match for a carrot cake than cream cheese frosting, but this updated version, made with brown butter, takes the frosting to the next level. You need to use Philadelphia brand cream cheese (or something similar) for the frosting, one that comes in a block, wrapped in foil, not an artisanal product that comes in a tub or from a cheese shop. I'm sure those are delicious, but they won't give the frosting the right consistency.

Makes one 8-inch Bundt cake

What You Need—
The Essential Special Equipment

Cooking spray

6-cup Bundt pan (I used a Nordic Ware Heritage Bundt Pan)

Large disposable piping bag

Large star tip

For the Frosting

226 grams (2 sticks) unsalted butter, cubed

1 tablespoon pure vanilla bean paste or vanilla extract

340 grams (12 ounces) cold cream cheese, cubed

270 grams (2¼ cups) powdered sugar

¾ teaspoon Diamond Crystal kosher salt

For the Cake

100 grams (1 cup) walnut halves

6 large carrots (1 to 1¼ pounds)

107.5 grams (½ cup) extra-virgin olive oil, plus more for drizzling

2 teaspoons grated peeled fresh ginger (grated on a fine Microplane) including the ginger juices

200 grams (1 cup lightly packed) dark brown sugar

2 extra-large eggs

1 tablespoon pure vanilla bean paste or vanilla extract

2 teaspoons ground cinnamon

1¼ teaspoons baking powder

1 teaspoon baking soda

¾ teaspoon Diamond Crystal kosher salt

140 grams (1 cup) unbleached all-purpose flour

100 grams (⅔ cup) golden raisins (halved if very large)

For Topping

1 teaspoon extra-virgin olive oil

½ teaspoon Diamond Crystal kosher salt →

Carrot Cake with Brown Butter Cream Cheese Frosting (continued)

1. To make the frosting, place the butter in a small saucepan or skillet with a light-colored bottom. Warm the butter over medium heat until it melts and begins to bubble, swirling the pan occasionally so the butter cooks evenly. Continue to cook the butter, swirling often, until the melted butter is caramel colored and the solids are the color of coffee grounds, 5 to 8 minutes. Remove from the heat. Working quickly so the butter doesn't continue to brown, transfer the butter to a medium bowl. Stir in the vanilla and set aside to cool to room temperature. Cover the bowl with plastic wrap and refrigerate for at least several hours, until solid.

2. To make the cake, adjust an oven rack to the center position and preheat the oven to 325°F. Coat the Bundt pan with cooking spray.

3. Spread the walnuts on a baking sheet and toast them on the center rack of the oven until they're lightly browned and fragrant, 10 to 12 minutes, shaking the baking sheet and rotating it front to back halfway through the toasting time so the walnuts brown evenly. Remove the walnuts from the oven and set aside to cool to room temperature. (If you think the nuts are on the verge of being overtoasted, transfer them to a plate so they don't continue to cook from the residual heat of the pan). Coarsely chop the walnuts.

4. Increase the oven temperature to 350°F.

5. Rinse and dry the carrots. Trim both ends and discard the trimmings. Put 2 of the carrots on the baking sheet the walnuts were on, drizzle lightly with olive oil, and rub the oil into the carrots to coat them evenly. Roast the carrots on the center rack of the oven until they are tender when pierced with a fork, about 1 hour 30 minutes, rotating the baking sheet front to back halfway through the roasting time. Remove the carrots from the oven and set aside to cool to room temperature.

6. Transfer the roasted carrots to a food processor and puree. Weigh out 87 grams (⅓ cup) of the puree and put it in a small bowl. (Reserve the remaining puree for another use.) Add the ginger (and juices) to the bowl with the puree and stir to combine.

7. Grate the remaining carrots on the large holes of a box grater (or the grating disc of a food processor). Weigh out 170 grams (or measure 2 cups) of the grated carrots and discard the rest (or reserve it for another use).

8. Combine the brown sugar and eggs in a stand mixer fitted with the whisk and beat on medium-high speed until the mixture has lightened in color, about 4 minutes. Stop the mixer, add the vanilla, cinnamon, baking powder, baking soda, and salt and beat on medium speed for about 15 seconds to distribute the additions. Add the flour and 107.5 grams (½ cup) oil alternately in three additions for the flour and two for the oil, starting and ending with the flour; mix on low speed until combined and stopping to scrape down the mixer after each addition. Add the pureed carrots and mix on medium-low speed to combine. Stop the mixer, remove the bowl and paddle from the stand, and clean them with the spatula. Add the grated carrots, raisins, and ⅔ cup of the walnuts and stir them in with the spatula, scraping the bowl from the bottom up to release any ingredients that may be stuck there. Set the remaining walnuts aside; you will sprinkle them over the cake.

9. Pour the batter into the prepared pan and smooth out the top with an offset spatula. Place the Bundt pan on a baking sheet.

10. Place the baking sheet with the cake on it on the center rack of the oven and bake until it is golden brown, is beginning to pull away from the sides of the pan, and a toothpick inserted into the center comes out clean, 40 to 50 minutes, rotating the baking sheet front to back halfway through the baking time so the cake bakes evenly. Remove the cake from the oven and set it aside to cool to room temperature.

11. While the cake is cooling, to finish the frosting, if you don't have another bowl for your stand mixer, wash the mixer bowl that you made the cake batter in and dry it thoroughly.

12. Remove the brown butter from the refrigerator and place the bowl in a large bowl of hot water to help release the butter. Dry off the bowl and invert it to release the butter onto a cutting board. (Alternatively, you may be able to wedge a knife under the butter and pop it out.) Cut the butter into roughly ½-inch cubes.

13. Put the butter in the clean stand mixer bowl. Fit the mixer with the paddle and beat on medium speed until the butter is smooth, 1 to 2 minutes. Add the cream cheese and mix on medium speed until the butter and cream cheese are combined, creamy, and glossy, 1 to 2 minutes, stopping to →

scrape the sides and bottom of the bowl as needed; do not mix longer than needed. Reduce the speed to medium-low, add the powdered sugar and salt, and mix until no lumps remain, 1 to 2 minutes, stopping to scrape down the bowl and paddle as needed.

14. Invert the cake onto a cake round or platter and invert it again so it is right-side up on another cake round or platter.

15. Fit a large piping bag with a large star tip. Put the bag in a tall container or glass so the bag flops over the top of the container. (This makes it easier to fill the bag.) Spoon the frosting into the bag and push it down toward the tip. Twist the top of the bag until it puts enough pressure on the frosting that it will squeeze out of the bottom of the bag. Holding the top of the bag with one hand, steer the tip with the other. Starting in the center hole, pipe along the crevices of the cake from the center up and over the hump and back down to the outside edge. Continue frosting along the crevices, refilling the piping bag as needed, until you've frosted the entire cake.

16. To top the cake, place the reserved walnuts in a small bowl. Add the oil and salt and toss to coat the nuts. Sprinkle them over the cake. Transfer the cake to a serving platter.

German Chocolate Cake

If I were to ask Americans what their favorite layer cake is, I think German chocolate cake, which consists of a chocolate cake layered with coconut pecan caramel, would come in toward the top of the list. The cake isn't from Germany at all; it is named for a man whose last name was German who worked for Baker's brand chocolate and who invented a type of sweet chocolate used to make the cake. No offense to Mr. German or Baker's chocolate, but when you make the cake with "German's" chocolate, it comes out a tannish-coffee color; it doesn't look or taste very chocolatey. The cake is also typically dry. For this version, I start with my Original Chocolate Birthday Cake (page 265), which is moist and so chocolatey it's almost black, layered with caramel pecan sauce, topped with dark chocolate frosting, and dusted with cocoa powder. It may not be exactly true to the original; I think it's better. This and the Original Chocolate Birthday Cake are the only three-layer cakes in the book. I tried to avoid making three-layer cakes because it can be challenging to get the third cake layer to sit on the cake evenly, so often you end up with a lopsided cake. In both cases, I felt that the third layer was important to the balance of frosting (and in this case caramel filling) and cake layers. I don't frost the sides of this cake because I don't want to cover up the caramel that oozes out and down the sides of the cake.

Makes one 8-inch three-layer cake

What You Need—
The Essential Special Equipment

3 (8-inch) round cake pans

Cooking spray

3 or more (12-inch) cardboard cake rounds (optional)

Candy thermometer (optional)

For the Cake

113 grams (4 ounces) bittersweet chocolate (70% cacao), coarsely chopped (heaping ¾ cup); halved if you're using feves

255 grams (1 cup plus 2 tablespoons) boiling water

425 grams (2 cups plus 2 tablespoons) granulated sugar

227 grams (1½ cups plus 2 tablespoons) unbleached all-purpose flour

127.5 grams (1¼ cups) natural cocoa powder

2 teaspoons baking soda

2 teaspoons Diamond Crystal kosher salt

255 grams (1 cup plus 2 tablespoons) buttermilk (preferably whole-milk or low-fat), shaken

170 grams (¾ cup) grapeseed oil (or other neutral-flavored oil, such as safflower)

2 extra-large eggs

2 tablespoons pure vanilla bean paste or vanilla extract

For the Chocolate Frosting

195 grams (1½ cups plus 2 tablespoons) powdered sugar

51 grams (½ cup) natural cocoa powder, sifted, plus more for dusting

113 grams (1 stick) unsalted butter, cubed and left at room temperature until pliable but not greasy

75 grams (one-third of an 8-ounce package) Philadelphia brand cream cheese, cubed, at room temperature

½ teaspoon pure vanilla bean paste or vanilla extract

½ teaspoon Diamond Crystal kosher salt

For the Caramel Filling

200 grams (2 cups) pecan halves

120 grams (1½ cups) unsweetened shredded coconut

226 grams (¾ cup plus 2 tablespoons) canned evaporated milk

200 grams (1 cup packed) dark brown sugar

113 grams (1 stick) cold unsalted butter, cubed

3 extra-large egg yolks

1 teaspoon pure vanilla bean paste or vanilla extract

½ teaspoon Diamond Crystal kosher salt

1. To make the cake, adjust an oven rack to the center position and preheat the oven to 350°F. Coat the bottom and sides of the cake pans with cooking spray. Cut three pieces of parchment paper to fit the bottom of the pans and place them in the pans. Coat the parchment with cooking spray.

2. Put the chocolate in a heatproof medium bowl and pour the boiling water over it. Stir with a whisk until the chocolate is melted and combined with the water. Set aside to cool to room temperature.

3. Sift the granulated sugar, flour, cocoa powder, baking soda, and salt into a large bowl. Sift it a second time into another large wide bowl.

4. Combine the buttermilk, oil, eggs, and vanilla in a medium bowl and stir with a whisk to combine. Add the melted chocolate and stir it in.

5. Create a well in the center of the dry ingredients with your hands. Pour half of the buttermilk/chocolate mixture into the well and use a whisk to draw the dry ingredients from the edges to the center to form a thick paste. Add the remaining buttermilk/chocolate mixture and stir with the whisk to combine.

6. Pour the batter into the prepared pans, dividing it evenly. Smooth out the tops with an offset spatula.

7. Bake the cakes on the center rack of the oven until they pull away from the sides of the pans, feel firm to the touch, and a toothpick inserted into the center of the cakes comes out clean, 30 to 35 minutes, rotating them front to back halfway through the baking time so they bake evenly. Remove the cakes from the oven and set them aside until they are cool enough to handle.

8. Leave the oven on and reduce the oven temperature to 325°F.

9. While the cakes are baking, to make the chocolate frosting, sift the powdered sugar and cocoa powder into a medium bowl or onto a sheet of parchment paper. →

10. Put the butter and cream cheese in a stand mixer fitted with the paddle and beat on medium speed until no lumps remain, 3 to 4 minutes, stopping to scrape down the sides and bottom of the bowl and the paddle with a rubber spatula whenever ingredients are accumulating. Add the powdered sugar/cocoa powder mixture, the vanilla, and salt and beat on low speed for 30 seconds to moisten the dry ingredients. Increase the speed to high and beat until no lumps remain, about 1 minute. Stop the mixer, remove the bowl and paddle from the stand, and clean them with the spatula, scraping the bowl from the bottom up to release any ingredients that may be stuck there. Set the frosting aside until you are ready to use it.

11. To remove the cakes from the pans, run the tip of a paring knife around the inside edges of each pan to loosen any stuck bits. One at a time, invert a cake onto a cake round or plate, lift off the cake pan, set aside to cool to room temperature.

12. While the cakes are cooling, to make the caramel filling, spread the pecans on a baking sheet and toast them on the center rack of the oven until they're lightly browned and fragrant, 15 to 20 minutes, shaking the baking sheet and rotating it front to back halfway through the toasting time so the pecans toast evenly. Remove the baking sheet from the oven and set aside until the pecans are cool enough to touch. (If you think the nuts are on the verge of being overtoasted, transfer them to a plate so they don't continue to cook from the residual heat of the pan.) Coarsely chop the pecans.

13. Spread the coconut on a small baking sheet (a quarter-sheet pan, if you have one) and toast it on the center rack of the oven until it is golden brown, 6 to 8 minutes, shaking the baking sheet and rotating it front to back halfway through the toasting time so the coconut browns evenly.

14. Fasten a candy thermometer, if you have one, to the side of a medium saucepan. Add the evaporated milk, brown sugar, butter, and egg yolks and bring to a boil over medium-high heat, stirring constantly with a silicone spatula. Boil the mixture for about 5 minutes, stirring often with the spatula, until it thickens and the candy thermometer registers 210° to 215°F. Remove from the heat and stir in the vanilla, toasted pecans, toasted coconut, and salt. Set aside to cool slightly. →

15. Using a long serrated knife with the blade held parallel to the work surface, trim the domes off the tops of the cakes to make them flat. (Reserve the trimmings to snack on.)

16. Place 2 of the cake layers cut-side up on your work surface. Pour 1½ cups of the caramel filling onto the center of each cake layer and use an offset spatula to spread it to the edges. Pour more caramel filling onto the layers if desired and spread it to the edges. (Reserve any remaining caramel to spoon over ice cream.) Place the cake layers in the refrigerator until the filling is firm, at least 30 minutes.

17. Invert the third cake layer onto a cake round or your work surface bottom-side up. Spoon two-thirds of the chocolate frosting onto the center of the cake layer and use the offset spatula to spread it to the edges, leaving ½ inch around the edges of the cake visible and free of frosting. Add the remaining frosting if desired, otherwise discard it or reserve it for another use. Use the spatula to create pretty swirls over the top.

18. Remove the cake layers with the caramel topping from the refrigerator and stack them on top of one another, lining them up evenly. Place the frosted cake layer on top, aligning it. Dust the top of the cake with cocoa powder.

Chocolate Decadence Cake with Cocoa-Covered Almonds and Hot Fudge Sauce

Back in the '80s, there was a very popular chocolate dessert called Chocolate Decadence. Every restaurant and every bakery had their version. I always liked the name, and the idea of it: a cake so chocolaty it was almost obscene. In developing an homage to that cake, I put together three of my favorite chocolate components: Julia Child's flourless chocolate cake, hot fudge, and chocolate-dipped almonds. We make the cake at Osteria Mozza and serve it with these accompaniments. The combination couldn't possibly be any more chocolatey. Or more decadent.

The cake isn't difficult to make, but for best results and a smooth baking experience, read through the recipe and have all the necessary ingredients and equipment ready before you begin. (It's important to keep ingredients at the correct temperature, so being organized is key.) This recipe calls for you to bake the cake in a 10-inch round cake pan. The ideal, for me, would be to make a 12-inch cake, but the cake is baked in a bain-marie, or water bath, so the cake pan must fit inside a roasting pan with room around all sides for the water; and not many people have such a large roasting pan. If you do have one, make this in a 12-inch cake pan. It makes for a very low-profile cake, which you cut into long, slender slices; it's very elegant. If you are anything like me, you'll want to double the almond recipe, so you have plenty to snack on. You may have hot fudge sauce left over, but that's never a bad thing.

Makes one 10- or 12-inch cake

**What You Need—
The Essential Special Equipment**

Cooking spray

Pastry brush

10-inch or 12-inch round cake pan

Roasting pan large enough to hold the cake pan with at least 2 inches around it

For the Cocoa-Covered Almonds

300 grams (2 cups) skin-on whole almonds

400 grams (2 cups) granulated sugar

204 grams (2 cups) natural cocoa powder

280 grams (9.8 ounces) bittersweet chocolate (70% cacao), roughly chopped (about 2 cups); whole if you're using feves

Flaky sea salt

For the Cake

180 grams (¾ cup) heavy cream

4 extra-large eggs

2 extra-large egg yolks

100 grams (½ cup) granulated sugar

½ teaspoon Diamond Crystal kosher salt

453.5 grams (1 pound) bittersweet chocolate (70% cacao), roughly chopped (heaping 3 cups); halved if you're using feves

36 grams (¼ cup) brewed espresso or strong coffee

For the Hot Fudge Sauce

170 grams (½ cup) Lyle's Golden Syrup

76 grams (¾ cup) natural cocoa powder

75 grams (¼ cup plus 2 tablespoons) granulated sugar

1 tablespoon coffee extract

1 teaspoon Diamond Crystal kosher salt

226 grams (8 ounces) bittersweet chocolate (70% cacao), roughly chopped (heaping 1½ cups); whole if you're using feves

3 tablespoons brandy (or 1 tablespoon pure vanilla bean paste or vanilla extract) →

Chocolate Decadence Cake with Cocoa-Covered Almonds (continued)

1. To make the cocoa-covered almonds, adjust an oven rack to the center position and preheat the oven to 325°F.

2. Spread the almonds out on a baking sheet and toast them on the center rack of the oven until they're lightly browned and fragrant, 12 to 14 minutes, shaking the baking sheet and rotating it front to back halfway through the toasting time so the almonds brown evenly. Remove the almonds from the oven and set aside until they're cool enough to touch. (If you think the nuts are on the verge of being overtoasted, transfer them to a plate so they don't continue to cook from the residual heat of the pan.)

3. Line a large baking sheet with parchment paper and coat the parchment with cooking spray. If you have a cooling rack that fits inside the baking sheet, place it on the lined baking sheet and coat it with cooking spray.

4. Put the sugar in a heavy-bottomed, light-colored medium saucepan. Add 240 grams (1 cup) water and stir with your finger to combine. Bring the water to a boil over medium-high heat without stirring, using a wet pastry brush to remove any sugar granules that may be stuck to the sides. Boil, tilting and swirling the pan so the sugar cooks evenly, until it is an auburn color, 7 to 9 minutes. While the sugar is cooking, fill a medium bowl with ice water to create an ice bath. Remove the saucepan from the heat and set it in the ice bath for 1 minute to stop the sugar from cooking from the residual heat of the pan. Remove the saucepan from the ice bath and set it on your work surface.

5. Working quickly as the sugar will harden as it cools, drop a handful of almonds into the pot of caramel. Use a fork to remove one almond at a time from the sugar and use a second fork to push the almond off the fork and onto the baking sheet (or cooling rack). Repeat until you have coated all the nuts with the melted sugar. (If the melted sugar starts to get hard and stringy, warm it over low heat until it returns to a liquid consistency.) Break off any extruded bits of sugar from the almonds and transfer the almonds to a small bowl; discard the bits and the melted sugar.

6. Line a second large baking sheet with parchment paper. Pour the cocoa powder on the baking sheet and spread it out in a thin layer.

7. Fill a small saucepan with 1½ to 2 inches of water and set a small stainless steel bowl atop the saucepan to make a double boiler, making sure the water doesn't touch the bottom of the bowl. Bring the water to a simmer over medium heat. Put the chocolate in the bowl and melt it, stirring and scraping the bowl with a silicone spatula to prevent the chocolate from burning. Turn off the heat and leave the bowl on the double boiler.

8. Put a handful of almonds in the melted chocolate. Lift one or two almonds out of the chocolate at a time with a fork. Hold a fork in your other hand and tap the fork with the almonds against it to shake off the excess chocolate. Drop the chocolate-covered almonds onto the cocoa powder, not touching one another and sprinkle with the flaky salt. Repeat with the remaining almonds, dropping them in a single layer on the baking sheet with the cocoa powder. (Strain the leftover melted chocolate to reserve it for another use, such as the hot fudge sauce below.)

9. Put the baking sheet with cocoa powder and almonds in the freezer for 30 minutes to harden the chocolate coating. Remove the baking sheet from the freezer. Using your hands, roll the almonds in the cocoa powder to thoroughly coat them. (Sift the leftover cocoa powder and reserve it for another use, such as the hot fudge sauce below.)

10. To make the cake, coat the bottom and sides of the cake pan with cooking spray. Cut a piece of parchment paper to fit the bottom of the pans and place it in the pan. Coat the parchment paper with cooking spray. Locate a roasting pan that the cake pan will fit inside of with at least 2 inches of space around it and set both pans aside.

11. Pour the cream into a stand mixer fitted with the whisk and whip the cream on low speed for about 1 minute until it thickens enough not to spatter. Increase the speed to medium-high and whip until stiff peaks form, about 3 minutes. If you don't have a second bowl for your stand mixer, transfer the whipped cream to another large bowl. Cover the bowl with plastic wrap and refrigerate the whipped cream until you're ready to use it.

12. Clean the mixer bowl (if you're using the same bowl) and the whisk and dry them thoroughly. →

Chocolate Decadence Cake with Cocoa-Covered Almonds (continued)

13. Place the whole eggs, egg yolks, sugar, and salt in the clean stand mixer bowl and whisk to combine.

14. Fill a small saucepan with 1½ to 2 inches of water and set a small stainless steel bowl atop the saucepan to make a double boiler, making sure the water doesn't touch the bottom of the bowl. (You will be using the double boiler twice, first to melt chocolate, and then you will put the bowl of your stand mixer on it to cook the eggs and sugar. Make sure the saucepan you choose is sufficiently large to place the mixer bowl on top of.) Bring the water to a simmer over medium heat. Put the chocolate in the bowl and melt it, stirring and scraping the bowl with a rubber spatula to prevent the chocolate from burning. Take the bowl off the double boiler but leave the water simmering.

15. Place the mixer bowl with the egg mixture on the double boiler and cook for about 1 minute, whisking constantly with a silicone spatula, until the sugar melts and the mixture no longer feels grainy when you rub it between your fingers. Turn off the heat and remove the bowl from the double boiler. Return the bowl with the chocolate to the double boiler to stay warm from the residual heat.

16. Place the mixer bowl on the stand, fit the mixer with the whisk, and whisk the egg mixture at medium-high speed until it is light yellow, foamy, and has tripled in volume, about 5 minutes, stopping to scrape down the sides and bottom of the bowl with the spatula whenever ingredients are accumulating. Stop the mixer, remove the whisk and bowl from the stand, and tap the whisk against the bowl to remove the egg mixture. Add the espresso and 1 tablespoon warm tap water, but don't stir. (This is to warm the liquids slightly, so all the ingredients are at the same temperature.)

17. Bring a kettle of water to a boil to make a bain-marie, or water bath.

18. Remove the whipped cream from the refrigerator. Remove the bowl with the melted chocolate from the double boiler and dry the bottom of the bowl. Pour the chocolate mixture into a large wide bowl. Add half of the whipped egg/sugar mixture and mix with the rubber spatula until the batter is streaky but not fully combined, scraping down the sides and bottom of the bowl →

and cleaning the chocolate off the spatula as you mix. Add the remaining egg/sugar mixture and fold it in, again just until the batter is streaky. Add the whipped cream to the batter and fold it in, scraping down the sides and bottom of the bowl, until no white streaks remain, scraping from the bottom up to release any ingredients from the bottom of the bowl.

19. Pour the batter into the prepared cake pan and smooth out the top with an offset spatula. Set the cake pan inside the roasting pan. Pull out the center oven rack and place the roasting pan on it. Carefully pour enough boiling water into the roasting pan to come halfway up the sides of the cake pan, taking care not to get any water on the batter. Cover the roasting pan tightly with aluminum foil and pierce the foil in several places with a sharp knife.

20. Gently slide the rack back in and bake the cake for 15 minutes. Gently pull out the oven rack and carefully lift a corner of the foil to release steam. Put the foil back down on the roasting pan. Rotate the roasting pan from front to back and slide the oven rack back in. Bake the cake until the center is set and not shiny, another 15 minutes. To test for doneness, slide out the oven rack, fold back the foil, and gently touch the cake; if it is done, it will feel foamy and some will come off on your finger, but it will not feel like raw batter. When it's done, carefully remove the roasting pan from the oven and remove the foil. Lift the baking pan out of the water and dry the bottom of the pan. Set the cake aside to cool to room temperature. Cup your hands around the sides of the pan to confirm that the cake has completely cooled, then cover the pan with plastic wrap and place it in the refrigerator to chill at least 2 hours, until the cake is firm.

21. To remove the cake from the pan, 2 hours before you are ready to serve it, line a cake round or cutting board with parchment paper. Remove the cake from the refrigerator and unwrap. Place the cake round or cutting board over the cake pan and quickly invert the cake onto it. Invert the cake again onto a flat serving platter or cutting board. Slice the cake using a long sharp knife, wiping the blade with a warm wet towel between cuts. Bring the cake to room temperature before serving.

22. While the cake is coming to room temperature, to make the hot fudge sauce, combine the golden syrup, cocoa powder, sugar, coffee extract, and salt in a medium saucepan. Add 180 grams (¾ cup) water and bring to a boil over medium-high heat, stirring constantly with a whisk to prevent the cocoa from burning. Remove from the heat, add the chocolate, and stir until the chocolate melts, 1 to 2 minutes. Stir in the brandy (or vanilla). Serve warm. (If needed, warm it over low heat, stirring constantly with a rubber spatula, until it is warm but not boiling.)

23. To serve, slide a long metal spatula under each cake slice and place it on a dinner plate. Drizzle hot fudge sauce over the cake slice and sprinkle with a small handful of cocoa-covered almonds. Serve the remaining hot fudge sauce and almonds on the side.

Spice Cake with Caramel Glaze and Pecans

One of the few sweets my mom bought regularly when I was growing up was Sara Lee Spice Cake. It came in a square foil tray with a cardboard top and she always stored it in the freezer. I have such vivid memories of sneaking into the kitchen late at night, opening the freezer, and taking out the cake. With the door still open, I would bend back the lip of the foil pan, slip off the cardboard lid, cut a thin slice, and return the cake to the freezer, as if nobody would know I was ever there. This is my re-creation of that cake, and that memory.

I recommend that you grind the spices for this recipe. Since spices have the title role in this cake, using freshly ground spices makes the difference between a good cake and one that is sublime. (You can use a spice grinder or most coffee grinders to grind the spices.)

Makes one 10-inch square cake

What You Need—
The Essential Special Equipment

10-inch square cake pan

Cooking spray

Candy thermometer (optional)

For the Cake

1 tablespoon plus 2 teaspoons ground cinnamon (preferably freshly ground)

1 tablespoon ground cardamom (preferably freshly ground)

1 tablespoon ground ginger

1 tablespoon baking powder

1½ teaspoons baking soda

1½ teaspoons Diamond Crystal kosher salt

1 teaspoon freshly grated nutmeg

1 teaspoon ground cloves (preferably freshly ground)

224 grams (1 cup) buttermilk (preferably whole-milk or low-fat), shaken

4 extra-large eggs

254 grams (2 sticks plus 2 tablespoons) cold unsalted butter, cubed

450 grams (2¼ cups packed) dark brown sugar

40 grams (1 tablespoon) grated peeled fresh ginger (grated on a fine Microplane), including the ginger juices

1 tablespoon pure vanilla bean paste or vanilla extract

455 grams (3¼ cups) all-purpose flour

250 grams (1 cup) unsweetened applesauce

For the Glaze and Pecans

100 grams (1 cup) pecan halves

150 grams (¾ cup packed) dark brown sugar

113 grams (1 stick) unsalted butter, cubed

85 grams (¼ cup) Lyle's Golden syrup

1 teaspoon pure vanilla bean paste or vanilla extract

1 teaspoon Diamond Crystal kosher salt

Flaky sea salt

---

1. To make the cake, adjust an oven rack to the center position and preheat the oven to 350°F. Coat the bottom and sides of the cake pan with cooking spray. Cut two pieces of parchment paper to 9 × 16 inches. Lay one sheet of paper in the pan so it travels up and over two of the sides. Lay the other sheet perpendicular so it travels up and over the remaining two sides of the pan. Coat the paper with cooking spray. →

2. Stir the cinnamon, cardamom, ground ginger, baking powder, baking soda, salt, nutmeg, and cloves together in a small bowl. Whisk the buttermilk and eggs together in a separate small bowl.

3. Put the butter in a stand mixer fitted with the paddle and beat on medium speed until the butter is softened but still cold, 3 to 4 minutes, stopping to scrape down the sides and bottom of the bowl and the paddle with a rubber spatula whenever butter is accumulating. Add the brown sugar and beat on medium speed until light and fluffy, 2 to 3 minutes, scraping down the bowl as needed. Add the spice mixture and mix on low speed for about 15 seconds to distribute. Add the fresh ginger (and juices) and vanilla and mix on medium speed for about 15 seconds to distribute them. Stop the mixer and scrape down the bowl and paddle. Add the flour and the buttermilk/egg mixture in four additions for the flour and three for the buttermilk/egg mixture, starting and ending with the flour; mix on low speed until the additions are combined and stop to scrape down the bowl before the next addition. Add the applesauce and mix on low speed for about 30 seconds to combine, scraping the bowl from the bottom up to release any ingredients that may be stuck there.

4. Scrape the batter into the prepared pan and smooth out the top with an offset spatula.

5. Bake the cake on the center rack of the oven until it is golden brown, firm to the touch, and a toothpick inserted into the center comes out clean, 60 to 70 minutes, rotating the pan front to back halfway through the baking time so the cake bakes evenly. Remove the cake from the oven and set it aside to cool to room temperature.

6. Reduce the oven temperature to 325°F.

7. While the cake is cooling, to make the glaze, spread the pecans on a baking sheet and toast them on the center rack of the oven until they're lightly browned and fragrant, 15 to 20 minutes, shaking the baking sheet and rotating it front to back halfway through the toasting time so the pecans brown evenly. Remove the pecans from the oven and set aside to cool to room temperature. (If you think the nuts are on the verge of being overtoasted, transfer them to a plate so they don't continue to cook from the residual heat of the pan.) Cut the pecans lengthwise in thirds along their natural ridges.

8. Have a heatproof dish handy. Fasten a candy thermometer, if you have one, to the side of a small saucepan. Add the brown sugar, butter, golden syrup, vanilla, and salt, and bring to a simmer over medium-high heat, stirring with a silicone spatula. Boil, stirring with the spatula, until the thermometer registers 235°F, 1 to 1½ minutes. If you do not have a candy thermometer, remove from the heat, dip a teaspoon into the glaze, and set the spoon on a plate for 1 minute to let the caramel cool. If it is thick and tacky, it's done. If it is still thin, return it to the heat and boil for another 30 seconds. Remove from the heat and pour the caramel into the heatproof dish to stop it from cooking.

9. To remove the cake from the pan, lift on both ends of the bottom sheet of parchment paper to lift the cake out of the pan. Gently peel off the parchment paper and discard it. Place the cake on the platter you will be serving it from. (If the surface of the cake is uneven and you want a more square-topped cake, invert the cake onto the platter so the bottom is facing up.) Pour the glaze over the cake and use an offset spatula to spread it in uneven swooshes toward the edges, letting the cake peek through in places and leaving ½ inch of cake visible around the edges. Scatter the pecans over the top and sprinkle generously with flaky salt. (If you don't use all the caramel, serve it on the side.)

Chocolate Almond Dot Cake

Sumi Chang started making this chocolate cake in the 1980s at Campanile. We often made it for Passover because it doesn't contain flour or leavening. Almond paste makes the cake moist and dense, in a nice way. It's not a cake for everyone. It is not super sweet, and it is very strong in its almond flavor.

I was taught early on in my pastry career that a simple chocolate glaze dressed up the look of a tart or cake, but on this cake, I always thought it looked a little messy. Instead of coating the entire cake in glaze, I decided to apply the glaze in circles over the surface of the cake. Now that, to me, looks dressed up, like the couture version of a glazed cake. If you have a tablespoon of golden butter (butter that is cooked just shy of brown butter) left over from another recipe, use it in place of the butter called for in this cake.

Makes one 10-inch cake

What You Need—
The Essential Special Equipment

10-inch fluted tart pan with a removable bottom

Cooking spray

Round cookie cutters (various sizes)

For the Cake

142 grams (1½ cups plus 2 tablespoons) natural cocoa powder, such as Valrhona

4 extra-large eggs

1 tablespoon pure vanilla bean paste or vanilla extract

150 grams (¾ cup) granulated sugar

168 grams (6 ounces) almond paste (preferably unblanched)

168 grams (1½ sticks) cold unsalted butter, cubed

½ teaspoon Diamond Crystal kosher salt

For the Toasted Almonds and Glaze

25 grams (¼ cup) skin-on thin-sliced almonds

227 grams (8 ounces) bittersweet chocolate (70% cacao), coarsely chopped (heaping 1½ cups); halved if you're using feves

28 grams (1 tablespoon) Lyle's Golden Syrup

184 grams (¾ cup) whole milk

14 grams (1 tablespoon) unsalted butter, left at room temperature until pliable but not greasy

Boiling water or hot coffee (optional)

1. To make the cake, adjust an oven rack to the center position and preheat the oven to 350°F. Coat the bottom and sides of the tart pan with cooking spray.

2. Sift the cocoa powder into a large bowl or onto a sheet of parchment paper. Whisk the eggs and vanilla together in a small bowl.

3. Put the sugar in the bowl of a stand mixer. Crumble the almond paste into the bowl, fit the mixer with the paddle, and beat on medium speed until the paste is combined with the sugar and the mixture is smooth, →

3 to 4 minutes. Stop the mixer, add the butter, and mix until the butter is combined with the almond paste mixture and no lumps remain, 4 to 5 minutes, stopping to scrape down the sides and bottom of the bowl and the paddle with a rubber spatula whenever ingredients are accumulating. Add the salt and beat on medium speed for about 15 seconds to distribute it. Stop the mixer and scrape down the bowl. With the mixer on low speed, drizzle the egg/vanilla mixture into the bowl, making sure it is incorporated and stopping to scrape down the bowl before adding more. Once all the egg/vanilla mixture is incorporated, stop the mixer and scrape down the bowl and paddle. Add the cocoa powder and mix on low speed for about 1 minute to combine. Stop the mixer, remove the bowl and paddle from the stand, and clean them with the spatula, scraping the bowl from the bottom up to release any ingredients that may be stuck there.

4. Pour the batter into the prepared pan and smooth out the top with an offset spatula.

5. Place the cake on a baking sheet, place the baking sheet on the center rack of the oven, and bake until the cake is cracked on top and begins to pull away from the sides of the pan, 28 to 35 minutes, rotating the baking sheet front to back halfway through the baking time so the cake bakes evenly. Remove the cake from the oven and set it aside to cool to room temperature.

6. Reduce the oven temperature to 325°F.

7. To toast the almonds and make the glaze, spread the almonds on a baking sheet (a quarter-sheet pan if you have one) and toast them on the center rack of the oven until they are light golden brown, 8 to 10 minutes, rotating the baking sheet front to back and stirring the almonds halfway through the toasting time so they brown evenly. Remove the baking sheet from the oven. Transfer the almonds to a plate to prevent them from toasting further and set aside to cool. Turn off the oven.

8. After the cake has cooled, put the chopped chocolate and golden syrup in a small heatproof bowl. Bring the milk to a boil over medium heat, then pour the milk over the chocolate and syrup. Stir with a whisk until the chocolate is melted. Add the butter and stir with the whisk to combine. (If the glaze is too thick to pour, stir in boiling water or hot coffee, 1 tablespoon at a time, until it reaches a pourable consistency.)

9. To remove the cake from the pan, press up on the bottom of the pan to remove the outer ring. Invert the cake onto a serving platter and gently pry the bottom of the pan off the top of the cake.

10. To create decorative rounds of glaze on the cake, coat several round cookie cutters of different sizes with cooking spray and set them on the cake in an artful fashion. Press gently on the cutters so they sink ever so slightly into the cake; this prevents the glaze from leaking and makes for perfect rounds of glaze. Scoop the glaze with a small measuring cup and pour it into the rings, filling each ring with about ⅛ inch of glaze. Put the cake in the refrigerator for about 20 minutes to chill until the glaze is set. Remove the cake from the refrigerator and gently remove the cookie cutters. Sprinkle the almonds over the glaze dots. Bring the cake to room temperature to serve.

I love pies and tarts. I like texture and contrast in my baked goods, and pies and tarts, because they are comprised of a crust and a filling, give me both. I use many shapes and sizes of pans for these pies and tarts: sheet pans for slab pies, pie pans and baking dishes for traditional pies, fluted tart shells, straight-sided flan rings, and miniature pans for individual pies. I also use several different doughs—a flaky, salty pie dough; a sweet tart dough, or *pâte sucrée*; a cookie-like crust, or *pâte sablée*; two types of puff pastry; and a good old-fashioned graham cracker crust.

Pies and tarts aren't difficult to make, but they require time and patience, because they need to be done in stages. Except for graham cracker crust, pie and tart crust starts by making a dough that then needs to be chilled and rolled out. Once that's out of the way, making pie is as easy as, well, pie. Just put together a simple filling, pour it into the crust, bake it, and you have something beautiful and that feels truly special. If you are organized and plan for it, having to make the dough ahead of time works in your favor. Make it in advance, refrigerate or even freeze it, and then you're halfway there.

I bake many of the tarts in a flan ring, which is basically a tart pan with no bottom. To use a flan ring, you place the ring on a baking sheet lined with parchment paper; the baking sheet serves as the bottom of the tart. When I started baking professionally, half a century ago, removable-bottom tart pans were not available. When they did become available, it was only those with fluted edges. While fluted-edged tarts are pretty, often I want the clean look of the smooth edges.

Pies
and Tarts

Chicken Pot Pies

Who doesn't love chicken pot pie? In developing this recipe, I was inspired by The Pie Room in the Holborn Dining Room, a fancy, old-school restaurant in the Rosewood hotel in London, where they sell nothing but pot pies. From the window you can look inside The Pie Room's jewel box of a kitchen—the shelves lined with beautiful copper molds in all sizes and shapes, and racks of individual pies for sale—and see the pies being formed. Their former chef Calum Franklin, who developed this concept, is wonderful, and each of his pies is extraordinary. He has a cookbook, *The Pie Room*, devoted to all things pie. I was so inspired by him and his pies that at my restaurant, Chi Spacca, we now have an entire pot pie section on the menu, including pork pie; bone marrow pie; shepherd's pie; Comté, potato, and leek pie; and, of course, chicken pot pie.

Makes seven 5-inch pies

What You Need—
The Essential Special Equipment

Cooking spray

7 (5-inch) pie pans

For the Pie Crusts

2 recipes Savory Pie Dough (recipe follows)

Unbleached all-purpose flour for dusting

For the Chicken

1¾ pounds boneless, skinless chicken thighs

1¾ teaspoons Diamond Crystal kosher salt

½ cup whole garlic cloves

2 cups unsalted chicken stock, homemade or store-bought

½ cup extra-virgin olive oil

3 fresh thyme sprigs

3 bay leaves (preferably fresh)

For the Carrots

3 large carrots (1 to 1⅓ pounds/ 500 to 600 grams), peeled and cut into ½- to ¾-inch cubes (about 2 cups)

113 grams (1 stick) unsalted butter, cubed

1½ teaspoons Diamond Crystal kosher salt

226 grams (2 sticks) unsalted butter, cubed

227 grams (1½ cups plus 2 tablespoons) unbleached all-purpose flour

3 quarts unsalted chicken stock, homemade or store-bought

2 tablespoons plus 1 teaspoon Diamond Crystal kosher salt

1 cup finely chopped fresh tarragon

For the Egg Wash

5 extra-large egg yolks

1. To prepare the pie crusts, coat the bottom and sides of the pie pans with cooking spray. Line two large baking sheets with parchment paper.

2. Lightly dust a work surface with flour. Remove one disk of dough from the refrigerator, unwrap, and place on the floured surface. Pound the dough with a rolling pin to soften it until it is malleable and as flat as possible. (The more you flatten the dough by pounding it, the easier it will be to roll out.) →

Dust the dough and rolling pin lightly with flour. Applying firm, steady pressure with the rolling pin, roll the dough to ⅛ inch thick, dusting with flour as needed.

3. Place one of the pie pans upside down on the dough and use a paring knife or kitchen shears to cut as many rounds as you can from the dough. (You'll cut the dough more precisely later; you're trimming at this point to make the sheet of dough easier to work with.) Repeat with the remaining 3 disks of dough, rolling and cutting a total of 14 rounds. Use a 2-inch cutter (preferably shaped like a chicken) to cut 7 shapes from the dough. (Gather the trimmings, pat them into a disk, and wrap them in plastic wrap to use another time, or discard them.)

4. Lay 7 of the dough rounds on one of the prepared baking sheets, dusting with flour between the layers of rounds to prevent them from sticking together. Place the cutouts on top.

5. Working with the remaining 7 dough rounds, lay one dough round in each of the prepared pie tins, centering the dough. Lift the edges of the dough and let it drop into the tins; dip the knuckle of your index finger in flour and use it to gently press the dough into the creases. Don't stretch the dough to fit, or it will shrink when baked. Place the pie pans on the second baking sheet and place both baking sheets in the refrigerator to chill until the dough is firm, at least 1 hour.

6. To prepare the chicken, place the chicken thighs in a baking dish. Sprinkle them all over with the salt. Cover the dish and place it in the refrigerator for at least 1 hour or overnight to allow the salt to penetrate.

7. Adjust an oven rack to the center position and preheat the oven to 300°F.

8. Remove the chicken thighs from the refrigerator and uncover them. Scatter the garlic cloves over the bottom of a large Dutch oven and lay the chicken on top of the garlic. Pour in the stock, drizzle with the olive oil, and scatter the thyme and bay leaves over the chicken. Place the lid on the Dutch oven and place it on the center rack of the oven to cook for 1 hour.

9. Remove the Dutch oven from the oven. Set the lid ajar by an inch or two and set aside until the chicken is cool enough to touch. Remove the chicken from the Dutch oven and pull it into long ½-inch-thick pieces and put the

pieces in a large bowl. Remove the garlic cloves from the Dutch oven and add them to the bowl with the chicken. Discard the remaining contents of the Dutch oven.

10. To cook the carrots, place them in a large sauté pan. Add the butter, salt, and 120 grams (½ cup) water and heat until the butter melts. Cover the pan, reduce the heat to medium, and simmer until the carrots are al dente and the liquid has reduced by half, 10 to 15 minutes. Drain the carrots in a colander (discard the cooking liquid). Spread the carrots on a large plate and put them in the refrigerator to stop them from cooking further.

11. To make the gravy, melt the butter in a medium saucepan over medium heat. Add the flour and whisk until there are no lumps. Cook the butter and flour together for 2 to 3 minutes to create a roux, whisking constantly to prevent the butter from burning, until the roux is a deep brown color. Gradually add the chicken stock, whisking as you add it to prevent lumps from forming. Increase the heat to high and bring the gravy to a boil. Reduce the heat to low and simmer the gravy, stirring with the whisk occasionally, until it is thick enough to coat the back of a spoon, about 10 minutes. Remove from the heat and stir in the salt and tarragon.

12. Pour the gravy into the bowl with the chicken and garlic. Remove the carrots from the refrigerator and add them to the bowl. Stir with your hands or a rubber spatula to combine the ingredients and coat the chicken with the gravy. Set aside to come to room temperature, then cover the bowl with plastic wrap and refrigerate overnight or for at least several hours to chill.

13. To assemble the pies, remove the pie shells and the dough rounds from the refrigerator and set them aside for about 5 minutes to soften the dough slightly.

14. Whisk the egg yolks together in a small bowl.

15. Remove the chicken filling from the refrigerator. Remove the pie shells from the baking sheet. Dividing evenly, spoon the filling into the pie shells. Using your hands, mound the filling in the center and smooth it out with your hands or a rubber spatula.

16. Lay one round of dough on top of each pie, centering it. Press the top and bottom crusts together at the point where they meet the edge of the pie pan to seal them together. Using kitchen shears, trim the sealed dough →

so there are 1½ inches of dough overhanging. (Discard the trimmings.) Set the baking sheet that the dough was on aside; you will use it to bake the pies on.

17. Working with one pie at a time, roll the edge of the dough under itself to create a thick lip of dough that rests on the edge of the pie tin. Press the thumb of one hand on the lip to create an indentation in the dough and press the thumb and forefinger of the other hand on either side of the first thumb, creating a U-shaped indentation. Continue around the perimeter of the crust, creating a crimped, scalloped edge. Repeat with the remaining pies. Brush the dough generously with the egg yolks (you won't use it all at this time). Return the pies to the baking sheet and place them in the refrigerator to chill until the dough is firm, at least 1 hour. Cover the bowl of egg yolks with plastic wrap and refrigerate it until you're ready to use it again.

18. To bake the pies, adjust the oven racks so one is in the top third and the other is in the bottom third of the oven and preheat the oven to 350°F.

19. Remove the pies and egg yolks from the refrigerator. Brush the pies with the remaining egg yolk. Place one cutout in the center of each pie and brush the cutout with the wash. One at a time, insert the tip of a paring knife into the center of the cutout through both layers of dough, creating a hole to allow steam to escape.

20. Divide the pies between the two baking sheets, spacing them evenly. Place one baking sheet on each oven rack and bake the pies until the tops are golden brown, 50 to 60 minutes, switching racks and rotating the baking sheets front to back halfway through the baking time so the pies brown evenly. Remove the baking sheets from the oven and let the pies cool slightly before serving.

Savory Pie Dough

This dough is a workhorse in my kitchens. It's everything I want in a pie dough: It's flaky, buttery, and a little bit salty. I use this at my restaurants and in this book, for both sweet and savory pies.

90 grams (3 tablespoons) ice-cold water

60 grams (¼ cup) heavy cream

560 grams (4 cups) unbleached all-purpose flour, plus more for dusting

1 tablespoon plus 1 teaspoon Diamond Crystal kosher salt

454 grams (4 sticks) cold unsalted butter, cubed

1. Whisk the water and cream in a small bowl.

2. Combine the flour and salt in a stand mixer fitted with the paddle and mix on low speed for a few seconds to distribute the salt. Add the butter and mix on low speed until the flour and butter look like wet sand. Add the cream/water mixture and mix on low speed until the dough just comes together.

3. Lightly dust a work surface with flour and transfer the dough to the floured surface. Consider what you are making with the dough before forming it. If you are making pot pies, gather the dough with your hands and pat it into one 1-inch-thick disk. If you are making quiche, pat it into two 1-inch-thick rectangular blocks. If you are making a classic round pie, pat it into two 1-inch-thick disks. For slab pies, pat the dough into one 1-inch-thick rectangular block. Wrap each disk or block of dough in plastic wrap and place it in the refrigerator to chill until it's firm, at least 2 hours. (You can also freeze the dough for up to 3 months. Place the frozen dough in the refrigerator overnight to thaw it.)

Bacon, Potato, and Comté Quiche

My rule of thumb when tinkering is, if you can't make it as good or better, then leave it alone. Quiche Lorraine, made with Gruyère cheese and bacon, is the beloved classic, and it's so delicious that to improve upon it was a challenge. So, I tinkered away and came up with this version, which includes bacon, and leeks, and Comté in place of Gruyère. I'm confident in saying it tastes as good as the classic, but better? You'll have to be the judge.

Comté is an Alpine cheese, made in a similar style to Gruyère. If you can't find it, use Gruyère. This recipe makes two slender rectangular quiches, baked in shallow fluted French tart pans.

Makes two 13 × 4-inch rectangular quiches

What You Need—
The Essential Special Equipment

Cooking spray

2 (13¾ × 4¼-inch) rectangular tart pans with removable bottoms

Pie weights (or dried beans)

Mandoline

For the Tart Shells

Unbleached all-purpose flour for dusting

½ recipe Savory Pie Dough (page 313)

For the Filling

2 slices thick-cut applewood-smoked bacon (about 2 ounces)

¼ pound medium Yukon Gold potatoes

1 pound leeks (about 2 medium)

1 large or 2 medium yellow Spanish onions (about 1 pound), cut into 1-inch chunks

57 grams (4 tablespoons) unsalted butter

½ teaspoon Diamond Crystal kosher salt

113 grams (4 ounces) Comté cheese, shredded (about 1 cup)

For the Custard

3 extra-large eggs

2 extra-large egg yolks

240 grams (1 cup) heavy cream

122.5 grams (½ cup) whole milk

85 grams (about ¾ cup) finely grated Parmesan cheese

43.5 grams (3 tablespoons) crème fraîche (or 45.75 grams/3 tablespoons sour cream)

1 teaspoon Diamond Crystal kosher salt

1 small yellow onion

1 tablespoon fresh thyme leaves

---

1. To make the tart shells, coat the bottoms and sides of the tart pans with cooking spray.

2. Lightly dust a work surface with flour. Remove one of the blocks of dough from the refrigerator, unwrap, and place on the floured surface. Pound the dough with a rolling pin to soften it until it is malleable and as flat as possible. (The more you flatten it by pounding it, the easier it will be to roll out.) Dust the dough and rolling pin lightly with flour. Using firm, steady pressure, roll the dough into a large rectangle about ⅛ inch thick, rotating the dough as you roll, and dusting the dough, rolling pin, and work surface with flour as needed. →

3. Place one of the tart pans upside down on the dough and use a paring knife or kitchen shears to cut 2 rectangles of dough that are at least 2 inches larger all around than the pan. (You'll cut the dough more precisely later; you're trimming at this point to make the sheet of dough easier to work with.)

4. Working with one pan at a time, loosely wrap the dough around the rolling pin and lower it over the prepared pan, centering it so that it overhangs evenly around the edges. Lift the edges of the dough and let it drop into the creases of the pan; dip the knuckle of your index finger in flour and use it to gently press the dough into the creases. Don't stretch the dough to fit or it will shrink when it is baked. Using kitchen shears, trim the dough so there are 1½ inches of dough overhanging all around. (Gather the trimmings, pat them into a disk, and wrap them in plastic wrap to use another time, or discard them.) Dot the bottom of the tart shell all over with the tines of a fork. Line and dot the second pan in the same way. Place the tart shells in the refrigerator to chill until the dough is firm, at least 1 hour.

5. Adjust an oven rack to the center position and preheat the oven to 350°F. Line a large baking sheet with parchment paper.

6. Remove the tart shells from the refrigerator. Coat two pieces of parchment on one side with cooking spray. Gently press a piece of parchment, sprayed-side down, into each tart shell to cover the dough. Fill the tart shells with pie weights (or dried beans), pressing them into the corners of the shells. Place the tart shells on the baking sheet.

7. Place the baking sheet with the tart shells on the center rack of the oven and bake until the edges of the crusts are light golden, 35 to 45 minutes, lifting the parchment to peek under it and gauge the color. Remove the shells from the oven and remove the weights and parchment paper. (Set the weights aside to cool to room temperature, then put them away to use again for the same purpose. Discard the parchment paper.) Return the shells to the oven, rotating the baking sheet from front to back, and bake until the shells are rich golden brown and uniform in color, another 15 to 20 minutes. Remove the tart shells from the oven and set aside to cool to room temperature. Leave the oven on for the bacon.

8. To prepare the filling, lay the bacon on a baking sheet and bake it on the center rack of the oven until it is cooked all the way through but not crisp, 15 to 17 minutes, rotating the baking sheet front to back halfway through the cooking time so the bacon cooks evenly. Remove the bacon from the oven and transfer it to paper towels to drain and cool to room temperature. Slice the bacon at an extreme angle into ¼-inch-wide strips. Set aside to sprinkle over the filling.

9. Place a steamer basket in a large saucepan and fill the saucepan 1 inch deep with water. Bring the water to a boil over high heat. Place the potatoes in the steamer basket, cover the saucepan, and steam the potatoes until they are tender when pierced with a paring knife, 20 to 25 minutes. Turn off the heat, uncover the pan, and set aside until the potatoes are cool enough to touch. Gently peel them with your hands and discard the peels. Break the potatoes up into roughly ¾-inch pieces and place them in a bowl.

10. Halve the leeks lengthwise. Lay each half flat and cut them at an extreme angle into 1-inch segments, white and light-green parts only (discard the dark green ends). Rinse them well and drain in a colander.

11. Put the leeks, onion, and 2 tablespoons of the butter in a large sauté pan. Sprinkle with the salt and cook over medium-high heat, stirring occasionally, until the leeks and onion begin to soften, about 10 minutes. Add 1 tablespoon of the butter and cook for another 10 minutes, stirring occasionally. Add the remaining 1 tablespoon butter and cook, stirring occasionally, until the vegetables are caramelized, 10 or 15 minutes. Remove from the heat. Add the potatoes and Comté and gently fold them in.

12. To make the custard, whisk the whole eggs and egg yolks in a large measuring cup or medium bowl to break up the yolks. Add the cream, milk, Parmesan, crème fraîche, and salt and stir with the whisk to combine the ingredients.

13. Peel the small onion and trim off and discard the stem end; leave the root end intact. Holding on to the root end, place the onion on a mandoline and slice 10 rings that are ⅛ inch thick or thinner. (Reserve the remaining onion for another use, such as to make stock, or discard it.) →

14. To assemble the quiches, spoon the filling into the tart shells, dividing it evenly, and smooth out the surface with your hands. Slowly pour or ladle the custard into the shells, moving from one end of the shell to the other, until the custard reaches ¼ inch from the top. (Discard the remaining custard.) Sprinkle the bacon over the custard, dividing it evenly. Lay the onion slices down the center of each quiche, overlapping them. Sprinkle the thyme over the quiches, dividing it evenly.

15. Bake the quiches until the tops are golden brown and the custard is set (when you gently shake the baking sheet, the custard will jiggle but it won't seem liquid), 35 to 45 minutes, rotating the baking sheet front to back halfway through the baking time so the quiches bake evenly. Remove the baking sheet from the oven and set aside for the quiches to cool for at least 1 hour for the filling to set before slicing them.

16. To remove the quiches from the pans, one at a time, push up on the bottom of the pans to remove the outer walls. Slide the quiches off the pan bottoms onto a large rectangular serving platter or boards.

Lattice-Topped Apple Pie

There are two camps when it comes to apple pie: the raw camp and the cooked. Much to my friend food writer Ruth Reichl's frustration, I am in the "cooked" camp. I sauté the apples in butter and sugar before baking them in the pie shell. Apples collapse a lot when cooked, so especially for a two-crusted pie such as this one, if you don't sauté the apples first, instead of a deep-dish apple pie full of apples, you end up with a deep-dish pie with a giant pocket of air between the apples and the top crust. The apples are cooked in five batches, to avoid overcrowding the pan. And they're cooked slowly to allow them to absorb the flavors of the cinnamon-sugar, cream, and bourbon they're cooked in. So this recipe takes some time. But I think you'll agree that it's worth it.

I use Granny Smith apples for this pie. They're tart and flavorful, they hold their shape when cooked, and they're consistently good year-round. For the ultimate experience, serve the pie warm, with a scoop of vanilla ice cream.

Makes one 9-inch pie

**What You Need—
The Essential Special Equipment**
Ruler
Rolling pastry cutter
9-inch (5-cup capacity) metal pie pan
Cooking spray

For the Crust
Unbleached all-purpose flour for dusting
Savory Pie Dough (page 313), formed into 1 disk and 1 block of equal size

For the Apples
6 pounds Granny Smith apples
400 grams (2 cups) granulated sugar
1 tablespoon ground cinnamon

454 grams (4 sticks) unsalted butter
1 tablespoon pure vanilla bean paste or vanilla extract
240 grams (1 cup) heavy cream
240 grams (1 cup) bourbon (or other whiskey)

To Assemble and Bake
30 grams (2 tablespoons) heavy cream

1. To make the crust, coat the pie pan with cooking spray. Line a baking sheet with parchment paper.

2. Lightly dust a work surface with flour. Remove the block of dough from the refrigerator and place on the floured surface. Pound the dough with a rolling pin to soften it until it is malleable and as flat as possible. Roll the dough out to a rectangle ⅛ inch thick. Using a ruler and rolling pastry cutter or a paring knife, cut the dough into strips 2½ to 3 inches wide. Lay the lattice strips in a single layer on the prepared baking sheet and place it in the refrigerator. →

3. Dust the surface with additional flour, remove the disk of dough from the refrigerator, unwrap, and place on the floured surface. Pound the dough with a rolling pin and roll it out into a round ⅛ inch thick, dusting with flour as needed. Place the pie pan upside down on the dough and use a paring knife or kitchen shears to cut a round of dough that is at least 3 inches larger all around than the pan. (You'll cut the dough more precisely later; you're trimming at this point to make the sheet of dough easier to work with.)

4. Loosely wrap the dough around the rolling pin and lower it over the prepared pan, centering it so that the dough overhangs evenly around the pan's rim. Lift the edges of the dough and let it drop into the pan; dip the knuckle of your index finger in flour and use it to gently press the dough into the creases of the pan. Don't stretch the dough to fit or it will shrink when it is baked. Using kitchen shears, trim the dough so there are 1½ inches of dough overhanging all around. (Gather the trimmings, pat them into a disk, and wrap them in plastic wrap to use another time, or discard them.) Place the pie shell in the refrigerator. Chill the pie shell and the lattice strips until the dough is firm, at least 1 hour.

5. To prepare the apples, line a large baking sheet with parchment paper.

6. Peel the apples and then, one at a time, place them upright on a cutting board. Make four cuts from top to bottom around the core, leaving you with four clean slabs of apple. Discard the core and repeat with the remaining apples. Lay the apple slabs flat-side down and cut them into ¼-inch-thick slices.

7. Stir the sugar and cinnamon together in a small bowl. Measure out 3 tablespoons of the cinnamon-sugar and set it aside to sprinkle over the pie.

8. Melt 1 stick (113 grams) of the butter in a large sauté pan with high sides over medium-high heat until it begins to bubble; do not let it brown. Stir in the vanilla. Lay one-quarter of the apple slices in a single layer in the pan and sauté them until they have begun to soften but not brown, 6 to 8 minutes, folding them with a silicone spatula and swirling the pan so the butter doesn't burn. Reduce the heat to medium-low and sprinkle with one-fifth of the cinnamon-sugar. Gently fold the apple slices to distribute the cinnamon-sugar evenly. Continue cooking the apples

for about 5 minutes, folding them, and swirling the pan, until the juices released from the apples have reduced to a thick syrup and the apples are translucent and caramelized, but still holding their shape, about 5 minutes; reduce the heat if your apples are starting to brown or fall apart. Add one-quarter of the cream and tilt the pan to distribute it. Increase the heat to medium-high and simmer for about 5 minutes, until the cream has reduced to a thick sauce and the apples are shiny. Remove from the heat and pour in one-fifth of the bourbon. Return the heat to medium-high and cook the apples until the sauce has reduced to a thick caramel, about 2 minutes. (Don't be alarmed if the alcohol in the pan ignites; it will extinguish by itself as the alcohol cooks off.) Gently transfer the apples to a colander to drain them. (Reserve the liquid for another use.)

9. Rinse and dry the pan you cooked the apples in and repeat, cooking the remaining apples with the remaining butter, vanilla, cinnamon-sugar, cream, and bourbon in three more batches. While you are sautéing the next batch, transfer the already sautéed apples to the baking sheet so the colander is free. Add each batch of drained apples to the baking sheet. When you have sautéed all the apple slices, set them aside to cool to room temperature. Cover the baking sheet with plastic wrap and place it in the refrigerator for several hours until the apples are chilled.

10. Remove the pie shell and lattice strips from the refrigerator and set aside for about 5 minutes to soften slightly. Remove the apples from the refrigerator and lay them in the shell, cupping your hands around the apples to bring them into a smooth, high mound.

11. Lay one lattice strip across the center of the pie. Lay another strip across the center of the pie at a 90-degree angle to the first strip. Lay one strip on either side of the first, with no space between the strips, weaving each strip under and over the existing strips. Lay one strip on each side of the strip that you placed at a 90-degree angle, weaving them under and over the existing strips. Set aside the parchment-lined baking sheet that the strips of dough were on to bake the pie on. Press the top and bottom crusts together at the point where they meet the edge of the pie pan to seal them together. Using kitchen shears, trim the sealed dough so there are 1½ inches of dough overhanging. (Discard the trimmings.) Roll the edge of the dough under itself to create a thick lip of dough that rests on the rim of the pie pan. →

Press the thumb of one hand on the lip to create an indentation in the dough and press the thumb and forefinger of the other hand on either side of the first thumb, creating a U-shaped indentation. Continue around the perimeter of the crust, creating a crimped, scalloped edge.

12. To assemble and bake the pie, pour the cream into a small bowl and brush it over the lattice strips and around the edges of the pie shell. Sprinkle with the reserved 3 tablespoons of cinnamon-sugar.

13. Arrange an oven rack to the lowest position and preheat the oven to 425°F. Line a large baking sheet with parchment paper.

14. Remove the pie from the refrigerator and place it on the prepared baking sheet.

15. Place the baking sheet with the pie on the lowest rack of the oven and bake for 30 minutes. Rotate the baking sheet front to back so the pie browns evenly. Reduce the oven temperature to 375°F and bake the pie until the crust is deep golden brown and the juices from the fruit are bubbling through the gaps in the crust, another 35 to 45 minutes. Remove the baking sheet from the oven and let the pie cool slightly.

16. Serve warm or at room temperature, with vanilla ice cream.

Chess Pie

Chess pie, also called vinegar pie, is a Southern classic. There are many stories about how it got its name. One is that it was whipped up by a formerly enslaved cook and, when somebody thought it was delicious, she said it was "Just pie," which, with her Southern accent, sounded like "chess pie." Another story is that it was made from "whatever's in the chest." And yet another explanation is that the name derives from the fact that the pie is kept in a pie chest. I combined the idea of chess pie with another Southern classic, buttermilk pie, and came up with my version of "just pie." Both pies belong to a category of Southern pies called Desperation Pies, so named because they were made in times of desperation, with humble, inexpensive ingredients. I love the acidity of chess pie, but what really sells me on it is the texture. I don't think I've ever had anything like it. It contains a lot of egg, so it's a custard, but it utilizes bread crumbs and cornmeal as thickeners. The result is a unique, silky, luscious texture—and a pie that tastes unmistakably homemade.

A lot of recipes tell you to serve chess pie while it's still warm from the oven, but I like it best the day after it's made, chilled. It sets up in the refrigerator and that's when its unique texture really shines.

Makes one 9½-inch pie

What You Need—
The Essential Special Equipment

9½-inch (6-cup capacity) glass or metal pie pan

Cooking spray

Pie weights (or dried beans)

For the Crust

Unbleached all-purpose flour for dusting

½ recipe Savory Pie Dough (page 313)

For the Filling

339 grams (3 sticks) unsalted butter, cubed

100 grams (3½ ounces) country bread, crusts removed, cut into large cubes

90 grams (¼ cup plus 2 tablespoons) champagne vinegar (or white wine vinegar)

140 grams (½ cup plus 2 tablespoons) buttermilk (preferably whole-milk or low-fat), shaken

1½ teaspoons pure vanilla bean paste or vanilla extract

9 grams (1 tablespoon) unbleached all-purpose flour

22.5 grams (2 tablespoons) fine yellow stoneground polenta

1½ teaspoons Diamond Crystal kosher salt

6 extra-large egg yolks

225 grams (1 cup plus 2 tablespoons) granulated sugar →

1. To make the crust, coat the pie pan with cooking spray.

2. Lightly dust a work surface with flour. Remove the dough from the refrigerator, unwrap, and place on the floured surface. Pound the dough with a rolling pin to soften it until it is malleable and as flat as possible. (The more you flatten the dough by pounding it, the easier it will be to roll out.) Dust the dough and rolling pin lightly with flour and, applying firm, steady pressure, roll the dough into a round ⅛ inch thick, dusting with flour as needed.

3. Place the pie pan upside down on the dough and use a paring knife or kitchen shears to cut a round of dough that is at least 3 inches larger all around than the pan. (You'll cut the dough more precisely later; you're trimming at this point to make the sheet of dough easier to work with.)

4. Loosely wrap the dough around the rolling pin and lower it over the prepared pan, centering it so that the dough overhangs evenly around the edge. Lift the edges of the dough and let it drop into the pan; dip the knuckle of your index finger in flour and use it to gently press the dough into the creases of the pan. Don't stretch the dough to fit or it will shrink when it is baked. Using kitchen shears, trim the dough so there are 1½ inches of dough overhanging all around. (Gather the trimmings, pat them into a disk, and wrap them in plastic wrap to use another time, or discard them.) Fold the edge of the dough under itself to create a thick lip that rests on the edge of the pie pan.

5. Press the thumb of one hand on the lip to create an indentation in the dough and press the thumb and forefinger of the other hand on either side of the first thumb, creating a U-shaped indentation. Continue around the perimeter of the crust, creating a crimped, scalloped edge. Dot the bottom of the pie shell all over with the tines of a fork and place the pie shell in the refrigerator to chill until the dough is firm, at least 1 hour.

6. Adjust an oven rack to the center position and preheat the oven to 350°F. Line a large baking sheet with parchment paper.

7. Remove the pie shell from the refrigerator, coat a piece of parchment on one side with cooking spray, and gently press the paper sprayed-side down into the shell to cover the dough. Fill the shell with pie weights (or dried beans), pressing them into the creases of the pie shell. Place the pie shell on the baking sheet.

8. Bake the pie shell on the center rack of the oven until the edges of the crust are light golden, 30 to 40 minutes, lifting the parchment to peek under it and gauge the color. Remove the shell from the oven and lift out the weights and parchment paper. (Set the weights aside to cool to room temperature, then put them away to use again for the same purpose. Discard the parchment paper.) Return the shell to the oven, rotating it from front to back, and bake until it is evenly golden brown, 8 to 10 minutes longer. Remove the shell from the oven and set aside to cool to room temperature. Leave the oven on.

9. To make the filling, place the butter in a small saucepan or skillet with a light-colored bottom to make golden butter. Warm the butter over medium heat until it melts and begins to bubble, swirling the pan occasionally. Cook the butter, swirling often so it cooks evenly, until it is golden and the milk solids are caramel colored, 3 to 6 minutes. Remove from the heat. Working quickly so the butter doesn't continue to cook, weigh out 227 grams (or measure 1 cup plus 1 tablespoon) of butter, making sure to include the milk solids. (Reserve the remaining butter for another use.) Transfer the butter to a bowl and set it aside to cool to room temperature. Cover the bowl with plastic wrap and place it in the refrigerator to chill until the butter is solid.

10. Put the bread cubes in a food processor (or mini food processor) and pulse to fine crumbs. Weigh out 55 grams (or measure 1 cup) of bread crumbs. (Reserve any remaining crumbs for another use or discard them.) Place the bread crumbs in a small bowl and pour the vinegar over them. Set aside for at least 20 minutes to let the bread crumbs absorb the vinegar.

11. Combine the buttermilk and vanilla in a small bowl. Combine the flour, polenta, and salt in a separate small bowl. Whisk the egg yolks together in a medium bowl.

12. Remove the butter from the refrigerator and place the bowl in a large bowl of hot water to help release the butter. Dry off the bowl and invert it to release the butter onto a cutting board. (Alternatively, you may be able to wedge a knife under the butter and pop it out.) Cut the butter into roughly ½-inch cubes.

13. Put the butter in a stand mixer fitted with the paddle and beat on medium-high speed until the butter is soft and smooth but still cold, →

about 1 minute, stopping to scrape down the sides and bottom of the bowl and the paddle with a rubber spatula whenever the butter is accumulating. Add the sugar and beat on medium speed until the mixture is smooth, about 1 minute; do not mix longer than necessary. With the mixer on medium speed, drizzle in the egg yolks, stopping to scrape down the mixer and making sure the egg is incorporated before adding more. Add the bread crumbs and the vinegar they were soaked in and mix on low speed for about 15 seconds until combined. Stop the mixer and scrape down the bowl with the spatula. Return the mixer to low speed, add the buttermilk/vanilla mixture and the flour/polenta mixture alternately, in four additions for the buttermilk and vanilla and three additions for the flour and polenta mixture, starting and ending with the buttermilk mixture; mix until the additions are incorporated before the next addition, stopping to scrape down the bowl and paddle as needed. Stop the mixer, remove the bowl and paddle from the stand, and clean them with the spatula, scraping the bowl from the bottom up to release any ingredients that may be stuck there. (The batter may look separated; this is normal.)

14. Scrape the filling into the crust and smooth out the top with an offset spatula.

15. Place the pie on a baking sheet and bake it on the center rack of the oven until the top is browned and a thin crust has formed on top (it will still jiggle when you shake it but will set up when it cools), 55 to 60 minutes, rotating it front to back halfway through the baking time so it browns evenly. Remove the pie from the oven and set aside to cool to room temperature.

16. Place the pie in the refrigerator, uncovered, overnight or for at least several hours to chill and set the filling. Serve cold.

Sweet Tart Dough

I learned to make this classic tart dough at Michael's restaurant in the 1980s and I've never deviated from it. It is a *pâte sucrée,* or sweet dough, which is enriched with egg, cream, and sugar. It's buttery and crispy and tastes like a cookie. (In fact, if you have scraps left over, roll them out, cut them, and bake them to make delicious buttery cookies. You can sprinkle them with sugar, or spices, or bake the dough plain.) It is strong enough to hold up to any filling, and it's so versatile. It is the only *pâte sucrée* recipe you will ever need.

Makes enough for one
10- or 12-inch tart

2 extra-large egg yolks

60 grams (¼ cup) heavy cream

385 grams (2¾ cups) unbleached all-purpose flour, plus more for dusting

100 grams (½ cup) granulated sugar

1½ teaspoons Diamond Crystal kosher salt

226 grams (2 sticks) cold unsalted butter, cubed

1. To make the dough, whisk the egg yolks and cream together in a small bowl.

2. Combine the flour, sugar, and salt in a stand mixer fitted with the paddle and mix on low speed to incorporate the ingredients. Add the butter and mix on low speed until the ingredients form the consistency of a fine meal. Add the egg yolk/cream mixture and mix on medium-low speed until the dough just comes together.

3. Lightly flour a work surface and turn the dough out onto it. Gather the dough into a ball in your hands and press it into a 1-inch-thick disk. Wrap the disk tightly in plastic wrap and refrigerate until firm, at least 2 hours. You can also freeze the dough for up to 3 months. Place the frozen dough in the refrigerator overnight to thaw it.

Pumpkin Tart with Dates (top);
Pecan Tart (bottom)

Pumpkin Tart with Dates

If you're setting out to make Thanksgiving pies, I offer you two options in the pumpkin category: this tart, made with canned pumpkin puree, and the Honeynut Squash Pie (page 437), made with fresh roasted Honeynut squash. Pumpkin puree is one of the few canned items that I can get behind, because it doesn't contain extraneous, unpronounceable, or unnecessary ingredients: just pumpkin. It's also the ideal consistency; fresh pumpkin is way too watery to use in this recipe. Although I appreciate the integrity of the Honeynut Squash Pie, made with fresh winter squash, this tart, with its silky, custardy texture and its sleek, low profile, is equally special, and closer to the pumpkin pie of our childhood holiday memories. Because the spices play such an important role in this filling, I recommend (even more strongly than I usually would!) that you freshly grind them.

Makes one 10-inch tart

**What You Need—
The Essential Special Equipment**

Cooking spray

10-inch flan ring

Pie weights (or dried beans)

12-inch cardboard cake round

For the Tart Shell

½ recipe Sweet Tart Dough (page 329)

Unbleached all-purpose flour for dusting (optional)

For the Filling

10 large Medjool dates

5 extra-large egg yolks

75 grams (¼ cup plus 2 tablespoons) granulated sugar

113 grams (½ cup) canned unsweetened pumpkin puree (preferably organic)

375 grams (1½ cups plus 1 tablespoon) heavy cream

¼ teaspoon freshly ground cinnamon

¼ teaspoon freshly grated nutmeg

½ teaspoon Diamond Crystal kosher salt

1. To prepare the tart shell, lay a sheet of parchment paper on a work surface. Remove the dough from the refrigerator, unwrap, and place in the center of the paper. Pound the dough with a rolling pin to soften it until it is malleable and as flat as possible. Lay a sheet of parchment paper on top of the dough, lining it up with the lower sheet. Applying firm, steady pressure with the rolling pin, roll the dough out between the parchment paper to ³⁄₁₆ inch thick. (Alternatively, you can skip the parchment paper and roll the dough on a flour-dusted work surface.) Lay the dough on a baking sheet and place it in the refrigerator to chill until it is firm, at least 1 hour.

2. Coat the inside of the flan ring with cooking spray.

3. Remove the baking sheet with the sheet of dough from the refrigerator. Transfer the dough to a work surface. Peel the top sheet of parchment →

off the dough and lay it back down on the dough. Flip the sheet of dough over. Peel off the top sheet of parchment paper and lay it clean-side up on the baking sheet to line it. Place the flan ring on the dough and use it as a guide to cut a round of dough that is at least 1 inch larger all around than the ring.

4. Place the ring on the prepared baking sheet. Loosely wrap the dough around a rolling pin and lower it over the ring, centering it so that the dough overhangs evenly around the rim. To fit the dough into the ring, lift the edges and let the dough drop into the ring; dip the knuckle of your index finger in flour and use it to gently press the dough into the creases where the ring meets the baking sheet. Don't stretch the dough to fit or it will shrink when it is baked. Run a rolling pin at a 45-degree angle around the edge of the ring to trim off the excess dough. (Pat the scraps into a 1-inch-thick disk, wrap in plastic, and refrigerate to use another time, or discard them.) Dot the bottom of the tart shell all over with the tines of a fork and place the baking sheet in the refrigerator to chill the dough until firm, at least 1 hour.

5. Adjust an oven rack to the center position and preheat the oven to 350°F.

6. Remove the tart shell from the refrigerator. Coat a piece of parchment on one side with cooking spray and gently press it, sprayed-side down, into the shell to cover the dough. Fill the shell with pie weights (or dried beans), pressing them into the creases of the tart shell.

7. Bake the tart shell on the center rack of the oven until the edges of the crust are light golden, 30 to 40 minutes, lifting the parchment to peek under it and gauge the color. Remove the shell from the oven and remove the weights and parchment paper. (Set the weights aside to cool to room temperature, then put them away to use again for the same purpose. Discard the parchment paper.) Return the shell to the oven, rotating the baking sheet from front to back, and bake until it is evenly golden brown, 8 to 10 minutes longer. Remove the shell from the oven and set it aside to cool to room temperature.

8. Reduce the oven temperature to 300°F.

9. To prepare the filling, fill a bowl with hot water and submerge the dates in the water for about 10 minutes to loosen the skins. Remove the dates from the water and pat them dry with paper towels. Cut a lengthwise slit down the

center of each date and discard the pits. Pat the dates with a paper towel to dry them.

10. Whisk the egg yolks and sugar together in a medium bowl until they're smooth. Pour the pumpkin puree into a large bowl.

11. Combine the cream, cinnamon, nutmeg, and salt in a medium saucepan over medium-high heat. When the cream just begins to boil, remove from the heat. Add 1 cup of the cream in a slow stream to the bowl with the eggs, whisking to prevent the cream from cooking the eggs. Add the warmed egg/cream mixture to the rest of the cream in the saucepan, whisking as you add it. Return the heat to medium and cook the custard, stirring with a silicone spatula, until there are no bubbles on the surface and the cream thickens slightly, about 1½ minutes. Pour the custard through a fine-mesh sieve into a large heat-resistant pitcher or spouted measuring cup. Pour about one-third of the custard into the bowl with the pumpkin puree, stirring with a rubber spatula to combine them. Add the rest of the custard and stir to combine. Set aside to cool slightly.

12. Arrange the dates slit-side down on the surface of the tart shell, splayed out like a sunburst, about 1 inch from the outer edge and spaced evenly so that when you slice the tart, each slice will have a whole date in its center.

13. Pour the filling into the tart shell until it is almost flush with the top of the shell. The filling should be the perfect amount, but if you have any left over, discard it; don't overfill the tart.

14. Place the baking sheet with the tart on it in the oven, taking care not to spill the filling. Bake until the filling is firm and the very center still jiggles slightly when you gently shake the pan, 20 to 30 minutes, rotating the baking sheet front to back halfway during baking time so the tart browns evenly. Remove the tart from the oven and set aside to cool to room temperature.

15. To remove the tart from the ring, run the tip of a paring knife around the inside edges of the ring to loosen any stuck bits. Slide the tart onto a cake round and slide it off the round onto a serving platter. Remove the ring. Slice the tart into 10 equal wedges, with each slice getting one date.

Pecan Tart

The best pecan pie is a pecan tart. A tart pan has a lower profile than the shallowest pie pan, which means that when I turn this classic goopy pie into a tart, I get a lot of crust, and just enough of that gooey, sticky sweet stuff to bind the enormous quantity of pecans that I use in this recipe. In the time it takes to get the crust a nice golden brown, the goop toward the outer edges of the pie cooks to the point where it's almost chewy, which is another bonus. Corn syrup is the base of traditional pecan pie; I replace it with Lyle's Golden Syrup, a thick, amber-colored syrup made from sugar cane that is common in British baking. It helps to make the goop in this tart, what little there is, flavorful and nuanced, and not just sweet. (See photo page 330.)

Makes one 10-inch tart

**What You Need—
The Essential Special Equipment**

Cooking spray

10-inch flan ring

12-inch cardboard cake round

For the Tart Shell

Sweet Tart Dough (page 329)

Unbleached all-purpose flour for dusting

For the Filling

400 grams (4 cups) pecan halves

255 grams (¾ cup) Lyle's Golden Syrup

75 grams (¼ cup plus 2 tablespoons packed) dark brown sugar

75 grams (¼ cup plus 2 tablespoons) granulated sugar

¼ cup bourbon

1 tablespoon pure vanilla bean paste or vanilla extract

2 extra-large egg yolks

1 extra-large egg

28 grams (2 tablespoons) unsalted butter, cubed

1 teaspoon Diamond Crystal kosher salt

1. To prepare the tart shell, lay a sheet of parchment paper on a work surface. Remove the dough from the refrigerator, unwrap, and place in the center of the parchment paper. Pound the dough with a rolling pin to soften it until it is malleable and as flat as possible. (The more you flatten it, the easier it will be to roll out.) Lay another sheet of parchment paper on top of the dough, lining it up with the lower sheet of parchment. Applying firm, steady pressure with the rolling pin, roll the dough out between the parchment paper to ³⁄₁₆ inch thick. (Alternatively, you can skip the parchment paper and roll the dough on a flour-dusted work surface, dusting the surface, the dough, or the pin with flour as needed.) Lay the dough on a baking sheet and place it in the refrigerator to chill until it is firm, at least 1 hour.

2. Coat the inside of the flan ring with cooking spray.

3. Remove the baking sheet with the sheet of dough from the refrigerator and transfer the dough to a work surface. Peel the top sheet of parchment off the dough and lay it back down on the dough. (This loosens the parchment so you will be able to lift the dough off without it sticking.) Flip the sheet of dough over. Peel off the top sheet of parchment paper and lay it clean-side up on the baking sheet to line it. Place the flan ring on the dough and use it as a guide to cut a round of dough that is at least 1 inch larger all around than the ring. (You will trim the dough to fit the ring in the next step; this just makes the dough easier to work with.)

4. Place the ring on the prepared baking sheet. Loosely wrap the dough around a rolling pin and lower it over the ring, centering it so that the dough overhangs evenly around the rim. To fit the dough into the ring, lift the edges and let the dough drop into the ring; dip the knuckle of your index finger in flour and use it to gently press the dough into the creases where the ring meets the baking sheet. Don't stretch the dough to fit or it will shrink when it is baked. Run a rolling pin at a 45-degree angle around the edge of the ring to trim off the excess dough. (Pat the scraps into a 1-inch-thick disk, wrap in plastic, and refrigerate to use another time, or discard them.) Place the tart shell in the refrigerator to chill until the dough is firm, at least 1 hour.

5. To make the filling, adjust an oven rack to the center position and preheat the oven to 350°F.

6. Pick out 2 cups of the best-looking pecans and set them aside to use for the top of the tart.

7. Spread the remaining pecans on a baking sheet and toast them on the center rack of the oven until they're lightly browned and fragrant, 15 to 20 minutes, shaking the baking sheet and rotating it front to back halfway through the toasting time so the pecans brown evenly. Remove the baking sheet from the oven. (If you think the nuts are on the verge of being overtoasted, transfer them to a plate so they don't continue to cook from the residual heat of the pan.) Set aside until the pecans cool enough to touch, then coarsely chop them.

8. Put the golden syrup, brown sugar, granulated sugar, bourbon, and vanilla in a medium bowl and whisk to combine.

9. Whisk the egg yolks and whole egg together in a small bowl. →

Pecan Tart (continued)

10. Place the butter in a small saucepan or skillet with a light-colored bottom to make brown butter. Warm the butter over medium heat until it melts and begins to bubble, swirling the pan occasionally so the butter cooks evenly. Continue to cook the butter, swirling often, until the melted butter is caramel colored and the solids are the color of coffee grounds, 5 to 8 minutes. Remove from the heat. Working quickly so the butter doesn't continue to cook, pour it into the bowl with the sugars. Add the salt and stir with a whisk to combine. Add the egg yolk mixture and whisk to combine. Stir in the chopped toasted pecans.

11. Remove the tart shell from the refrigerator and pour the filling into it.

12. Starting on the outside and working your way toward the center, arrange the pecan halves rounded-side up in concentric circles to cover the filling; the lines in the pecans will run perpendicular to the edge of the tart so in the end, they spread out from the center like a sunburst. Place the baking sheet with the tart on the center rack and bake until the filling has risen in a low dome and the edges of the crust are deep brown, 40 to 50 minutes, rotating the baking sheet front to back halfway through the baking time so the tart bakes evenly. Remove the tart from the oven and set it aside to cool to room temperature.

13. To remove the tart from the ring, run the tip of a paring knife around the inside edges of the ring to loosen any stuck bits. Slide the tart onto a cake round and slide it off the round onto a serving platter. Remove the ring.

Chocolate Ganache Tart

The next time you need to make a simple, sophisticated dessert for adult friends, this is your answer. Made with bittersweet chocolate and booze and dusted with cocoa powder, it is essentially a chocolate truffle in a tart shell. In my opinion, this tart is even better than a truffle because the truffle filling—dense, silky smooth, and not too sweet—is complemented by the crunchy, buttery crust. It is a portrait of simplicity. Because it is so straightforward, it really allows you to taste and appreciate the nuances of the chocolate itself. The ganache is poured into a low-profile tart shell, which makes for the ideal ratio of crust to ganache. I like to serve it in narrow slices; it's so dense and rich, a little goes a long way.

Makes one 12-inch tart

**What You Need—
The Essential Special Equipment**

12-inch flan ring

Cooking spray

Pie weights (or dried beans)

12-inch cardboard cake round

For the Tart Shell

Unbleached all-purpose flour for dusting (optional)

Sweet Tart Dough (page 329)

For the Filling

540 grams (19 ounces) bittersweet chocolate (70% cacao), coarsely chopped (about 3¾ cups); whole if you're using feves

400 grams (1⅔ cups) heavy cream

200 grams (¾ cup plus 2 tablespoons) crème fraîche (or 213 grams/¾ cup plus 2 tablespoons sour cream)

½ cup plus ½ tablespoon whiskey (or brandy)

63 grams (3 tablespoons) Lyle's Golden Syrup

1 teaspoon Diamond Crystal kosher salt

Natural cocoa powder for dusting

1. To prepare the tart shell, lay a sheet of parchment paper on a work surface. Remove the dough from the refrigerator, unwrap, and place in the center of the parchment paper. Pound the dough with a rolling pin to soften it until it is malleable and as flat as possible. (The more you flatten it, the easier it will be to roll out.) Lay a sheet of parchment paper on top of the dough, lining it up with the lower sheet of parchment. Applying firm, steady pressure with the rolling pin, roll the dough out between the parchment paper to ³⁄₁₆ inch thick. (Alternatively, you can skip the parchment paper and roll the dough on a flour-dusted work surface, dusting the surface, the dough, or the pin with flour as needed.) Lay the dough on a baking sheet and place it in the refrigerator to chill until it is firm, at least 1 hour.

2. Coat the inside of the flan ring with cooking spray. →

3. Remove the baking sheet with the sheet of dough from the refrigerator and transfer the dough to a work surface. Invert the baking sheet so the underside is facing up. (The 12-inch ring will not fit inside the pan.) Peel the top sheet of parchment off the dough and lay it back down on the dough. (This loosens the parchment so you will be able to lift the dough off without it sticking.) Flip the sheet of dough over. Peel off the top sheet of parchment paper and lay it clean-side up on the inverted baking sheet to line it. Place the flan ring on the dough and use it as a guide to cut a round of dough that is at least 1 inch larger all around than the ring. (You will trim the dough to fit the ring in the next step; this just makes the dough easier to work with.)

4. Place the ring on the prepared baking sheet. Loosely wrap the dough around a rolling pin and lower it over the ring, centering it so that the dough overhangs evenly around the edge. To fit the dough into the ring, lift the edges and let the dough drop into the ring; dip the knuckle of your index finger in flour and use it to gently press the dough into the creases where the ring meets the baking sheet. Don't stretch the dough to fit or it will shrink when it is baked. Run a rolling pin at a 45-degree angle around the edge of the ring to trim off the excess dough. (Pat the scraps into a 1-inch-thick disk, wrap in plastic, and refrigerate to use another time, or discard them.) Dot the bottom of the tart shell all over with the tines of a fork and place the baking sheet in the refrigerator to chill the dough until firm, at least 1 hour.

5. Adjust an oven rack to the center position and preheat the oven to 350°F.

6. Remove the tart shell from the refrigerator. Coat a piece of parchment on one side with cooking spray and gently press it, sprayed-side down, into the shell to cover the dough. Fill the shell with pie weights (or dried beans), pressing them into the creases of the tart shell.

7. Bake the tart shell on the center rack of the oven until the edges of the crust are light golden, 30 to 40 minutes, lifting the parchment to peek under it and gauge the color. Remove the shell from the oven and remove the weights and parchment paper. (Set the weights aside to cool to room temperature, then put them away to use again for the same purpose. Discard the parchment paper.) Return the shell to the oven, rotating the baking sheet front to back, and bake until it is evenly golden brown, 8 to 10 minutes. Remove the shell from the oven and set it aside to cool to room temperature. →

8. Reduce the oven temperature to 300°F.

9. To make the ganache, place the chocolate in a large heatproof bowl.

10. Put the cream, crème fraîche, and whiskey in a small saucepan and stir with a whisk to combine. Bring the mixture to a simmer over medium heat, stirring with the whisk to prevent the liquid from scorching. Remove from the heat, pour the mixture over the chopped chocolate, and let it sit for 5 minutes without stirring to allow the hot liquid to melt the chocolate. Stir with the whisk to combine the ingredients. Add the golden syrup and salt and stir to combine. Pour the chocolate mixture into a food processor and pulse to emulsify the mixture, stopping when the ganache is shiny and smooth.

11. Pour enough ganache into the prepared tart shell to reach ¼ inch from the top of the tart. Pour the remaining ganache into a small bowl and set aside to cool to room temperature without stirring or touching it. (Touching it may cause the ganache to separate.) Set the tart aside for several hours until the ganache is firm and solid to the touch.

12. Spoon the reserved ganache onto the center of the tart. Using an offset spatula, spread it toward the edges in swirling motions, leaving about ½ inch of the first layer of ganache visible around the edges.

13. To remove the tart from the ring, run the tip of a paring knife around the inside edges of the ring to loosen any stuck bits. Slide the tart onto a cake round and slide it off the round onto a serving platter. Remove the ring.

14. Dust with cocoa powder before serving.

Raisin Brown Butter Tart

I started making a brown butter tart at my first baking job at the legendary restaurant Michael's, in Santa Monica. In the forty years since, I've included the recipe in all my baking books and served some version of it in nearly every one of my restaurants—and I've never changed a thing about it. The tart is composed of a moist, buttery, cake-like filling baked into a cookie crust. It is so easy to make, and so versatile. I have included two versions in this book. This one is dotted with plump, brandy-soaked raisins and finished with a dusting of powdered sugar. And the other is topped with fresh in-season blueberries (see Brown Butter Tart with Blueberries, page 419).

You can use black, flame, or golden raisins; what's important is not the variety, but that the raisins are moist, plump, and large. I garnish mine with raisins on the stem, which you can find at some farmers' markets and at cheese shops.

Makes one 12-inch tart

**What You Need—
The Essential Special Equipment**

12-inch flan ring

Cooking spray

12-inch cardboard cake round

For the Tart Shell

Unbleached all-purpose flour for dusting (optional)

Sweet Tart Dough (page 329)

For the Filling

225 grams (1 cup) raisins

¼ cup brandy (or whiskey)

250 grams (1¼ cups) granulated sugar

3 extra-large eggs

1 tablespoon pure vanilla bean paste or vanilla extract

1 teaspoon Diamond Crystal kosher salt

170 grams (1½ sticks) unsalted butter

70 grams (½ cup) unbleached all-purpose flour

Raisins on the vine (optional)

Powdered sugar for dusting

---

1. To prepare the tart shell, lay a sheet of parchment paper on a work surface. Remove the dough from the refrigerator, unwrap, and place in the center of the parchment paper. Pound the dough with a rolling pin to soften it until it is malleable and as flat as possible. (The more you flatten it, the easier it will be to roll out.) Lay a sheet of parchment paper on top of the dough, lining it up with the lower sheet of parchment. Applying firm, steady pressure with the rolling pin, roll the dough out between the parchment paper to ³⁄₁₆ inch thick. (Alternatively, you can skip the parchment paper and roll the dough on a flour-dusted work surface, dusting the surface, the dough, or the pin with flour as needed.) Lay the dough on a baking sheet and place it in the refrigerator to chill until it is firm, at least 1 hour. →

2. Coat the inside of the flan ring with cooking spray.

3. Remove the baking sheet with the sheet of dough from the refrigerator and transfer the dough to a work surface. Invert the baking sheet so the underside is facing up. (The 12-inch ring will not fit inside the pan.) Peel the top sheet of parchment off the dough and lay it back down on the dough. (This loosens the parchment so you will be able to lift the dough off without it sticking.) Flip the sheet of dough over. Peel off the top sheet of parchment paper and lay it clean-side up on the inverted baking sheet to line it. Place the flan ring on the dough and use it as a guide to cut a round of dough that is at least 1 inch larger all around than the ring. (You will trim the dough to fit the ring in the next step; this just makes the dough easier to work with.)

4. Place the ring on the prepared baking sheet. Loosely wrap the dough around a rolling pin and lower it over the ring, centering it so that the dough overhangs evenly around the edge. To fit the dough into the ring, lift the edges and let the dough drop into the ring; dip the knuckle of your index finger in flour and use it to gently press the dough into the creases where the ring meets the baking sheet. Don't stretch the dough to fit or it will shrink when it is baked. Run a rolling pin at a 45-degree angle around the edge of the ring to trim off the excess dough. (Pat the scraps into a 1-inch-thick disk, wrap in plastic, and refrigerate to use another time, or discard them.) Place the tart shell in the refrigerator to chill until the dough is firm, at least 1 hour.

5. To make the filling and bake the tart, adjust an oven rack to the bottom third and preheat the oven to 350°F.

6. Combine the raisins with the brandy in a small saucepan and bring to a boil over high heat. Remove from the heat, cover the pan, and set aside to absorb the liquid and come to room temperature.

7. Combine the sugar, eggs, vanilla, and salt together in a large bowl and stir with a whisk to combine. Fill a medium saucepan with water. Place the bowl on top of the saucepan. (The weighted saucepan anchors the bowl, so it remains stable when you whisk ingredients in it.)

8. Place the butter in a small saucepan or skillet with a light-colored bottom to make brown butter. Warm the butter over medium heat until it melts and begins to bubble, swirling the pan occasionally so the butter cooks evenly. →

Continue to cook the butter, swirling often, until the melted butter is caramel colored and the solids are the color of coffee grounds, 5 to 8 minutes. Remove from the heat. Working quickly so the butter doesn't continue to brown, gradually add the brown butter to the bowl with the eggs in a slow, steady stream, whisking constantly so the warm butter doesn't cook the eggs. Add the flour and stir with the whisk until no lumps remain.

9. Remove the tart shell from the refrigerator. Pour the filling into the tart shell and use an offset spatula to smooth out the top. Drain the raisins, discarding the soaking liquid, and scatter them evenly over the top of the tart.

10. Place the baking sheet on the lower rack of the oven and bake the tart until the top is deep golden brown, 45 minutes to 1 hour, rotating the baking sheet front to back halfway through the baking time so the tart browns evenly. Remove the tart from the oven and set it aside to cool to room temperature.

11. To remove the tart from the ring, run the tip of a paring knife around the inside edges of the ring to loosen any stuck bits. Slide the tart onto a cake round and slide it off the round onto a serving platter. Remove the ring.

12. If you were lucky enough to find raisins on the vine, place a small bunch on each slice. Dust the tart with powdered sugar before serving.

Raspberry Crumble Bars

For me, these bars are the most craveable dessert in this book. They consist of three contrasting textures: tender, buttery shortbread crust, a raspberry jam filling, and topped with a crunchy crumble streusel. The streusel topping contains egg, which makes it hard and crunchy and prevents it from melting into the jam. The bars are baked until the streusel gets golden brown and, in the process, the butter in the shortbread crust caramelizes; the result is nothing you could really plan for, and it's so delicious.

Use a quality, artisanal seedy jam for these; the seeds add yet another texture to the bars—and enhance the overall experience. Raspberry, for me, makes the ultimate bar, but blackberry or apricot jam would also be delicious.

Makes one 10 × 16-inch slab

For the Crust

560 grams (4 cups) unbleached all-purpose flour, plus more for dusting

50 grams (½ cup) granulated sugar

50 grams (½ cup packed) dark brown sugar

56 grams (½ cup) potato starch

1 teaspoon Diamond Crystal kosher salt

452 grams (4 sticks) cold unsalted butter, cubed

For the Streusel

1 extra-large egg

350 grams (2½ cups) unbleached all-purpose flour

75 grams (½ cup plus 2 tablespoons) granulated sugar

1¼ teaspoons baking powder

1 teaspoon Diamond Crystal kosher salt

141 grams (1 stick plus 2 tablespoons) cold unsalted butter, cubed

For the Filling

640 grams (2 cups) seedy raspberry jam

---

1. To make the crust, put the flour, granulated sugar, brown sugar, potato starch, and salt in a stand mixer fitted with the paddle and mix on low speed to combine the ingredients and distribute the salt. Add the butter and mix on low speed until the dough comes together. (Don't mix the dough any longer than necessary.) Lightly flour a work surface and turn the dough out onto it. Lightly dust your hands with flour and form the dough into a 1-inch-thick block. Wrap the dough in plastic wrap and refrigerate until it's chilled and firm, at least 2 hours.

2. To make the streusel, beat the egg in a small bowl to break up the yolk.

3. Combine the flour, granulated sugar, baking powder, and salt in a stand mixer fitted with the paddle and mix on low speed for a few seconds to combine the ingredients. Add the butter and mix on low speed until the mixture is the texture of a coarse meal. Stop the mixer and remove the →

Raspberry Crumble Bars (continued)

bowl and paddle from the stand. Drizzle the egg over the flour/butter mixture and use your hands to incorporate it, forming uneven clumps. Don't work the ingredients so much that they come together into a dough. Cover the bowl and refrigerate the streusel until you're ready to use it.

4. Adjust the oven racks so one is in the center position and the other is in the top third of the oven and preheat the oven to 350°F.

5. Lay a sheet of parchment paper on your work surface. Draw a 10 × 16-inch rectangle on the paper; you will use this as a guide to shape the crust. Turn the parchment paper over and dust it lightly with flour. Remove the dough from the refrigerator, unwrap, and place on the floured parchment. Pound the dough with a rolling pin to soften it until it is malleable. Using your hands, form the dough into a 10 × 16-inch rectangle using the one you drew as a guide, dusting your hands as needed. Dot the dough all over with the tines of a fork.

6. Slide the parchment with the dough onto a large baking sheet and bake it on the center rack of the oven until the crust is light golden brown, 25 to 30 minutes, rotating the baking sheet front to back halfway through the baking time so the crust browns evenly. Remove the crust from the oven and set aside to cool to room temperature. Leave the oven on.

7. For the filling, spoon the jam onto the crust and use an offset spatula to spread it toward the edges, leaving ½ inch of crust free of jam. Remove the streusel from the refrigerator and scatter it in large clumps over the jam, leaving about ¼ inch of jam around the edges free of streusel.

8. Place the baking sheet on the upper rack of the oven and bake the bars until the streusel is deep golden brown and the jam is caramelized and chewy, 55 to 65 minutes, rotating the baking sheet front to back halfway through the baking time so the streusel browns evenly. Remove the baking sheet from the oven and set aside for the bars to cool to room temperature.

9. Slide the parchment paper with the bars onto a large cutting board or a work surface. Use a large sharp knife to cut into whatever size and shape you like.

Lemon Bars

If you are a purist, someone who doesn't like to mess with tradition, and you are also a lover of lemon bars, then you might want to turn the page. Because these are not the lemon bars of your childhood. People talk about lemon bars with nostalgia, but I didn't grow up eating them. And my experience of them as an adult was not positive. I found them to be way too sweet, as well as visually unappealing. The crust is too white, the filling is too wet and often cracked, and the powdered sugar melts into the filling and looks sticky.

My first several attempts at trying to improve upon lemon bars in the way they're usually made were failures. Traditionally, the goopy lemon topping is thickened with flour and cooked only in the oven. Every time I bit into one, my thought was "Why can't this be more like a French lemon curd tart?" So, I changed my course, and went in the direction of lemon curd. After about a dozen tries, I give you this: a tender, buttery shortbread crust topped with a rich, tart, bright, lemony curd. The crust contains ground pine nuts, which add a unique, nutty flavor. If you are lucky enough to find Sicilian pine nuts, use those. This is not a dessert to take on a picnic. The bars need to be served straight from the refrigerator. While writing this book, I sat in on a baking class taught by Claudia Fleming at the Food & Wine Classic in Aspen. It was there that I learned, after all these decades baking, that the secret to perfect lemon curd was to cook it to 180°F. Until then, I had always cooked it to a certain thickness. I just love the way that bakers share their secrets, and that even at the professional level, we always have something to learn from, and to teach, one another.

Makes one 8-inch square

What You Need—
The Essential Special Equipment

8-inch square baking dish

Cooking spray

For the Crust

57 grams (scant ½ cup) pine nuts

25 grams (2 tablespoons) granulated sugar

15 grams (2 tablespoons) powdered sugar

140 grams (1 cup) unbleached all-purpose flour

½ teaspoon Diamond Crystal kosher salt

113 grams (1 stick) cold unsalted butter, cubed

1 tablespoon pure vanilla bean paste or vanilla extract

For the Lemon Curd

6 extra-large eggs

6 extra-large egg yolks

300 grams (1½ cups) granulated sugar

1 teaspoon Diamond Crystal kosher salt

8 to 10 large lemons

14 grams (2 tablespoons) potato starch

226 grams (2 sticks) unsalted butter, cubed and left at room temperature until pliable but not greasy

Powdered sugar for dusting →

1. To make the crust, adjust an oven rack to the center position and preheat the oven to 350°F. Coat the bottom and sides of the baking dish with cooking spray.

2. Put the pine nuts, granulated sugar, and powdered sugar in a food processor and pulse until the nuts are the texture of a coarse meal. Add the flour and salt and pulse to combine. Add the butter and vanilla and pulse until the mixture is wet and crumbly; do not pulse so long that it comes together into a dough.

3. Turn the crumbly mixture out into the prepared baking dish and use your fingers to press it evenly over the bottom of the dish.

4. Bake the crust on the center rack of the oven until it is golden brown, 25 to 30 minutes, rotating it front to back halfway through the baking time so it browns evenly. Remove the crust from the oven and set it aside to cool to room temperature.

5. To make the lemon curd, fill a medium saucepan with 1½ to 2 inches of water and set a small stainless steel bowl atop the saucepan to make a double boiler, making sure the water doesn't touch the bottom of the bowl. Now that you know you have the correct size bowl, remove it from the saucepan and bring the water to a simmer over medium heat.

6. Fasten an instant-read thermometer to the side of the bowl, if you have one. Put the whole eggs, egg yolks, granulated sugar, and salt in the bowl. Use a fine Microplane to grate the zest (the bright-yellow outer layer) of 5 lemons into the bowl. Halve and juice enough lemons to get 372 grams (1½ cups) juice. Add 310 grams (1¼ cups) of the juice and whisk to break up the yolks and combine the ingredients. Put the remaining ¼ cup lemon juice in a small bowl and set it aside. (Reserve any remaining lemons for another use.) Return the bowl to the saucepan. With the water at a consistent simmer, cook the curd, stirring often with a silicone spatula, until the thermometer reaches 180°F, or until it is thick enough to coat the spatula, 20 to 25 minutes.

7. While the curd is cooking, add the potato starch to the bowl with the reserved lemon juice and whisk to combine. Gradually add this mixture to the curd, whisking constantly. Cook the curd for 2 minutes, stirring with the whisk, to cook out the starch.

8. Turn off the heat and remove the bowl from the saucepan. Dry off the bottom of the bowl to prevent water from getting into the curd and pass the curd through a fine-mesh sieve into a bowl to strain out the zest, pushing the curd with a rubber spatula to force it through. Set the curd aside for about 20 minutes, until the thermometer reaches 130°F; it will feel barely warm. Add the butter and whisk until it is melted and combined.

9. Pour the curd into the crust and smooth out the top with an offset spatula. Set aside to cool to room temperature. Cover the baking dish with plastic wrap and refrigerate the lemon bars overnight or for at least several hours, until the curd is completely set.

10. Remove the lemon bars from the refrigerator. Use a large sharp knife to cut into whatever size and shape you like. Dust the lemon bars with powdered sugar just before serving. Serve chilled.

Tarte Tatin

A tarte Tatin is a classic French tart that is baked upside down, with the crust on the top, and then flipped before serving. I worked at Michael's in Santa Monica, my first pastry job, for a year and a half, and it is hardly an exaggeration to say that I made a tarte Tatin every day during my tenure there. Some days, my tarte Tatin turned out perfect, other days it did not; flipping that tarte was either the highlight or the disappointment of my day. I never bragged as much when my tarte came out just right. And when it didn't, I was never so glum. The whole day it would be on my mind; I would analyze the steps to try to see what went wrong. I didn't take solace in the fact that everyone still loved the "failures."

Making tarte Tatin is unlike anything else you'll ever do in the kitchen. It's more cooking than baking. I almost didn't include this recipe because it is such an unusual technique, and I wasn't sure it was something that could be taught in a book. But I decided it belonged in any baking book of "classic bests." A true tarte Tatin is made by cooking halved and cored apples in butter and sugar. The butter and sugar turn into caramel, and the apples cook very slowly in that shallow puddle of caramel; the apples soak up that caramel as they cook, while the caramel continues to brown. The trick is to cook the apples slowly enough that they cook through, but without burning the caramel in the process. Once the apples are cooked, you lay a sheet of puff pastry over the top and bake the tarte Tatin just to brown the crust.

I didn't do anything to make the tarte Tatin different; tarte Tatin doesn't need to be altered. My challenge here wasn't to make improvements (a well-made tarte Tatin can't be improved upon), but to try to properly communicate how to make it correctly. In any case, making tarte Tatin takes practice. You will learn something about the process every time. And let me tell you: there is nothing more joyous than when you invert your tarte Tatin, lift off the pan, and see that it is perfect.

There is no getting around it: Tarte Tatin is a sweet dessert. That sweetness begs to be cut with whipped cream or vanilla ice cream.

Use Delicious apples, either Golden Delicious or Red Delicious, which break down just the way they need to. You may want to line the burners on your stove with aluminum foil before cooking the apples on the stovetop; the caramel they're cooked in will bubble and may splatter out, creating quite a mess. And don't worry if your tarte isn't perfect; just scoop it into a bowl and put ice cream on top. It'll be wonderful. I understand that a copper tarte Tatin pan is not inexpensive, but from my experience, →

there is no substitute; it's essential to the success of a tarte Tatin. To save the time of making and rolling out the dough, start with 1 pound store-bought puff pastry; just make sure to buy one that's made with butter.

Makes one 9½-inch tarte Tatin

**What You Need—
The Essential Special Equipment**

9½-inch copper tarte Tatin pan

Apple corer or melon baller

For the Crust

½ recipe Rough Puff Pastry Dough (recipe follows)

Unbleached all-purpose flour for dusting

For the Apples

12 Red Delicious or Golden Delicious apples (4½ to 5 pounds)

284 grams (2½ sticks) cold unsalted butter

2 tablespoons pure vanilla bean paste or vanilla extract

340 grams (1½ cups plus 3 tablespoons) granulated sugar

For the Whipped Cream (optional)

360 grams (1½ cups) heavy cream

116 grams (½ cup) crème fraîche (or 122 grams/½ cup sour cream)

---

1. To prepare the crust, line a large baking sheet with parchment paper.

2. Remove the puff pastry dough from the refrigerator and set it aside to soften at room temperature until it is pliable but not soft, 20 to 30 minutes.

3. Lightly dust a work surface with flour. Unwrap the dough and place the dough in front of you. Dust the dough and rolling pin with flour and apply firm, steady pressure with the rolling pin to roll the dough out to a ¼-inch-thick round shape, dusting with flour as needed. Using the tarte Tatin pan as a guide, use a paring knife or kitchen shears to cut the dough about 2 inches larger than the pan all the way around. Loosely roll the dough around the rolling pin and then roll it out onto the prepared baking sheet. Dust off the excess flour and dot it all over with the tines of a fork, making sure to penetrate through the dough. Place the baking sheet in the refrigerator to chill the dough until it is firm, at least 1 hour.

4. To prepare the apples, peel them. If you're using an apple corer, remove the cores and cut the apples in half through the core. If you're using a melon baller, cut the apples in half through the stem and use a small melon baller to cut out the cores.

5. Place the butter on a cutting board and pound it with a rolling pin to flatten and soften it. Spread the butter over the bottom of the pan to cover it. Spread the vanilla bean paste (or sprinkle the vanilla extract) over the butter. Sprinkle the granulated sugar evenly over the butter and vanilla. Stand a row of apple halves, facing the same direction, around the perimeter of the pan, squeezing in as many as will fit. Place 3 or 4 more apple halves in the center of the pan to fill the pan completely. Pile the remaining apple halves cut-side down on top of the standing apples. (You want to fit as many of the apple halves as you can into a pile in the center of the pan; you will add more apples in the next step, as the first batch cooks down.)

6. Cook the apples over low heat without stirring until they begin to shrink, about 20 minutes, rotating the pan as needed so the caramel created by the butter and sugar browns evenly. Remove from the heat and gently nudge a few of the apples to confirm they have shrunk and that there is space between them. Add as many of the remaining apple halves as will fit into the spaces, gently wedging them in without forcing them; if you force the apples in, they will break when they cook. If the apples have not cooked down enough to create space in the pan, cook them for another 5 or 7 minutes and then check again. (You may not need to add all of the apples to the pan; snack on any that are left over.) Continue to cook the apples in the caramel until the caramel in the pan is a rich, dark amber color and all of the apples in the pan are caramelized and soft, 15 to 25 minutes, rotating the pan so the apples and caramel brown evenly. Remove from the heat.

7. While the apples are cooking, adjust an oven rack so it is in the center position and preheat the oven to 350°F.

8. Remove the baking sheet with the dough from the refrigerator. Place the dough on top of the tarte Tatin pan, centering it. Use kitchen shears or a paring knife to trim the dough so it is just barely larger than the pan. Ease the dough inside the edges of the pan; when it shrinks, it will cover the apples perfectly. Place the tarte Tatin on the baking sheet that the dough was on.

9. Place the baking sheet on the center rack of the oven and bake until the crust is golden brown, about 30 minutes, rotating the baking sheet front to back halfway through the baking time so the crust brows evenly. Remove →

the tarte Tatin from the oven and set it aside for a few minutes until it is cool enough to handle. Place a large serving platter on top of the tarte Tatin pan, invert the tarte Tatin onto the platter, and lift off the pan. Set aside to continue to cool.

10. If you're serving the tarte Tatin with whipped cream, pour the heavy cream into a stand mixer fitted with the whisk and whip it on low speed for about 1 minute until it thickens enough not to spatter. Increase the speed to medium-high and whip until soft peaks form, for 2 to 3 minutes. Add the crème fraîche and whip on medium-low speed until medium peaks form, about 1 minute.

11. Serve the tarte Tatin barely warm or at room temperature with the whipped cream or vanilla ice cream.

Rough Puff Pastry Dough

Rough puff pastry, also called a "blitz," is a type of puff pastry. It's made using the same ingredients and the same turning method (which is how this and other doughs get their flaky layers) as is used to make classic puff pastry. But instead of folding in a precisely measured block of butter, the butter is chopped into large chunks and folded in with the dough; it's so "rough" that you'll see big chunks of butter in the dough when you're rolling it out.

When I learned to make puff pastry as a student at Le Cordon Bleu in London, they presented rough puff as a lazy baker's alternative to the classic version. Since then, I've learned that rough puff is not an inferior option, it is simply a different dough. Rough puff doesn't rise as evenly or as high as traditional puff pastry, but it's just as delicious. It's light, flaky, buttery, and a beautiful golden-brown color when baked. This recipe was developed by Anna Nguyen while working on pastry recipes for one of my newer restaurants, The Barish. Anna added whole wheat flour to the dough to give it a bit of flavor and a pretty, burnished color. I use it in this book to make Cheese Twists (page 463) and for a classic Tarte Tatin (page 353).

This dough is turned a total of five times. The dough takes several hours to make because it needs to rest between turns and then, ideally, again overnight. It can be refrigerated for up to 4 days or frozen for up to several months. If you freeze the dough, place it in the refrigerator overnight to thaw it.

Makes about 2½ pounds

326 grams (2⅓ cups) unbleached all-purpose flour, plus more for dusting

110.5 grams (¾ cup plus 1 tablespoon) whole wheat flour

2¼ teaspoons Diamond Crystal kosher salt

565 grams cold unsalted European-style butter, cut into 1-inch pieces

113 to 170 grams (7½ to 11 tablespoons) ice-cold water

1. Put the all-purpose flour, whole wheat flour, and salt in a stand mixer fitted with the dough hook. Mix on low speed for about 15 seconds to combine the ingredients. Add the butter and mix on low speed for 1 minute. Increase the speed to medium-low and mix until about half of the butter is mixed with the flour to form a coarse meal and the other half of the →

Rough Puff Pastry Dough (continued)

butter remains in larger, flour-covered chunks, 1 to 2 minutes longer. Stop the mixer and remove the bowl from the stand. Squeeze the flour/butter mixture in your fists to form big chunks.

2. Return the bowl to the stand. Add about 110 grams (7 tablespoons) of the water and mix on low speed, adding more water if needed to bring the ingredients together into a shaggy, crumbly dough. (The amount of water you will need changes from day to day; add as little as you can get away with. The more water you add, the heavier the dough will turn out.)

3. Lightly dust a work surface with flour and turn the dough out onto it. Use your hands to bring the dough together into a 9 × 7-inch block. Wrap the dough tightly with plastic wrap and place it in the refrigerator to chill until the dough is firm, at least 30 minutes.

4. Lightly dust a work surface. Remove the dough from the refrigerator. Remove and reserve the plastic wrap and place the block of dough with a short side facing you. Place a rolling pin on the dough parallel to the counter's edge and press the pin into the dough to create a ridge in the dough. Continue, working your way to the top edge of the dough, making a total of 5 or 6 ridges in the dough. Lightly dust the dough and rolling pin with flour and gently roll the pin back and forth along the ridges to flatten them slightly, elongating the dough. When you've reached the ridge closest to you, roll the dough away from you to create a rough 8 × 20-inch rectangle, dusting the dough, rolling pin, and counter as needed; gently tug at the corners of the dough and press on the sides of the dough with the rolling pin during the rolling process to achieve squared corners. You don't want the dough to be wider than 8 inches; if it starts to widen, gently push on the edges with your hands to shape it.

5. Brush off the excess flour with a pastry brush or your hands and fold the bottom edge of the dough up by one-third and the top edge down to meet it, lining up the edges and corners; this is a "letter" fold. Turn the dough counterclockwise so the folded edge is facing left. You have just made your first turn.

6. Make ridges in the dough and then flatten them as you did previously, then roll the dough out again to 8 × 20 inches, dusting with flour as needed. Make a second letter fold in the dough. You have now completed two turns. Dust off the excess flour and wrap the dough tightly in the reserved plastic wrap. Place the dough in the refrigerator for 30 minutes to rest the dough and chill the butter.

7. Lightly dust your work surface. Remove the dough from the refrigerator and remove the plastic wrap and set it aside. Place the dough with the folded edge facing left and repeat, making three more turns of the dough as you did previously. (You may need to rest the dough in the refrigerator between the fourth and fifth turns if it is springing back so much that you can't roll it out.) After you have made a total of five turns, wrap the dough in plastic wrap and place it in the refrigerator overnight or for at least 1 hour to chill and rest.

Coconut Cream Slab Pie with Bittersweet Chocolate and Toasted Almonds

I am very much on the fence when it comes to cream pie; I find them to be lacking in texture, and I don't like all that pudding-like filling. That said, I had no choice but to include a coconut cream pie in this book, because so many people told me it was their favorite. I found a compromise: in the form of a slab pie, which makes for a lower-profile pie, which means less filling, more crust. To give the pie more texture, I added a layer of almond-studded chocolate between the crust and the filling, and I top the pie with candied coconut.

It's not a difficult pie to make, but it does require several steps, so plan accordingly. I suggest you take the steps in the following order: (1) Make the dough. (2) Form and parbake the crust. (3) Prepare the pudding filling. (4) Make the chocolate-almond layer. (5) Make the whipped cream. (6) Make the candied coconut. The dough and pie shell can be made and formed up to a day in advance and refrigerated until you're ready to parbake it. The almonds can be toasted a day in advance and stored at room temperature. And the filling can be made up to 2 days in advance; refrigerate until you're ready to assemble the pie. The candied coconut is so good, you may want to double it and serve the remaining coconut on the side. The big news in this recipe (and that for Banana Cream Slab Pie, page 367), is that I use rice flour in the pudding filling. This is a new discovery for me, and I love it. The rice flour makes the pudding strong enough to stand up in the pie, so it doesn't fall apart or get weepy. The rice flour also gives the pudding a wonderful silky texture. I'm very happy to have learned this "trick" in time for this book of bests.

Save this and the Banana Cream Slab Pie to serve for a party. Both are large, and both desserts lose their luster after a few hours. If you do have leftover pie, store it in the refrigerator. (See photo page 366.)

Makes one 9 × 13-inch slab pie

**What You Need—
The Essential Special Equipment**
9 × 13-inch rimmed baking sheet (also called a quarter-sheet pan)
Cooking spray
Pie weights (or dried beans)
Pastry brush
Large disposable piping bag

For the Crust
Unbleached all-purpose flour, plus more for dusting
Savory Pie Dough (page 313)

For the Pudding Filling
12 extra-large egg yolks
150 grams (¾ cup) granulated sugar
21 grams (3 tablespoons) potato starch
24 grams (2½ tablespoons) stone-ground white rice flour (not sweet rice flour)
15 grams (3 tablespoons) coconut cream powder or coconut milk powder
840 grams (3½ cups) canned coconut cream
1 tablespoon pure vanilla bean paste or vanilla extract
¾ teaspoon pure almond extract

¼ teaspoon Diamond Crystal kosher salt

¼ teaspoon grated nutmeg

For the Chocolate and Almond Layer

75 grams (1 cup) skin-on whole almonds

140 grams (5 ounces) bittersweet chocolate (70% cacao), coarsely chopped (about 1 cup); whole if you're using feves

For the Whipped Cream

480 grams (2 cups) heavy cream

15 grams (2 tablespoons) powdered sugar

4.5 grams (1½ teaspoons) potato starch

1 teaspoon pure vanilla bean paste or vanilla extract

For the Candied Coconut Chips

25 grams (2 tablespoons) granulated sugar

60 grams (1 cup) unsweetened coconut chips

1. To prepare the crust, coat the baking sheet with cooking spray.

2. Lightly dust a work surface with flour. Remove the dough from the refrigerator, unwrap, and place on the floured surface. Pound the dough with a rolling pin to soften it until it is malleable and as flat as possible. (The more you flatten it, the easier it will be to roll out.) Dust the dough and rolling pin lightly with flour. Applying firm, steady pressure with the rolling pin, roll the dough into a ⅛-inch-thick rectangle, dusting with flour as needed. Place the baking sheet on the dough and use it as a guide to cut a rectangle of dough that is at least 2 inches larger all around than the baking sheet. (You will trim the dough to fit the baking sheet in the next step; this just makes the dough easier to work with.)

3. Loosely wrap the dough around the rolling pin and lower it over the baking sheet, centering it. To fit the dough into the baking sheet, lift the edges of the dough and let it drop into the baking sheet; dip the knuckle of your index finger in flour and use it to gently press the dough into the creases. Don't stretch the dough to fit or it will shrink when it is baked. Using kitchen shears, trim the overhanging dough so there are 1½ inches of dough overhanging all around. (Pat the scraps into a 1-inch-thick disk, wrap in plastic, and refrigerate to use another time, or discard them.)

4. To crimp the pie shell, roll the edge of the dough under itself to create a thick lip of dough that rests on the rim of the baking sheet. Press the thumb of one hand on the lip to create an indentation in the dough and press the thumb and forefinger of the other hand on either side of the first thumb, creating a U-shaped indentation. Continue around the perimeter of the crust, creating a crimped, scalloped edge. Place the shell in the refrigerator to chill until the dough is firm, at least 1 hour. →

5. Adjust an oven rack to the center position and preheat the oven to 350°F.

6. Remove the pie shell from the refrigerator, coat a piece of parchment on one side with cooking spray, and gently press it sprayed-side down on the shell to cover the dough. Fill the shell with pie weights (or dried beans), pressing them into the creases of the pie shell.

7. Bake the pie shell on the center rack of the oven until the edges of the crust are light golden, 30 to 40 minutes, lifting the parchment to peek under it and gauge the color. Remove the shell from the oven and lift out the weights and parchment paper. (Set the weights aside to cool to room temperature, then put them away to use again for the same purpose. Discard the parchment paper.) Return the shell to the oven, rotating it front to back, and bake until it is evenly golden brown, 15 to 20 minutes. Remove the shell from the oven and set aside to cool to room temperature.

8. Reduce the oven temperature to 325°F for the almonds.

9. To make the pudding filling, combine the egg yolks and sugar in a stand mixer fitted with the whisk and beat on medium-high speed until the eggs and sugar are very thick, pale yellow, and form a ribbon when the whisk is lifted from the bowl, about 1½ minutes, stopping to scrape down the sides of the bowl with a rubber spatula as needed. Add the potato starch, flour, and coconut powder and mix on low speed for about 30 seconds to combine.

10. Place the coconut cream in a heavy-bottomed medium saucepan, making sure to get all the solids out of the can. Whisk the cream if needed to integrate the milk and the solids. Add the vanilla, almond extract, salt, and nutmeg and warm the mixture over medium heat until the cream begins to bubble around the edges, whisking constantly so it doesn't scorch. Remove from the heat. Slowly drizzle ½ cup of the hot coconut cream into the bowl with the egg mixture, whisking constantly to prevent the hot cream from cooking the eggs. Continue adding the coconut cream mixture to the eggs, drizzling it in ½ cup at a time and stirring constantly with the whisk, until you have added about half of the coconut cream mixture. Gradually add the warmed egg mixture to the remaining coconut cream mixture in the saucepan, stirring constantly with the whisk. Set the saucepan over medium heat and warm the mixture, whisking constantly, until it bubbles in the center. Continue to cook, stirring with the whisk, until thickened to the consistency of pudding, about 3 minutes, reducing the heat if it seems to be

scorching. Remove from the heat. Set a fine-mesh sieve over a medium bowl and pass the filling through the strainer, pushing it through with a rubber spatula. Place the bowl over a bowl full of ice and set aside until the pudding is chilled, stirring often to prevent a skin from forming on the surface. (If you make the pudding in advance, after it has cooled, cover the bowl tightly with plastic wrap and refrigerate for up to 2 days.)

11. To make the chocolate and almond layer, spread the almonds on a baking sheet (a quarter-sheet pan, if you have one) and toast them on the center rack of the oven until they're lightly browned and fragrant, 10 to 15 minutes, shaking the baking sheet and rotating it front to back halfway through the toasting time so the almonds brown evenly. Remove the almonds from the oven and set them aside until they're cool enough to handle. (If you think the nuts are on the verge of being overtoasted, transfer them to a plate so they don't continue to cook from the residual heat of the pan.) Coarsely chop the almonds.

12. While the almonds are toasting, fill a small saucepan with 1½ to 2 inches of water and set a small stainless steel bowl atop the saucepan to make a double boiler, making sure the water doesn't touch the bottom of the bowl. Bring the water to a simmer over medium heat. Put the chocolate in the bowl and melt it, stirring and scraping the bowl with a silicone spatula to prevent the chocolate from burning. Turn off the heat and remove the bowl from the double boiler; dry off the bottom of the bowl.

13. Pour the melted chocolate into the parbaked pie shell and use an offset spatula to spread it to the edges in an even layer. Sprinkle the toasted almonds over the chocolate. Place the pie shell in the refrigerator to chill until the chocolate is solid, at least several hours.

14. Remove the pie shell from the refrigerator. Remove the filling from the ice bath. Spoon the filling into the shell and use an offset spatula to spread it to the edges in an even layer. Put the pie in the refrigerator to chill about 1 hour to set the filling.

15. While the pie is chilling, to make the whipped cream, combine 120 grams (½ cup) of the heavy cream, the powdered sugar, and potato starch in a heavy-bottomed medium saucepan and cook over medium heat, stirring constantly with a whisk, until the mixture just comes to a boil. Remove from the heat and transfer the cream mixture to a medium bowl. →

(If there are burnt bits on the sides of the pot, leave them there rather than scraping them into the bowl.) Place a sheet of plastic wrap on top of the cream mixture, pressing it down so it touches the cream mixture to keep a skin from forming. Refrigerate the cream mixture until it is completely chilled, at least 1 hour.

16. Put the bowl and whisk attachment of a stand mixer in the freezer for at least 10 minutes to chill. Add the remaining 360 grams (1½ cups) heavy cream and the vanilla to the chilled bowl. Put the bowl on the mixer stand, fit the mixer with the chilled whisk, and beat on medium speed until the cream forms soft peaks, 2 to 3 minutes. Stop the mixer. Remove the bowl of cream/sugar/potato starch mixture from the refrigerator. Add the mixture to the mixer bowl and beat on medium speed until the whipped cream is smooth and shiny and has thickened to medium peaks, about 1 minute. (Don't overwhip the cream or it will become grainy, and you'll have to start over.)

17. Remove the pie and the whipped cream from the refrigerator. Put the piping bag in a tall container or glass so the bag flops over the top of the container. (This makes it easier to fill the bag.) Spoon the whipped cream into the bag and push it down toward the tip. Twist the top of the bag until it puts enough pressure on the whipped cream that it will squeeze out of the bottom of the bag and cut a ½-inch hole in the tip of the bag. Holding the top of the bag with one hand and steering the tip with the other, pipe the whipped cream around the perimeter of the pie filling in loose teardrop-like shapes, with the points facing the center of the pie. Continue piping the whipped cream in the same way, working toward the center and refilling the piping bag as needed, until you reach the center of the pie. (You may not need all the whipped cream; use the remaining whipped cream to dress any dessert or enjoy it with fresh berries.) Return the pie to the refrigerator for at least 2 hours to set the whipped cream.

18. While the whipped cream is setting, to make the candied coconut chips, adjust an oven rack to the center position and preheat the oven to 325°F. Line a baking sheet (a quarter-sheet pan, if you have one) with parchment paper.

19. Put the granulated sugar in a medium saucepan. Add 2 tablespoons water, stir with your finger to combine, and bring to a boil over medium-high heat. Gently boil for about 1 minute, brushing down the sides of the pot with a wet pastry brush, until it thickens to the consistency of thin syrup. Add the coconut chips and stir to coat them in the syrup. Lift them out of the syrup with a small strainer and spread them out onto the prepared baking sheet.

20. Bake the coconut chips on the center rack of the oven until they are golden brown, 12 to 15 minutes, rotating the sheet front to back halfway through the toasting time so they brown evenly. Watch them carefully, as coconut goes from untoasted to burnt very quickly. Remove the baking sheet from the oven and set aside for the coconut chips to cool on the pan. Set aside or transfer the chips to an airtight container and store at room temperature until you are ready to garnish the pie, or for up to several hours. The chips soften as they sit, so ideally you should make them as close to serving time as possible.

21. To serve, remove the pie from the refrigerator and sprinkle the coconut chips over the top.

Coconut Cream Slab Pie with Bittersweet Chocolate and Toasted Almonds (top);
Banana Cream Slab Pie with Caramel and Salted Toasted Peanuts (bottom)

Banana Cream Slab Pie with Caramel and Salted Toasted Peanuts

During the year-plus that I worked on this book, I did a lot of informal research, which means I asked just about everyone I encountered what their favorite baked goods were. A surprising number of people mentioned banana cream pie. I wasn't totally shocked, because we serve banana cream pie at my restaurant, Chi Spacca, and when we have leftovers, the staff goes absolutely nuts over it. Since I already published that recipe in the *Chi Spacca* cookbook, not to plagiarize myself, I wanted to make this different. So I added a layer of caramel to the filling and sprinkled crunchy roasted and salted Spanish peanuts over the top. (It would be equally delicious topped with toasted walnuts, pecans, or hazelnuts.) This recipe makes double the number of peanuts you'll need to top the pie. They're so addictive, I'm predicting you are going to eat quite a few before they make their way onto the pie.

Making this pie isn't difficult, but it does require several steps, so plan accordingly. I suggest you take the steps in the following order: (1) Make the dough. (2) Form and parbake the crust. (3) Toast the peanuts. (4) Make the pudding filling. (5) Make the caramel. (6) Make the whipped cream. The dough and pie shell can be made and formed up to a day in advance and refrigerated until you're ready to parbake it. The peanuts can be toasted a day in advance and stored at room temperature. And the caramel and filling can be made up to 2 days in advance (warm the caramel over low heat before using).

Save this and the Coconut Cream Slab Pie to serve for a party. Both desserts lose their luster after a few hours. If you do have leftover pie, store it in the refrigerator.

Makes one 9 × 13-inch slab pie

What You Need—
The Essential Special Equipment

9 × 13-inch rimmed baking sheet (also called a quarter-sheet pan)

Cooking spray

Pie weights (or dried beans)

Pastry brush

Large disposable piping bag

Large star tip

For the Crust

Unbleached all-purpose flour for dusting

Savory Pie Dough (page 313)

For the Toasted Peanuts

250 grams (2 cups) skin-on Spanish peanuts

2 tablespoons grapeseed oil (or other neutral-flavored oil, such as safflower)

1 tablespoon Diamond Crystal kosher salt

For the Pudding Filling

5 extra-large egg yolks

125 grams (½ cup plus 2 tablespoons) granulated sugar

50 grams (7 tablespoons) potato starch

490 grams (2 cups) whole milk

1 tablespoon pure vanilla bean paste or vanilla extract

¼ teaspoon Diamond Crystal kosher salt

70 grams (5 tablespoons) unsalted butter, cubed and left at room temperature until pliable but not greasy →

For the Caramel Sauce

240 grams (1 cup) heavy cream

113 grams (1 stick) unsalted butter, cubed

1 tablespoon pure vanilla bean paste or vanilla extract

½ teaspoon Diamond Crystal kosher salt

200 grams (1 cup) granulated sugar

85 grams (¼ cup) Lyle's Golden Syrup

For the Whipped Cream

480 grams (2 cups) heavy cream

15 grams (2 tablespoons) powdered sugar

4.5 grams (1½ teaspoons) potato starch

1 teaspoon pure vanilla bean paste or vanilla extract

For Assembling the Pie

6 ripe unpeeled bananas (1½ pounds/680 grams)

1. To prepare the crust, coat the baking sheet with cooking spray.

2. Lightly dust a work surface with flour. Remove the dough from the refrigerator, unwrap, and place on the floured surface. Pound the dough with a rolling pin to soften it until it is malleable and as flat as possible. (The more you flatten it, the easier it will be to roll out.) Dust the dough and rolling pin lightly with flour. Applying firm, steady pressure with the rolling pin, roll the dough into a ⅛-inch-thick rectangle, dusting with flour as needed. Place the baking sheet on the dough and use it as a guide to cut a rectangle of dough that is at least 2 inches larger all around than the baking sheet. (You will trim the dough to fit the baking sheet in the next step; this just makes the dough easier to work with.)

3. Loosely wrap the dough around the rolling pin and lower it over the baking sheet, centering it. To fit the dough into the baking sheet, lift the edges of the dough and let it drop into the baking sheet; dip the knuckle of your index finger in flour and use it to gently press the dough into the creases. Don't stretch the dough to fit or it will shrink when it is baked. Using kitchen shears, trim the overhanging dough so there are 1½ inches of dough overhanging all around. (Pat the scraps into a 1-inch-thick disk, wrap in plastic, and refrigerate to use another time, or discard them.)

4. To crimp the pie shell, roll the edge of the dough under itself to create a thick lip of dough that rests on the rim of the baking sheet. Press the thumb of one hand on the lip to create an indentation in the dough and press the thumb and forefinger of the other hand on either side of the first thumb, creating a U-shaped indentation. Continue around the perimeter of the crust, creating a crimped, scalloped edge. Place the shell in the refrigerator to chill until the dough is firm, at least 1 hour.

5. Adjust an oven rack to the center position and preheat the oven to 350°F.

6. Remove the pie shell from the refrigerator, coat a piece of parchment on one side with cooking spray, and gently press it sprayed-side down on the shell to cover the dough. Fill the shell with pie weights (or dried beans), pressing them into the creases of the pie shell.

7. Bake the pie shell on the center rack of the oven until the edges of the crust are light golden, 30 to 40 minutes, lifting the parchment to peek under it and gauge the color. Remove the shell from the oven and lift out the weights and parchment paper. (Set the weights aside to cool to room temperature, then put them away to use again for the same purpose. Discard the parchment paper.) Return the shell to the oven, rotating it front to back, and bake until it is evenly golden brown, 15 to 20 minutes. Remove the shell from the oven and set aside to cool to room temperature.

8. Reduce the oven temperature to 325°F.

9. To toast the peanuts, put them on a baking sheet (a quarter-sheet pan, if you have one), drizzle them with the oil, sprinkle with the salt, and toss to coat them. Spread the peanuts out in an even layer and toast them on the center rack of the oven until they are dark mahogany in color, 18 to 20 minutes, shaking the pan occasionally and rotating the pan front to back halfway through the toasting time so the peanuts brown evenly. Remove the baking sheet from the oven and set aside to cool the nuts to room temperature. (If you think they are on the verge of being overtoasted, transfer them to a plate so they don't continue to cook from the residual heat of the pan.)

10. Turn off the oven.

11. To make the pudding filling, combine the egg yolks and sugar in a stand mixer fitted with the whisk and beat on medium-high speed until the eggs and sugar are very thick, pale yellow, and form a ribbon when the whisk is lifted from the bowl, about 1½ minutes, stopping to scrape down the sides of the bowl with a rubber spatula when needed. Add the potato starch and mix on low speed for about 30 seconds to combine.

12. Combine the milk, vanilla, and salt in a heavy-bottomed medium saucepan and warm over medium heat, whisking constantly so the →

milk doesn't scorch, until it begins to bubble around the edges. Remove from the heat. Slowly drizzle ½ cup of the hot milk into the bowl with the egg and potato starch mixture, whisking constantly to prevent the hot milk from cooking the eggs. Continue adding the milk to the eggs, drizzling it in ½ cup at a time and stirring constantly with the whisk, until you have added about half of the milk. Gradually add the warmed egg mixture to the saucepan with the remaining milk, stirring constantly with the whisk. Warm the milk and eggs over medium heat, whisking constantly, until it bubbles in the center. Continue to cook, stirring with the whisk, until it thickens to the consistency of pudding, about 3 minutes, reducing the heat if the filling seems to be scorching. Remove from the heat. Place a fine-mesh sieve over a medium bowl and pass the filling through the sieve, pushing it through with a rubber spatula. Add the butter and whisk until it is melted and combined. Place the filling over a bowl full of ice and set aside until it is chilled, stirring often to prevent a skin from forming on the surface. (If you make the filling in advance, after it has cooled, cover the bowl tightly with plastic wrap and refrigerate for up to 2 days.)

13. To make the caramel sauce, warm the cream in a medium saucepan over medium-high heat until it begins to bubble around the edges. Remove from the heat, add the butter, vanilla, and salt and stir until the butter melts.

14. Combine the granulated sugar, golden syrup, and 60 grams (¼ cup) water in a large heavy-bottomed saucepan with a light-colored bottom. Cook the sugar mixture over medium-high heat until it is medium amber in color, about 8 minutes, swirling the pan so the sugar cooks evenly and using a wet pastry brush to remove any sugar crystals from the sides of the pan to keep them from burning. Remove from the heat. Add the cream mixture, taking care as it will cause the sugar syrup to bubble up and steam. Stir with a whisk until the caramel sauce is smooth. Set aside to cool slightly.

15. Pour ½ cup of the warm caramel into the parbaked pie shell and use an offset spatula to spread it to the edges in an even layer. Place the pie shell in the refrigerator to chill until the caramel is set, at least 1 hour.

16. While the pie is chilling, to make the whipped cream, combine 120 grams (½ cup) of the heavy cream, the powdered sugar, and potato starch in a heavy-bottomed medium saucepan and cook over medium heat, stirring constantly with a whisk, until the mixture just comes to a boil.

Remove from the heat and transfer the cream mixture to a medium bowl. (If there are burnt bits on the sides of the pot, leave them there rather than scraping them into the bowl.) Place a sheet of plastic wrap on top of the cream mixture, pressing it down so it touches the cream mixture to keep a skin from forming. Refrigerate the cream mixture until it is completely chilled, about 1 hour.

17. Put the bowl and whisk attachment of a stand mixer in the freezer for at least 10 minutes to chill. Add the remaining 360 grams (1½ cups) heavy cream and the vanilla to the chilled bowl. Put the bowl on the mixer stand, fit the mixer with the chilled whisk, and beat on medium speed until the cream forms soft peaks, 2 to 3 minutes. Stop the mixer. Remove the bowl of cream/sugar/potato starch mixture from the refrigerator. Add the mixture to the mixer bowl and beat on medium speed until the whipped cream is smooth and shiny and has thickened to medium peaks, about 1 minute. (Don't overwhip the cream or it will become grainy, and you'll have to start over.)

18. To assemble the pie, peel the bananas and slice them into ¼-inch-thick rounds.

19. Remove the pie shell from the refrigerator. Remove the filling from the ice bath or the refrigerator. Whisk the pudding to loosen it to a spreadable consistency. Spoon ¾ cup of the filling onto the shell and use an offset spatula to spread it to the edges in an even layer. Lay half of the banana slices on the filling in a single layer so that they are touching but not overlapping. Spoon ¾ cup of the remaining filling over the bananas and use the spatula to spread it out toward the edges. Create another layer, laying the remaining banana slices in a single layer. (Reserve any remaining banana slices to snack on or put them in a smoothie.) Spoon the remaining filling onto the bananas and use the spatula to spread it to the edges. Put the pie in the refrigerator to chill about 1 hour to set the filling.

20. Remove the pie from the refrigerator. Fit a large piping bag with a large star tip. Put the bag in a tall container, such as a 1-quart deli container, so the edges flop over the edge of the container. (This is simply to make it easier to fill the piping bag.) Spoon the whipped cream into the bag and push it down toward the tip. Twist the top of the bag until it puts enough pressure on the whipped cream that it squeezes out of the bottom of the bag. Holding the →

top of the bag with one hand and steering the tip with the other, pipe rosettes over the surface of the pie, leaving space between them for the pudding to peek through and refilling the piping bag as needed. (You may not need all the whipped cream for the pie; use any left over to dress any dessert or enjoy it with fresh berries.) Return the pie to the refrigerator for at least 2 hours to set the whipped cream.

21. To serve, remove the pie from the refrigerator. Drizzle ¼ cup of the remaining caramel sauce over the pie. Sprinkle with ½ cup of the peanuts. Serve the remaining caramel and peanuts on the side for people to personalize their serving.

Rice Pudding

Discovering Italian rice pudding, or *budino di riso,* changed my entire rice pudding perspective. I like to eat with my teeth, to chew my food, and the only rice pudding I had ever tried consisted of a bowl of mushy, milky rice, so it was like baby food or porridge. Not so in Italy. There, the rice pudding is baked inside individual oval-shaped molds, so it's less creamy, but still comforting and delicious. But the crust is what really makes the difference. Combining the rice pudding with a crunchy, buttery crust turns the rice pudding into something appealing and luxurious. I got the idea to bake them in fluted brioche molds, instead of the traditional oval shape, from Vivoli, a gelateria and bakery in Florence. I also borrowed from Vivoli the idea of finishing the tarts with a little knob of rice on top. When the tarts are dusted with powdered sugar, that knob detail stands out and gives the tart a finished look, like a finial on a lamp. I didn't give this recipe the name "rice pudding tarts," because in Italy, they just call it rice pudding; the fact that the pudding is in a tart shell goes without saying. As far as I'm concerned, that's the way rice pudding should be. I take one bite of this rice pudding and I am transported to Italy. I wish the same sensation for you!

Arborio is an Italian rice variety used to make risotto that, when cooked, gets creamy while the individual grains stay firm. It is essential to the success of this pudding.

Makes 12 individual tarts

What You Need— The Essential Special Equipment

12 (3-inch, ¼-cup capacity) nonstick brioche molds

Cooking spray

3½- to 3¾-inch round cutter

Pie weights (or dried beans)

8-inch ovenproof sauté pan (2 inches deep) with a lid

For the Crust

2 extra-large egg yolks

30 grams (2 tablespoons) heavy cream

2 tablespoons pure vanilla bean paste or vanilla extract

80 grams (⅔ cup) powdered sugar, plus more for dusting

226 grams (2 sticks) cold unsalted butter, cubed

2 teaspoons Diamond Crystal kosher salt

350 grams (2½ cups) unbleached all-purpose flour, plus more (optional) for dusting

For the Rice Pudding

100 grams (½ cup) Arborio rice

245 grams (1 cup) whole milk

240 grams (1 cup) heavy cream

50 grams (¼ cup) granulated sugar

1 tablespoon pure vanilla bean paste or vanilla extract

1 teaspoon Diamond Crystal kosher salt

1 cinnamon stick

1 large lemon

1 medium orange

2 extra-large egg yolks

28 grams (2 tablespoons) unsalted butter, cubed and left at room temperature until pliable but not greasy →

Rice Pudding (continued)

1. To make the crust, combine the egg yolks, cream, and vanilla together in a small bowl and whisk to combine. Sift the powdered sugar into a medium bowl or onto a sheet of parchment paper.

2. Put the butter in a stand mixer fitted with the paddle and beat on medium speed until the butter is soft but still cold, 3 to 4 minutes, stopping to scrape down the bowl and paddle with a rubber spatula whenever butter is accumulating. Add the powdered sugar and beat on medium speed until the mixture is light and creamy, 3 to 4 minutes, scraping down the bowl as needed. Add the salt and beat on low speed for about 15 seconds to distribute it. Stop the mixer and scrape down the bowl. With the mixer on medium speed, gradually add the egg yolk mixture, making sure the addition is incorporated before adding more. Add the flour and mix on low speed for about 30 seconds, until no flour is visible. Stop the mixer. Remove the bowl and paddle from the stand and clean them with the spatula, scraping from the bottom up to release any ingredients from the bottom of the bowl.

3. Turn the dough out onto a work surface and gather it into a ball. Press the dough into a 1-inch-thick disk and wrap it in plastic wrap. Refrigerate the dough until it is chilled and firm, at least 1 hour.

4. Lay a sheet of parchment paper on your work surface. Remove the dough from the refrigerator, unwrap, and place in the center of the parchment. Place another sheet of parchment on the dough, lining up the two sheets. Applying firm, steady pressure with the rolling pin, roll the dough out between the parchment to ¼ inch thick. (Alternatively, you can skip the parchment paper and roll out this dough on a flour-dusted work surface.) Lay the parchment-sandwiched dough on a baking sheet and place it in the refrigerator to chill until the dough is firm, at least 1 hour.

5. Coat the molds with cooking spray.

6. Remove the baking sheet with the dough from the refrigerator and transfer the dough to your work surface. Peel the top sheet of parchment off the dough and lay it back down on the dough. (This loosens the parchment so after you cut the dough, you will be able to lift it off the parchment without it sticking.) Flip the sheet of dough over. Peel off the top sheet of parchment paper and lay it clean-side up on the baking sheet to line it.

7. Use the cutter to cut as many rounds as you can from the dough. Gather the scraps, reroll them, and cut until you have a total of 12 rounds. (Gather any remaining scraps of dough and reserve for another use; for example, roll it out, cut it into shapes for cookies, sprinkle with sugar and/or spices, and bake them to snack on.)

8. Lay one dough round in each of the molds, centering the dough. Lift the edges of the dough and let it drop into the molds; dip the knuckle of your index finger in flour and use it to gently press the dough into the creases. Don't stretch the dough to fit, or it will shrink when baked. Place the brioche molds on the prepared baking sheet and refrigerate until the dough is firm, at least 1 hour.

9. Adjust an oven rack to the center position and preheat the oven to 350°F.

10. Cut out twelve 4-inch squares of parchment paper. Coat one side of the parchment paper with cooking spray. Remove the brioche molds from the refrigerator and gently press one piece of parchment paper, sprayed-side down, in each mold to cover the dough. Fill the molds with pie weights (or dried beans), pressing them into the corners of the molds.

11. Place the baking sheet in the oven to bake the shells until the edges are golden brown, 18 to 20 minutes, rotating the baking sheet front to back halfway through the baking time so the shells bake evenly. (The bottoms of the shells will not look thoroughly cooked. If you bake them any longer at this point, they will be too crunchy and hard after you bake them again with the filling.) Remove the baking sheet from the oven and remove the pie weights (or dried beans) and parchment paper. (Let the weights cool to room temperature, and then store them to use another time. Discard the parchment paper.) Set the shells aside to cool to room temperature.

12. To make the pudding, put the rice, milk, cream, sugar, vanilla, and salt in the ovenproof sauté pan. Add the cinnamon stick. Use a fine Microplane to grate the zest (the brightly colored outer layer) of the lemon and orange into the pot. (Reserve the fruit for another use.) Warm the mixture over medium-high heat, stirring occasionally with a silicone spatula to keep it from scorching, until it starts to bubble around the edges. →

13. Cover the sauté pan and transfer to the oven to bake until the rice is tender, 35 to 40 minutes. (When checking the rice for doneness, be careful of the steam that will arise from the pot when you remove the lid.) Remove the sauté pan from the oven.

14. Increase the oven temperature to 375°F.

15. Uncover the pan and run a silicone spatula across the bottom; if the empty streak from the spatula doesn't fill immediately, then proceed to the next step. If the rice pudding is so thin that it immediately fills the streak, it needs to be cooked longer: Set the sauté pan over low heat and simmer the rice pudding, uncovered and stirring often with the spatula, until the liquid thickens, 5 to 10 minutes. Remove from the heat. Set the rice pudding aside for a few minutes to cool slightly. Discard the cinnamon stick.

16. Meanwhile, whisk the egg yolks together in a medium bowl. Add the softened butter to the bowl with the eggs and whisk to combine. Pour the rice over the eggs and butter and stir with the whisk to combine.

17. Spoon about 3 tablespoons of the rice pudding into each of the tartlet shells, filling each shell to the rim.

18. Put the baking sheet in the oven and bake the rice pudding tartlets until a thick skin has formed on top, about 15 minutes. Remove the baking sheet from the oven. Pinch the pudding in the center to create a knob on each tartlet. Return the baking sheet to the oven, rotating it front to back, and bake the tartlets until the rice pudding is tinged with color and firm to the touch, another 10 to 15 minutes.

19. Remove the baking sheet from the oven and set aside to cool to room temperature. To remove the tartlets from the molds, run the tip of a paring knife around each tartlet to loosen them. One at a time, slide the knife under each tartlet and pop it out. Place the tartlets right-side up on the baking sheet.

20. Dust the tartlets generously with powdered sugar before serving.

Peanut Butter Pies and Key Lime Pies

Peanut Butter Pies

Think of these as peanut butter cups, in pie form. The filling is a rich, sweet peanut butter mousse, which is topped with milk chocolate sauce and salted toasted Spanish peanuts. I made the pies individual size, which is part of what makes them perfect. They are so rich, you would regret eating more than this small portion.

Seek out common supermarket varieties of peanut butter, not health food or artisanal varieties; I use Skippy Creamy Peanut Butter. These pies must be eaten the day they're made, and straight from the refrigerator. At room temperature, the filling gets too soft and the pies will just fall apart.

Makes 12 individual pies

**What You Need—
The Essential Special Equipment**

12 (3-inch; 6-tablespoon capacity) aluminum pie pans

Candy thermometer

Pastry brush

For the Pie Shells

188 grams Spiced Graham Crackers (page 165), or quality store-bought graham crackers

37.5 grams (3 tablespoons) granulated sugar

¼ teaspoon Diamond Crystal kosher salt

¼ teaspoon ground cinnamon (if you are not using Spiced Graham Crackers)

85.75 grams (6 tablespoons) unsalted butter, melted

For the Peanuts

154 grams (1 cup) skin-on Spanish peanuts

1 tablespoon grapeseed oil (or other neutral-flavored oil, such as safflower)

1½ teaspoons Diamond Crystal kosher salt

For the Peanut Butter Filling

30 grams (¼ cup) powdered sugar

4 extra-large egg yolks

133 grams (⅔ cup) granulated sugar

226 grams (2 sticks) unsalted butter, cubed and left at room temperature until pliable but not greasy

340 grams (1¼ cups) creamy peanut butter

2 teaspoons Diamond Crystal kosher salt

For the Chocolate Sauce

113.5 grams (4 ounces) milk chocolate (preferably 46% cacao), coarsely chopped (scant 1 cup); halved if you're using feves

1½ teaspoons Lyle's Golden Syrup

1½ teaspoons pure vanilla bean paste or vanilla extract

72.5 grams (about ¼ cup plus 1 tablespoon) heavy cream

1. To make the pie shells, adjust an oven rack to the center position and preheat the oven to 350°F.

2. Break the graham crackers into pieces, place them in a food processor, and process to fine crumbs. Turn the crumbs out into a large bowl. Add the granulated sugar, salt, and cinnamon (if using) and stir to combine. Add the melted butter and stir with your hands to combine and break up any lumps. →

3. Working with one at a time, spoon 24 grams (3 tablespoons) of the graham cracker mixture into the bottom of each pie pan and use a small measuring cup to firmly press the crumbs to evenly line the bottom and sides. (The process of lining these tiny pans can, admittedly, be a bit tedious. Shiri, who tested these recipes, suggested that we call for you to make a cocktail at this point in the recipe. I'm not saying it's a terrible idea.)

4. Place the pans on a baking sheet and place it on the center rack of the oven to bake until the pie shells are firm to the touch, 10 to 15 minutes, rotating the baking sheet front to back halfway through the baking time so the shells bake evenly. Remove the baking sheet from the oven and set aside to cool the shells to room temperature. Place in the refrigerator to chill for at least 1 hour. Leave the oven on.

5. To toast the peanuts, put them in a small bowl, drizzle with the oil, sprinkle with the salt, and toss to coat. Spread the peanuts out in an even layer on a small sheet pan and toast them on the center rack of the oven until they are dark mahogany in color, 18 to 20 minutes, shaking the pan occasionally and rotating the pan front to back halfway through the toasting time so the peanuts brown evenly. Remove the pan from the oven and set aside to cool the peanuts to room temperature.

6. Turn off the oven.

7. To make the peanut butter filling, sift the powdered sugar into a bowl or onto a sheet of parchment paper and set aside.

8. Put the egg yolks in a stand mixer fitted with the whisk and set aside.

9. Fasten a candy thermometer to the side of a small saucepan. Add the granulated sugar and 155 grams (⅓ cup) water and stir with your finger to combine. Bring the sugar and water to a boil over medium-high heat, brushing down the sides of the pan with a wet pastry brush as needed to remove any sugar crystals from the sides of the pan. Continue boiling until the thermometer registers 235°F, about 5 minutes. Remove from the heat.

10. Turn the mixer on low speed and pour the sugar mixture down the side of the bowl, taking care not to pour it directly onto the whisk. Increase the speed to medium-high and beat until the eggs and sugar are thick and

mousse-like and the sugar has cooled to room temperature. (To check the temperature, cup your hands around the bottom of the mixer bowl; if it feels cool, the sugar has cooled.) Stop the mixer and scrape down the sides of the bowl with a rubber spatula. Add the butter and beat on medium-high speed for about 1 minute to combine. Add the peanut butter and beat on medium-high speed for about 1 minute to combine. Stop the mixer, scrape down the bowl, and add the powdered sugar and salt. Beat on medium-high speed for about 1 minute to combine. Stop the mixer, remove the bowl from the stand, and clean it with the spatula, scraping the bowl from the bottom up to release any ingredients that may be stuck there.

11. To assemble the pies, scoop 50 grams (¼ cup) of the filling into each of the prepared pie shells and use the back of a spoon to create a pretty indentation on top of each pie. Cover the baking sheet with plastic wrap and refrigerate to chill until the filling is firm, about 2 hours.

12. When you're ready to serve the pies, to make the chocolate sauce, put the chocolate in a food processor and pulse to finely chop. Add the golden syrup and vanilla and pulse to combine.

13. Heat the cream in a heavy-bottomed medium saucepan over medium-high heat until it just begins to boil. Remove from the heat and with the food processor running, stream it into the feed tube, running the food processor until the chocolate and cream are combined, stopping the food processor to scrape the chocolate off the sides of the bowl with a rubber spatula once or twice in the process. (When you first add the cream, the mixture will tighten up and look like it's going to seize; keep mixing and it will loosen up and become soft and shiny.) Transfer the chocolate to a medium bowl and set aside to cool to room temperature, about 10 minutes. (If the chocolate gets so cold that it is too stiff to pour, warm it slightly and then let it cool again.)

14. Remove the pies from the refrigerator.

15. Spoon 1 tablespoon of the milk chocolate into each indentation and tilt the pies so the ganache spreads out over the surface. Scatter about 10 of the salted peanuts on top of each. (You will have some peanuts left over to snack on.) Serve the pies chilled.

Key Lime Pies

There's not a lot you can do to improve upon Key lime pie. The "classic," as far as I know, starts with canned sweetened condensed milk and a packaged graham cracker crust, and it's delicious. I wasn't thrilled about calling for canned milk in my key lime pie recipe, so I tried making it substituting cream and other ingredients, but I couldn't get the same right silky texture without it. So, I came to terms with using the canned milk. (I used Eagle Brand.) The good news is, there are no weird ingredients in sweetened condensed milk: just milk and sugar. Although the proportions of ingredients are like those on the standard, back-of-the-can recipe, I upgraded the quality of the ingredients, calling for fresh (as opposed to bottled) Key lime juice and a homemade graham cracker crust, both of which make the flavor of the pie pop. These are individual-sized pies, which give you more crust in every bite, and I think that also improves the experience.

Key limes are a variety of small limes associated with the Florida Keys. They're smaller than conventional limes, and yellowish in color. They have an intense, tart lime flavor. Don't try to substitute conventional limes in this recipe; they aren't tart enough or flavorful enough. You can often find Key limes (also called Mexican limes) at Hispanic grocery stores and farmers' markets in addition to some grocery stores. You will have more whipped cream than you need for these pies, but it's challenging to make whipped cream in a smaller amount. I'm confident you can find a way to use it. These pies must be eaten the day they're made, and straight from the refrigerator. At room temperature, the filling melts and the pies will just fall apart. (See photo page 378.)

Makes 14 individual pies

**What You Need—
The Essential Special Equipment**

14 (3-inch; 6-tablespoon capacity) aluminum pie pans

For the Pie Shells

250 grams Spiced Graham Crackers, homemade (page 165), or quality store-bought graham crackers

50 grams (¼ cup) granulated sugar

½ teaspoon Diamond Crystal kosher salt

¼ teaspoon ground cinnamon (if you are not using Spiced Graham Crackers)

113 grams (1 stick) unsalted butter, melted

For the Filling

2 (14-ounce) cans sweetened condensed milk

77 grams (⅓ cup) crème fraîche (or 81 grams/⅓ cup sour cream)

20 to 25 Key limes (also called Mexican limes)

½ teaspoon Diamond Crystal kosher salt

For the Whipped Cream

360 grams (1½ cups) heavy cream

116 grams (½ cup) crème fraîche (or 122 grams/½ cup sour cream)

1 regular lime (if you have one, not a Key lime, for a brighter green color), for zesting over the finished pie

1. To make the pie shells, adjust an oven rack to the center position and preheat the oven to 350°F.

2. Break the graham crackers into pieces, transfer to a food processor, and process to fine crumbs. Turn out the crumbs into a large bowl. Add the sugar, salt, and cinnamon (if using) and stir to combine. Add the melted butter and stir with your hands to combine and break up any lumps.

3. Working one at a time, spoon 24 grams (3 tablespoons) of the graham cracker mixture into the bottom of each pie pan and use a small measuring cup to firmly press the crumbs to evenly line the bottom and sides of the pans. (Reserve any remaining crumbs for another use, or discard them.)

4. Place the pans on a baking sheet and place it on the center rack of the oven to bake until the pie shells are firm to the touch, 10 to 15 minutes, rotating the baking sheet front to back halfway through the baking time so the shells bake evenly. Remove the baking sheet from the oven and set aside to cool the shells to room temperature. Place in the refrigerator to chill for at least 1 hour.

5. When you are ready to make the filling, turn the oven temperature to 325°F.

6. To make the filling, combine the sweetened condensed milk and crème fraîche in a medium bowl and whisk to combine. Use a fine Microplane to grate the zest (the greenish-yellow outer layer) of 4 Key limes into the bowl. Halve and juice as many of the remaining limes as needed to get to 166 grams ($\frac{2}{3}$ cup) of juice. Add the juice to the bowl with the condensed milk mixture. (Reserve any extra limes for another use.) Add the salt and stir with a whisk to combine the ingredients.

7. Remove the baking sheet with the pie shells on it from the refrigerator. Scoop 70 grams (¼ cup) of the filling into each of the prepared pie shells.

8. Place the baking sheet with the pies on the center rack of the oven for 3 minutes. Remove the baking sheet from the oven and set aside to cool the pies to room temperature. Cover the baking sheet with plastic wrap and place the pies in the refrigerator to chill until firm, about 2 hours. →

9. Before serving, to make the whipped cream, pour the heavy cream into a stand mixer fitted with the whisk and whip the cream on low speed for about 1 minute until it thickens enough not to spatter. Increase the speed to medium-high and whip until soft peaks form, 2 to 3 minutes. Add the crème fraîche and whip on medium-low speed until medium peaks form, about 30 seconds.

10. Remove the pies from the refrigerator and dollop about 2 tablespoons of whipped cream on top of each pie, leaving the edges of the filling visible, and use the back of a spoon to create a pretty swoosh in the whipped cream. Using the fine Microplane, grate the zest (the bright-green outer layer) of the regular lime over the pies.

Portuguese Custard Tarts

Every time I am finishing a cookbook, just as it is about to go to press, I get obsessed with a recipe, old or new, that I feel *must* be included. "Stop the presses!" I yell. "I need to add one more recipe!" This is that recipe. A Portuguese custard tart, *tarta de nata* consists of a delicate, eggy custard baked in a puff pastry shell until it has an almost burnt, mottled top. When you bite into the custard, it's clear to anyone who has ever made or eaten custard before that this is something different. It's not a curd. It's not panna cotta. And it's not crème brûlée. But neither is it a typical egg custard. It leaves a baker such as me asking, "What exactly is it? And how is it made?"

I've been obsessed with Portuguese custard tarts for years, but it wasn't until I was working on this book that I started the quest to learn how to make them. And let me tell you: It wasn't an easy one. I've never seen so many recipes, so varied, and each one led me down a path to failure. It so happened that around this time, a salesman, Felipe Madeira, came into Mozza offering Portuguese olive oil. Of course, I took the opportunity to pick his brain about the classic tart of his homeland. And he told me that the baker who makes the best version he had ever tasted just moved to London. Lucky for me, I was going to London the next day to check on my restaurant there. Felipe arranged for me to meet his chef friend, João Diaz. João invited me, along with Mozza's executive chef, Liz Hong, to his home, where he put out the most beautiful spread of Portuguese meats, cheeses, and other delicious dishes for lunch. But first, he took us into his kitchen. He had all the ingredients and components for the tart prepped out at different stages, like on a cooking show. Liz and I sat at the counter in front of him and he set about showing us how to make the tarts. He showed us how to make the puff pastry dough, the art of forming the dough into the molds, and the nuances of making the unique custard. None of his techniques were available in books or online. The whole day was memorable, and now I have this recipe to memorialize the experience, and to share with you.

I first made these with my rough puff pastry dough, which is easier than João's traditional puff pastry dough recipe, but it didn't work. The dough puffed up too much when baked. So, this recipe requires you to make a puff pastry dough with three folds (aka turns). I believe that these tarts will follow in the footsteps of their neighbor and cousin, Basque Cheesecake (page 252), escaping the confines of their native land to become an international →

sensation. When that moment comes, you will be glad to hold the keys to the Portuguese Custard Tart Kingdom. You'll know that you've truly succeeded in making a traditional Portuguese custard tart when, after taking the tarts out of the pans, you look at the bottoms of the shells. If there is a spiral pattern in the layers of dough, you've done it! If you don't achieve the spirals, you'll just have to try again. Perfection takes practice.

The custard needs to rest overnight in the refrigerator, as does the dough, so plan ahead. As João told me, the most important ingredient to making these tarts is time.

Makes 20 individual tarts

What You Need—
The Essential Special Equipment

15 (2¾-inch; 5-tablespoon capacity) aluminum or stainless steel (nondisposable) pie pans

For the Dough

280 grams (2 cups) unbleached all-purpose flour

15 grams cold unsalted European-style butter, cubed; plus 140 grams unsalted European-style butter, cubed and left at room temperature until pliable but not greasy

8 grams (2 teaspoons) distilled white vinegar

2 teaspoons Diamond Crystal kosher salt

¾ teaspoon granulated sugar

150 grams (½ cup plus 2 tablespoons) cold water

Unbleached all-purpose flour for dusting

For the Syrup

712.5 grams (3½ cups plus 1 tablespoon) granulated sugar

37.5 grams (about ¼ cup plus 1 tablespoon) Lyle's Golden Syrup

1 tablespoon pure vanilla bean paste or vanilla extract

2 cinnamon sticks

1 large lemon

For the Custard

78 grams (about ½ cup plus 1 tablespoon) unbleached all-purpose flour

18 grams (2 tablespoons) potato starch

585 grams (about 2 cups plus 6 tablespoons) whole milk

9 extra-large egg yolks

1½ teaspoons Diamond Crystal kosher salt

1. To make the dough, combine the flour, the 15 grams of cold butter, the vinegar, salt, sugar, and water in a stand mixer. Fit the mixer with the dough hook and mix on medium speed for 5 minutes to develop the gluten. Transfer the dough to the counter and form it into a ball. Wrap the dough in plastic wrap and refrigerate for at least 12 and up to 24 hours.

2. Lay a sheet of parchment on your work surface. Draw a 6½ × 4½-inch rectangle in the center of the paper to use as a guide and flip the paper. Put the 140 grams of room-temperature butter on the parchment within the parameters of the line drawing; use an offset spatula to smear it into an

even ¼-inch-thick layer and to square off the sides and corners. Fold the parchment paper to enclose the sheet of butter and refrigerate until it is cool and firm, at least 1 hour.

3. To make the syrup, combine the sugar, golden syrup, vanilla, cinnamon sticks, and 375 grams (1½ cups plus 1 tablespoon) water in a small saucepan. Use a vegetable peeler to peel 2 strips of zest (the bright-yellow outer layer) from the lemon and add the strips to the saucepan. (Reserve the lemon for another use.) Bring the ingredients to a boil over medium-high heat, stirring occasionally, to dissolve the sugar and combine the ingredients. Remove from the heat and set aside to cool to room temperature. Remove the cinnamon sticks and lemon zest strips from the syrup and discard them. Weigh out 705 grams (or about 3 cups plus 3 tablespoons) of the syrup and set it aside. (Use the remaining syrup for another use, such as to sweeten your iced coffee, or discard it.)

4. To make the custard, put the flour, potato starch, and 122.5 grams (½ cup) of the milk in a small bowl and whisk until no lumps remain. Fill a medium saucepan with water. Place the bowl on top of the saucepan. (The weighted saucepan anchors the bowl, so it remains stable when you whisk ingredients in it.)

5. Pour the remaining 463 grams (1½ cups plus 6 tablespoons) milk into a small saucepan and heat it over medium-high heat until it begins to bubble around the edges. Remove from the heat. Gradually add the warm milk to the bowl with the milk mixture, whisking to prevent lumps from forming. Pour the milk mixture back into the saucepan and cook over medium-high heat until it just comes to a boil; the mixture will have thickened from the added starch. Remove from the heat and transfer to a large bowl. Set it aside to cool to room temperature. Place the bowl on a saucepan filled with water to anchor it.

6. Whisk the egg yolks and salt together in a medium bowl. Gradually add them to the bowl with the cooled milk mixture, whisking constantly and making sure the egg is incorporated before adding more. Drizzle in the reserved syrup, whisking constantly. Pass the custard through a fine-mesh sieve into a container with a lid, pushing it through with a rubber spatula. Cover the container and refrigerate the custard for 1 to 3 days, until you are ready to form the tarts. (The custard is best after it's had some time to rest.) →

7. Remove the rectangle of butter from the refrigerator and set it on your work surface to soften for 10 to 20 minutes, until it is pliable but not soft, and still cool.

8. Lightly dust a large work surface with flour. Remove the dough from the refrigerator, remove and reserve the plastic wrap, and place the dough on the floured surface. Lightly dust the top of the dough and the rolling pin with flour and roll the dough out into a roughly 8 × 10-inch rectangle with a long side facing you. Open up the parchment enclosing the butter and flip the butter onto the center of the rectangle of dough with the 4½-inch side of the butter block facing you. Peel the parchment from the butter and discard it. Fold the top and bottom of the dough toward the center to envelop the butter packet. Fold the left and right sides of the dough to meet in the middle and gently press the seam together to seal the dough closed. The butter is now completely locked into the dough.

9. Lightly flour the dough, work surface, and rolling pin with flour and roll the dough out to a 9 × 17-inch rectangle with the long side moving away from you, dusting with flour as needed and squaring off the edges of the dough with the rolling pin or your hands. Fold the bottom edge toward the top by one-third and fold the top edge down to meet the bottom edge. You have completed one letter fold. Wrap the dough in plastic wrap and refrigerate for 30 minutes to relax the dough.

10. Remove the dough from the refrigerator, remove the plastic wrap and reserve it. Place the dough on your countertop, rotating a quarter-turn counterclockwise so the closed side is facing left. Dust the dough, work surface, and rolling pin with flour and roll the dough out to a 9 × 17-inch rectangle with the long side moving away from you, dusting with flour as needed and squaring off the edges. Make another letter fold by folding the bottom edge of the dough toward the top by one-third and folding the top edge down to meet the bottom edge. Wrap the dough in plastic wrap and refrigerate for 30 minutes to relax the dough. Remove the dough from the refrigerator and roll it out and turn it a third time. Wrap it in plastic wrap and refrigerate for 30 minutes to relax the dough.

11. To prepare the tart shells, remove the dough from the refrigerator, unwrap, and place on the floured surface. Dust the dough, work surface, →

and rolling pin with flour and roll it out to a 16-inch square, dusting with flour as needed. Cut the dough in half to form two 8 × 16-inch strips of dough.

12. Lay one strip of dough in front of you with a long side facing you. Fill a small bowl with water. Dip your fingers in the water and flick the water off them onto the dough. Use your fingertips to paint additional water onto both the top and the edge of the dough closest to you. Begin to tightly roll the dough away from you to create a log: To roll the dough as tightly as it needs to be, start the roll by using your fingertips to fold the first ¼ inch of dough over itself; it will feel more like you are pinching the dough than rolling it. Once you have it started, put your palms on the dough and it will roll up easily. When you reach the end of the log, paint water on the edge of the dough and gently roll the log back and forth to seal the end closed. Wrap the log tightly in plastic wrap and place it in the refrigerator to chill. Repeat with the second log. Chill the dough until it is firm, at least 1 hour.

13. When you are ready to shape the dough, coat the pie pans with cooking spray.

14. Lightly dust a work surface with flour. Remove a log of dough from the refrigerator, unwrap, and place on your work surface. Slice the log into 15 coins ¾ to 1 inch thick (about 20 grams each), placing the coins in the pie pans. (Do not slice the next log until you have more pie pans available.)

15. To form the tart shells, fill a small bowl with water. Place a tart pan on your work surface. Dip the thumb of one hand in the water and press on the dough until your thumb almost touches the bottom of the pan. Rotate the pan and press on the dough a few more times to begin to flatten it. Then place both thumbs on the dough and steadily rotate the pan, applying constant pressure with your thumbs to mold the dough to fit the pan. (The shells will not be perfect at this point, as the dough will tend to bounce back. The shells will be refrigerated to relax the dough and then you can finish forming them.) Set the pan aside and form the remaining tart shells in the same way, dipping your thumb in more water as needed. Place the shells on a baking sheet, cover with plastic wrap, and refrigerate for 8 hours to relax the dough.

16. To bake the tarts, adjust an oven rack to the center position and preheat the oven to 550°F (500°F if you're using a convection oven).

17. Remove the tart shells from the refrigerator. One by one, finish the shells: Dip your thumbs in water and press on the dough until the dough is pressed all the way to the top edge of the tart shell.

18. Remove the custard from the refrigerator. Skim off and discard the bubbles that have formed on the surface of the custard. Pour 45 grams (3 tablespoons) of custard into each tart, filling them almost to the top. After you've filled all the tarts, space them evenly apart on the baking sheet.

19. Bake the tarts on the center rack of the oven until the tops are dark and splotchy, 10 to 12 minutes, rotating the baking sheet front to back halfway through the baking time so the tarts bake evenly. Remove the baking sheet from the oven.

20. To remove the tarts from the pans, one at a time, run the tip of a paring knife around each tart to loosen them. Slide the knife under the tart and pop it out of the pan.

There is only one reason to make any of the recipes in this chapter: because you have an abundance of the seasonal fruit that stars in the title role. Simple as it sounds, fruits have a season. That's when they are at their optimal flavor, and that's when they should be used. Fruit desserts made with out-of-season fruit, flown in from some faraway place (where either they are in season or grown in a greenhouse), will never live up to the flavor of the same dessert made with local seasonal fruit—no matter how much butter and sugar are involved!

The recipes in this chapter will take you through the year, from winter's Meyer Lemon Meringue Tart (page 395) to springtime's Strawberry Rhubarb Pie (page 401). You'll experience summer's bounty of plums in the Hazelnut Plum Tart (page 411), and welcome fall with a delicious Apple Crisp (page 429) and Rustic Pear Tarts (page 432). When deciding what to make in this chapter, let the fruit make that decision for you. When it's springtime and you see nothing but fresh strawberries at the market, consider the Almond Tart with Fresh Strawberries (page 407). When you have a bowl of peaches, plums, and nectarines so juicy you have to eat them over the sink, Stone Fruit and Berry Crumble (page 423) is in your future. Once you start thinking and baking this way, your baking life will be transformed.

Seasonal Fruit Desserts

Meyer Lemon Meringue Tart

I like the idea of lemon meringue pie, but I've always felt that the texture and proportions were not right. There is too much lemony filling in relation to the crust and too much meringue piled on top that offers no textural contrast, just sweetness and fluff. To remedy these issues, I bake this lemon meringue in a tart shell, which isn't as deep as a pie, so there is relatively more crust and less filling. And I bake the meringue before placing it on the tart, so it gets a nice golden brown. The result is a perfectly proportioned, not-too-sweet tart with a crispy, buttery crust, a smooth lemony filling, and a slightly crunchy, slightly chewy meringue that you can sink your teeth into.

Meyer lemons—a hybrid of a citron, a mandarin, and a pomelo—are ideal for this pie. They're sweeter and less acidic than conventional lemons. They're only in season during winter and early spring. If you don't have access to Meyer lemons or they aren't in season, use conventional lemons; in this case, they will work.

This tart is best eaten the day it is made. Store it at room temperature to ensure the crust stays crunchy.

Makes one 12-inch tart

**What You Need—
The Essential Special Equipment**

12-inch flan ring

Cooking spray

Pie weights (or dried beans)

12-inch cardboard cake round

Large disposable piping bag

Large star tip

For the Tart Shell

Sweet Tart Dough (page 329)

Unbleached all-purpose flour for dusting (optional)

For the Filling

6 extra-large eggs

180 grams (¾ cup) heavy cream

340 grams (about 1¼ cups plus 2 tablespoons) freshly squeezed Meyer lemon juice (about 8 large Meyer lemons)

150 grams (¾ cup) granulated sugar

For the Meringues

30 grams (heaping ¼ cup) skin-on thin-sliced almonds

2 extra-large egg whites

65 grams (about ⅓ cup) superfine sugar (or 65 grams/5 tablespoons plus ½ teaspoon) granulated sugar

½ teaspoon Diamond Crystal kosher salt

65 grams (½ cup plus 2 teaspoons) powdered sugar, plus more for dusting

1 teaspoon pure vanilla bean paste or vanilla extract

1. To prepare the tart shell, lay a sheet of parchment paper on a work surface. Remove the dough from the refrigerator, unwrap, and place in the center of the parchment paper. Pound the dough with a rolling pin to soften it until it is malleable and as flat as possible. (The more you flatten it, the easier it will be to roll out.) Lay a sheet of parchment paper on top of the dough, lining →

it up with the lower sheet of parchment. Applying firm, steady pressure with the rolling pin, roll the dough out between the parchment paper to ³/₁₆ inch thick. (Alternatively, you can skip the parchment paper and roll the dough on a flour-dusted work surface, dusting the surface, the dough, or the pin with flour as needed.) Lay the dough on a baking sheet and place it in the refrigerator to chill until it is firm, at least 1 hour.

2. Coat the inside of the flan ring with cooking spray.

3. Remove the sheet of dough from the refrigerator and transfer the dough to a work surface. Invert the baking sheet so the underside is facing up. Peel the top sheet of parchment off the dough and lay it back down on the dough. (This loosens the parchment so you will be able to lift the dough off without it sticking.) Flip the sheet of dough over. Peel off the top sheet of parchment paper and lay it clean-side up on the inverted baking sheet to line it. Place the flan ring on the dough and use it as a guide to cut a round of dough that is at least 1 inch larger all around than the ring. (You will trim the dough to fit the ring in the next step; this just makes the dough easier to work with.)

4. Place the ring on the prepared baking sheet. Loosely wrap the dough around a rolling pin and lower it over the ring, centering it so that the dough overhangs evenly around the edge. To fit the dough into the ring, lift the edges and let the dough drop into the ring; dip the knuckle of your index finger in flour and use it to gently press the dough into the creases where the ring meets the baking sheet. Don't stretch the dough to fit or it will shrink when it is baked. Run a rolling pin at a 45-degree angle around the edge of the ring to trim off the excess dough. (Pat the scraps into a 1-inch-thick disk, wrap in plastic, and refrigerate to use another time, or discard them.) Dot the bottom of the tart shell all over with the tines of a fork and place the baking sheet in the refrigerator to chill the dough until firm, at least 1 hour.

5. Adjust an oven rack to the center position and preheat the oven to 350°F.

6. To make the filling, whisk the eggs and cream together in a medium bowl.

7. Combine the lemon juice and granulated sugar in a small saucepan and warm over medium heat, whisking constantly, until the sugar dissolves, 1 to 2 minutes. Remove from the heat. Gradually pour the lemon juice mixture into the bowl with the eggs and cream, whisking constantly to prevent the

warm liquid from cooking the eggs. Pass the filling through a fine-mesh sieve into a large heatproof pitcher or spouted measuring cup to strain out any lumps, pushing it through with a rubber spatula.

8. Pull out the center oven rack and place the baking sheet with the tart shell on it. Carefully pour the filling into the shell until it reaches ¼ inch from the rim of tart. (You may not use all the filling. Bake it in a small dish until it is set to snack on.) Gently slide the rack back in and bake until the filling is firm around the edges and slightly jiggly in the center when you shake it, 20 to 27 minutes, rotating the baking sheet front to back halfway through the baking time so the tart bakes evenly. Remove the tart from the oven and set aside to cool to room temperature. (Don't worry if the filling cracks when it bakes or after it cools; you will cover it up with the meringue.)

9. Reduce the oven temperature to 325°F.

10. While the tart is cooling, to make the meringues, spread the almonds on a baking sheet and toast them on the center rack of the oven until they are light golden brown, 5 to 6 minutes, rotating the baking sheet front to back and stirring the nuts halfway through the toasting time so they brown evenly. (The nuts will be baked again on top of the meringues, so they are only lightly toasted here.) Remove the almonds from the oven. Transfer them to a plate to prevent them from toasting from the residual heat of the pan and set aside to cool to room temperature.

11. Line a large baking sheet with parchment paper. Using a bold pen, draw two 6-inch circles on the parchment, leaving about 2 inches of space between them. Flip the parchment paper; you will be able to see the circles through the paper.

12. Place the egg whites in a stand mixer fitted with the whisk and beat the whites on medium speed until they are foamy, 1½ to 2 minutes. Increase the speed to medium-high and mix until soft peaks form, 1½ to 2 minutes. Increase the speed to high, and with the mixer running, gradually add the superfine sugar and salt and beat until the peaks are stiff and shiny but not dry, 1½ to 2 minutes. Add the powdered sugar and vanilla and beat on medium speed for about 30 seconds until the additions are combined. Stop the mixer, remove the whisk and bowl from the stand, and tap the whisk against the bowl to remove the egg whites. →

13. Scoop up ¼ cup of the meringue and drop it in an organic coif on the prepared baking sheet. Use the back of a spoon to create a pretty whisp in the top of the meringue. Repeat with the remaining meringue, dropping a total of 12 coifs on the baking sheet, spacing them evenly apart. Sprinkle the toasted almonds over the meringues, dividing them evenly.

14. Bake the meringues on the center rack of the oven until the surfaces look dry with some cracks in them and they lift easily off the baking sheet, 35 to 45 minutes, rotating the baking sheet front to back halfway through the baking time so the meringues bake evenly. Remove the meringues from the oven and set them aside to cool to room temperature.

15. To remove the tart from the ring, run the tip of a paring knife around the inside edges of the ring to loosen any stuck bits. Slide the tart onto a cake round and slide it off the round onto a serving platter. Slice the tart into 10 equal slices. Lightly dust the meringues with powdered sugar. Pick the 10 prettiest meringues and place one on each slice; arrange them strategically if necessary to cover up any cracks or imperfections in the tart. (Snack on the 2 remaining meringues.)

Meyer Lemon Polenta Cake

I am often disappointed by lemon cake because it doesn't taste enough like lemon, so in creating two lemon cakes for this book—this cake and the Lemon Bundt Cake (page 208)—my main goal was to make sure they were sufficiently lemony. I also wanted them to be very different from each other. Where the Bundt cake feels like a classic American bake sale treat, this one, made with Meyer lemons, ground almonds, polenta, and Italian leavening, feels more Italian—and more sophisticated.

Meyer lemons are a hybrid of a citron, a mandarin, and a pomelo; they're sweeter and less acidic than conventional lemons. They're in season in the winter and spring. The lemons are pureed whole for this cake, so it's very aggressive in its lemon flavor. You can't substitute conventional lemons in this recipe; if you were to puree conventional lemons, the cake would be way too bitter.

I bake this in a long narrow pan called a *Rehrücken,* or German almond cake pan. The batter is so dense, it wouldn't work in a deeper loaf or a Bundt pan. If you can't find the pan I call for, use a fluted 12-inch tart pan instead (see page 200 for photo).

Makes one 12-inch-long cake

What You Need—
The Essential Special Equipment

12½ × 4½-inch *Rehrücken*/almond cake loaf pan (or another 5-cup capacity cake pan)

Cooking spray

89 grams (½ cup) coarse yellow stoneground polenta

85 grams (about ¾ cup plus 2 tablespoons) unblanched almond meal (or 85 grams, a heaping ½ cup skin-on whole almonds)

70 grams (½ cup) unbleached all-purpose flour

3½ large Meyer lemons

90 grams (¾ cup) powdered sugar

42.5 grams (2 tablespoons) Lyle's Golden Syrup

2 extra-large eggs

170 grams (1½ sticks) cold unsalted butter, cubed

150 grams (¾ cup) granulated sugar

1½ teaspoons Italian leavening (or ¾ teaspoon baking powder and ¾ teaspoon baking soda)

1 teaspoon Diamond Crystal kosher salt

---

1. Adjust an oven rack to the center position and preheat the oven to 350°F. Coat the pan generously with cooking spray and place it on a large baking sheet.

2. Whisk the polenta, almond meal, and flour together in a small bowl. (If you're using whole almonds instead of almond meal, put the almonds in a food processor with 2 tablespoons of the total granulated sugar and pulse to a fine meal, then combine this mixture with the flour and polenta.) →

3. Cut 1½ of the lemons into roughly ½-inch pieces and discard the seeds. Place the lemon pieces in a food processor, add the powdered sugar and golden syrup, and pulse for about 15 seconds, until the lemons are very finely chopped. Transfer to a medium bowl. Add the eggs and whisk to combine.

4. Put the butter in a stand mixer fitted with the paddle and beat on medium speed until it is soft but still cold, 3 to 4 minutes, stopping to scrape down the sides and bottom of the bowl and the paddle with a rubber spatula whenever butter is accumulating. Add the granulated sugar and beat on medium speed until the mixture is light and fluffy, 3 to 4 minutes, scraping down the bowl as needed. Stop the mixer. Add the Italian leavening and salt. Using a fine Microplane, grate the zest (the bright-yellow outer layer) of the 2 remaining lemons into the mixer bowl. (Reserve the lemons for another use.) Beat on low speed for about 15 seconds to distribute the additions. Stop the mixer and scrape down the bowl and paddle. Add the dry ingredients and the wet ingredients alternately in five additions for the dry ingredients and four for the lemon mixture, starting and ending with the dry ingredients; mix on low speed until the additions are combined and stop to scrape down the bowl before the next addition. Stop the mixer, remove the bowl and paddle from the stand, and clean them with the spatula. Stir the dough with the spatula, scraping the bowl from the bottom up to release any ingredients from the bottom of the bowl.

5. Scrape the batter into the prepared pan and smooth out the top with an offset spatula.

6. Place the baking sheet with the cake on it on the center rack of the oven and bake until the cake begins to pull away from the sides of the pan, the top is deep browned, and a toothpick inserted in the center of the cake comes out clean, about 1 hour 15 minutes, rotating the baking sheet front to back halfway through the baking time so the cake bakes evenly. Remove the cake from the oven.

7. To remove the cake from the pan, run the tip of a paring knife around the top inside edge of the pan to release any stuck bits and invert the cake onto a large rectangular serving platter or board.

Strawberry-Rhubarb Pie

When I think of a double-crust, baked fruit pie, strawberry-rhubarb is the iconic image that comes to mind. Rhubarb, often called "pie plant," because the plant is most often used to make pie, is a vegetable with long, thin, crimson-colored stalks and a tart, earthy flavor. Rhubarb comes into season in the spring, the same time as strawberries, so it makes sense that strawberry-rhubarb is the classic combo. You don't normally see strawberries baked into pie because they're too watery, but in strawberry-rhubarb pie, the rhubarb is cooked until it turns into a sort of stew, which absorbs the water from the berries. My dad loved strawberry-rhubarb pie. You don't see it often in California, so maybe he developed his taste from his South Dakota roots. Whenever I make it, I feel like I am making it for him.

The success of this pie is totally dependent on using tender, in-season rhubarb and sweet, flavorful strawberries. Made with tough, out-of-season rhubarb and white-in-the-center strawberries, the filling will be flavorless and watery; don't waste your time. I like this pie best cold, with a scoop of vanilla ice cream.

Makes one 9-inch pie

**What You Need—
The Essential Special Equipment**

9-inch (5-cup capacity) metal pie pan

Cooking spray

For the Crust

Unbleached all-purpose flour for dusting

Savory Pie Dough (page 313; formed into 2 equal disks)

For the Filling

3 pounds rhubarb stalks

312.5 grams (1½ cups plus 1 tablespoon) granulated sugar

1 cup brandy (or whiskey)

1 tablespoon pure vanilla bean paste or vanilla extract

2 pounds (about 6 cups) seasonal strawberries

28 grams (¼ cup) potato starch

For Assembly

30 grams (2 tablespoons) heavy cream

25 grams (2 tablespoons) demerara, turbinado, or granulated sugar

1. To make the crust, coat the pie pan with cooking spray. Line a large baking sheet with parchment paper.

2. Lightly dust a work surface with flour. Remove one disk of the dough from the refrigerator, unwrap, and place on the floured surface. Pound the dough with a rolling pin to soften it until it is malleable and as flat as possible. (The more you flatten the dough by pounding it, the easier it will be to roll out.) Dust the dough and rolling pin lightly with flour and, →

applying firm, steady pressure, roll the dough into a ⅛-inch-thick round, dusting with flour as needed. Transfer the dough to a baking sheet and place it in the refrigerator.

3. Dust the surface with additional flour, remove the second disk of dough from the refrigerator, unwrap, and place on the floured surface. Pound the dough with a rolling pin and roll it out into a ⅛-inch-thick round, dusting with flour as needed. Place the pie pan upside down on the dough and use a paring knife or kitchen shears to cut a round of dough that is at least 3 inches larger all around than the pan. (You'll cut the dough more precisely in the next step; you're trimming at this point to make the sheet of dough easier to work with.)

4. Loosely wrap the dough around the rolling pin and lower it over the prepared pan, centering it so that the dough overhangs evenly around the rim. Lift the edges of the dough and let it drop into the pan; dip the knuckle of your index finger in flour and use it to gently press the dough into the creases of the pan. Don't stretch the dough to fit or it will shrink when it is baked. Using kitchen shears, trim the dough so there are 1½ inches of dough overhanging all around. (Gather the trimmings, pat them into a disk, and wrap them in plastic wrap to use another time, or discard them.) Place the pie shell in the refrigerator. Chill the dough until it is firm, at least 1 hour.

5. To make the filling, rinse and dry the rhubarb. Trim and discard the ends and cut the remaining stalks into batons 3 inches long and ½ inch thick.

6. Put 150 grams (¾ cup) of the sugar in a large sauté pan. Add 60 grams (¼ cup) water and bring to a boil over high heat without stirring. Reduce the heat to medium-low and cook the sugar until it is a medium caramel color, 3 to 4 minutes, tilting and swirling the pan so the sugar cooks evenly. Remove the pan from the heat. Add half of the rhubarb, taking care as the sugar mixture may spatter when you add it, and stir the rhubarb to mix it in with the melted sugar. (The sugar will seize when you add the rhubarb. Don't worry, it will melt again as you cook the rhubarb.) Add half of the brandy and half of the vanilla, return the pan to high heat, and cook, stirring often, until the rhubarb has softened but still holds its shape and the liquid has thickened slightly, 1 to 2 minutes. Remove from the heat. Transfer the rhubarb, including the cooking liquid, to a shallow baking dish. Add the remaining

¾ cup of sugar to the pan along with 60 grams (¼ cup) water and bring to a boil over high heat without stirring. Cook the sugar for 3 to 4 minutes as you did previously, until it is a medium caramel color. Add the remaining rhubarb and cook it as you did the first batch, adding the remaining brandy and vanilla. Add the second batch of rhubarb to the baking dish and set aside to cool to room temperature. Cover the dish with plastic wrap and refrigerate until chilled, about 1 hour.

7. While the rhubarb is chilling, prep the strawberries. Hull the strawberries and if they are small, leave them whole. If they are medium-sized, cut them in half. If they are large, cut them into thirds. Place the strawberries in a large bowl. Sprinkle with the remaining 1 tablespoon sugar and the potato starch and gently toss with your hands or a rubber spatula to coat the strawberries with the sugar and starch. Set aside for 20 minutes to macerate the strawberries.

8. Remove the chilled rhubarb from the refrigerator. Add the strawberries and gently stir them into the rhubarb with a rubber spatula.

9. To assemble the pie, remove the pie shell and round of dough from the refrigerator and set aside for about 5 minutes to soften slightly. Spoon the strawberry-rhubarb mixture into the shell, making sure to get all the sugary goop out of the bowl with a rubber spatula. Using your hands, mound the filling in the center and use the rubber spatula to smooth the fruit.

10. Lay the round of dough on top of the pie, centering it. Press the top and bottom crusts together at the point where they meet the edge of the pie pan to seal them together. Using kitchen shears, trim the sealed dough so there are 1½ inches of dough overhanging. (Discard the trimmings.) Roll the edge of the dough under itself to create a thick lip of dough that rests on the edge of the pie tin. Press the thumb of one hand on the lip to create an indentation in the dough and press the thumb and forefinger of the other hand on either side of the first thumb, creating a U-shaped indentation. Continue around the perimeter of the crust, creating a crimped, scalloped edge.

11. Pour the cream into a small bowl and brush it onto the surface of the pie shell, including the crimped edges, and sprinkle with the sugar. Place the pie in the freezer for 20 minutes to chill. →

12. Arrange the oven racks so there are no racks near the oven floor; place the parchment-lined baking sheet on the oven floor to preheat it. (If you have an electric oven or another oven where you can't put anything on the floor, place one rack as close to the floor as possible and put a pizza steel or stone, if you have one, on the rack. Put the baking sheet on the pizza stone or the rack.) Preheat the oven to 500°F.

13. Remove the pie from the freezer. Insert the tip of a paring knife into the center and twist the knife, creating a hole to allow steam to escape. Score the crust four times (at 12 o'clock, 3 o'clock, 6 o'clock, and 9 o'clock) around the center hole without cutting through the dough. Make four small scores (again, not cutting all the way through the dough) between the bigger ones to create a starburst look.

14. Slide the baking sheet out of the oven and place the pie on it, then slide the baking sheet back in. Reduce the oven temperature to 425°F and bake the pie for 30 minutes. Reduce the oven temperature to 375°F, rotate the baking sheet front to back so the pie bakes evenly, and bake until the crust is deep golden brown and the filling is bubbling up through the steam holes, about 1 hour. Remove the baking sheet from the oven and set the pie aside to cool to room temperature. Place the pie in the refrigerator for at least 2 hours until the filling is chilled and set.

15. Serve chilled or at room temperature, with vanilla ice cream.

Almond Tart with Fresh Strawberries

Strawberries and almonds are a classic pairing. This tart is French in spirit, but it's unique in how the strawberries are arranged, or rather, not arranged, on top. I don't know what French pastry chef or baker decided that the strawberries on a tart had to be arranged with the points facing up, in concentric circles. It only gets worse when the berries are shellacked in a thick layer of currant jelly. It all looks so artificial and unappetizing, not to mention outdated. But people are still doing it, so I guess someone likes it. Not me. For this tart, I start with a sweet cookie-like crust *(pâte sucrée)* in which I bake a chewy almond cake-like filling. The strawberries are macerated, releasing their juices and enhancing their flavor, and then piled on top of the finished tart just before serving it. The tart is so fresh and bright—both in color and flavor. It's the perfect dessert to make in the springtime and early summer, when sweet, flavorful strawberries are in abundance.

While you can find strawberries in grocery stores year-round, strawberries that are hard, with white centers, and no flavor, are not what you are looking for. Buy your strawberries at farmers' markets. Only tender, juicy strawberries—that taste like strawberries—will do.

Makes one 10-inch tart

What You Need—
The Essential Special Equipment

10-inch flan ring

Pie weights (or dried beans)

Cooking spray

12-inch cardboard cake round

For the Tart Shell

½ recipe Sweet Tart Dough (page 329)

Unbleached all-purpose flour for dusting (optional)

Cooking spray

For the Filling

4 extra-large egg whites

1 tablespoon pure vanilla bean paste or vanilla extract

2 teaspoons pure almond extract

112.5 grams (1 cup plus 2 tablespoons) unblanched almond meal (or 112.5 grams/¾ cup, skin-on whole almonds)

100 grams (½ cup) granulated sugar

90 grams (¾ cup) powdered sugar

35 grams (¼ cup) unbleached all-purpose flour

1 teaspoon Diamond Crystal kosher salt

169.5 grams (1½ sticks) unsalted butter

For the Strawberries

1 pound (about 3 cups) seasonal strawberries

16 grams (1 heaping tablespoon) granulated sugar →

1. To prepare the tart shell, lay a sheet of parchment paper on a work surface. Remove the dough from the refrigerator, unwrap, and place in the center of the parchment paper. Pound the dough with a rolling pin to soften it until it is malleable and as flat as possible. (The more you flatten it, the easier it will be to roll out.) Lay a sheet of parchment paper on top of the dough, lining it up with the lower sheet of parchment. Applying firm, steady pressure with the rolling pin, roll the dough out between the parchment paper to ³⁄₁₆ inch thick. (Alternatively, you can skip the parchment paper and roll the dough on a flour-dusted work surface, dusting the surface, the dough, or the pin with flour as needed.) Lay the dough on a baking sheet and place it in the refrigerator to chill until it is firm, at least 1 hour.

2. Coat the inside of the flan ring with cooking spray.

3. Remove the baking sheet with the sheet of dough from the refrigerator and transfer the dough to a work surface. Peel the top sheet of parchment off the dough and lay it back down on the dough. (This loosens the parchment so you will be able to lift the dough off without it sticking.) Flip the sheet of dough over. Peel off the top sheet of parchment paper and lay it clean-side up on the baking sheet to line it. Place the flan ring on the dough and use it as a guide to cut a round of dough that is at least 1 inch larger all around than the ring. (You will trim the dough to fit the ring in the next step; this just makes the dough easier to work with.)

4. Place the ring on the prepared baking sheet. Loosely wrap the dough around a rolling pin and lower it over the ring, centering it so that the dough overhangs evenly around the edge. To fit the dough into the ring, lift the edges and let the dough drop into the pan; dip the knuckle of your index finger in flour and use it to gently press the dough into the creases where the ring meets the baking sheet. Don't stretch the dough to fit or it will shrink when it is baked. Run a rolling pin at a 45-degree angle around the edge of the ring to trim off the excess dough. (Pat the scraps into a 1-inch-thick disk, wrap in plastic, and refrigerate to use another time, or discard them.) Place the tart shell in the refrigerator to chill until the dough is firm, at least 1 hour.

5. To prepare the filling and bake the tart, adjust an oven rack to the bottom third of the oven and preheat the oven to 350°F.

6. Combine the egg whites, vanilla, and almond extract in a small bowl and whisk to combine.

7. Combine the almond meal, granulated sugar, powdered sugar, flour, and salt together in the bowl of a stand mixer. (If you are using whole almonds instead of almond meal, put the almonds in a food processor with 2 tablespoons of the powdered sugar and pulse to a fine meal. Transfer to a stand mixer and add the sugar, flour, salt, and the remaining powdered sugar.) Fit the mixer with the paddle attachment and mix on low speed to combine the ingredients. Stop the mixer, remove the paddle and bowl, and clean them with the rubber spatula.

8. Place the butter in a small saucepan or skillet with a light-colored bottom to make brown butter. Warm the butter over medium heat until it melts and begins to bubble, swirling the pan so it cooks evenly. Continue to cook the butter, swirling often, until it is caramel colored and the solids are the color of coffee grounds, 5 to 8 minutes. Remove from the heat. Working quickly, pour the butter, including the browned bits, into the mixer bowl and mix on medium speed for about 1 minute to incorporate.

9. Remove the tart shell from the refrigerator. Pour the filling into the shell and use an offset spatula to smooth out the surface.

10. Place the baking sheet on the lower rack of the oven and bake the tart for 20 minutes. Rotate the baking sheet front to back; if you see that the tart is puffing up, push it down with the palms of your hands. Bake the tart until a crust has formed on top and the outer edges of the tart are deep brown, an additional 15 to 20 minutes. Remove the tart from the oven and set aside to cool to room temperature.

11. While the tart is cooling, to prepare the strawberries, remove the hulls. If the strawberries are small or medium-sized, cut them in half. If they are large, cut them into thirds. Place the strawberries in a large bowl. Sprinkle the granulated sugar over them and gently toss with your hands or a spatula to coat the strawberries with the sugar. Set aside for about 30 minutes to macerate the strawberries.

12. To remove the tart from the ring, run the tip of a paring knife around the inside edges of the ring to loosen any stuck bits. Slide the tart onto a cake round and slide it off the round onto a serving platter. Remove the ring.

13. Pile the strawberries in a mound in the center of the tart, leaving the edges visible.

Hazelnut Plum Tart

Made with ground nuts, egg whites, and brown butter, the cake portion of this tart is light, chewy, and redolent of the nutty flavor of brown butter. It is my favorite application for a baked plum dessert.

This recipe calls for ground hazelnuts, but if you want to use almonds, they will make for a delicious tart as well. I prefer to make this with red plums, such as Santa Rosa or Elephant Heart. The important thing is that you make this tart when plums are in season (which is in the summer!) and with plums that are ripe but firm, not mushy.

Makes one 12-inch tart

What You Need—
The Essential Special Equipment

12-inch flan ring

12-inch cardboard cake round

Cooking spray

For the Tart Shell

Sweet Tart Dough (page 329)

Unbleached all-purpose flour for dusting (optional)

For the Filling

150 grams (about 1 cup plus 2 tablespoons) hazelnuts (preferably skinless)

1 generous pound plums, such as Santa Rosa or Elephant Heart

3 extra-large egg whites

1 tablespoon pure vanilla bean paste or vanilla extract

150 grams (1¼ cups) powdered sugar

25 grams (about 3 tablespoons) unbleached all-purpose flour

¾ teaspoon Diamond Crystal kosher salt

150 grams (about ½ cup plus 3 tablespoons) unsalted butter, cubed

1. To prepare the tart shell, lay a sheet of parchment paper on a work surface. Remove the dough from the refrigerator, unwrap, and place in the center of the parchment paper. Pound the dough with a rolling pin to soften it until it is malleable and as flat as possible. (The more you flatten it, the easier it will be to roll out.) Lay a sheet of parchment paper on top of the dough, lining it up with the lower sheet of parchment. Applying firm, steady pressure with the rolling pin, roll the dough out between the parchment paper to ³⁄₁₆ inch thick. (Alternatively, you can skip the parchment paper and roll the dough on a flour-dusted work surface, dusting the surface, the dough, or the pin with flour as needed.) Lay the dough on a baking sheet and place it in the refrigerator to chill until it is firm, at least 1 hour.

2. Coat the inside of the flan ring with cooking spray.

3. Remove the baking sheet with the sheet of dough from the refrigerator and transfer the dough to a work surface. Invert the baking sheet so the →

Hazelnut Plum Tart (continued)

underside is facing up. Peel the top sheet of parchment off the dough and lay it back down on the dough. (This loosens the parchment so you will be able to lift the dough off without it sticking.) Flip the sheet of dough over. Peel off the top sheet of parchment paper and lay it clean-side up on the inverted baking sheet to line it. Place the flan ring on the dough and use it as a guide to cut a round of dough that is at least 1 inch larger all around than the ring. (You will trim the dough to fit the ring in the next step; this just makes the dough easier to work with.)

4. Place the ring on the prepared baking sheet. Loosely wrap the dough around a rolling pin and lower it over the ring, centering it so that the dough overhangs evenly around the edge. To fit the dough into the ring, lift the edges and let the dough drop into the ring; dip the knuckle of your index finger in flour and use it to gently press the dough into the creases where the ring meets the baking sheet. Don't stretch the dough to fit or it will shrink when it is baked. Run a rolling pin at a 45-degree angle around the edge of the ring to trim off the excess dough. (Pat the scraps into a 1-inch-thick disk, wrap in plastic, and refrigerate to use another time, or discard them.) Dot the bottom of the tart shell all over with the tines of a fork and place the baking sheet in the refrigerator to chill the dough until firm, at least 1 hour.

5. To prepare the filling and bake the tart, adjust an oven rack to the center position and preheat the oven to 350°F.

6. Spread the hazelnuts on a baking sheet and place them on the center rack of the oven to toast until they are fragrant and golden brown, 15 to 18 minutes, gently shaking the baking sheet and rotating it front to back halfway through the toasting time so the nuts brown evenly. Remove the baking sheet from the oven. (If you think they are on the verge of being overtoasted, transfer them to a plate so they don't continue to cook from the residual heat of the pan.) Set the hazelnuts aside until they are cool enough to touch. If the hazelnuts have skins, place them in the center of a clean dish towel; close the towel into a bundle and rub the hazelnuts together inside the towel to remove the skins; discard the skins.

7. Leave the oven on, but reposition a rack to the bottom third of the oven.

8. Cut the plums in half lengthwise and discard the pits. Cut the plum halves into ¾-inch-thick wedges. Set aside.

9. Whisk the egg whites and vanilla together in small bowl.

10. Put the hazelnuts and 60 grams (½ cup) of the powdered sugar in a food processor and pulse until the nuts are ground to a coarse meal. Scrape down the food processor bowl and lid to loosen any nuts that may be stuck there. Add the flour, salt, and remaining 90 grams (¾ cup) powdered sugar and pulse to combine. Slowly drizzle the egg white/vanilla mixture through the feed tube and pulse until the ingredients come together. Transfer the mixture to a stand mixer fitted with the paddle.

11. Place the butter in a small saucepan or skillet with a light-colored bottom to make brown butter. Warm the butter over medium heat until it melts and begins to bubble, swirling the pan occasionally. Cook the butter, swirling often so it cooks evenly, until the butter is caramel colored and the milk solids are the color of coffee grounds, 4 to 8 minutes. Remove from the heat. Working quickly so the butter doesn't continue to brown, turn the mixer on medium speed and add the butter, including the browned bits, pouring it down the side of the bowl so the warm butter doesn't hit the paddle. Continue to mix for about 1 minute until the butter is combined. Stop the mixer, remove the paddle and bowl, and clean them with the rubber spatula.

12. Remove the tart shell from the refrigerator. Pour the filling into the shell and use an offset spatula to smooth out the surface. Lay a circle of plum wedges with the tips facing the center around the perimeter of the tart shell. Place 1 plum half or quarter in the center. Lay a second circle of plums inside the first one and then fit the rest of the plums into the remaining space so the surface of the tart is completely covered.

13. Place the baking sheet on the lower rack of the oven and bake the tart until a thin, golden crust has formed on top and the outer edges of the tart are deep brown, 40 minutes to 1 hour. Remove the tart from the oven and set it aside to cool to room temperature.

14. To remove the tart from the ring, run the tip of a paring knife around the inside edges of the ring to loosen any stuck bits. Slide the tart onto a cake round and slide it off the round onto a serving platter. Remove the ring.

Cherry Cobbler

Think of this as a cherry cobbler, disguised as a clafoutis. I love the look of a cherry clafoutis when it is cooked in a copper pan and the cherries sink down in the custardy base, but I find the flavor too eggy. I took the same idea and used it to make this cobbler. The cherries sink into the batter, leaving deep indentations around each cherry where the batter browns around the edges. I top the cobbler with toasted thinly sliced almonds and then dust it with powdered sugar, as you would a clafoutis. The result is simple, rustic, and homey—everything I love in a dessert. It also couldn't be easier to make. If cherries are in season and you need to make a last-minute dessert, this is it. It may be the simplest recipe in the book. It takes about 15 minutes to get it in the oven, and requires next to zero technique.

Fresh sour (also called "tart") cherries, which are in season during the summer, are ideal, but any variety of ripe, in-season cherries will do. If cherries aren't in season, use blueberries, raspberries, blackberries, or a combination; even when these berries aren't in season, the cobbler is delicious. I guess that's the magic of cobbler. And berries.

Makes 1 cobbler

What You Need—
The Essential Special Equipment

9-cup capacity baking dish or pan (I used a 12-inch oval All-Clad gratin pan)

Cooking spray

For the Toppings

37.5 grams (¼ cup plus 2 tablespoons) skin-on thin-sliced almonds

25 grams (2 tablespoons) granulated sugar

½ teaspoon ground cinnamon

½ pound (1¼ to 1½ cups) sour cherries

For the Batter

113 grams (1 stick) unsalted butter, cubed

336 grams (1½ cups) buttermilk (preferably whole-milk or low-fat), shaken

1½ tablespoons pure almond extract

1 teaspoon pure vanilla bean paste or vanilla extract

1 large lemon

210 grams (1½ cups) unbleached all-purpose flour

225 grams (1 cup plus 2 tablespoons) granulated sugar

19 grams (3 tablespoons) unblanched almond meal

1 tablespoon baking powder

1 teaspoon Diamond Crystal kosher salt

Powdered sugar for dusting →

1. To prepare the toppings, adjust an oven rack to the center position and preheat the oven to 325°F.

2. Spread the almonds on a baking sheet and toast them on the center rack of the oven until they are light golden brown, 8 to 10 minutes, rotating the baking sheet front to back and stirring the almonds halfway through the toasting time so they brown evenly. Remove the baking sheet from the oven. Transfer the almonds to a plate to prevent them from browning further and set aside to cool.

3. Leave the oven on and increase the temperature to 350°F.

4. Stir the granulated sugar and cinnamon together in a small bowl and set aside.

5. Stem the cherries and cut them in half, leaving some of them still connected on one side so they open like a book. Discard the pits. Put the cherries in a medium bowl.

6. To make the batter, coat the baking dish or pan with cooking spray.

7. Place the butter in a small saucepan or skillet with a light-colored bottom to make golden butter. Warm the butter over medium heat until it melts and begins to bubble, swirling the pan occasionally. Cook the butter, swirling often so it cooks evenly, until it is golden and the milk solids are caramel colored, 3 to 6 minutes. Remove from the heat and pour the butter into a large wide bowl. Working quickly so the butter doesn't continue to cook, weigh out 81 grams (or measure 6 tablespoons) of butter, making sure to include the milk solids, and transfer to a medium bowl. (Reserve the remaining butter for another use.)

8. Warm the buttermilk in a small saucepan over medium heat until it is warm to the touch. Remove from the heat and stir in the almond extract and vanilla. Add the buttermilk mixture to the bowl with the golden butter and stir with a whisk to combine. Use a fine Microplane to grate the zest (the bright-yellow outer layer) of the lemon into the bowl and stir it in. (Reserve the lemon for another use.)

9. Sift the flour, granulated sugar, almond meal, baking powder, and salt into a large bowl and whisk to combine. Create a well in the center with your hands. Pour half of the buttermilk/butter mixture into the well and use a whisk to draw the dry ingredients from the edges to the well to make a thick paste. Add the remaining buttermilk/butter mixture and stir with the whisk to combine.

10. Pour the batter in the prepared baking dish or pan and smooth out the top with an offset spatula. Scatter the cherries evenly on top of the batter. Sprinkle the cinnamon-sugar on the batter and scatter the toasted almonds unevenly over the top, leaving some of the batter and cherries visible.

11. Bake the cobbler on the center rack of the oven until it is evenly browned, 35 to 45 minutes, rotating it front to back halfway through the baking time so it browns evenly. Remove the cobbler from the oven and set it aside to cool to room temperature.

12. Dust with powdered sugar before serving.

Brown Butter Tart with Blueberries

This tart, with a cake-like brown butter filling, is my answer to a French fruit tart. Before I was introduced to this recipe—back in the 1980s, while working at Michael's restaurant in Santa Monica—the only French tarts I knew were the old-school variety, filled with pastry cream and decorated with various types of fruit arranged in concentric circles and covered in a shiny glaze. Even under the best of circumstances, these tarts were never appealing to me.

Once I was introduced to this tart, I started using it as a base for all my fresh fruit tarts. The brown butter filling, which is like a delicious soft cookie, is the ideal vehicle for soft, seasonal fruit, such as peaches, nectarines, plums, raspberries, blackberries, or my favorite—blueberries—and since the theme of this book is "the best of the best," I am leaving it at that. In this recipe, the blueberries are baked into the filling as well as piled on top.

Makes one 12-inch tart

**What You Need—
The Essential Special Equipment**

12-inch flan ring

12-inch cardboard cake round

Cooking spray

Pastry brush

For the Tart Shell

Sweet Tart Dough (page 329)

Unbleached all-purpose flour for dusting

For the Filling

250 grams (1¼ cups) granulated sugar

3 extra-large eggs

1 tablespoon pure vanilla bean paste or vanilla extract

1 teaspoon Diamond Crystal kosher salt

170 grams (1½ sticks) unsalted butter

70 grams (½ cup) unbleached all-purpose flour

5 ounces (1 cup) blueberries

For Finishing

1 pound 5 ounces (5 cups) blueberries

500 grams (2½ cups) granulated sugar

Powdered sugar for dusting

1. To prepare the tart shell, remove the dough from the refrigerator, unwrap, and place in the center of the parchment paper. Pound the dough with a rolling pin to soften it until it is malleable and flatten it as much as possible. (The more you flatten it, the easier it will be to roll out.) Lay another sheet of parchment paper on top of the dough, lining it up with the lower sheet. Applying firm, steady pressure, roll the dough between the parchment to ³⁄₁₆ inch thick. (Alternatively, you can skip the parchment paper and roll the dough on a flour-dusted work surface, dusting the surface, the dough, or the pin with flour as needed.) Lay the dough on a baking sheet and place it in the refrigerator to chill until it is firm, at least 1 hour. →

2. Coat the inside of the flan ring with cooking spray.

3. Remove the sheet of dough from the refrigerator and lay it on your work surface. Invert the baking sheet so the underside is facing up. Peel the top sheet of parchment off the dough and lay it right back down on the dough. (This loosens the parchment so you will be able to lift it off without it sticking.) Flip the sheet of dough over. Peel off the top sheet of parchment paper and lay it clean-side up on the inverted baking sheet to line it. Place the ring on the sheet of dough and use it as a guide to cut a round of dough that is at least 1 inch larger all around than the ring. (You will trim the dough to fit the ring in the next step; this just makes it easier to work with.)

4. Place the ring on the prepared baking sheet. Loosely wrap the dough around a rolling pin and lower it over the prepared ring, centering it so that the dough overhangs evenly around the edge. To fit the dough into the ring, lift the edges of the dough and let the dough drop into the creases of the ring, dipping the knuckle of your index finger in flour and using it to gently press the dough into the creases of the ring rather than stretching it to fit. Don't stretch the dough to fit, or it will shrink when baked. Run a rolling pin at a 45-degree angle around the edge of the ring to trim off the excess dough. (Pat the scraps into a 1-inch-thick disk, wrap in plastic, and refrigerate to use another time, or discard them.) Place the baking sheet in the refrigerator to chill the tart shell until the dough is firm, at least 1 hour.

5. To make the filling and bake the tart, adjust an oven rack to the bottom third of the oven and preheat the oven to 350°F.

6. Combine the granulated sugar, eggs, vanilla, and salt together in a large bowl and stir with a whisk to combine. Fill a medium saucepan with water. Place the bowl on top of the saucepan. (The weighted saucepan anchors the bowl, so it remains stable when you whisk ingredients in it.)

7. Place the butter in a small saucepan or skillet with a light-colored bottom to make brown butter. Warm the butter over medium heat until it melts and begins to bubble, swirling the pan occasionally so the butter cooks evenly. Continue to cook the butter, swirling often, until the melted butter is caramel colored and the solids are the color of coffee grounds, 5 to 8 minutes. Remove from the heat. Working quickly so the butter doesn't continue to brown, gradually add the brown butter to the bowl with the eggs in a slow,

steady stream, whisking constantly so the warm butter doesn't cook the eggs. Add the flour and stir with the whisk until no lumps remain.

8. Remove the tart shell from the refrigerator. Pour the filling into the shell, scraping the bowl clean with a rubber spatula. Use an offset spatula to smooth out the filling. Scatter 1 cup of the blueberries evenly over the surface of the tart.

9. Place the baking sheet with the tart on it in the lower third of the oven and bake until the top is deep golden brown, 45 minutes to 1 hour, rotating the tart front to back halfway through the baking time so it bakes evenly. Remove the tart from the oven and set it aside to cool to room temperature.

10. To remove the tart from the ring, run the tip of a paring knife around the inside edges of the ring to loosen any stuck bits. Slide the tart onto a cake round and slide it off the round onto a serving platter. Remove the ring.

11. While the tart is cooling, to finish the tart, rinse the remaining 5 cups of berries in a fine-mesh sieve and transfer them to a heatproof medium bowl. Place the sieve in the sink, ready to use in the next step.

12. Put the granulated sugar in a medium saucepan. Add 590 grams (2½ cups) water and bring it to a boil over medium-high heat, stirring with a whisk to dissolve the sugar. Gently boil for about 3 minutes, brushing down the sides of the pot with a wet pastry brush, until it is the consistency of thin syrup. Remove from the heat and pour the sugar syrup over the blueberries in the bowl. Count to five, then drain the blueberries in the sieve; the point is not to cook the blueberries but to bring out and preserve their deep blue color. Shake the sieve to remove any excess syrup and pile the glazed blueberries on the tart, leaving at least 1 inch of filling visible around the edges.

13. Dust the tart with powdered sugar before serving.

Stone Fruit and Berry Crumble

This is most definitely a summer dessert. Stone fruit refers to any fruit that contains a stone, or pit, including peaches, plums, nectarines, apricots, pluots, or cherries. Other than the exterior appearance, there is no resemblance between a ripe, farmers' market peach in the summertime, so juicy you eat it over the sink, and a mealy, dry, and flavorless out-of-season peach. They shouldn't even be called the same name. This stone fruit crumble is the perfect use for all that stone fruit you couldn't resist buying at the farmers' market, and that you need to use before it gets overripe. Stone fruit season is also berry season, so I often add a pint or two of berries to this crumble for color and flavor. Make this only when you're staring down some beautiful summer fruit that is begging to be baked.

The streusel topping has eggs in it, so it's like a cookie dough that, when baked in clumps on the crumble, gets crunchy and hard. I just love it in contrast with the soft fruit. As with all crumbles and crisps, a big scoop of vanilla ice cream is the perfect finish.

Makes one 12-inch crumble

What You Need—
The Essential Special Equipment

12 × 7-inch oval baking dish
(or another 12-cup capacity baking dish)

For the Streusel

1 extra-large egg

1 tablespoon pure vanilla bean paste
or vanilla extract

272 grams (2 cups minus 1 tablespoon) unbleached all-purpose flour

91 grams (⅓ cup plus 2 tablespoons) granulated sugar

1¼ teaspoons baking powder

1¾ teaspoons Diamond Crystal kosher salt

1 teaspoon grated nutmeg

136 grams (1 stick plus 1½ tablespoons) cold unsalted butter, cubed

For the Fruit Filling

4¼ pounds seasonal fruit and berries (any combination of apricots, peaches, plums, pluots, nectarines, cherries, raspberries, blackberries, and boysenberries)

350 grams (1¾ cups) granulated sugar

77 grams (⅓ cup) crème fraîche (or 81 grams/⅓ cup sour cream)

37 grams (⅓ cup) potato starch

½ teaspoon Diamond Crystal kosher salt

1. To make the streusel, whisk the egg and vanilla together in a small bowl.

2. Combine the flour, sugar, baking powder, salt, and nutmeg in a stand mixer fitted with the paddle and mix on low speed to combine the ingredients and distribute the salt and baking powder. Add the butter and mix on low speed until the mixture is the texture of a coarse meal. Remove the bowl and paddle from the stand. (If the butter has softened, which will →

happen in a warm kitchen, put the bowl in the freezer for 20 to 30 minutes to firm it up before moving on to the next step.) Drizzle the egg/vanilla mixture over the flour/butter mixture and use your hands to incorporate it, forming uneven clumps. Don't work the ingredients so much that they come together into a dough. Transfer the streusel to a covered container and refrigerate until you're ready to use it.

3. To make the fruit filling, halve and pit the stone fruit and cut the fruit into quarters or eighths, depending on the size, to create long wedges of fruit. (If you're using small Italian prune plums or apricots, you can leave those halved.) Put the stone fruit in a large bowl and add the berries if you're using them. (You want a total of 13 cups of fruit.) Sprinkle with the sugar and set aside to macerate for at least 30 minutes and up to 2 hours, stirring occasionally to distribute the sugar evenly.

4. While the fruit is macerating, adjust an oven rack to the center position and preheat the oven to 375°F. Line a large baking sheet with parchment paper.

5. Drain the accumulated juices from the fruit into a medium bowl. (You can drain the fruit in a sieve set over a bowl or simply hold the fruit back with your hand and pour the juices into the second bowl.) To the bowl of fruit juices, add the crème fraîche, potato starch, and salt and whisk until no lumps remain. Return this liquid to the bowl with the fruit and mix with a rubber spatula to coat the fruit with the liquid.

6. Transfer the fruit to the baking dish. Crumble the streusel over the fruit in big clumps, leaving bits of fruit peeking through.

7. Put the dish on the lined baking sheet and bake it on the center rack of the oven until the streusel topping is evenly golden brown and the fruit is bubbling around the edges, 60 to 75 minutes, rotating the baking sheet front to back halfway through the baking time so it bakes evenly. (If the topping is browning unevenly, reduce the oven temperature to 350°F.) Remove the crumble from the oven and remove the baking dish from the baking sheet. (Otherwise, the juices that bubbled over will cause it to stick to the parchment paper. Please resist the temptation to wipe down the outside of the cobbler dish after the cobbler is baked; the baked fruit juices add to the character and make it look even more tempting.) Serve warm or at room temperature.

Vanilla Custard Tart with Raspberries

I love the combination of raspberries and creamy vanilla custard. In this tart, the raspberries are baked into the custard, so they don't seem like an afterthought as they can in classic French tarts made with pastry cream. Raspberries are available these days year-round, and admittedly, they're pretty good as far as out-of-season fruit goes. Still, I think of this as a summer tart. I can't decide whether I like this tart better still slightly warm from the oven, or the next day, cold from the refrigerator. I'll leave it to you to be the judge.

Make the custard a day in advance; this helps prevent bubbles from forming on the top.

Makes one 10-inch tart

**What You Need—
The Essential Special Equipment**

10-inch flan ring

Pie weights (or dried beans)

12-inch cardboard cake round

Cooking spray

For the Custard

4 extra-large egg yolks

100 grams (½ cup) granulated sugar

360 grams (1½ cups) heavy cream

1 tablespoon pure vanilla bean paste or vanilla extract

For the Tart Shell

½ recipe Sweet Tart Dough (page 329)

Unbleached all-purpose flour for dusting (optional)

For Assembly

24 ounces raspberries
(4 pint-size clamshell containers)

1. To make the custard, whisk the egg yolks and sugar together in a medium bowl. Fill a medium saucepan with water. Place the bowl on top of the saucepan. (The weighted saucepan anchors the bowl, so it remains stable when you whisk ingredients in it in the next step.)

2. Bring the cream to a simmer in a medium saucepan over medium heat, stirring occasionally with a silicone spatula. Remove from the heat. Gradually ladle about half of the hot cream into the bowl with the egg/sugar mixture, whisking constantly to prevent the cream from cooking the eggs. Gradually add the warmed egg/cream mixture to the saucepan with the remaining cream, stirring constantly. Cook the custard over medium heat, stirring gently from the edges toward the center with a silicone spatula until it thickens slightly, becomes more yellow in color, and the bubbles subside. Remove from the heat. Pass the custard through a fine-mesh sieve into a large heatproof pitcher or spouted measuring cup. Set aside to cool to room temperature. Cover with plastic wrap and refrigerate overnight or for at least several hours. →

3. To prepare the tart shell, lay a sheet of parchment paper on a work surface. Remove the dough from the refrigerator, unwrap, and place the dough in the center of the parchment paper. Pound the dough with a rolling pin to soften it until it is malleable and as flat as possible. (The more you flatten it, the easier it will be to roll out.) Lay another sheet of parchment paper on top of the dough, lining it up with the lower sheet of parchment. Applying firm, steady pressure with the rolling pin, roll the dough out between the parchment paper to ¾₆ inch thick. (Alternatively, you can skip the parchment paper and roll the dough on a flour-dusted work surface, dusting the surface, the dough, or the pin with flour as needed.) Lay the dough on a baking sheet and place it in the refrigerator to chill until it is firm, at least 1 hour.

4. Coat the inside of the flan ring with cooking spray.

5. Remove the baking sheet with the sheet of dough from the refrigerator and transfer the dough to a work surface. Peel the top sheet of parchment off the dough and lay it back down on the dough. (This loosens the parchment so you will be able to lift the dough off without it sticking.) Flip the sheet of dough over. Peel off the top sheet of parchment paper and lay it clean-side up on the baking sheet to line it. Place the flan ring on the dough and use it as a guide to cut a round of dough that is at least 1 inch larger all around than the ring. (You will trim the dough to fit the ring in the next step; this just makes the dough easier to work with.)

6. Place the ring on the prepared baking sheet. Loosely wrap the dough around a rolling pin and lower it over the ring, centering it so that the dough overhangs evenly around the edge. To fit the dough into the ring, lift the edges and let the dough drop into the tin; dip the knuckle of your index finger in flour and use it to gently press the dough into the creases where the ring meets the baking sheet. Don't stretch the dough to fit or it will shrink when it is baked. Run a rolling pin at a 45-degree angle around the edge of the ring to trim off the excess dough. (Pat the scraps into a 1-inch-thick disk, wrap in plastic, and refrigerate to use another time, or discard them.) Dot the bottom of the tart shell all over with the tines of a fork and place the baking sheet in the refrigerator to chill the dough until firm, at least 1 hour.

7. Adjust an oven rack to the center position and preheat the oven to 350°F. →

8. Remove the tart shell from the refrigerator. Coat a piece of parchment on one side with cooking spray and gently press it, sprayed-side down, into the shell to cover the dough. Fill the shell with pie weights (or dried beans), pressing them into the creases of the tart shell.

9. Bake the tart shell on the center rack of the oven until the edges of the crust are light golden, 30 to 40 minutes, lifting the parchment to peek under it and gauge the color. Remove the shell from the oven and remove the weights and parchment paper. (Set the weights aside to cool to room temperature, then put them away to use again for the same purpose. Discard the parchment paper.) Return the shell to the oven, rotating the baking sheet front to back, and bake until it is evenly golden brown, 8 to 10 minutes. Remove the shell from the oven and set it aside to cool to room temperature.

10. Reduce the oven temperature to 325°F.

11. To assemble and bake the pie, arrange a row of raspberries, each touching the other, around the perimeter of the tart shell, then place one raspberry in the center of the tart. Working outward from the center berry, place the berries in concentric circles until the shell is covered in rings of raspberries. (You may have some raspberries left over to snack on.)

12. Remove the custard from the refrigerator. Skim off and discard any bubbles that may have formed on the top of the custard.

13. Pull the center rack of the oven out and place the baking sheet with the tart on the rack. Gradually pour the custard mixture into the tart shell, pouring slowly to prevent the raspberries from moving. (You may not use all the custard. Bake any remaining custard in a ramekin to snack on or discard it.) Gently push the oven rack in, taking care not to spill the custard. Bake the tart until the custard jiggles but is not liquid when you shake the pan, 35 to 40 minutes, rotating the baking sheet front to back halfway through the baking time so the tart bakes evenly. To test for doneness, jiggle the center raspberry with your finger; the custard beneath it should feel soft and jiggly, but not runny. Remove the tart from the oven and set aside to set for at least 2 hours before serving.

14. To remove the tart from the ring, run the tip of a paring knife around the inside edges of the ring to loosen any stuck bits. Slide the tart onto a cake round and slide it off the round onto a serving platter. Remove the ring.

Apple Crisp

I hate to break it to you, but apple crisp is *not* a year-round dessert. To earn its name, a dessert as simple and straightforward as apple crisp requires that each element be ideal: The topping needs to be crunchy but not tough and hard. The proportion of apple filling to topping needs to be just right. And then, yes, there's the filling itself. I can't stress enough how important it is to use seasonal apples; that's what gives this simple dessert its flavor and complexity. It's so crucial, in fact, that I forbid you from calling this an apple crisp if you make it with common types of apples sold out of season, such as Granny Smith, or Red or Golden Delicious apples.

I made so many versions before arriving at this recipe that it became very clear just how bad an apple crisp could be when made with the wrong type of apple. I started the process in Italy over the Christmas holidays and made versions using apples that I bought from a nearby farm that sells nothing but apples—good ones! The crisp was wonderful: The apples, when baked, were soft but still intact, glossy, and glazed, and they exuded enough juice that they had an almost caramel-like sauce around them.

I like to use several varieties of apples in this, since each one has a subtly different flavor and cooks slightly differently; the mixture adds complexity and flavor to the finished crisp. There are many great baking apples out there, including Northern Spy, Jonathan, Mutsu, Honeycrisp, Fuji, Pink Lady, and Pippin.

This crisp is best still warm from the oven, served with vanilla ice cream.

Makes one 10-inch crisp

What You Need—
The Essential Special Equipment

10-inch ovenproof skillet (or another 10-cup capacity baking dish)

For the Crisp Topping

175 grams (1¼ cups) unbleached all-purpose flour

125 grams (1¼ cups) rolled oats

1 teaspoon Diamond Crystal kosher salt

½ teaspoon ground cinnamon

¼ teaspoon grated nutmeg

280 grams (2½ sticks) unsalted butter, cubed and left at room temperature until pliable but not greasy

250 grams (1¼ cups) granulated sugar

For the Apples

113 grams (1 stick) unsalted butter

4½ pounds baking apples, such as Pink Lady, Braeburn, Fuji, Northern Spy, Jonathan, Mutsu, Honeycrisp, Fuji, Pink Lady, or Pippin

150 grams (¾ cup) granulated sugar

50 grams (¼ cup packed) dark brown sugar

1 tablespoon pure vanilla bean paste or vanilla extract

1 teaspoon ground cinnamon

¼ teaspoon grated nutmeg

½ teaspoon Diamond Crystal kosher salt

7.5 grams (2 tablespoons) unbleached all-purpose flour →

---

1. To make the crisp topping, put the flour, oats, salt, cinnamon, and nutmeg in a bowl and stir with a whisk to combine. Add the butter and press each cube between your fingers to work it together with the dry ingredients. Add the granulated sugar and work it in with your fingers until the topping comes together in big chunks with no dry patches; don't work the mixture so much that it comes together into a dough. Cover the bowl with plastic wrap and refrigerate until you are ready to use the topping.

2. To prepare the apples, adjust an oven rack to the center position and preheat the oven to 400°F. Line a large baking sheet with parchment paper.

3. Place the butter in a small saucepan or skillet with a light-colored bottom to make golden butter. Warm the butter over medium heat until it melts and begins to bubble, swirling the pan occasionally. Cook the butter, swirling often so it cooks evenly, until it is golden and the milk solids are caramel colored, 3 to 6 minutes. Remove from the heat.

4. Peel the apples. Working one at a time, stand an apple upright on a cutting board. With a large knife, cut down on the apple around the core four times so that you end up with 4 slabs of apple. Discard the core and repeat with the remaining apples. Cut each slab in half lengthwise into 2 wedges and cut each wedge in 2 or 3 pieces across the middle into roughly ¾ × 1-inch pieces and put them in a large bowl.

5. Add the granulated sugar, brown sugar, vanilla, cinnamon, nutmeg, and salt to the apples and toss to coat. Set aside for about 15 minutes, until the apples are sticky from the released juices. Add the flour and toss to coat the apples. Add the golden butter and toss to combine.

6. Transfer the apples to the skillet (or baking dish), scraping the juices out of the bowl and into the skillet. Drop the topping over the apples in large chunks. Move the topping with your fingers to create space for the apples to show through. (Bake any remaining topping on a separate baking sheet to snack on or sprinkle it over yogurt or ice cream.)

7. Place the skillet on the prepared baking sheet. Place the baking sheet on the center rack of the oven and bake the crisp for 1 hour, rotating the baking sheet halfway through the baking time so the crisp bakes evenly. Increase the oven temperature to 450°F. Bake the crisp until the topping is golden brown and crunchy and the juices from the apples are bubbling through, about 10 minutes longer.

Rustic Pear Tarts

I call these tarts "rustic," because they are free-form, meaning the crust is freely formed on the baking sheet, not constricted inside a tart or pie pan. This type of tart is also called a galette, in French, or a crostata, in Italian. The first time I ever saw a free-form tart was about thirty years ago, at Johanne Killeen and George Germon's Italian restaurant, Al Forno, in Rhode Island. At that time, it was groundbreaking: a tart that is not baked in a mold? Since then, free-form tarts have become commonplace, but seeing them for the first time was life-changing. I gravitate toward anything that is irregular or organic looking, and I added them to my repertoire right away.

When I make free-form tarts, I always make them individually sized. Because they don't have outside walls, you need to fold the crust up over the fruit, and the resulting proportions—the amount of crust around the edge, the look of the pleats in the crust, and the ratio of fruit peeking through the crust around it—are out of balance with the larger tarts. With the smaller tart, the proportions of filling and crust are prettier, and tastier. I top this with streusel topping made with whole wheat flour, which gives it a nice brown color. I add wheat flakes to the topping, instead of typical rolled oats, to keep with the wheat theme. If you can't find the flakes, use rolled oats in their place.

I love all kinds of pears, but after extensive research, I've decided that hands down, the best variety for baking is Bartlett. They break down and become soft when baked, without becoming dry; they're not watery; and they hold their shape and don't turn into mush. They also have great flavor. If you can't find Bartletts, use Anjou, and if you can't find either, bake something else. Also, make sure the pears are ripe (but still firm, not mushy). Unripe pears have little flavor and are too hard, even when baked. If you have any golden butter left over from another recipe, use it in place of the melted butter in the filling.

Makes 10 individual tarts

For the Streusel

63 grams (½ cup plus 1 tablespoon) wheat flakes (or rolled oats)

112.5 grams (½ cup plus 1 tablespoon) granulated sugar

79 grams (½ cup plus 1 tablespoon) whole wheat flour

1 teaspoon Diamond Crystal kosher salt

½ teaspoon ground cinnamon

¼ teaspoon ground cardamom

¼ teaspoon grated nutmeg

113 grams (1 stick) unsalted butter, cubed and left at room temperature until pliable but not greasy

For the Crust

30 grams (2 tablespoons) heavy cream

2 tablespoons pure vanilla bean paste or vanilla extract

420 grams (3 cups) unbleached all-purpose flour, plus more for dusting

75 grams (¼ cup plus 2 tablespoons) granulated sugar

1 teaspoon Diamond Crystal kosher salt

339 grams (3 sticks) cold unsalted butter, cubed

For the Filling

3 pounds firm-ripe Bartlett pears (6 to 8 pears)

50 grams (¼ cup) granulated sugar

28 grams (2 tablespoons) unsalted butter, melted

1 tablespoon pure vanilla bean paste or vanilla extract

½ teaspoon Diamond Crystal kosher salt

For Assembly and Finishing

60 grams (¼ cup) heavy cream

50 grams (¼ cup) granulated sugar

1 teaspoon ground cinnamon

¼ teaspoon ground cardamom

¼ teaspoon grated nutmeg

1. To make the streusel, adjust an oven rack to the center position and preheat the oven to 350°F. Line a baking sheet with parchment paper (a quarter-sheet pan would be ideal).

2. Spread the wheat flakes on the prepared baking sheet and toast on the center rack of the oven until golden brown and fragrant, 6 to 8 minutes, stirring the wheat flakes and rotating the baking sheet halfway through that time so the wheat flakes toast evenly. Remove the baking sheet from the oven and set it aside for the wheat flakes to cool to room temperature.

3. Turn off the oven.

4. Using the parchment paper as a funnel, transfer the wheat flakes to a medium bowl. Add the sugar, whole wheat flour, salt, cinnamon, cardamom, and nutmeg and stir to combine. Add the butter and press it between your fingers to work it in with the flour until the streusel comes together in big chunks; don't mix it so much that it becomes a homogeneous dough. Cover the bowl with plastic wrap and place it in the refrigerator.

5. To make the crust, whisk the cream and vanilla together in a small bowl.

6. Combine the all-purpose flour, sugar, and salt in a stand mixer fitted with the paddle and mix on low speed to incorporate the ingredients. Add the butter and mix on low speed until the ingredients form the consistency of a fine meal. Add the cream/vanilla mixture and mix on medium-low speed until the dough just comes together.

7. Lightly flour a work surface and turn the dough out onto it. Gather the dough together and divide it into three equal portions. Roll each portion into a ball in your hands and press each ball into a 1-inch-thick disk. Wrap the disks in plastic wrap and refrigerate until the dough is firm, about 1 hour.

8. Lay a sheet of parchment paper on a work surface. Dust the paper lightly with flour. Working with one disk of dough at a time (leaving the others in →

the refrigerator), place a disk of the dough in the center of the parchment paper, dust the dough with flour, and lay another sheet of parchment paper on top of the dough, lining it up with the lower sheet. Roll the dough between the parchment to ³⁄₁₆ inch thick. Lay the parchment paper–sandwiched dough on a baking sheet and place it in the refrigerator. Repeat, rolling out the second and third disks of dough in the same way, between two fresh sheets of parchment paper. Add them to the refrigerator, laying them on top of the first sheet of dough. Refrigerate the dough until it is firm, at least 1 hour.

9. Remove one sheet of dough from the refrigerator and lay it on your work surface. Peel the top sheet of parchment off the dough and lay it right back down on the dough. (This loosens the parchment so you will be able to lift it off without it sticking.) Flip the sheet of dough over. Peel off the top sheet of parchment paper and lay it clean-side up on the inverted baking sheet to line it. Using a plate as a stencil, use a paring knife to cut the dough into 6-inch rounds. Place the rounds in a single layer on the prepared baking sheet. Repeat, cutting rounds out of the second and third sheets of dough and adding them to the baking sheet, separating each layer with parchment paper (you can use the paper the dough was rolled between). Place the baking sheet in the refrigerator to chill the dough until it is firm, at least 1 hour. (You can cut the rounds up to 1 day in advance; if you do this, cover the baking sheet with plastic wrap to prevent the dough from drying out.)

10. To make the filling, peel the pears. Working with one at a time, stand a pear upright on a cutting board. With a large knife, cut down on the pear around the core four times, so that you end up with 4 slabs of pear. Discard the core and repeat with the remaining pears. Cut each slab in half lengthwise into 2 wedges; cut each wedge in 2 or 3 pieces across the middle into roughly ½ × ¾-inch chunks. Measure out 5 cups of pear chunks and place in a large bowl. (Reserve any remaining pears to snack on.) Add the sugar, melted butter, vanilla, and salt to the pears and toss with your hands to coat. (Proceed quickly with the recipe; you don't want to macerate the pears with the sugar.)

11. Line two large baking sheets with parchment paper and coat the parchment paper with cooking spray.

12. Pour the heavy cream in a small bowl.

13. To assemble the tarts, remove 1 round of dough from the refrigerator. Hold the round in front of you so it's hanging, like a pizza maker making →

dough, and turn the round with your hands a few times to soften the edges. Place the dough on one of the prepared baking sheets. Brush 1 inch of the outer edge of the dough with some of the heavy cream. Pile ⅓ cup of the pear filling in the center of the dough, leaving the edge brushed with the cream free of filling, and spoon some of the liquid from the bottom of the bowl over the pears. Fold the outside edges of the dough toward the center in 5 pleats, pressing on each pleat to seal it. Repeat to make 2 or 3 more tarts (the number that will fit on the baking sheet), then place the baking sheet in the refrigerator. Continue forming the remaining tarts in the same way until you have used all the dough rounds and filling (including the liquid), putting 3 or 4 tarts on each baking sheet and keeping the formed tarts in the refrigerator as you form the remaining tarts. (If you don't have enough baking sheets to form the tarts all at once, bake them in two batches, keeping all the components refrigerated in the meantime.)

14.   To finish the tarts, pour the remaining cream into a small bowl. Stir the sugar, cinnamon, cardamom, and nutmeg together in a separate small bowl. Remove the tarts and streusel from the refrigerator. Brush the dough generously with the cream and sprinkle 1 teaspoon of the spiced sugar mixture over the dough. If the opening in the tart is not at least 2 inches wide, use your fingers to gently pull the dough back to widen the opening. Drop about ¼ cup of streusel in clumps over the opening on each tart.

15.   Place the tarts in the refrigerator to chill until the dough is firm, about 30 minutes.

16.   Adjust the oven racks so one is in the top third and the other is in the bottom third of the oven and preheat the oven to 400°F.

17.   Remove the baking sheets with the tarts from the refrigerator. Place one baking sheet on each oven rack and bake the tarts for 30 minutes. Switch racks and rotate the baking sheets front to back. Reduce the oven temperature to 375°F. Bake the tarts until the edges are deep brown and the juices begin to bubble out of the tarts, another 10 to 20 minutes. Remove the baking sheets from the oven. While the tarts are still warm, slide an offset spatula or another metal spatula under them and slide the tarts away from any juices that may have spilled out. When they are cooled, use a large spatula to carefully transfer the tarts to individual plates or a large flat board or slab, taking care as the tarts are very fragile.

Honeynut Squash Pie

Pumpkin pie on the Thanksgiving table is one of those traditions that we just *must* honor—it's too close to our hearts to let it go. That said, in my opinion, pumpkin pie can often be better in memory than reality. (Naturally I would say my Pumpkin Tart with Dates, page 331, is the exception.) This pie, made with a winter squash variety called Honeynut, is my nod to traditional pumpkin pie, but with a more authentic, natural squash flavor. Honeynut squash is similar in shape and color to butternut, but smaller; it is a relatively new variety, developed by the chef Dan Barber, at his farm, Blue Hill at Stone Barns, in upstate New York. Without question, it has more flavor than any other winter squash I've tried, and it's not at all watery, which makes it ideal for this pie. I added maple syrup, brandy, golden butter (butter that is cooked just shy of brown butter), and a lot of freshly ground "pumpkin pie" spices to the squash filling to elevate the flavor while keeping with the sensibility of a classic pumpkin pie. Because the spices play such a big role in this pie filling, I call for freshly ground spices. It really makes a difference.

If you can't find Honeynut squash, substitute another winter squash, such as butternut, cheese pumpkin, or kabocha, or even orange-fleshed sweet potatoes. Your pie will be delicious. Chill the pie overnight and serve it chilled. Not only is the pie at its best this way, this also means you'll have one less task—and a free oven!—on Thanksgiving day.

Makes one 9½-inch pie

**What You Need—
The Essential Special Equipment**

9-inch (4-cup capacity) glass or metal pie pan

Cooking spray

Pie weights (or dried beans)

Large disposable piping bag

Large star tip

For the Crust

Unbleached all-purpose flour for dusting

½ recipe Savory Pie Dough (page 313)

For the Filling

3 pounds Honeynut (or butternut) squash

Extra-virgin olive oil for drizzling

1 teaspoon Diamond Crystal kosher salt

113 grams (1 stick) unsalted butter, cubed

116 grams (½ cup) crème fraîche

96.5 grams (¼ cup) sweetened condensed milk

56 grams (3 tablespoons) artisanal maple syrup (preferably barrel-aged)

2 tablespoons brandy (or whiskey)

1 tablespoon pure vanilla bean paste or vanilla extract

2 extra-large egg yolks

1 extra-large egg

37.5 grams (3 tablespoons packed) dark brown sugar

¾ teaspoon freshly ground cinnamon

½ teaspoon freshly ground allspice

½ teaspoon ground ginger

¼ teaspoon freshly grated nutmeg

⅛ teaspoon freshly ground cloves →

Honeynut Squash Pie (continued)

For the Spice Topping

25 grams (2 tablespoons) granulated sugar

¼ teaspoon freshly ground cinnamon

¼ teaspoon freshly grated nutmeg

For the Whipped Cream

360 grams (1½ cups) heavy cream

116 grams (½ cup) crème fraîche (or 122 grams/½ cup sour cream)

1. To make the crust, coat the pie pan with cooking spray.

2. Lightly dust a work surface with flour. Remove the dough from the refrigerator, unwrap, and place on the floured surface. Pound the dough with a rolling pin to soften it until it is malleable and as flat as possible. (The more you flatten the dough by pounding it, the easier it will be to roll out.) Dust the dough and rolling pin lightly with flour and, applying firm, steady pressure, roll the dough into a ⅛-inch-thick round, dusting with flour as needed.

3. Place the pie pan upside down on the dough and use a paring knife or kitchen shears to cut a round of dough that is at least 3 inches larger all around than the pan. (You'll cut the dough more precisely in the next step; you're trimming at this point to make the sheet of dough easier to work with.)

4. Loosely wrap the dough around the rolling pin and lower it over the prepared pan, centering it so that the dough overhangs evenly around the edge. Lift the edges of the dough and let it drop into the pan; dip the knuckle of your index finger in flour and use it to gently press the dough into the creases of the pan. Don't stretch the dough to fit or it will shrink when it is baked. Using kitchen shears, trim the dough so there are 1½ inches of dough overhanging all around. (Gather the trimmings, pat them into a disk, and wrap them in plastic wrap to use another time, or discard them.)

5. Roll the edge of the dough under itself to create a thick lip of dough that rests on the rim of the pie pan. Press the thumb of one hand on the lip to create an indentation in the dough and press the thumb and forefinger of the other hand on either side of the first thumb, creating a U-shaped indentation. Continue around the perimeter of the crust, creating a crimped, scalloped edge. Dot the bottom of the pie shell all over with the tines of a fork and place the pie shell in the refrigerator to chill until the dough is firm, at least 1 hour.

6. Adjust an oven rack to the center position and preheat the oven to 350°F. Line a large baking sheet with parchment paper.

7. Remove the pie shell from the refrigerator, coat a piece of parchment on one side with cooking spray, and gently press the paper sprayed-side down into the shell to cover the dough. Fill the shell with pie weights (or dried beans), pressing them into the creases of the pie shell. Place the pie shell on the baking sheet.

8. Bake the pie shell on the center rack of the oven until the edges of the crust are light golden, 30 to 40 minutes, lifting the parchment to peek under it and gauge the color. Remove the shell from the oven and lift out the weights and parchment paper. (Set the weights aside to cool to room temperature, then put them away to use again for the same purpose. Discard the parchment paper.) Return the shell to the oven, rotating it front to back, and bake until it is evenly golden brown, 8 to 10 minutes. Remove the shell from the oven and set aside to cool to room temperature.

9. Leave the oven on but increase the temperature to 425°F.

10. To prepare the filling, line a baking sheet with parchment paper.

11. Using a large knife, cut the squash in half lengthwise and use a spoon to scoop out and discard the seeds. Place the squash cut-sides up on the prepared baking sheet. Drizzle with the olive oil, sprinkle with ½ teaspoon of the salt, and massage to coat the squash evenly with the oil and salt. Turn the squash cut-side down on the baking sheet and place it in the oven to roast until it is tender when pierced with a fork, 30 to 40 minutes. Remove the squash from the oven and set aside until it is cool enough to touch.

12. Leave the oven on.

13. Place the butter in a small saucepan or skillet with a light-colored bottom to make golden butter. Warm the butter over medium heat until it melts and begins to bubble, swirling the pan occasionally. Cook the butter, swirling often so it cooks evenly, until it is golden and the milk solids are caramel colored, 3 to 6 minutes. Remove from the heat. Working quickly so the butter doesn't continue to cook, weigh out 54 grams (or measure ¼ cup) of butter, making sure to include the milk solids and transfer it to a large bowl. (Reserve the remaining butter for another use.) →

14. Scoop the squash out of its skin and discard the skin. Put the squash in a food processor fitted with a metal blade and puree it. Pass the pureed squash through a fine-mesh sieve, pushing it through the holes with a rubber spatula. Weigh out 510 grams (or measure 2 cups) of the squash puree and put it in a large bowl. (Reserve any remaining squash for another use.) While the squash is still warm, add the warm golden butter and stir with a whisk until it is thoroughly combined. Add the crème fraîche, sweetened condensed milk, maple syrup, brandy, and vanilla and stir them in with the whisk just until they are combined. Do not overmix.

15. Combine the egg yolks, whole egg, brown sugar, cinnamon, allspice, ginger, nutmeg, cloves, and remaining ½ teaspoon salt in a stand mixer fitted with the whisk. Beat on medium-high speed until the eggs have lightened in color and thickened slightly, about 3 minutes. Stop the mixer and scrape down the sides and bottom of the bowl with a rubber spatula. Add the squash mixture and beat on low speed for about 30 seconds to combine. Stop the mixer and remove the whisk and bowl from the stand and scrape the bowl from the bottom up to release any ingredients that may be stuck there.

16. To make the spice topping, stir the sugar, cinnamon, and nutmeg together in a small bowl. Set aside.

17. Place the prepared pie shell on a baking sheet, pour the filling into the shell, and smooth the top with an offset spatula. Sprinkle the sugar and spice topping evenly over the surface.

18. Place the baking sheet with the pie in the oven and bake for 15 minutes. Rotate the baking sheet front to back and reduce the oven temperature to 350°F. Bake the pie until it is evenly colored, puffs up around the edges, and sets up slightly, 25 to 35 minutes longer. The center will still jiggle when you gently shake the pan, but it won't be liquid. Remove the pie from the oven and set aside to cool to room temperature. Place the pie in the refrigerator to chill overnight.

19. To make the whipped cream, pour the heavy cream into a stand mixer fitted with the whisk and whip the cream on low speed for about 1 minute until it thickens enough not to spatter. Increase the speed to medium-high and whip until soft peaks form, 2 to 3 minutes. Add the crème fraîche and whip on medium-low speed until medium peaks form, about 1 minute.

20. Serve the pie chilled, with the whipped cream on the side.

I am not a big sweets eater, so the recipes for salted biscuits, rolls, and crackers in this chapter are some of my favorites in the book. The crackers are ideal for a cheese or sliced meat board, to snack on with wine. And the biscuits and breads are a delicious addition to any breakfast, lunch, or dinner spread. The next time you're thinking of baking holiday cookies, consider making something from this chapter instead. Who wouldn't want a lovely bag full of buttery Cheese Twists (page 463), thin, crispy Onion Crackers (page 466), or homemade, whole-grain Spelt Digestivi (page 476). Any baked goods involving yeast, which many of these do, need to be made in stages to give the dough time to rest. Read the recipe through and see what it entails before getting started. (A good rule of thumb when baking anything, but essential when working with yeast.) If you plan, this can work to your advantage because you can make the recipe in stages.

Bread Basket

Barish Farmhouse Rolls

After baking for a half century as I have, it's rare that I make something that is truly nothing like anything I have made in the past. But that's the case with these dinner rolls, which we serve at The Barish, my steakhouse in Hollywood. The buttery dough is folded several times and cut into squares, and then each square is placed on its side into the cup of a muffin tin with the layers facing up; they fan out when they're baked, so you get more of the good, delicious, crusty parts. I love playing with my food, pulling things apart and eating bits at a time, so these are perfect for me; I can pull these rolls apart and eat one layer at a time. I also love when I discover something so tiny, like this little trick of turning the layered dough on its side, that makes something as simple as a dinner roll look and even taste that much better. Rolls that fan out like this are often called fantails, but I call them Barish Farmhouse Rolls. The Barish is a nod to my father's side of my family, who were farmers in Saskatchewan, Canada. If I'd had the opportunity to meet my grandparents or eat with them in their farmhouse, I imagine these dinner rolls, warm from the oven, would have been on the table.

If you choose to bake the second dozen rolls another day, freeze the dough and thaw it overnight in the refrigerator, then proceed with the recipe.

Makes 24 dinner rolls

What You Need—
The Essential Special Equipment

At least two (6-cup) jumbo muffin tins

For the Dough

128 grams (2 sticks plus 1 tablespoon) unsalted butter, cubed and left at room temperature until pliable but not greasy, plus more for greasing

1.08 kilograms (7½ cups plus 2 tablespoons) unbleached all-purpose flour

150 grams (¾ cup plus 1 tablespoon plus 1 teaspoon) potato flour

676 grams (2¾ cups) whole milk

3 extra-large eggs

116 grams (about ½ cup plus 1 tablespoon) granulated sugar

2 tablespoons plus 2 teaspoons instant (rapid-rise) yeast (I use Fleischmann's)

2 tablespoons Diamond Crystal kosher salt

For Forming and Finishing the Rolls

84 grams (6 tablespoons) unsalted butter, melted

Flaky sea salt →

1. To make the dough, grease a large bowl with butter.

2. Put the butter, all-purpose flour, potato flour, milk, eggs, sugar, yeast, and salt in a stand mixer fitted with the dough hook. Mix on low speed (speed 4 on a KitchenAid) until the dough is smooth, about 15 minutes. (To check to see if the dough is ready, stop the mixer and pull out a small handful of dough. Work the dough into a square, then pull on the square, and do the windowpane test: If the dough is strong enough, you will be able to pull it until it is translucent, like a windowpane. If the dough rips, it is too weak and needs to be mixed for longer.) Stop the mixer and remove the bowl and dough hook; wipe the hook clean.

3. Transfer the dough to the greased bowl. Cover the bowl with plastic wrap and set aside until the dough has doubled in size, 1 to 1½ hours.

4. While the dough is rising, grease the cups of the jumbo muffin tins with butter.

5. To form and finish the rolls, punch down the dough with your fists and turn out onto a work surface. Divide the dough into 2 equal portions. Wrap one half-portion of the dough and put it in the refrigerator. Working with the other half-portion, cut it in half to make 2 quarter-portions. Set one quarter-portion aside and set the other one in front of you. Roll out to a 9 × 12-inch rectangle. The dough will want to snap back; when it does, apply more pressure and keep rolling. Brush the dough with some melted butter.

6. With a short side of the rectangle facing you, use a ruler and a large knife to cut the dough lengthwise into 6 strips 1½ inches wide. Stack 3 strips on top of one another and cut the stacked strips into 6 equal pieces, each about 2 × 1½ inches. Put 2 stacks (a total of 6 pieces) sideways (so the layers are facing up) in each cup of the muffin tin. Repeat with the reserved quarter-portion, rolling, cutting strips, stacking, cutting into pieces, and placing 2 stacks (a total of 6 pieces) into each cup of the muffin tin. You should now have 12 rolls.

7. Repeat with the refrigerated half-portion of dough until you have filled both muffin tins. Cover the tins with a clean damp towel and set aside to proof the dough until it has nearly doubled in size, 45 minutes to 1 hour; the dough will look puffy and fill the muffin tins.

8. Thirty minutes into the proofing time, adjust an oven rack to the center position and preheat the oven to 350°F.

9. To finish the rolls, brush them with melted butter and sprinkle a big pinch of flaky salt on each roll.

10. Place both muffin tins on the center rack of the oven and bake until the rolls are golden brown, 20 to 25 minutes, switching the muffin tins from side to side and rotating them front to back halfway through the baking time so the rolls brown evenly.

11. Remove the rolls from the oven. Brush them with melted butter and set them aside to cool slightly. Serve warm or at room temperature.

Layered Buttermilk Biscuits
(right); Cream Biscuits (left)

Layered Buttermilk Biscuits

Imagine this: a biscuit so buttery that you don't even want to put butter on it. Yup, these biscuits are a game changer. I included this recipe in my book *Mozza at Home,* but I couldn't write a baking book without biscuits, and, frankly, I couldn't improve upon these. The recipe originated with New Orleans chef Alon Shaya, who shared his recipe with me. The biscuits get their layers from laminating the dough, a baker's term for folding the dough to create layered pastries, such as croissants. But laminating biscuits is no secret. The real secret behind Shaya's biscuits is frozen butter. He grates the butter on a box grater, mixes it in with the flour and then freezes it again, so the shards of butter are intact when they go into the oven, where they melt into the dough, creating biscuits that are light, airy, and incredibly buttery. My version is in fact even more buttery than the original. Where Shaya's recipe calls for four sticks of butter, I use five. It's so much butter, in fact, that some oozes out when they're baked.

At the end of this recipe, I give you instructions for turning the biscuits into flaky, buttery crackers. You could make the crackers with leftover biscuits or bake biscuits for the purpose of turning them into crackers.

Makes 12 biscuits

For the Dough

700 grams (5 cups) unbleached all-purpose flour, plus more for dusting

2 tablespoons plus 2 teaspoons baking powder

1 teaspoon baking soda

1 tablespoon Diamond Crystal kosher salt

12.5 grams (1 tablespoon) granulated sugar

566 grams (5 sticks) unsalted butter, frozen for 2 hours (but not frozen solid)

448 grams (2 cups) buttermilk (preferably whole-milk or low-fat), shaken, plus more as needed

For Finishing

28 grams (2 tablespoons) unsalted butter, melted

Flaky sea salt

1. To make the dough, put the flour, baking powder, baking soda, salt, and sugar in a large bowl and whisk to combine.

2. Lay a piece of parchment or wax paper on a work surface and grate the butter onto the paper using the largest holes of a box grater. Using the paper as a funnel, add the butter to the bowl with the dry ingredients. Stir to combine the ingredients. Put the bowl in the freezer until the butter is frozen solid, at least 30 minutes. →

3. Remove the bowl from the freezer. Add the buttermilk and gently work the dough together with your hands to create a shaggy mess. Press the mess together into a homogeneous dough.

4. Line a large baking sheet with parchment paper. Lightly dust a work surface and turn the dough out onto the floured surface. Using your hands, press the dough into a 10 × 7-inch rectangle with the short side facing you. Use your hands or a bench scraper to square the dough off as much as possible. Fold the top edge of the dough down two-thirds and the bottom edge to meet the top edge so the dough is folded in thirds, like a letter. (Pat the dough together with your hands as needed; it may be crumbly.) Rotate the dough 90 degrees clockwise so the open edge is facing you. This completes the first of three turns.

5. Roll the dough out again, dusting with flour as needed, and make another letter fold. Turn the dough clockwise 90 degrees and roll it out a third time. Make another letter fold and turn the dough 90 degrees clockwise. Roll out the dough to an approximately ½-inch-thick rectangle (at least 10 × 12½ inches). Using a ruler and a long sharp knife, trim the edges to make a clean 10 × 12½-inch rectangle. Use the ruler and knife to cut the dough into 2½-inch squares. (Bake the trimmings to snack on or discard them.)

6. Put the squares on the prepared baking sheet and put them in the freezer until they are frozen solid, at least 1 hour.

7. To finish and bake the biscuits, adjust the oven racks so one is in the top third and the other is in the bottom third of the oven and preheat the oven to 425°F. Line a second large baking sheet with parchment paper.

8. Remove the biscuits from the freezer and place half of them on the second baking sheet, evenly spacing the biscuits on both baking sheets. Brush the tops with the melted butter and sprinkle them with flaky salt.

9. Bake the biscuits for 10 minutes. Switch racks and rotate the baking sheets front to back and reduce the oven temperature to 400°F. Bake the biscuits until the tops are golden brown, for 10 to 15 minutes longer. (A lot of butter will run out of the biscuits as they bake. Don't be alarmed, this is the proof of just how buttery these biscuits are.) Remove the biscuits from the oven.

Biscuit-Top Crackers

These thin, layered, seasoned crackers are like eating the top layer off a biscuit, which we all know is the best part! To turn biscuits into crackers, line a large baking sheet with parchment paper. Turn the biscuits upside down and use a long serrated knife to slice them horizontally as thinly as possible without them crumbling, about ¼ inch thick. Lay the slices on the prepared baking sheet. Brush them with melted butter and sprinkle them with flaky sea salt or the Italian Herb Seasoning (see below). Bake the crackers in a 350°F oven until they're golden brown and crispy, 15 to 20 minutes.

Italian Herb Seasoning (optional)

1 tablespoon plus 1 teaspoon dried oregano

1 tablespoon dried onion flakes

½ teaspoon chile flakes

If you are using the Italian Herb Seasoning, stir the oregano, onion, and chile flakes together and sprinkle over the crackers before baking.

Cream Biscuits

Biscuits, shortcake, scones—they're all so similar, it's easy to confuse them. Cream biscuits, however, are in a category of their own. They get their name because they're made with heavy cream. Traditional cream biscuits don't contain any butter; the cream, which contains butterfat, is what makes them moist and flavorful. I cheated and added 2 tablespoons of melted butter to this recipe. I just couldn't make them perfectly delicious without it. You can serve them with butter and jam or in your savory bread basket, like you would a dinner roll. This may be the simplest recipe in the book. Not only does it not require any skill, it also requires the least amount of equipment. You just need a pot to melt the butter in, a bowl to mix the dough in, and a hand to mix it with. (See photo page 448.)

Makes 8 biscuits

For the Dough

200 grams (about 1¼ cups plus 3 tablespoons) unbleached pastry flour

37.5 grams (3 tablespoons) granulated sugar

2¼ teaspoons baking powder

1 teaspoon Diamond Crystal kosher salt

240 grams (1 cup) heavy cream

28 grams (2 tablespoons) unsalted butter, melted and cooled to room temperature

For Finishing

28 grams (2 tablespoons) unsalted butter, melted

1 teaspoon flaky sea salt

Italian Herb Seasoning (optional)

1 tablespoon plus 1 teaspoon dried oregano

1 tablespoon dried onion flakes

½ teaspoon chile flakes

1. Adjust an oven rack to the center position and preheat the oven to 425°F. Line a large baking sheet with parchment paper.

2. Stir the flour, sugar, baking powder, and salt together in a large bowl. Create a large well in the center with your hands and pour the cream and melted butter into the well. Draw the wet and dry ingredients together with your hands or a rubber spatula until just combined.

3. Using your hands, pick up a handful (about ¼ cup) of the dough and plop it onto the prepared baking sheet. Continue plopping the dough in uneven shaped mounds onto the baking sheet, leaving about 2 inches between them.

4. To finish, brush the surface of each biscuit with the melted butter and sprinkle with a generous pinch of flaky sea salt. If you are using the Italian Herb Seasoning, stir the oregano, onion, and chile flakes together and sprinkle over the crackers.

5. Bake the biscuits on the center rack of the oven for 7 minutes. Slide the oven rack out and use your hands or a spoon to reshape the biscuits, which will have drooped in the oven, to the shape you dropped them in. Slide the rack back in and bake the biscuits for another 5 minutes. Open the oven again, rotate the baking sheet front to back and slide a second baking sheet under the baking sheet of biscuits. Increase the oven temperature to 450°F and bake the biscuits until they are light golden brown all over, with one or two peaks that are deep brown on top, 5 to 7 minutes longer. Remove the biscuits from the oven. Serve warm.

Onion and Sage Focaccia

Every region in Italy, it seems, makes focaccia, and they are all very different from one another. Some denser, some lighter. Some dry, others oily. Some are very simple and others are heavy on the toppings. This is based on Puglia-style focaccia, which is a light, airy deep-dish bread, baked in a pan that is heavily coated with olive oil so the bottom of the bread essentially fries, making it crunchy and oily, and the top dimpled with ingredients, usually cherry tomatoes. I've made this focaccia with many different toppings, but this combination, with onion and sage, is my favorite. This makes two large focaccias. This recipe requires some patience because the dough needs time to rise. After the wait, and as delicious as this focaccia is, you'll be glad to have two.

Makes two 10-inch square focaccias

What You Need—
The Essential Special Equipment

Two 10-inch square cake pans

For the Poolish

0.25 gram fresh (cake) yeast (the size of a pea)

70 grams (½ cup) unbleached all-purpose flour

For the Dough

490 grams (3½ cups) unbleached all-purpose flour, plus more for dusting

61 grams (¼ cup plus 2 tablespoons plus 2 teaspoons) spelt flour

61 grams (¼ cup plus 2 tablespoons plus 1 teaspoon) stone-ground white rice flour (not sweet rice flour)

48 grams (¼ cup plus 1 tablespoon plus 1 teaspoon) high-gluten flour

3.5 grams (¾ teaspoon) fresh (cake) yeast

20 grams (1½ tablespoons) olive oil, plus more for oiling the bowl

2 tablespoons plus 2 teaspoons Diamond Crystal kosher salt

For the Pans and Topping

100 grams (about 7 tablespoons) extra-virgin olive oil, plus more for drizzling

1 large Spanish yellow onion

142 grams (5 ounces) low-moisture mozzarella cheese

8 large fresh sage leaves, each ripped into 3 pieces

4 teaspoons flaky sea salt

1. To make the poolish, put the yeast in a 1-quart container with a tight-fitting lid. Add 70 grams (½ cup) room-temperature water and stir with a fork to dissolve the yeast. Add the flour and stir to combine. Make a mark on the side of the container at the level of the ingredients so you can later judge their increase in size. Cover the container and set it aside in a warm place in your kitchen to proof until it has increased by half, 4 to 6 hours. Place the container in the refrigerator overnight to ferment the poolish, which develops the flavor of the dough. →

2. To make the dough, place 522.5 grams (2¼ cups plus 2 tablespoons plus 2 teaspoons) cold tap water in the bowl of a stand mixer. Add the all-purpose flour, spelt flour, rice flour, and high-gluten flour to the bowl. Fit the mixer with the dough hook and mix on low speed for 2 to 3 minutes, until no flour is visible. Stop the mixer and cover the bowl with a damp cloth, resting the cloth around the dough hook. Let the dough rest for 10 minutes to hydrate the flours. (This step, called the autolyze, gives the dough elasticity, resulting in a lighter, airier bread.)

3. Remove the poolish from the refrigerator. Uncover the mixer bowl and use a rubber spatula to scrape the poolish into the bowl with the dough. Crumble the yeast into the bowl. Mix on low speed until there are no visible lumps of flour or yeast, about 6 minutes. With the mixer running, slowly drizzle the olive oil into the bowl and sprinkle in the kosher salt. Mix for about 1 minute to distribute the oil and salt. Increase the speed to medium-high and mix until the dough pulls away from the sides of the bowl, about 8 minutes; you will need to hold on to the mixer during this time to keep it steady, as the bowl will tend to move along the countertop. Turn off the mixer.

4. Generously oil a large bowl with olive oil. Use a spatula or your hand to scrape the dough out of the mixer and into the oiled bowl. Cover the bowl with plastic wrap, making sure the plastic doesn't touch the dough, and set the dough aside to rest for 1 hour. Uncover the bowl, reserving the plastic wrap. To turn the dough, imagining the round of dough as the face of a clock, fold the 9 and 3 toward the center. Rotate the bowl a quarter-turn and fold the 12 and 6 toward the center. Flip the dough so the folded edges are facing down. Re-cover the bowl and set the dough aside for 1 hour. Uncover the bowl and repeat, folding the four sides of the dough toward the center and then flipping it. Wrap the bowl in a fresh sheet of plastic wrap and refrigerate overnight to allow the flavors of the dough to develop.

5. To prepare the pans, pour 50 grams (about 3½ tablespoons) of extra-virgin olive oil into each of the cake pans and use your fingers to spread the oil to cover the bottom and sides of the pans.

6. Dust a work surface lightly with flour. Remove the bowl from the refrigerator and turn the dough out onto the floured surface. Gently shape it into a rectangle roughly 6 × 12 inches. Use a bench scraper or knife to cut the dough in half to make two roughly 6-inch squares and place one square in each pan.

7. Working with one pan of dough at a time, gently lift the dough with both hands and stretch it toward the edges of the pan (it won't reach the edges at this stage) to obtain a roughly square shape. Repeat with the second pan of dough. Cover the pans with plastic wrap, making sure the plastic is taut across the pans so it doesn't touch the dough, and set aside to rest until the dough does not immediately spring back when pulled on, about 1 hour.

8. To prepare the topping, cut the onion into roughly 1-inch pieces, taking care to try to keep the layers of the onion intact. Cut the cheese into 24 roughly 1-inch cubes.

9. Uncover the pans of dough. Keeping the onion pieces in chunks of at least two layers, press one chunk into each corner of a focaccia, about ½ inch away from the sides of the pan, pressing the onion so deep that it touches the bottom of the pan and then pushing outward to encourage the dough toward the edges of the pan. Repeat in all four corners of the pan. Press 8 more chunks of onion into the focaccia, distributing them evenly throughout, each time pushing the dough toward the edges of the pan. Place 1 cube of mozzarella on top of each piece of onion. Repeat with the second focaccia using the remaining onion and cheese. Drop a piece of sage onto the dough alongside each piece of onion. Press the dough about 10 times with your fingers, pressing almost all the way through the dough. Cover the focaccia with plastic wrap and set aside in a warm place to proof until the dough has risen and is light and fluffy and bubbles have formed on the surface, 1 to 2 hours.

10. Adjust an oven rack to the lowest position and preheat the oven to 500°F.

11. Uncover the focaccia. Drizzle 1 tablespoon of olive oil over each focaccia and sprinkle each with 2 teaspoons flaky salt.

12. Place the pans side by side on the lowest rack of the oven and bake until the focaccias are deep golden brown and crispy in places, 20 to 25 minutes, rotating the pans front to back halfway through the baking time so the focaccias brown evenly. While the focaccias are baking, place a cooling rack inside a large baking sheet.

13. Remove the focaccias from the oven. One at a time, slide a metal spatula around the inside edges of the pans and under the bread to lift them out of the pans and onto the rack. The focaccia are cooled on the rack to prevent the bottoms from getting soggy from the oil in the baking pans.

Corn Bread with Honey Butter

If there's one recipe in this book that I think everyone needs to make—and that confirms this book's reason for being—it's this recipe for corn bread. Developing it almost killed me. Simple as it seems and try as I did, I just couldn't get it right. To be fair, I've been making and eating corn bread for almost my entire baking life, and I never thought it was bad. It just never tasted enough of corn, even though I always made it with fresh corn. In fact, most American corn bread doesn't even contain corn kernels. It's made from cornmeal. But I wasn't content with cornmeal bread. I wanted my corn bread to taste like corn. I was so desperate that I even stooped so low as to add a can of creamed corn to the batter in one try. It didn't work.

After countless attempts, I finally figured out a solution. Start with fresh summer corn and shave it on a tool called a corn creamer (more on that below). The creamer also breaks down the walls of the corn and creates a lot of liquid in the process, and then—here's the big secret. I cook that liquid down until it is a thick and starchy, intensely corn-flavored "pudding." (Pudding after all is made with cornstarch.) Typically, I would drain off the liquid, knowing it would make the batter too watery. I guess I'm getting smarter in my old age. Folding that pudding into the batter turned out to be the secret to the ultimate corn bread experience.

This recipe relies on your having some key equipment and ingredients: You need a corn creamer, which is a clever grating gadget in a shape that hugs the ear of corn and scrapes it clean of kernels. You also need a cast-iron skillet to bake the bread in. And, of course, you need fresh corn, which is in season in the summer. Seek out quality polenta, such as Anson Mills fine yellow polenta, which is available at gourmet stores and from online sources.

Serve this corn bread on its own, with the honey butter on the side, like a snacking cake. Or serve it as a side, with a pot of chili or Southern-style barbecue. The recipe for honey butter makes a lot. It's delicious, and I don't want you to run out. Spoon the rest on oatmeal, toast, or anywhere else that honey and butter would be welcome.

Makes one 10-inch round corn bread

What You Need—
The Essential Special Equipment

Corn creamer

10-inch cast-iron skillet

For the Corn Bread

141.5 grams (1 stick plus 2 tablespoons) unsalted butter

105 grams (¾ cup) unbleached all-purpose flour

1½ teaspoons baking powder

¼ teaspoon baking soda

2 teaspoons Diamond Crystal kosher salt

150 grams (1 cup) fine yellow stoneground polenta

25 grams (2 tablespoons) granulated sugar

112 grams (½ cup) buttermilk (preferably whole-milk or low-fat), shaken

80 grams (¼ cup) artisanal maple syrup (preferably barrel-aged)

2 extra-large eggs

2 pounds fresh summer corn (4 to 6 ears), husked

For the Honey Butter

113 grams (1 stick) unsalted butter, cubed and left at room temperature until pliable but not greasy

85 grams (⅓ cup) mild-flavored honey, such as clover or wildflower

1 teaspoon Diamond Crystal kosher salt

¼ teaspoon Aleppo pepper (or cayenne)

For Finishing

1 teaspoon fresh thyme leaves

¼ teaspoon flaky sea salt

1. To make the corn bread, adjust an oven rack to the center position and preheat the oven to 350°F.

2. Place the butter in a small saucepan or skillet with a light-colored bottom to make golden butter. Warm the butter over medium heat until it melts and begins to bubble, swirling the pan occasionally. Cook the butter, swirling often so it cooks evenly, until it is golden and the milk solids are caramel colored, 3 to 6 minutes. Remove from the heat. Strain the butter through a fine-mesh sieve into a measuring cup or a bowl; reserve the strained milk solids. Weigh out 81.5 grams (or measure ¼ cup plus 2 tablespoons) of the strained golden butter and set it aside to cool slightly. Pour another 2 tablespoons into the cast-iron skillet and set it aside. (Reserve the remaining butter for another use.)

3. Sift the flour, baking powder, baking soda, and salt into a large bowl. Add the polenta and sugar and stir with a whisk to combine. Put the buttermilk, maple syrup, and eggs in a medium bowl and stir with a whisk to combine.

4. Grate the corn on a corn creamer and discard the cobs. Drain the corn in a fine-mesh sieve set over a medium sauté pan so the liquid falls into the pan, pressing on the corn with a spatula to squeeze as much liquid out as possible. Measure out 1 packed cup of the corn. (Reserve any remaining corn for another use, such as to use in a salad.) Cook the liquid →

over medium-high heat, stirring constantly with a silicone spatula, until it thickens to the consistency of pudding, about 5 minutes. Remove from the heat, weigh out 110 grams (or measure ½ cup) of "pudding," and transfer it to a medium bowl (discard any remaining "pudding"). Set aside to cool to room temperature. Add the buttermilk mixture to the bowl with the corn "pudding" and stir with a whisk to combine. Add the golden butter and the reserved strained milk solids and stir to combine.

5. Create a well in the center of the dry ingredients with your hands. Pour half of the wet ingredients into the well and use a whisk to draw the dry ingredients from the edges to the center into a thick paste. Add the remaining wet ingredients and stir with the whisk to combine. Stir in the corn.

6. Place the skillet with the golden butter on the stovetop over medium-high heat, tilting the pan so the butter coats it evenly, and heat until it just begins to smoke and a drop of batter sizzles when you drop it in the pan, 2 to 3 minutes. Remove from the heat and pour the batter into the hot pan. Smooth out the top with an offset spatula.

7. Transfer the skillet to the oven and bake the corn bread on the center rack until it starts to brown and is slightly firm to the touch, 40 to 45 minutes. Rotate the skillet front to back and increase the temperature to 400°F. Bake until the top is nicely browned and firm to the touch, 5 to 10 minutes.

8. While the corn bread is baking, to make the honey butter, put the butter, honey, salt, and Aleppo pepper in a stand mixer fitted with the paddle and beat on medium-high speed to combine the ingredients, stopping to scrape down the bottom and sides of the bowl as needed. Transfer the butter to a covered container and refrigerate until you are ready to use it.

9. Remove the corn bread from the oven. To finish, remove the honey butter from the refrigerator and spread 2 tablespoons in uneven clumps over the surface of the still-warm corn bread. Sprinkle the thyme leaves and flaky sea salt on the corn bread. Transfer the remaining butter to a serving dish and serve it on the side.

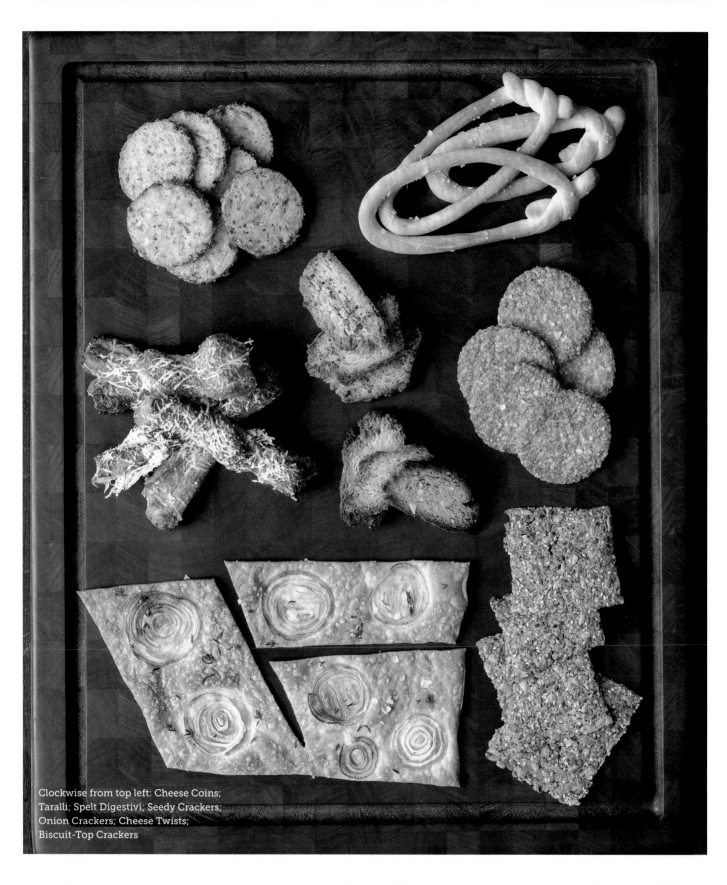

Clockwise from top left: Cheese Coins;
Taralli; Spelt Digestivi; Seedy Crackers;
Onion Crackers; Cheese Twists;
Biscuit-Top Crackers

Cheese Twists

There are a million versions of cheese twists (aka "cheese straws," or "cheese sticks"), but these are based on one in particular: the cheese sticks from Murray's Cheese in New York City. The sign of great cheese twists is that they're so buttery and cheesy, your hands are greasy after eating one. I start with a rough puff pastry (a slightly less time-consuming to make, but equally buttery, alternative to traditional puff pastry) and then layer in additional butter, and pack as much cheese on top as possible. The result is a buttery, cheesy, very crispy cracker with a dough so tender that it almost shatters when you bite into it.

This recipe makes a lot of cheese twists—about six dozen. They're so addictive, and so labor-intensive, it didn't make sense to make fewer. They're a great party snack. Also, you can freeze them after twisting and bake them off frozen.

Makes about 72 cheese twists

Rough Puff Pastry Dough (page 357)
Unbleached all-purpose flour for dusting

236 grams unsalted European-style butter, left at room temperature until pliable but not greasy
1½ teaspoons Diamond Crystal kosher salt

1 large chunk (at least ½ pound) Pecorino Romano cheese

1. Line a large baking sheet with parchment paper.

2. Remove the dough from the refrigerator, unwrap, and divide into 2 equal portions. Rewrap one portion in plastic wrap and return it to the refrigerator. Set the other portion aside to soften at room temperature for 20 to 30 minutes, until it is pliable but not soft.

3. Lightly dust a work surface with flour. Place the dough on the floured surface and dust the top of the dough and rolling pin with flour. Applying firm, steady pressure, roll the dough out to a 14 × 10-inch rectangle, dusting with flour as needed. Using a ruler and a large knife, trim the dough to square off the edges. (Bake the trimmings to snack on.) Loosely roll the dough around a rolling pin and then roll it out onto the prepared baking sheet. Dust off the excess flour. Repeat, rolling out the second block of dough and lay it on top of the first sheet of dough, separated by the parchment →

paper. Wrap the baking sheet in plastic wrap and place in the refrigerator to chill until the dough is firm, at least 1 hour.

4. Combine the butter and salt in a large bowl and use your hands or a rubber spatula to mix them together and soften the butter.

5. Remove the baking sheet of dough from the refrigerator. Invert a large baking sheet underside up on your work surface. Slide the parchment with the top sheet of dough onto the inverted baking sheet. Rewrap the first baking sheet and return it to the refrigerator.

6. Divide the butter into four portions. Spoon one-quarter of the butter over the surface of the dough and use an offset spatula to spread it to the edges. Using a fine Microplane, grate a generous layer of Pecorino Romano over the dough. Press down on the cheese with your hands to compact it. Grate another layer of cheese on top of the first. Gently press the second layer of cheese into the dough so it sticks. Lay a sheet of parchment paper on the dough. Gently rest a baking sheet on top of the dough; the dough will now be sandwiched between two baking sheets. Quickly invert them. Lift off the top baking sheet and top sheet of parchment paper. Repeat, spreading one-quarter of the butter over the dough and grating two layers of cheese on top, pressing each layer of cheese into the dough. (Repeat, layering the second half of the dough with the remaining butter and cheese.)

7. With a short side of the dough rectangle facing you, use a ruler and paring knife to cut the dough lengthwise into two equal roughly 14 × 5-inch sections. Then cut the dough across the sections to create ¾-inch-wide strips. One at a time, pick up both ends of each strip, pull gently on each end, and then twist them two times in opposite directions so that the whole piece of dough is gently twisted. (If at any time in this process the dough becomes so soft that it is difficult to work with, put it back in the refrigerator for 15 minutes or more to firm it up.)

8. Place the cheese twists on the prepared baking sheets, dividing them evenly and leaving at least 2 inches between them. Refrigerate the twists for at least 1 hour to chill until the dough is firm.

9. Adjust the oven racks so one is in the top third and the other is in the bottom third of the oven and preheat the oven to 375°F.

10. Remove the cheese twists from the refrigerator. Grate a layer of Romano cheese over them.

11. Place one baking sheet on each rack of the oven and bake for 15 minutes. Switch racks, rotate the baking sheets front to back, and bake until the twists are golden brown and crispy, 5 to 10 minutes longer.

12. Remove the baking sheets from the oven and grate another layer of cheese over them while they're hot. Set aside to cool to room temperature.

Onion Crackers

I'm rarely original; everything I create is inspired by something I've seen or tasted somewhere else. And then I bring it home and make it my own. These crisp buttermilk crackers are a good example. I'd been making delicious, unadorned buttermilk crackers for years and was perfectly happy with them. Then I went to Maine to do an event at the restaurant Primo. The chef, Melissa Kelly, was hosting me, and in my hotel room she had left a welcome gift of beautiful crackers topped with thinly sliced onion and sea salt. I liked the way they looked with the almost-burnt onion on top. And what flavor! I came home and applied those touches to my tried-and-true buttermilk crackers, and these delicious and beautiful crackers are the result.

The onion needs to be sliced paper thin, so you need to use a mandoline to slice it. And to get whole onion rings, you need to start with a small onion in order to fit it on a standard home cook's mandoline without first cutting it in half (which doesn't look as pretty). (See photo page 462.)

Makes 4 large sheets

**What You Need—
The Essential Special Equipment**

Mandoline

Ruler

Fluted rolling pastry cutter (optional)

490 grams (3½ cups) unbleached all-purpose flour, plus more for dusting

25 grams (2 tablespoons) granulated sugar

¾ teaspoon baking powder

½ teaspoon Diamond Crystal kosher salt

142 grams (1 stick plus 2 tablespoons) cold unsalted butter, cubed

280 grams (1¼ cups) buttermilk (preferably whole-milk), shaken

1 small onion (such as white spring onions, red torpedo onions, or another smaller onion)

½ cup extra-virgin olive oil

¼ cup fresh thyme leaves

Flaky sea salt

---

1. Put the flour, sugar, baking powder, and salt in a food processor and pulse to combine the ingredients. Add the butter and pulse until the mixture is the consistency of fine, wet crumbs. Turn the crumbs out into a large bowl and create a well in the center. Pour the buttermilk into the well with one hand while using the other hand to draw the dry ingredients in toward the center. Continue mixing in this way until the wet and dry ingredients are combined into a sticky dough.

2. Wash and dry your hands and dust them with flour. Dust a work surface with flour and turn the dough out onto the floured surface. Knead the dough to gather it into a ball. Cut the ball into 4 equal portions. Use your hands to pat each portion into a rectangular block 1 to 2 inches thick and wrap each

one individually in plastic wrap. Place the dough in the refrigerator until it is chilled and firm, about 2 hours.

3. Lay a large sheet of parchment paper on a work surface and dust it with flour. Remove one block of dough from the refrigerator, unwrap, and place in the center of the parchment paper. Dust the top of the dough and a rolling pin with flour and roll the dough out to no thicker than 1/16 inch, dusting with more flour as needed. (This dough requires a lot of flour when rolling.) Slide the parchment with the dough onto a large baking sheet. Repeat, rolling a second block of dough on a separate sheet of parchment paper. Lay the second sheet of dough on top of the first one. Place the baking sheet in the refrigerator to chill the dough until it is firm, about 1 hour.

4. Remove the dough from the refrigerator. Slide one sheet of dough off the baking sheet and dot the surface of the dough several times with the tines of a fork. Return the dough to the baking sheet and place it in the freezer to chill for about 30 minutes, until it is very firm.

5. Adjust the oven racks so one is in the top third and the other is in the bottom third of the oven and preheat the oven to 350°F.

6. Peel the onion and trim the stem end. Holding the onion by the root end, slice it on a mandoline into paper-thin rounds.

7. Remove the baking sheet of dough from the freezer. Lay one sheet of dough on your work surface. Using a ruler and a fluted rolling pastry cutter (or a paring knife), cut the dough into crackers the size and shape you desire. You can also leave the dough in one large sheet to make one large cracker that you can break up when you serve it. Do the same with the second sheet of dough. Return one sheet of dough to the baking sheet and place the second sheet of dough on a second baking sheet.

8. Pour the olive oil into a bowl and brush an even, light layer over the dough. Separate the rings of the onion and lay one-third of the rings, slightly overlapping, over the surface of the dough, rumpling them if needed to fit within the cuts. Sprinkle the dough with one-third of the thyme leaves, dividing them evenly, and a generous sprinkling of flaky sea salt. Dip the pastry brush in the oil and use the brush like a mop to drizzle a light layer over each sheet of dough without touching it with the brush. →

9. Place the baking sheets in the oven and bake until the crackers are golden brown, crispy, and baked all the way through, 20 to 30 minutes, switching racks and rotating the baking sheets front to back halfway through the baking time so they bake evenly. Remove the crackers from the oven and set them aside to cool to room temperature before breaking them apart.

10. Repeat, rolling, cutting, dressing, and baking the remaining two blocks of dough in the same way.

Cheese Coins

Made with a combination of pungent cheeses—Parmesan, Romano, and sharp cheddar—these buttery little coins are a great addition to a cheese platter, or to serve along with olives, sliced meats, and, of course, wine. They're basically a savory version of a shortbread cookie: super buttery and tender. They're a slice-and-bake "cookie," and like all slice-and-bakes, you can put the dough in the refrigerator or freezer and slice and bake the crackers off as desired. I give you two choices for coating the logs: an Italian Herb Seasoning, which consists of dried oregano, dried onion flakes, sea salt, and chile flakes; or coarsely ground black pepper, which I call Cacio e Pepe, named for the famous pasta dish made with Pecorino Romano cheese and black pepper. (See photo page 462.)

Makes about 2 dozen coins

For the Garlic Oil

6 large garlic cloves

1 cup olive oil (or as needed)

For the Coins

57 grams (2 ounces) Pecorino Romano cheese, finely grated (½ cup)

57 grams (2 ounces) Parmigiano-Reggiano cheese, finely grated (½ cup)

57 grams (2 ounces) sharp white cheddar, shredded (½ cup)

315 grams (2¼ cups) unbleached all-purpose flour

1½ teaspoons Diamond Crystal kosher salt

¾ teaspoon chile flakes

169 grams (1½ sticks) unsalted butter, cold and cubed

116 grams (½ cup) crème fraîche (or 122 grams/½ cup sour cream)

Italian Herb Seasoning

1 tablespoon plus 1 teaspoon dried oregano

1 tablespoon dried onion flakes

1 teaspoon flaky sea salt

½ teaspoon chile flakes

Cacio e Pepe Seasoning

3 tablespoons fresh coarsely ground black pepper

1. To make the garlic oil, put the garlic in the smallest saucepan you have and add enough olive oil to barely cover it.

2. Heat the oil over high heat until you start to hear the first sizzling noises and see the first rapid bubbles bubbling up. Reduce the heat so the oil is barely simmering and simmer until the garlic is very soft and spreadable and just barely golden, about 30 minutes. (Keep a careful eye on the garlic and reduce the heat as needed so it doesn't brown.) Remove from the heat and cool to room temperature.

3. To make the coins, put the Romano, Parmigiano, and cheddar in a medium bowl and mix with your hands to combine. →

4. Put the flour, salt, and chile flakes in a large food processor and pulse to combine the ingredients. Add the butter, garlic cloves, and 2 tablespoons of garlic oil and pulse until the mixture looks like a coarse meal. Transfer the contents of the food processor to a large bowl. Add the mixed cheeses and toss gently with your hands to combine. Make a well in the center of the ingredients with your hands. Add the crème fraîche to the well and draw the dry ingredients toward the center with your hands to combine everything. As you are bringing the ingredients together, smash the bigger pieces between your fingers to break them up, stopping when the ingredients are still crumbly.

5. Transfer the rough dough to a work surface and bring the crumbs together with your hands. Knead to form a homogeneous dough. Lay a sheet of plastic wrap on your work surface. Divide the dough in half. Place one portion of dough on the plastic wrap and shape it into a log 2 inches in diameter. Wrap the log in the plastic, twisting the ends like a candy wrapper. Repeat, shaping and wrapping the remaining dough into a second log. Place the logs in the refrigerator to chill until firm, at least 1 hour.

6. Adjust the oven racks so one is in the top third and the other is in the bottom third of the oven and preheat the oven to 350°F. Line two large baking sheets with parchment paper.

7. While the oven is preheating, choose which seasoning mixture you want to roll the logs in (or choose both). For the Italian herb seasoning mix, combine the oregano, onion flakes, flaky salt, and chile flakes in a small bowl and spread them on a flat surface (such as a large plate, small baking sheet, or cutting board). For the cacio e pepe seasoning, coarsely grind the black pepper onto a flat surface. To make both seasonings, prepare half of each coating.

8. Remove one of the logs from the refrigerator and unwrap. Brush the log with the garlic oil. (Don't brush the ends.) Roll the log in the seasoning to coat it. If the dough has gotten soft in the process, return it to the refrigerator to chill until firm.

9. Place the log on a cutting board and use a long sharp knife to slice it into ¼-inch-thick rounds. Place the rounds on the prepared baking sheets, leaving 1 inch between them. (If the coins become misshapen when you transfer them, reshape by wrapping the thumb and index finger of one hand around the coin and turning the coin with the other hand.)

10. Place one baking sheet on each rack of the oven and bake until they are firm to the touch, the centers are golden brown, and the edges are darker brown, 16 to 18 minutes, switching racks and rotating the baking sheets front to back halfway through the baking time so the coins bake evenly. Remove the cheese coins from the oven.

11. Repeat, coating, slicing, and baking the second log in the same way.

Seedy Crackers

Every summer, I spend about two months at my home in Italy, and every Sunday, I walk about an hour to the next town over to have a coffee. There, I met a German woman who is also a baker, Lia Cornelia Kramer. For a short time, Lia had a bakery, where she offered, among other delights, these crispy seedy crackers. I quickly became addicted, so lucky for me, after closing down her bakery, she gave me the recipe. They're thin, crispy, and chock-full of a variety of seeds; they also happen to be gluten-free.

This recipe is easy, flexible, and forgiving. You put together a loose batter and roll it out between sheets of parchment paper on a baking sheet. (You'll need to look around your kitchen or beyond for something to improvise as a rolling pin that fits inside the walls of the baking sheet; most rolling pins are too long for this.) That said, the crackers do require some babysitting while baking. They bake unevenly, so you need to turn them and remove them from the oven one by one, as they're done. Use whatever gluten-free flour you want, including buckwheat, brown rice, oat, or quinoa flour, or a mix, such as Bob's Red Mill 1-to-1 Gluten Free Flour. You can also substitute different seeds or use more of one type of seed and skip another.

Store these crackers at room temperature, loosely covered. Don't put them in a sealed container, or they'll lose their signature crunch. (See photo page 462.)

Makes about 48 crackers
(depending on how you cut them)

What You Need—
The Essential Special Equipment

Bench knife (optional)

128 grams (1 cup) brown rice flour (or another gluten-free flour, or a mix)

120 grams (about 1¼ cups) buckwheat flakes

40 grams (⅓ cup) golden or brown flaxseeds

40 grams (½ cup) toasted golden sesame seeds (or unhulled sesame seeds)

40 grams (scant ⅓ cup) salted toasted sunflower seeds

2 tablespoons chia seeds

1 tablespoon plus 1 teaspoon Diamond Crystal kosher salt

20 grams (1½ tablespoons) olive oil, plus more for oiling the parchment paper

---

1. Combine the brown rice flour, buckwheat flakes, flaxseeds, sesame seeds, sunflower seeds, chia seeds, and salt in a large bowl. Add the olive oil and 375 grams (1½ cups plus 1 tablespoon) hot tap water and stir to combine. Set the batter aside for about 30 minutes for the water to absorb the flour, until it is the consistency of wet porridge or thick batter. (If the batter absorbs

too much liquid and is dry, like dough, add more hot water to achieve the desired consistency. It's better to err on the wetter side, so you can spread the batter thin; basically, what you're doing in the oven is drying the batter out, so if it is too wet, you'll just need to bake it for longer.)

2. Adjust the oven racks so one is in the top third and the other is in the bottom third of the oven and preheat the oven to 325°F. Line two large baking sheets with parchment paper and brush the paper with olive oil.

3. Scoop half of the batter onto the center of one of the baking sheets. Brush another sheet of parchment paper with olive oil and place it oiled-side down on the batter. Find an improvised tool such as a wine bottle that you can use as a rolling pin that fits within the walls of your baking sheet. Use this improvised rolling pin to roll the batter to meet the edges of the baking sheet, applying even pressure and rolling the batter as evenly as possible; rolling it out evenly is key to the success of these crackers, as this way they will bake more evenly. Peel off the parchment paper and reserve it to roll the second half of the batter. Scoop the remaining batter onto the second baking sheet. Oil the clean side of the parchment paper and place it oiled-side down on the batter. Roll it out as you did the first half.

4. Place one baking sheet on each oven rack and bake the crackers until they are firm and dry, about 15 minutes; to this point you are baking them just until the batter is firm enough for you to score the crackers. Remove the baking sheets and use the blade of a bench knife to score the crackers into whatever shapes and sizes you want. (I like to cut them into roughly 2 × 3-inch rectangles.)

5. Return the baking sheets to the oven, switching racks and rotating the baking sheets front to back, and bake until the tops are deep golden brown; begin to check the crackers for doneness after 45 minutes. Line a third baking sheet with parchment paper. Use an offset or another thin spatula to turn the crackers, one at a time, as they brown. (If the crackers stick to the baking sheet when you try to turn them, they're not ready to be turned.) After you have turned the crackers, bake them until the tops on the second side are deep golden brown and the crackers are crisp on both sides. Remove the crackers from the oven one at a time, as they are done, and place them on the prepared baking sheet to cool to room temperature.

Taralli

A few summers ago, I went to visit a pig farm in Campania, in the south of Italy. For our visit, the owner set out a spread of the cured meats that they make at the farm, and along with the meats were these taralli. *Taralli* means "tires" in Italian, and the crackers called taralli, traditionally from the region of Puglia, are round, like tires, and about the size of your fingers if you put them in an "OK" sign. These, on the other hand, are thin, giant, and misshapen, like old-fashioned bicycle tires that have gone flat. So eye-catching and beautiful! Simply by changing the scale and the shape, the crackers were transformed from good to spectacular. They're easy to make and they are a stunning addition to a cheese board or charcuterie board. At The Barish, we serve these giant taralli with prosciutto draped around them; it's a real showstopper. (See photo page 462.)

Makes about 20 very large taralli

**What You Need—
The Essential Special Equipment**

Dough scraper (optional)

Bench knife (optional)

315 grams (2¼ cups) unbleached all-purpose flour, plus more for dusting

1 tablespoon Diamond Crystal kosher salt

1 teaspoon instant (rapid-rise) yeast

121.5 grams (½ cup plus 1 tablespoon) extra-virgin olive oil, plus more for greasing

56 grams (½ stick) unsalted butter, left at room temperature until pliable but not greasy

Flaky sea salt

1. Put the flour, salt, and yeast in a stand mixer fitted with the dough hook and mix on low speed to distribute the salt and yeast. Add 70 grams (¼ cup plus 1 tablespoon) of the olive oil, the butter, and 150 grams (½ cup plus 2 tablespoons) of warm tap water and mix on medium-high speed until the ingredients come together into a cohesive (albeit lumpy) dough, 8 to 10 minutes. Turn off the mixer.

2. Remove the mixer from the stand and remove the hook. Grease a large bowl with olive oil and use a dough scraper or a wet hand to transfer the dough to the greased bowl. Cover the bowl with a clean kitchen towel and set it aside in a warm place in your kitchen for 1 hour to allow the dough to relax and ferment.

3. Place the dough on a work surface. Using a bench knife (or knife), cut the dough into 30-gram (about ¼-cup) pieces, setting them aside as you cut them. After you have cut all the pieces, place one piece in front of you and

form it into a 4-inch-long log, dusting your hands lightly with flour as needed. Move the log to the side and repeat with the remaining pieces of dough. After you have formed all the logs, place one in front of you. Dust the palms of your hands with flour and roll the log back and forth under your hands to form a foot-long rope. Set the rope to the side and roll the remaining logs into foot-long ropes, setting them to the side as they are done.

4. Cover the ropes with the kitchen towel and let them rest for about 15 minutes to relax the dough. (If you don't relax the dough, it will snap back when you roll them into longer strands in the next step.)

5. While the dough is resting, adjust the oven racks so one is in the top third and the other is in the bottom third of the oven and preheat the oven to 400°F. Line two large baking sheets with parchment paper.

6. Uncover the ropes. Place one rope in front of you, flour your hands, and roll it under your hands until it is about 18 inches long. (If the dough snaps back or breaks, piece it back together as needed and let it rest for about 10 minutes, then try rolling it out again.) Set the long strand aside and continue, rolling the remaining dough in the same way.

7. When you have rolled all the ropes, place one of the lined baking sheets in front of you with a long side facing you. Place one rope lengthwise on the baking sheet. Pick up both ends of the rope and bring them together to form a very long, flat circle with the ends of the rope gently flopped over each other, with about 2 inches of rope on either side of the point where they met. Gently press on the meeting point to seal the taralli closed. Repeat, forming 4 taralli on each baking sheet, and set aside until you are ready to put them in the oven.

8. Pour a few tablespoons of olive oil into a small bowl and brush the taralli with the oil and sprinkle generously with the flaky sea salt.

9. Place one baking sheet on each rack and bake the taralli until they are golden brown and crisp, 20 to 24 minutes, switching racks and rotating the baking sheets front to back halfway through the baking time so the taralli bake evenly. Remove the taralli from the oven.

10. Form and bake the remaining taralli in the same way. Serve the taralli while they're still warm or at room temperature. (If you want warm taralli, reheat them at 350°F for 5 minutes.)

Spelt Digestivi

These are basically crunchy, grainy, not-too-sweet cookies disguised as crackers. They're like a cross between Italian *digestivi,* packaged grainy cookies sold at every convenience store in Italy, and British oaten biscuits, grainy crackers that are not as sweet as digestivi and are meant to be enjoyed with cheese. This recipe comes to us thanks to James Lowe, the chef at Lyle's, one of my favorite restaurants in London. For years, I have made a similar "biscuit," inspired by oaten biscuits, but his had a grainier texture and was a bit sweeter. Frankly, I liked them better. They're great with cheese or a cup of coffee. (See photo page 462.)

Makes about 30 digestivi

**What You Need—
The Essential Special Equipment**

2½-inch round cutter (preferably fluted)

250 grams (2 cups) rolled oats

250 grams (2 cups) spelt flour

100 grams (½ cup packed) dark brown sugar

10 grams (3 tablespoons plus 1 teaspoon) flaky sea salt

2 teaspoons baking powder

250 grams (about 2 sticks plus 2 tablespoons) cold unsalted butter, cubed

Unbleached all-purpose flour for dusting (optional)

1. Put the oats, flour, brown sugar, salt, and baking powder in the bowl of a stand mixer. Fit the mixer with a paddle attachment and mix on low speed for about 15 seconds to combine the ingredients. Add the butter and mix on low speed to form a coarse meal. Turn the mixture out onto your work surface and use your hands to gather the dough into a ball. Divide the dough in half and form each half into a disk 1 to 2 inches thick.

2. Lay a sheet of parchment paper on a work surface and place one disk of dough in the center. Lay another sheet of parchment paper on top of the dough, lining it up with the lower sheet. Applying firm steady pressure to the rolling pin, roll the dough between the parchment to ⅛ inch thick. Lay the parchment paper–sandwiched dough on a baking sheet. (Alternatively, you can skip the parchment paper and roll the dough on a flour-dusted work surface, dusting the surface, the dough, or the pin with flour as needed.) Repeat, rolling out the second half of the dough in the same way, between two fresh sheets of parchment paper. Add it to the baking sheet in the refrigerator, laying it on top of the first sheet of dough. Chill the dough until it is firm, at least 1 hour.

3. Remove one sheet of dough from the refrigerator and lay it on your work surface. Peel the top sheet of parchment off the dough and lay it back down on the dough. (This loosens the parchment so you will be able to lift it off without it sticking.) Flip the sheet of dough over. Peel off the top sheet of parchment paper and lay it clean-side up on a large baking sheet to line it. Use the 2½-inch cutter to cut rounds from the dough, cutting the rounds as close together as possible to get as many rounds as you can from one sheet of dough. Use a thin metal spatula to lift the dough rounds off the work surface and place them on the prepared baking sheet, leaving ½ inch between them. Gather the scraps and set them aside. Use the bottom sheet of parchment paper to line a second baking sheet.

4. Remove the second sheet of dough from the refrigerator and repeat, peeling off the parchment paper, cutting the cookie rounds, and placing the rounds on the prepared baking sheet, leaving at least ½ inch between them. Gather the scraps and form them into a 1-inch-thick disk, refrigerate until the dough is firm, and roll out the scraps between two sheets of parchment. (You can reuse sheets that were removed from the dough, with the clean sides facing up.) Cut the scraps into rounds and add them to the baking sheets. Refrigerate the dough until it is chilled and firm, at least 30 minutes.

5. While the dough is chilling, adjust the oven racks so one is in the top third and the other is in the bottom third of the oven and preheat the oven to 350°F.

6. Place one baking sheet on each oven rack and bake the crackers until they are golden brown around the edges, 12 to 13 minutes, switching racks and rotating the baking sheets front to back halfway through baking time so the crackers bake evenly. Remove the baking sheets from the oven and set aside. Let the crackers cool on the baking sheets.

Gougères

Gougères are light and airy French cheese puffs made from a savory *pâte à choux,* an eggy dough from which cream puffs, profiteroles, and éclairs are made. They make a delicious one-bite cocktail-time snack. Admittedly, with this recipe I deviated from the theme of this book of sticking to the classics and making them as good as they could be. I took the traditional gougères base, made with Gruyère cheese, and went to town with them, adding Parmesan cheese, chopped ham, caraway seeds, and pickled mustard seeds. It's the combination of flavors I like in a ham and cheese deli sandwich. With all the add-ins, these are a bit denser than typical gougères, but what you lose in airiness, you gain in flavor and texture.

Pickled mustard seeds are very easy to make, just boil the pickling ingredients, pour them over the seeds, and after a few hours you have these delicious little seeds that pop like caviar in your mouth.

Makes about 42 gougères

For the Mustard Seeds

¼ cup yellow mustard seeds

½ cup apple cider vinegar

1½ teaspoons mild-flavored honey, such as clover or wildflower

1 dried chile de árbol

¾ teaspoon Diamond Crystal kosher salt

For the Gougères

18 grams (3 tablespoons) caraway seeds

7 extra-large eggs

360 grams (about 1½ cups) whole milk

180 grams (about 1½ sticks plus 1 tablespoon) unsalted butter

2½ teaspoons Diamond Crystal kosher salt

263 grams (about 1¾ cups plus 2 tablespoons) unbleached all-purpose flour

57 grams (2 ounces) quality cooked ham, cut into ¼-inch dice (½ cup)

85 grams (3 ounces) Gruyère cheese, shredded (1 cup)

28 grams (1 ounce) Parmesan cheese, finely grated (¼ cup)

For Garnish

42.5 grams (1½ ounces) Gruyère cheese, shredded (½ cup)

Flaky sea salt

A chunk of Parmesan for grating

1. To pickle the mustard seeds, put them in a half-pint canning jar with a lid or in a heatproof small bowl or mug.

2. Combine the vinegar, honey, chile, and salt in a small saucepan and bring to a boil over high heat. Remove from the heat, pour the boiling liquid over the mustard seeds, and set aside to cool to room temperature. Put the lid on the jar or cover the bowl or mug tightly with plastic wrap and set aside for 2 to 3 hours so the pickling liquid can saturate the seeds and it's like a →

seedy syrup. Drain the mustard seeds in a fine-mesh sieve and set aside (discard the liquid).

3. Adjust the oven racks so one is in the top third and the other is in the bottom third of the oven and preheat the oven to 425°F. Line two large baking sheets with parchment paper.

4. To make the gougères, toast the caraway seeds in a small skillet over medium-high heat until they are golden and fragrant, about 1 minute, shaking the pan often so they toast evenly. Remove from the heat and transfer the seeds to a plate to prevent them from burning from the residual heat of the pan. Measure out 2 tablespoons of the seeds for the dough; reserve the remaining 1 tablespoon seeds for garnish.

5. Beat the eggs in a medium bowl to break up the yolks.

6. Combine the milk, butter, and salt in a medium saucepan and warm over low heat until the butter melts and the mixture comes to a simmer, about 10 minutes, stirring gently with a wooden spoon to make sure the mixture heats evenly. (This is done over very low heat because you don't want the milk to come to a simmer before the butter melts.) Increase the heat to medium-high and bring the mixture to a boil, stirring occasionally. Remove from the heat, add the flour all at once, and stir it in with the wooden spoon. Return the saucepan to low heat and cook for about 1 minute, stirring constantly, until the dough comes away from the sides of the pan.

7. Transfer the dough to a stand mixer fitted with the paddle and beat on low speed for about 30 seconds to cool the dough enough so that you can add the eggs without fear that the warm dough will cook them. With the mixer on medium-low, add the eggs slowly, making sure the egg is incorporated into the dough before adding more. When all the egg is incorporated, stop the mixer and scrape down the sides and bottom of the bowl with a rubber spatula.

8. Turn off the mixer and add the mustard seeds, 2 tablespoons caraway seeds, ham, Gruyère, and Parmesan. Mix on medium-low for about 30 seconds to distribute them throughout the dough.

9. Using two dinner forks, scoop about 34 grams (3 tablespoons) of dough with one fork and scrape it off with another fork onto the prepared baking sheets, making the drops as tall as possible and leaving about 1½ inches between them; you will drop 12 gougères on each baking sheet.

10. To garnish the gougères, sprinkle the shredded Gruyère, reserved toasted caraway seeds, and flaky salt over each one.

11. Reduce the oven temperature to 375°F and put one baking sheet on each oven rack. Bake until the gougères are puffy and deep brown, 30 to 35 minutes, switching racks and rotating the baking sheets front to back halfway through the baking time so they brown evenly.

12. Remove the baking sheets from the oven. While the gougères are still hot, use a fine Microplane to grate a generous flurry of Parmesan over them.

Acknowledgments

This is my tenth cookbook, and you might think after writing nine I would know what I'm doing, and number ten would be a breeze. Wrong. I owe this one to as many people as ever.

First off, I am fortunate to have an extraordinary team at Penguin Random House led by my brilliant editor Peter Gethers. Peter actually baked—and loved—the peanut butter cookie recipe. What editor does that? He was ably backed by Tom Pold and Morgan Hamilton, both of whose attention never ceases to amaze me. The design team of Cassandra Pappas and Kristen Bearse were obviously stellar, as you can see. Copy editor Kate Slate saved the day about 714 times. This is an elite squad. Thank you.

My agent Janis Donnaud is ideal. She gets things done. Period.

Now to my kitchen team. Special thanks to my James Beard Award–winning pastry chef and friend Dahlia Narvaez, who let me take over the Mozza pastry kitchen to develop these recipes. Many of the recipes were tested during Covid shutdowns so I had the kitchen pretty much to myself, but when our Mozza restaurants reopened, her pastry team of Cecily Feng, Ashley Paredes, Carlo Dominguez, Diana Lael, Audrey Persall, Marissa Brown, and Adam Marka let me step on their toes and gently nudge their desserts to the side to make room for me and for that I am thankful.

Anne Fishbein did a fantastic job with the photographs. On her first cookbook, Anne really captured the essence of each dish. I look at the photographs and marvel at the individuality she was able to capture. Anne worked tirelessly. How many times she had to reshoot and Anne was so patient. She went above and beyond.

A special thanks goes out to Elizabeth "Liz" Hong, who has become my right-hand woman in our kitchens around the planet. Liz, known as "Go Go," go-goes indeed and swiftly moved during the lockdown from savory to help me with this book. Liz was there for every sweet—and sour—step and her transition to the pastry kitchen had us joking she was a "rising star pastry chef."

"Mozza Shiri!" "Mozza Shiri!" What would I have done without Mozza Shiri and our nightly speaker phone calls on 300-plus drives home from Mozza? Mozza Shiri is Shiri Nagar, whom I asked to help test the recipes but who became much more of a collaborator. She was not working at Mozza during the pandemic and was making wine when I asked her to help me with this book. Help me? She more like saved me! When something was good, it wasn't good enough for Shiri and she not only encouraged me but slowly and clearly articulated what flavors she thought could be more highly extracted. Many thanks to Kate Greenberg, who keeps me—and all the Mozza restaurants—running smoothly. Thank you in advance to Juliet Kapanjie, who came on as my personal assistant just as the book was going to print. I have confidence that in the year(s) ahead, I'll have many things to thank Juliet for. And to all of my guinea pigs—in particular Herbie, Kirby, and Juan—who tasted batch after batch of sugary, buttery confections and had the courage to tell me what they really thought so that I could continue on my perfection journey.

I live with Michael Krikorian, a crime reporter. But for this cookbook, he was our "Go Get This" guy. Countless times, I or someone on my team would need something from a market and one of us would yell "Michael!" And usually he was gone in sixty seconds, but not before his trademark line: "Ya know, I used to be a journalist." One of us would respond, "Yeah, sure. Just go to the Afghan market and get the raisins."

This is the fifth book that Carolynn Carreño has written for me and it's difficult to think I would ever have anyone else write my cookbooks. She gets me and has that ability to not only write in my voice but tweak it to improve my very own thoughts. That is a rare talent. If you ever meet me, you'll find out I'm not quite as articulate as Carolynn makes me out to be.

Index

bars:
    Blondies, *116*, 119–21
    Brownies, *116*, 117–18
    Granola Bar Bites, *70*, 71–3
    Lemon, *348*, 349–51
    Raisin, Iced, 173–6, *177*
    Raspberry Crumble, 345–6, *347*
Basque Cheesecake, *246*, 252–3
béchamel, Twice-Baked Ham and
    Cheese Croissants, smothered in,
    74, 75–7
bench knives, 9
Beramendi, Rolando, 232
Beran, David, 252
berry(ies):
    in Cherry Cobbler (substitution), 415
    and Stone Fruit Crumble, *422*,
    423–4
    see also blueberry(ies);
        raspberry(ies); strawberry(ies)
Big Sur Bakery, California, 265
Birthday Cake, The Original
    Chocolate, with White Mountain
    Frosting, *264*, 265–7
biscotti:
    Almond, 159–60, *161*
    crumbs, in Chocolate Salami, *161*,
    162–3
biscuits, 442
    Buttermilk, Layered, *448*, 449–50
    Cream, *448*, 452–3
Biscuit-Top Crackers, 449, 451
blackberry(ies):
    Stone Fruit and Berry Crumble, *422*,
    423–4
    Thumbprint Scones (substitution),
    43
black pepper, 24
    Cacio e Pepe Seasoning, 469, 470
    Parmesan and Pecorino Cheese
    Scones, 49–50, *51*

Twice-Baked Ham and Cheese
    Croissants, 75–77
Black Sesame White Chocolate
    Cookies, 100–1, *102*
"blitz" (Rough Puff Pastry Dough),
    357–9
Blondies, *116*, 119–21
blueberry(ies):
    Brown Butter Tart with, *418*, 419–21
    Millet Muffins, *34*, 38–9
Blue Hill at Stone Barns, Tarrytown,
    N.Y., 437
Bob's Red Mill:
    almond meal, 17
    gluten-free flour, 472
    oat products, 23
Bon Appétit, 261
bourbon
    Kentucky Butter Cake, *196*, 197–9
    Lattice-Topped Apple Pie, *vi*,
    319–22, *323*
    Pecan Tart, *330*, 334–6
    Pineapple Upside-Down Cake, *216*,
    217–19
bowls, 9–10
boysenberries, in Stone Fruit and
    Berry Crumble, *422*, 423–4
b. Patisserie, San Francisco, 75
brandy:
    Bran Muffins, *34*, 40–1
    Canelés, *224*, 230–1
    Chocolate Cake, *254*, 255–7
    Chocolate Ganache Tart, 337–40,
    339
    Chocolate Salami, *161*, 162–3
    Honeynut Squash Pie, 437–40, *441*
    Hot Fudge Sauce, 291, *295*, 297
    Raisin Brown Butter Tart, 341–4,
    342
    Strawberry-Rhubarb Pie, 401–4,
    405

Bran Muffins, *34*, 40–1
Brat, London, 252
bread basket, 442–81
    Barish Farmhouse Rolls, *444*, 445–7
    Biscuit-Top Crackers, 449, 451
    Cheese Coins, *462*, 469–71
    Cheese Twists (aka "cheese straws"
        or "cheese sticks"), *462*, 463–5
    Corn Bread with Honey Butter,
    458–60, *461*
    Cream Biscuits, *448*, 452–3
    Gougères, *478*, 479–81
    Layered Buttermilk Biscuits, *448*,
    449–50
    Onion and Sage Focaccia, *454*,
    455–7
    Onion Crackers, *462*, 466–8
    Seedy Crackers, *462*, 472–3
    Spelt Digestivi, *462*, 476–7
    Taralli, *462*, 474–5
bread crumbs, in Chess Pie, *324*,
    325–8
bread flour, 20
Bread Pudding (cake), 238–42, *241*
breads:
    Banana, *30*, 31–3
    Corn, with Honey Butter, 458–60,
    461
    Monkey, 81–4, *85*
    Onion and Sage Focaccia, *454*,
    455–7
    Orange Cranberry Tea Loaf, 57–8, *59*
breakfast baked goods, 28–89
    Almond Croissants, Twice-Baked,
    74, 78–80
    Apricot Thumbprint Scones, *42*,
    43–5
    Banana Bread, *30*, 31–3
    Blueberry Millet Muffins, *34*, 38–9
    Bran Muffins, *34*, 40–1
    British Scones, *52*, 55–6

cream slab pies:
  Banana, with Caramel and Salted
    Toasted Peanuts, *366*, 367–72
  Coconut, with Bittersweet Chocolate
    and Toasted Almonds, 360–5, *366*
crimping pie shell, 361, 368
Crisp, Apple, 429–30, *431*
croissants:
  Almond, Twice-Baked, *74*, 78–80
  Ham and Cheese, Twice-Baked, *74*,
    75–7
crostata, 432
Crumb Cake, New York, *64*, 65–6
crumble:
  Bars, Raspberry, 345–6, *347*
  Stone Fruit and Berry, *422*, 423–4
cupcakes, 259
  Chocolate, with Fudge Frosting,
    273–6, *275*
  Coconut, with Cream Cheese
    Frosting, *275*, 277–80
  filling tins for, with piping bag, 12
  muffins vs., 28
  piping frosting onto, 15, 280
  removing from pan, 279
currant(s):
  Bran Muffins, *34*, 40–1
  British Scones, *52*, 55–6
  Granola Bar Bites, *70*, 71–3
  in Iced Raisin Bars (substitution),
    173
  Oat Scones, *52*, 53–4
  Zante, 27
custard(s):
  Bacon, Potato, and Comté Quiche,
    314, 315–18
  Bread Pudding (cake), 238–42, *241*
  Canelés, *224*, 230–1
  Chess Pie, *324*, 325–8
  Pumpkin Tart with Dates, *330*,
    331–3

Tarts, Portuguese (*tarta de nata*),
  385–91, *389*
Vanilla, Tart with Raspberries,
  425–8, *427*
cutters, 10

dates:
  Pumpkin Tart with, *330*, 331–3
  Rugelach, *154*, 155–8
  Sticky Toffee Pudding (cake), *234*,
    235–7
Davis, Joni, 46
demerara sugar, 25
  Chinese Restaurant Almond
    Cookies, 147–8
  Linzer Cookies, 139–42
  Oat Currant Scones, 53–4
  Snickerdoodles, *106*, 107–9
  Strawberry-Rhubarb Pie, 401–4, *405*
Desperation Pies, 325
Devil's Food Cake with Fudge Frosting,
  268, 269–72
Dialogue, Los Angeles, 252
Diamond Crystal kosher salt, 23
Diaz, João, 385–6
Digestivi, Spelt, *462*, 476–7
digital kitchen scales, 10
dinner rolls, baked goods to serve as:
  Barish Farmhouse Rolls, *444*, 445–7
  Cream Biscuits, *448*, 452–3
  Parmesan and Pecorino Cheese
    Scones, 49–50, *51*
doughs:
  freezing, 8, 90
  laminating, 155, 449
  Rough Puff Pastry, 357–9
  Savory Pie Dough, *308*, 313
  sticky, rolling out between sheets of
    parchment paper, 16, 174
  Sweet Tart Dough (*pâte sucrée*), 306,
    329

dulce de leche:
  Alaska Cookies with Chocolate
    Chunks, Marshmallows, and, *112*,
    113–15
  making, 113–14

École Lenôtre, Paris, 78
eggs, 20
  in curd for Lemon Bars, *348*, 349–51
  see also custard(s)
egg whites:
  Angel Food Cake, *204*, 205–7
  Chewy Almond Cookies, *188*,
    189–90
  Coconut Macaroons, *188*, 191–2, *193*
  Meyer Lemon Meringue Tart, *394*,
    395–8
  Nut Clusters, 185–6, *187*
  Poppy Seed Cake, *200*, 201–3
  White Mountain Frosting, *264*, 265,
    266–7
egg yolks, grated hard-boiled, in
  doughs, 43, 139
equipment and tools, 8–16

Financiers, *224*, 228–9
flan rings, 11
  baking cookies in, 11, 90, 95
  baking tarts in, 11, 15, 306
flaxseeds:
  Granola Bar Bites, *70*, 71–3
  Oat Currant Scones, *52*, 53–4
  Seedy Crackers, *462*, 472–3
Fleming, Claudia, 5, 243, 349
flour, 20–1
  bread, 20
  cake, 20
  dark rye, 21
  pastry, 20
  rice, 20
  self-rising, 21

A Note About the Authors

Nancy Silverton is the co-owner of numerous restaurants around the world, including Osteria Mozza (which was awarded a Michelin star in 2019), Pizzeria Mozza, Chi Spacca, and Mozza2Go, in her hometown, Los Angeles, California. She is the founder of the La Brea Bakery and is the only person ever to be awarded both the Outstanding Chef and Outstanding Pastry Chef awards from the James Beard Foundation. In 2014, Silverton was listed as one of the Most Innovative Women in Food and Drink by both *Fortune* and *Food & Wine* magazines, and in 2017, she was profiled in an episode of Netflix's award-winning docuseries *Chef's Table*. Silverton is the author of ten cookbooks, including *Chi Spacca, Mozza at Home, The Mozza Cookbook, A Twist of the Wrist, Nancy Silverton's Sandwich Book, Nancy Silverton's Pastries from the La Brea Bakery* (recipient of a 2000 Food & Wine Best Cookbook Award), *Nancy Silverton's Breads from the La Brea Bakery,* and *Desserts.*

Carolynn Carreño is a writer whose essays and feature stories have been published in *The New York Times Magazine, Saveur, Gourmet, Bon Appétit, Food & Wine, Playboy,* the *Los Angeles Times,* and the *Los Angeles Times Magazine,* among other publications. She is the author or co-author of more than fifteen books and is currently working on a memoir, *Cooking My Way to Mexican,* about food and family, as well as a memoir about life with her late, beloved miniature Labradoodle, *RUFUS.* She lives in San Diego and Mexico City.

A Note on the Type

The text of this book is set in Museo Slab, a typeface based on the fonts
Museo and Museo Sans, designed by Dutch typeface designer Jos Buivenga
and released through the exljbris Font Foundry in 2009. The original Museo
has semi-slab serifs but Museo Slab is a full-on slab serif. It has a very friendly
and warm appearance for a slab serif.

Composed by North Market Street Graphics,
Lancaster, Pennsylvania

Printed and bound by C&C Offset, China

Designed by Cassandra J. Pappas